Representing People with Mental Disabilities

A Practical Guide for Criminal Defense Lawyers

SECOND EDITION

ELIZABETH KELLEY
EDITOR

AMERICAN BAR ASSOCIATION
ABA Publishing

Cover design by ABA Design

Printed in the United States of America.

28 27 26 25 24   5 4 3 2 1

A catalog record for this book is available from the Library of Congress.

Discounts are available for books ordered in bulk. Special consideration is given to state bars, CLE programs, and other bar-related organizations. Inquire at Book Publishing, ABA Publishing, American Bar Association, 321 N. Clark Street, Chicago, Illinois 60654-7598.

www.shopABA.org

Contents

Introduction

How the world has changed during the six years between the publication of the first edition of this book in 2018 and the second in 2024. The pandemic touched virtually every life and institution across the planet. And because of the pandemic, the awareness of mental health issues has heightened due to the impact of the lockdown during that time and the trauma many are still dealing with because of social isolation and the reordering of the world as we knew it.

To the degree that the criminal legal system reflects society at large, it too has become more aware of mental health issues. Indeed, even before the pandemic, a disproportionately high number of people in jails and prisons had mental health issues. But now, there is a growing awareness, a thirst for more information, and a quest for solutions. Thus, this is a perfect time for a second edition of *Representing People with Mental Disabilities: A Practical Guide for Criminal Defense Lawyers*.

This second edition is significantly different than the first. Several chapters are new: "Testing," "Substance Use Disorder," and "Post-Conviction Remedies." Some chapters have changed or expanded in scope; Chapter 10 about false confessions includes a more thorough discussion of *Miranda*, and Chapter 13 about mental health courts is now titled "Mental Health Courts and Other Diversion Options." The chapter on juveniles has been renamed "Youthful Offenders." Other chapters have been updated by their authors from the first edition.

The format remains the same. I have written a short introduction to each chapter. The content is still meant to be practical and readable. Chapters can be read in one sitting. All authors, notwithstanding their scholarly and professional qualifications, were asked to keep endnotes to a minimum. If readers want to learn more about a topic, they are encouraged to consult the Suggested Works section at the back of the book, which is arranged by chapter.

The content in one chapter may necessarily overlap with that in another. On the one hand, it is sufficient to read one chapter. On the other hand, for a broader understanding of a topic, a reader may want to explore a related chapter. For example, you may want to know the difference between competency and sanity (otherwise known as criminal responsibility). Thus, you should read Chapter 1, "Competency to Stand Trial" by Dr. Eric Y. Drogin and Chapter 2, "Criminal Responsibility" by Professor Lucy Guarnera and Professor Richard Bonnie. But curiosity takes you to Chapter 6 on malingering by Richard Rogers, Kamar Tazi, and Dr. Drogin. Similarly, you read Chapter 14 on veteran's courts by Professor Julie Marie Baldwin, which may lead you to Chapter 13 on mental health courts and other diversion options by defenders Katherine Bujak and Jeffery Berman. That discussion may motivate you to read Chapter 19 on ethical issues by federal public defender Peggy Cross-Goldberg.

As with the first edition, I am deliberate about my word choice. "Mental disabilities" is my global term for mental illness (issues like bipolar disorder and schizophrenia), intellectual/developmental disabilities (like autism spectrum disorder and fetal alcohol spectrum disorder), and neurological conditions like dementia. That being said, many people have co-occurring disorders or dual diagnoses. Moreover, it is important to understand what something is and is not; for example, some people on the autism spectrum do not have an intellectual disability but they may have a co-occurring disorder. In the meantime, autism is a developmental disability. All of this is important in terms of understanding a client's complexity, knowing what expert or experts to seek, and knowing how to most effectively advocate for your client.

I have many colleagues to thank for their contributions to this book. First and foremost, I would like to thank the authors of each chapter. I respect the time, knowledge, and creativity they channeled into their chapters.

I would also like to thank the ABA for again supporting one of my writing adventures. In particular, I thank Bryan Kay, who was a staunch advocate for this volume, as well as Lorraine Murray. Also, I appreciate the leadership of the Criminal Justice Section, namely Chairs Justin Bingham and Tina Luongo, who understood the need for a second edition.

Special recognition goes to those who peer-reviewed chapters, including Justin Murphy, Esq., Dr. Kenneth P. Rosenberg, Dr Charles Samenow, Dr. Michael Santa Maria, and Lizett M. Schreiber.

Finally, I thank the members of my team who help me in my law practice: Christine Andraus, Amber Fayerberg, Hannah Friedman, Kathryn Koontz, Julia Milan, and Starr Oldorff. In particular, I thank Lisa Johnson, who kept track of the thousands of moving parts that comprise this volume and always did so with grace and good humor.

I have devoted my practice and my life to representing people with mental disabilities. I am appalled by the fact that we criminalize people for manifesting the symptoms of their disabilities. In addition to advocating for my clients in my practice, I do a good deal of writing and speaking in order to educate criminal defense lawyers, judges, and anyone who will listen about the intersection of mental disabilities and the criminal legal system. But all the education in the world will not meaningfully help people with mental disabilities unless and until we first have a robust system of resources in the community to prevent criminal conduct from ever occurring; second, we return to rehabilitation and treatment as goals of our criminal legal system such that they are not eclipsed by punishment, incapacitation, and retribution; and finally, we modify our laws at the state and federal levels in order to give prosecutors and judges the discretion they need in order to wisely and humanely resolve these cases.

Elizabeth Kelley
Editor

Chapter

1

Competency to Stand Trial

Eric Y. Drogin

The following two chapters—"Competency to Stand Trial" and "Criminal Responsibility"—are deliberately placed next to each other because (1) lawyers and judges often confuse these two concepts; and (2) it is vital to know the differences and similarities between the two. Generally speaking, as Dr. Eric Y. Drogin, the author of this chapter points out, competency to proceed is the ability to understand the nature of the legal proceedings and the ability to assist counsel. It is a measure of the client's ability to participate in the legal proceedings at the current point in time. In contrast, as the next chapter on criminal responsibility by professors Lucy Guarnera and Richard Bonnie explains, the insanity defense is an attempt to take a snapshot of the client's mental condition at the time of the alleged incident. In order to determine competency and/or to pursue an insanity defense, an expert will be appointed or counsel must secure an expert. The expert will administer a range of tests; interview the client as well as others who know the accused such as family, friends, and coworkers; and review collateral materials such as school, medical, employment, and military records in addition to the case file.

As Dr. Drogin notes in this chapter, the decision to request a competency evaluation is not only one of the first decisions an attorney makes, but also one that will set the course for the entire criminal case. Indeed, competency remains a concern throughout the entire criminal proceeding. Although this chapter is self-contained, readers are encouraged to explore the abundant cross-references to other chapters as the issue of competency raises a host of other issues such as mitigation, malingering, working with the expert, and the ethical implications of arguing that a client is not competent to proceed.

This chapter is an update of Dr. Drogin's chapter in the first edition of this book. He has added scholarly works that have been published since the last edition. He discusses the restoration process in greater detail. And he answers the frequently asked question, "Is the standard for competency to stand trial the same as the standard to plead guilty?"

• • •

Competency to stand trial is a fundamental psycholegal issue that influences every subsequent interaction between defense counsel and clients with mental disabilities. Trust can be won or lost permanently at this critical stage of the attorney-client relationship, and the fashion in which counsel interacts with the criminal justice system concerning competency matters will have an impact on every other disability-related aspect of these proceedings, from initial pleadings through—under the most unfortunate of circumstances—post-conviction hearings and appeals.

In every jurisdiction, competency to stand trial encompasses two distinct but intertwined notions: the client's grasp of what is and could be happening, and the client's willingness and ability to collaborate with counsel in pursuing a desirable outcome. Although it touches upon many of the same diagnostic techniques and historical issues, competency to stand trial should not be confused with criminal responsibility (see Chapter 2, "Criminal Responsibility"). The former concerns what your client can do now and in the future. The latter concerns your client's mental health status at a particular point in the past.

This chapter will address the legal background of competency to stand trial, the expert's assessment techniques, counsel's familiarity with the assessment process, and counsel's practical management of issues that arise along the way—for example, a failure on the part of evaluating experts to conduct an appropriate clinical or forensic interview, or with implications of "competency restoration" in the event of success. All of this material will be offered with a particular guiding principle in mind: That should the court not prove willing to bring criminal proceedings to an end by rendering a finding of incompetency, counsel can still mine information gained at this stage in order to prevail in areas described in this book's subsequent chapters.

Legal Background

The fundamental appellate source for understanding modern competency matters is the seminal Supreme Court of the United States case of *Dusky v. United States.*[1] Milton Dusky was convicted at trial of transporting a female across state lines for immoral purposes. A federal district judge had found that Dusky was competent to stand trial because he was "oriented to time and place" and "had some recollection of events."[2] This decision was confirmed at the first appellate level by the U.S. Court of Appeals, Eighth Circuit, which held that "how much mental capacity or alertness a defendant must have to assist his counsel is a question of fact for the trial court [which] cannot be set aside on review unless clearly arbitrated or unwarranted."[3]

In fact, it was the solicitor general who eventually argued before the Supreme Court in *Dusky* that "a trial judge ought, at a minimum, [to] have other expert opinion before he undertakes to disregard the unanimous conclusion of disinterested experts."[4] The Court ultimately concluded in this matter that the appropriate test in competency to stand trial matters "must be whether [the defendant] has sufficient present ability to consult with his lawyer with a reasonable degree of rational understanding—and whether he has a rational as well as factual understanding of the proceedings against him."[5]

While *Dusky* establishes a federal standard below which competency schemes in other jurisdictions cannot stray, counsel must remain aware that there may be subtle nuances in a particular state's specific guidance on this topic. As one example, in Kentucky, one reads that

> "[i]ncompetency to stand trial" means, as a result of mental condition, lack of capacity to appreciate the nature and consequences of the proceedings against one or to participate rationally in one's own defense.[6]

Here, although *Dusky* refers to whether a defendant actually "has" the requisite "understanding" of relevant legal matters, Kentucky casts

---

1. Dusky v. United States, 362 U.S. 402 (1960).
2. *Id.*, at 402.
3. Dusky v. United States, 271 F.2d. 385 (8th Cir. 1959), at 397.
4. Dusky, *supra* note 1, at 430.
5. *Id.*, at 402–403.
6. Ky. Rev. Stat. Ann. § 504.060 (2) ("Definitions for chapter").

this in terms of whether a defendant possesses the "capacity" for such understanding. Similarly, the *Dusky* requirement that a defendant actually "has" a "sufficient present ability" to "consult" with counsel with a requisite level of "rational understanding" can arguably be distinguished from Kentucky's language concerning the "capacity" to "participate rationally."

As another example, in New Hampshire, one reads that

> [t]he *Dusky* test is thus two-pronged. First, the defendant must have a sufficient present ability to consult with and assist his lawyer with a reasonable degree of rational understanding. Second, he must have a rational as well as a factional understanding of the proceedings against him.[7]

Here, although the expressed intent is to cleave to the *Dusky* standard, New Hampshire attorneys are faced with the insertion of the phrase "and assist." This arguably distinct requirement could not only underscore the active nature of the role of a client with mental disabilities—or any other client, for that matter—but also lay the groundwork for asserting that a particular individual was able to, for example, share information with counsel, but not participate in more arduous activities such as helping to make tactical legal decisions on the fly.

Although it has long been acknowledged that not every state cleaves to the letter of *Dusky*, this is not to suggest that each jurisdiction expresses a unique take on competency to stand trial.[8] In any event, there is no substitute for knowing the competency standards in one's home jurisdiction inside and out. Subtle differences in wording, however casually proffered by legislatures or judges, could wind up making a very substantial difference for clients with mental disabilities. It is beyond the scope of this chapter to address such ancillary matters as specific legal standards for burdens and standards of proof; however, there are other easily accessible resources that explain these and other such matters in detail.[9]

It would be a mistake for counsel to assume that once competency to stand trial has initially been adjudicated its components are no longer relevant. For one thing, competency matters can arise any number of times going forward—particularly when one considers the cyclical nature

---

7. State v. Champagne, 127 N.H. 266 (1985), at 270.

8. *See* Alan R. Felthous, *Competence to Stand Trial Should Require Rational Understanding*, 39 J. Am. Acad. Psychiatry & L. 19 (2011).

9. *See, e.g.*, David Collins, *Re-Evaluating Competence to Stand Trial*, 82 L. Contemp. Probs. 157 (2019); Heidi Putney & Andrea Dinsmore, *Burden of Proof in Competence to Stand Trial Hearings*, 49 J. Am. Acad. Psychiatry & L. 445 (2021).

of many underlying disease processes. It may also be the trial process itself that eventually serves to overwhelm the defendant, as litigation stress (also known as "critogenic harms") plays an increasing role.[10] Competency to stand trial concerns may influence other critically important competency statuses, such as competency to be executed. The case of *Madison v. Alabama*[11] demonstrated this vividly, instantly garnering the attentions of the forensic as well as legal communities.[12]

Not every form of "competency" in criminal proceedings must spring from or bear a direct relationship to competency to stand trial. Throughout this book, for example, the reader will see treatments of such additional notions as competency to represent oneself (see Chapter 15, "Standby or Advisory Counsel") and competency to confess (see Chapter 10, "False Confessions and *Miranda* Waivers").[13]

Warning Signs

Experienced defense counsel will remain alert to signs of competency to stand trial issues from the time of appointment forward. Hints that a client may have problems in this regard will come from one or both of two sources: (1) the client's behavior during the first and subsequent meetings with counsel as well as records; and (2) remarks that emanate from other sources.

When first laying eyes upon the client, defense counsel does not have to be a doctor in order to run down a list of readily observable attributes that are typically included in the mental health professional's "mental status examination."[14] These include:

- *Appearance and General Behavior*: Are clients disheveled, oddly dressed, or malodorous? Is it likely that these conditions are due to more than

10. *See* Thomas G. Gutheil & Katharine Y. Joo, *"Critogenic Harms" and Criminal Law*, Crim. Just., Fall 2017, at 18.

11. 586 U.S. ___, 2019.

12. *See, e.g.*, Manish A. Fodzar, *Neuropsychiatric Reflections on Madison v. Alabama*, 48 J. Am. Acad. Psychiatry & L. 151 (2020); Alexander H. Updegrove & Michael S. Vaughn, *Evaluating Competency for Execution after Madison v. Alabama*, 48 J. Am. Acad. Psychiatry & L. 530 (2020).

13. *See also* Daniel C. Murrie & Heather Zelle, *Criminal Competencies*, in APA Handbook of Forensic Psychology 115 (Bruce L. Cutler & Patricia A. Zapf eds., 2015).

14. Components utilized here are adapted from David R. Norris et al., *The Mental Status Examination*, 94 Am. Fam. Physician 635 (2016) and Danielle Snyderman & Barry R. Rovner, *Mental Status Examination in Primary Care: A Review*, 80 Am. Fam. Physician 810 (2009).

just currently known circumstances of arrest or confinement? Are clients matter-of-fact and straightforward, or instead rude, evasive, or generally interpersonally bizarre? In jail settings, have staff found physical restraint to be necessary?

- *Motor Activity*: Are clients virtually catatonic or, at the other end of the psychomotor spectrum, are they pacing about in the office or jail cell, gesticulating wildly? Are clients staring off vacantly into space, or are they scratching, fidgeting, or toe-tapping restlessly? Counsel will do well to determine if such behaviors reflect acute intoxication, or perhaps medication withdrawal.
- *Language*: Is a client's speech "pressured," such that their flow of words is so torrential that counsel has a difficult time getting a comment in edgewise? Is a client's tone flat and even, or instead excitable and perhaps accusatory? Is it hard to hear clients, or are they perhaps virtually—or actually—shouting? Slurred words may suggest any of a number of acute or chronic conditions.
- *Mood and Affect*: "Mood" refers to a client's ongoing emotional state, while "affect" refers to a client's immediate expression of emotion. Clients may, for example, be observably sad, angry, fearful, or some combination thereof. When counsel is serious, inquisitive, friendly, or jocular, do clients have either the capacity or the inclination to respond appropriately?
- *Thought Process*: What can counsel observe of how clients attempt to convey information in the course of a face-to-face conversation? Are a client's statements crisp, organized, and sequential, or instead are they rambling, circuitous, and at times simply veering off course altogether? Is the same true when clients discuss everyday issues as well as emotionally laden ones?
- *Thought Content*: Distinct from—but likely related to—a client's thought process will be the personally held notions that such utterances contain. Is the client prey, for example, to paranoid statements of a general or specific nature? Particularly when these pertain directly to the matter at hand, counsel may want to file this information away for mitigation purposes (see Chapter 3, "Mitigation").
- *Perceptual Disturbances*: Counsel has often heard of mental health professionals referring to a client as "responding to internal stimuli." This is a reference to hallucinations. Different types of hallucinations

correspond to each of the five senses, in the following fashion: visual (seeing), auditory (hearing), tactile (feeling), olfactory (smelling), and gustatory (tasting).

- *Perceptual Capacity*: What if, instead of as a result of hallucinations or other acute psychiatric phenomena, clients are incapable of grasping what counsel is saying because of a simple inability to see or to hear? Clients may have been rousted from their homes without a chance to bring their eyeglasses to the jail. They may also seem to have limited vocabulary, when in fact ear blockage is the true culprit.
- *Insight*: Simply put, do clients have a seeming ability to understand what may be going on at all? Perhaps problems in this regard are betrayed by a blithe attitude toward the present situation, despite the direness of currently pending criminal charges. It may also be that clients, while understandably upset at being charged, just cannot connect this to what others are claiming they did.
- *Judgment*: Are clients capable of expressing what their roles might be as the representation process moves forward? What sorts of plans do clients share—marshalling evidence, avoiding contact with fellow arrestees, and remaining in touch with counsel, or instead dressing down the prosecutor in court, writing directly to the judge, or discussing evidence with relatives during jail visits?

In addition to tips derived from family members (see Chapter 17, "Working with Families"), jail personnel, educational records, legal records, employment records, and perhaps initially available reports or arraignment statements from arresting officers, counsel may have access to medical records, or the client may be able to convey some standing psychiatric diagnosis that has served as a focus of treatment or even disability benefits. The existence of certain diagnoses, even when counsel is not in a position to observe actively displayed symptoms firsthand, could inspire counsel to start thinking about a particular case in terms of competency to stand trial. These diagnoses may include:

- *Major Depressive Disorder*: Despite the fact that important decisions often must be made as soon as possible, clients with this disorder may adopt a frustratingly indifferent attitude concerning counsel's need for information and advice in the face of rapidly approaching deadlines. Often, the client with depression may dissolve into tears, seemingly incapable of taking an active role in his or her own defense. Some criminal defense attorneys conclude—erroneously—that a client must exhibit psychosis or intellectual disability to lack trial competency. In fact, some severe forms of clinical depression, in which the client is literally immobilized, will render clients utterly incapable of rational understanding or participation. Depression is associated with impaired memory as well as low energy or mood.

- *Intellectual Developmental Disability*: The client may be someone who has been masking this condition—formerly termed "mental retardation"—with intermittent success over the course of his or her entire life. Intellectual developmental disability may figure prominently not only in competency to stand trial matters but also when counsel seeks to exclude prior inculpatory statements (see Chapter 10, "False Confessions and *Miranda* Waivers"). Although counsel will want to attempt to converse with the client in an accessible fashion, this should not be taken as advice to speak as if the client were a child. Counsel will also attempt to anticipate and combat a prosecution expert's suggestion that incompetency can ultimately be cured by conducting courtroom proceedings with restricted legal vocabulary and with breaks for frequent explanations.
- *Paranoid Personality Disorder*: A primary concern in working with clients with paranoid personality disorder is that they should not be confused with those suffering from a full-blown delusional disorder; however, both conditions can be relevant to competency to stand trial. Predictably, constructing a viable working relationship with a client with paranoid personality disorder is fraught with complications. For example, any indication that any member of the defense team is less than fully prepared and supportive is likely to be interpreted as an expression of indifference, a heedless slight, or even an outright declaration of contempt for the client. Steadily building a track record of responsiveness and reliability may or may not result in trial competency.
- *Substance Use Disorders*: Often, the substance-dependent client is first encountered in the throes of withdrawal. Comprehension difficulties are a significant issue in these cases. While deficits are typically not as profound or as pervasive as those encountered with clients with intellectual disability, these still may provide a substantial barrier to collaboration. Withdrawal is a temporary circumstance, but it must

be managed with appropriate medical care, or death might actually result. Even subsequent to withdrawal, the trademark attitude (and primary defense mechanism) of the addicted client is denial. Counsel should not be surprised when such clients resolutely refuse to acknowledge circumstances that would readily be apparent to anyone else, with predictable competency implications. (See Chapter 11, "Substance Use Disorder.")

- *Schizophrenia*: Clearly, an active phase of this disorder will almost always render a client incapable of effective collaboration or communication, leading to an at least temporary lack of competency to stand trial. In those cases where psychotic symptoms are currently inactive, and thus at least temporarily in "remission," counsel may be in a position to garner useful information from such clients, in addition to forming at least an initial basis for a viable professional relationship. Similar to clients with paranoid personality disorder, those subject to the vicissitudes of schizophrenia may be prone to overreact to seemingly innocuous remarks or comments—even as more florid aspects of this illness are not readily observable—with predictably negative competency implications.
- *Bipolar Disorder*: A client with bipolar disorder may be prey to dramatic fluctuations between manic episodes of seemingly unrestrained agitation and excessive energy on one hand, and at times catatonic periods of depression on the other. Defense counsel may be able to obtain some much-needed factual material and forge some degree of cooperative bonding between more dramatic shifts in the client's overall mood and accompanying behavior. As with schizophrenia, a current forensic finding of competency to stand trial will often be tempered by the evaluator's stated observation that the client's abilities to understand and participate are only temporary, such that future mood swings may jeopardize competency and call for further assessment, perhaps on the eve of trial.

Expert Assistance

The Right Expert

Should a sufficient combination of the preceding concerns convince counsel that a legitimate problem with competency to stand trial may be present, the next task will be to obtain assistance from a qualified forensic mental health professional. A few considerations in particular will assist in this task (for a more in-depth review of issues in collaborating with the expert eventually chosen, see Chapter 4, "Working with the Expert: From the Perspective of Experts" and Chapter 5, "Working with the Expert: Guidance for Lawyers").

First, who is going to pay for the expert? Privately funded cases—especially those with solid financial backing—enable counsel to seek out assistance on his or her own, without having to disclose that expert's identity to the court or to the prosecution any time soon, if ever. With this protection, and in jurisdictions that do not compel disclosure even later in the course of criminal proceedings, counsel can afford (literally and figuratively) to weather an unhelpful initial expert opinion and seek supplemental support from an evaluator who is legitimately inclined to view competency matters more favorably.

Second, what expert discipline would be the most appropriate for a competency to stand trial evaluation? Should intellectual developmental disability (formerly termed "mental retardation") be a likely factor in the current case, the assistance of a psychologist will be particularly important because intelligence quotient (IQ) testing will be necessary in all but the most dramatic cases of cognitive impairment. If some form of brain damage is likely to be a relevant factor, a neuropsychological specialist, neuropsychiatrist, or forensic psychiatric generalist may be desirable, depending on how central to competency issues this issue is likely to become. In some jurisdictions—or in any event, in some courtrooms—a specifically "medical" opinion may be preferable.

Third, irrespective of discipline, what attributes should counsel be seeking in a competency to stand trial expert? As a general matter, "less important than searching for the narrowest discernible specialization is the quest for an expert who observes foundational requirements common to all branches of mental health science."[15] Based upon the experience of your attorney colleagues in employing a potential expert, is that expert well-credentialed, readily available, consistent, and sincere?[16] Experience

15. Eric Y. Drogin, *Determining the Need for, Identifying, and Selecting Experts*, *in* Coping with Psychiatric and Psychological Testimony 775, at 776 (David Faust ed., 6th ed., 2012).

16. Kristy A. Martire, Gary Edmond, & Danielle Navarro, *Exploring Juror Evaluations of Expert Opinions Using the Expert Persuasion Expectancy Framework*, 25 Legal Criminol. Psychol. 90 (2020).

with the threshold notion of trial competency will of course be desirable, and for cases in which funding is a concern, the expert chosen may need to be capable of addressing subsequently arising issues as well (see, for example, Chapter 2, "Criminal Responsibility" and Chapter 3, "Mitigation"). The competency to stand trial expert who seeks to evaluate a child or adolescent defendant should be well-versed in the clinical as well as legal issues pertinent to that age group (see Chapter 12, "Youthful Offenders").

Specialized Assessment Measures

Once the eventually chosen expert witness has identified the specific mental health condition that has given rise to what counsel is asserting as lack of competency to stand trial—using standard measures of intellectual capacity and psychopathology—that evaluator may also choose, in consultation with counsel, to administer one or more of a range of specifically forensic assessment measures as well. Commonly utilized examples[17] include:

- *Competency Screening Test (CST)*: The CST[18] employs hypothetical situations in a sentence completion format to identify defendants who might require a fuller, hospital-based competency evaluation. However, studies of the CST found problems in terms of classification, accuracy, and utility. The last major research published on the CST found that there was little stability in factor structure across studies for the CST, making it difficult to determine just what aspects of competency this instrument measures.
- *Competency to Stand Trial Assessment Instrument (CAI)*: The CAI,[19] a rating scale of 13 functions derived from the legal literature and clinical/courtroom experience, has generally been used as an interview guide rather than as a psychometric instrument. Studies indicated high levels of interrater reliability among trained examiners and

---

17. Information concerning these forensic assessment measures is adapted from Kathleen P. Stafford & Robert L. Sadoff, *Competence to Stand Trial*, *in* Handbook of Forensic Assessment: Psychological and Psychiatric Perspectives 3, at 14–17 (Eric Y. Drogin, Frank M. Dattilio, Robert L. Sadoff, & Thomas G. Gutheil eds., 2011).

18. *See also* Grant A. Blake, James R. P. Ogloff, & Won Sun Chen, *Meta-Analysis of Second Generation Competency to Stand Trial Assessment Measures: Preliminary Findings*, 64 Int'l J. L. Psychiatry 238 (2019).

19. *See also* Richard Rogers, Kamar Y. Tazi, & Eric Y. Drogin, *Forensic Assessment Instruments: Their Reliability and Applicability to Criminal Forensic Issues*, 41 Behav. Sci. & L. 415 (2023).

significant correlations between competency status and CAI ratings. Like the CST, this instrument served an important function in training mental health professionals about the concept of competency to stand trial, but is infrequently used now, as other measures have been developed to reflect changes in case law about decisional competence.

- *Interdisciplinary Fitness Interview—Revised (IFI-R)*: The IFI-R[20] was initially developed to assess symptoms of psychopathology and assess understanding of legal concepts and functions through a structured, joint interview by a psychologist and a lawyer. The potential strength of the instrument lies in its attempt to assess the defendant's functioning in the context of the anticipated demands of his or her particular legal situation. The IFI-R is a promising interview guide that tailors the assessment to the individual case, ensures lawyer input, and highlights the connection between psychopathology and psycholegal impairment.
- *Georgia Court Competency Test (GCCT)*: The GCCT[21] is a screening instrument that uses a courtroom drawing as a reference point for 12 questions about the physical positions and functional roles of court participants in a trial. It also consists of five questions about the defendant's charges and defense. A Mississippi State Hospital version (GCCT-MSH) added four questions about knowledge of courtroom proceedings and changed the weights of some items. Factor analytic research has confirmed that the GCCT-MSH yields stable, independent factors: general knowledge, courtroom layout, and specific legal knowledge. This screening instrument does not address ability to make decisions in consultation with counsel and to assist in one's defense.
- *Fitness Interview Test—Revised (FIT-R)*: This interview schedule functions as a screening measure to address legal issues and assessment of psychopathology. The FIT-R[22] has been described as a promising screening measure to determine whether an inpatient competency

---

20. *See also* Patricia A. Zapf, Amanda Beltrani, & Amanda L. Reed, *Psychological Assessment in Forensic Settings*, in The Cambridge Handbook of Clinical Assessment and Diagnosis 462 (Martin Sellbom & Julie A. Suhr eds., 2019).

21. *See also* Richard Rogers, Kamar Y. Tazi, & Eric Y. Drogin, *Forensic Assessment Instruments: Their Reliability and Applicability to Criminal Forensic Issues*, 41 Behav. Sci. & L. 415 (2023).

22. *See also* Ronald Roesch, *Social Worker Assessments of Competency to Stand Trial*, 5 J. Forensic Soc. Work 186 (2016).

evaluation is required, although in jurisdictions where thorough competency evaluations are routinely completed outside of a hospital setting, the utility of a screening measure may be somewhat limited.

- *Competence Assessment for Standing Trial for Defendants with Mental Retardation (CAST-MR)*: The CAST-MR[23] consists of three scales developed to assist in evaluation of competency to stand trial of defendants with intellectual disability (formerly termed "mental retardation"), including Basic Legal Concepts (multiple-choice items addressing essential courtroom notions); Skills to Assist Defense (multiple-choice items about hypothetical situations the defendant may face in working with his or her attorney); and Understanding Case Events (open-ended questions tapping understanding of aspects of case events in his or her own court case).
- *MacArthur Competence Assessment Tool—Criminal Adjudication (MacCAT-CA)*: The MacCAT-CA[24] is an abbreviated, clinical version of a more extensive research instrument designed to assess distinct competence-related abilities, rather than merely current knowledge. It attempts to measure the ability to understand information related to law and adjudicatory proceedings, and the ability to reason about specific choices that confront a defendant in the course of adjudication. The Understanding and Reasoning scales each contain eight items that are based on a hypothetical legal scenario. The Appreciation scale taps the ability to appreciate the meaning and consequences of the proceedings in the defendant's own case, through six items that refer to the specific legal situation. The authors noted that the MacCAT-CA does not include measures of response set, that the possibility of malingering needs to be assessed through other methods, and that the MacCAT-CA should be employed in the context of a comprehensive competency evaluation.

---

23. *See also* Mary E. Wood, Kimberly P. Brown, Amanda R. Bitting, Christopher Slobogin, & Brooke Bowerman, *Legal Admissibility of the Competence Assessment for Standing Trial for Defendants with Mental Retardation*, 104 J. PERSONALITY ASSESSMENT 289 (2022).

24. *See also* Mary E. Wood, Jaime L. Anderson, & David M. Glassmire, *The MacArthur Competence Assessment Tool-Criminal Adjudication: Factor Structure, Interrater Reliability, and Association with Clinician Opinion of Competence in a Forensic Inpatient Sample*, 29 PSYCHOL. ASSESSMENT 776 (2017).

- *Evaluation of Competency to Stand Trial—Revised (ECST-R)*: The ECST-R[25] was developed to assess aspects of the *Dusky* standard in the defendant's own case, and to assess feigned incompetency in a standardized manner. The ECST-R contains scales tapping Factual Understanding of the Courtroom Proceedings and Overall Rational Ability (combined measures of Rational Understanding of the Courtroom Proceedings and Consult with Counsel). The ECST-R also contains a measure of response style comprised of items tapping realistic, psychotic and nonpsychotic, and impairment types of items. The scales are reported to have high internal consistency and interrater reliability. It is a promising guide to systematically assessing competency to stand trial.

Clinical and Forensic Interview

Psychological testing is not intended as a stand-alone method of inquiry for forensic evaluations concerning competency to stand trial. There does not exist to date a measure that encompasses each and every relevant aspect of this legal construct. Counsel will want to ensure that his or her expert witness has taken the time to conduct an appropriate clinical and forensic interview, and correspondingly will be eager to cross-examine opposing experts on their apparent failure to do so.

When counsel seeks to cross-examine opposing experts regarding the results of psychological testing per se (see Chapter 2, "Criminal Responsibility"), an important issue may be whether the client possessed the requisite reading or oral vocabulary levels to comprehend certain test questions at all.[26] It is manifestly unfair for the client to be accused of malingering, poor cooperation, or some unflattering diagnosis, simply because of his or her lack of understanding. Consulting with one's own expert on the academic skill set necessary for taking a particular test is often a wise investment of time.

As noted earlier, various jurisdictions are likely to adhere to competency standards that diverge subtly from *Dusky* requirements. No psychological

---

25. *See also* Jaime L. Anderson, Jake Plantz, Sabine Glocker, & Patricia A. Zapf, *The MacCAT-CA and the ECST-R in Competency to Stand Trial Evaluations*, 104 J. Personality Assessment 281 (2022).

26. *See also* Kiera Himsl, Danielle Burchett, Anthony M. Tarescavage, & Davie M. Glassmire, *Assessing Reading Ability for Psychological Testing in Forensic Assessments: An Investigation with the WRAT-4 and MMPI-2-RF*, 16 Int'l J. Forensic Mental Health 239 (2017).

test could possibly be designed specifically to accommodate them all. What is the precise nature of your client's lack of understanding or capacity for rational discourse with counsel? Is it rooted in some collection of diagnoses that is subject to "cure" as opposed merely to temporary symptom reduction? Perhaps the latter situation reflects treatment initially received on an involuntary basis and is no longer being maintained in an outpatient or local jail setting.

Competency Restoration

When counsel has established to the trial court's satisfaction that his or her client is not competent to stand trial, that will not necessarily be the end of legal deliberations or consequences concerning this notion. Should your client be deemed only temporarily lacking in the requisite abilities, the judge may determine that an attempt at "competency restoration" is in order, for the purpose of addressing impediments based in either mental illness[27] or cognitive impairment.[28]

Counsel is likely to find the "restoration" label somewhat discomfiting and perhaps even misleading, since this term appears to suggest that the client was competent in the first place, but somehow lost his or her way. More problematic, from a practical standpoint, are those situations in which the trial court either turns to counsel for guidance in identifying treatment resources, or perhaps even orders counsel to arrange for these services. Counsel should also consider very carefully the possibility—depending upon the jurisdiction in question—that the client will languish in jail for an extended period of time while "restoration" services are being arranged, rendered, reported, and subjected to judicial review.

In most cases, it is to the client's advantage to remain incompetent to stand trial, despite the efforts of mental health professionals to supply missing information and instill coping mechanisms by means of psychoeducational counseling. Why, then, should counsel feel compelled to become an active participant in this process? Of course, it may ultimately be injurious to the client's standing to spurn requests or direction emanating from the

---

27. *See* Douglas R. Morris, *Change Severity and Aggression During Competency Restoration*, 50 J. Am. Acad. Psychiatry & L. 388 (2022).

28. *See* Graham S. Danzer, Elizabeth M. A. Wheeler, Apryl A. Alexander, & Tobias D. Wasser, *Competency Restoration for Adult Defendants in Different Treatment Environments*, 47 J. Am. Acad. Psychiatry & L. 68 (2019).

bench, and there may be some comfort to be gained from exerting at least some degree of control over the choice and instruction of those providing "restoration" services. Here, however, a potential conflict arises, as counsel would need to ensure that a needed opportunity for clinical treatment is not being sabotaged in the name of zealous advocacy.

Counsel may also wish to consider conducting—or enabling—broader legal interventions when faced with a systematic failure to provide necessary services. In Washington, for example, the Department of Social and Health Services was found in 2023 to be in contempt with respect to a range of matters including competency restoration.[29] Similarly, ongoing contempt lawsuits have been filed for over a decade in Colorado, citing repeated violations with respect to failures to meet competency restoration deadlines.[30]

Irrespective of counsel's level of involvement in the initiation and accountability of services, counsel will want to monitor the "restoration" process as closely as feasible. Similar to those problematic cases in which opposing experts may deem a client competent due to having him or her accept and parrot back supplied information, there is always a concern that "restoration" will involve little more than enabling the client to recite certain facts at a later date by mere dint of repetition. Counsel will want to have their own witnessed conduct follow-up examinations once the prescribed treatment regimen has run its course, in order to determine if the client has truly attained competency to stand trial.

• • •

Eric Y. Drogin, JD, PhD, ABPP, is a Fellow of the American Psychological Association, a Fellow of the American Academy of Forensic Psychology, and a Diplomate and former President of the American Board of Forensic Psychology. He currently holds faculty appointments with Harvard Medical School, the Harvard Mass General Brigham Forensic

---

29. *Court Again Holds WA DSHS in Contempt, Imposes $100M in Fines and Orders Changes to Hospital Admission Policies*, Disability Rights Washington (July 10, 2023), https://www.disabilityrightswa.org/court-again-holds-wa-dshs-in-contempt.

30. Allison Sherry, *Colorado Increasingly in Contempt as More Judges Recognize That Jail Isn't a Mental Health Answer* (September 11, 2018), Colorado Public Radio News, https://www.cpr.org/2018/09/11/colorado-increasingly-in-contempt-as-more-judges-recognize-that-jail-isnt-a-mental-health-answer.

Psychiatry Fellowship, the Brigham and Women's Hospital (BWH) Harvard Medical School Psychiatry Residency Training Program, and the Beth Israel Deaconess Medical Center (BIDMC) Harvard Psychiatry Residency Training Program. He is the Affiliated Lead of Psycholegal Studies for the Psychiatry, Law, and Society Program (at BWH), and participates in the Forensic Psychiatry Service (at BIDMC) and the Program in Psychiatry and the Law (at Massachusetts Mental Health Center). Dr. Drogin is a Life Fellow of the American Bar Foundation and a former Chair of the American Bar Association's Section of Science and Technology Law. His multidisciplinary practice encompasses mental health law, expert witness testimony, and trial consultation.

Chapter

2

Criminal Responsibility

Lucy Guarnera and Richard Bonnie

Lack of responsibility or insanity is probably one of the most misunderstood concepts in the criminal legal system. Contrary to popular belief, an insanity defense is mounted only in a small number of cases, and of those cases, only a small number are successful. Part of the reason is that, irrespective of the jurisdiction, the legal standard for insanity is difficult to meet. Whereas the legal standard for competency to proceed is relatively low, the standard for insanity is a demanding one.

This chapter by professors Lucy Guarnera and Richard Bonnie discusses all aspects of the insanity defense, including identifying mental disorders that may fit into the definition of insanity, through selecting the appropriate expert, understanding the components of an examination such as testing and interviews, and drafting and reviewing the written evaluation. As this chapter emphasizes, the mere diagnosis of a mental disorder in itself is insufficient to constitute insanity; rather, there must be a nexus between the disorder and the conduct charged, or it must, as the authors state, "have significantly altered your client's perception, rationality, or self-control at the time of the offense to the extent that they grossly misconceived the nature of the situation or were unable to control themselves."

• • •

Our system of laws generally defines a criminal offense as having two legal components: the *actus reus* (guilty act) and the *mens rea* (guilty mind). In other words, for someone to be considered legally blameworthy and deserving of criminal punishment, they must intentionally engage in prohibited conduct while having a basic understanding of the nature and likely consequences of the act they are committing (or they must at least be reckless or negligent in committing the act). Most of the time, the guilty act and guilty mind go together. For example, imagine a common situation in which a person drives their car onto someone else's property that is clearly marked "Do Not Enter." The person intentionally chose to trespass, knowing that their action is prohibited by law.

Now let us imagine that the trespassing driver is being chased by an armed assailant. It is likely that the law would recognize a defense of justification in this situation. In other words, the law typically exculpates a defendant who honestly believes (even if mistaken) that the otherwise illegal act was justified.

Now let us assume that there is no armed assailant, but that the driver is delusional and incorrectly believes that they are being chased by a homicidal aggressor. This shows that some mental disorders can impair a person's perception and judgment to such a degree that they commit a prohibited act *without* a "guilty mind." Most states have laws to accommodate these very rare situations—situations in which an individual may not be criminally responsible for a demonstrably illegal act due to a mental disorder or disability that led the defendant to believe that their behavior was legal or justifiable. The insanity defense is the most common and well-known of these exculpatory provisions and will be the focus of this chapter.

Legal Background

The insanity defense has existed in some form for hundreds of years in English common law, which forms the basis for American criminal law. Records exist of English courts acquitting defendants they considered to be "idiots" or "madmen" with the understanding of "wild beasts." The first modern codification of the insanity defense arose in 1843, after Scotsman Daniel M'Naghten was acquitted for killing the British prime minister's private secretary while suffering from paranoid delusions. The "M'Naghten rule" specified that a defendant qualified for the insanity defense if—as the result of "a defect of reason" or "disease of the mind"—they did not know "the nature and quality of the act" or "did not know [they were] doing what was wrong."[1]

1. *R. v. M'Naghten*, 8 E.R. 718 (1843).

Since these early days, one-half of U.S. states have retained some version of the M'Naghten rule, although the precise wording differs from state to state. Another 20 states and the District of Columbia have adopted the test recommended by the American Law Institute's Model Penal Code (1962), which uses different language with essentially the same purpose—asking whether the defendant was unable to "appreciate the criminality" (or wrongfulness) of their behavior due to mental disease or defect. In addition, about one-third of states have added a "volitional test" as an alternative basis for an insanity verdict. These states allow an insanity verdict if, due to mental disorder, the defendant was unable to resist the impulse to commit the act (or, as the Model Penal Code phrases it, was unable to "conform [their] conduct to the requirements of the law.") New Hampshire alone uses the "product rule," which states that a defendant is insane if their criminal behavior was the "product" of a mental disorder. Currently, four states (Kansas, Utah, Montana, and Idaho) have no traditional insanity defense at all.

States vary whether the burden of proof in an insanity case lies with the prosecution or the defense. Further, some states have other provisions that consider impaired criminal responsibility due to mental disorder (e.g., *mens rea* defenses, "guilty but mentally ill" verdicts). Attorneys should consult statute and case law to determine the legal language and application of criminal responsibility defenses in their area of practice.

Criminal responsibility defenses are often a political lightning rod due to unwarranted concerns about their overuse or misuse. For example, the federal government passed the Insanity Defense Reform Act in 1984 as a reaction to the insanity acquittal of John Hinckley, Jr., who shot President Ronald Reagan and others in an assassination attempt while mentally ill. Notwithstanding these concerns, criminal responsibility defenses have always been rare. For example, research indicates that insanity is raised in less than 1 percent of felony cases and that, when contested, an insanity defense prevails only about one-quarter of the time.

When to Consider a Criminal Responsibility Defense

When might a defense attorney consider a criminal responsibility defense for a client? First, you must have reason to think your client was experiencing some sort of mental illness or disability *at the time of the offense*. Unlike competency to stand trial—which is all about the defendant's *current* state—the insanity defense involves a retrospective analysis of the person's mental state at the time of the crime. Of course, the offense may have occurred weeks, months, or even years before you meet with a client, so their mental state may be quite different now. For example, a defendant may have been highly symptomatic at the time of the offense several months ago, but they have since been stabilized on psychiatric medications and are no longer displaying the same symptoms. A person's current symptoms, documented history of mental illness (e.g., prior hospitalizations), family accounts, and police reports of their behavior around the time of the offense are all factors that might lead you to suspect the defendant was experiencing a mental disorder at the time of the crime.

Second, the mental disorder must bear a plausible *relationship* to the offense conduct. In other words, the mental illness must have significantly altered your client's perception, rationality, or self-control at the time of the offense to the extent that they grossly misconceived the nature of the situation or were unable to control themselves. Many common mental disorders (such as depression, anxiety, ADHD, and eating disorders) are unlikely to meet this threshold. Thus, it will not be fruitful to pursue an insanity defense if the defendant has minor symptoms or symptoms without a plausible relationship to the offense conduct. Research indicates that just a handful of severe conditions account for most successful insanity pleas:

- **Psychotic disorders**: Most successful insanity pleas involve a psychotic disorder. Psychosis is a loss of contact with reality, which can include hallucinations (false sensory experiences, such as hearing voices), delusions (fixed, false beliefs that persist despite contrary evidence), and grossly disorganized speech or behavior. Individuals with psychosis may legitimately misperceive the nature of their behavior in a way that impairs criminal responsibility. For example, they may perceive life-threatening danger where none exists, or they may believe themselves to have official duties that justify their behavior (e.g., believing themselves to be a CIA agent ordered to shoot and kill terrorists; believing themselves to be the owner of the house in which they trespassed). The most common psychotic disorders you will encounter are schizophrenia and schizoaffective disorder (which involves both psychotic and mood symptoms). However, psychosis can also occur in individuals without a history of severe and persistent mental illness, such as in the case of postpartum psychosis or substance-induced psychosis.

- **Mood disorders**: Mania—abnormally and persistently elevated mood along with increased goal-directed activity or energy—may be relevant to criminal responsibility. People experiencing a manic episode may feel "on top of the world" or excessively irritable, often accompanied by racing thoughts and reduced need for sleep. As a result, they may engage in impulsive or disorganized behavior—possibly without adequate ability to think through or inhibit their behavior, which may impair criminal responsibility. For example, an individual experiencing a manic episode may drive recklessly, get into physical altercations, or repeatedly telephone the same person. Bipolar I disorder and schizoaffective disorder are the most common manic disorders you will encounter. Severe depression is rarely relevant to criminal responsibility.
- **Neurocognitive disorders**: A neurocognitive disorder entails acquired organic damage to the brain that results in impaired cognitive skills, such as attention, learning, memory, decision-making, and language. This may result from acute damage (e.g., traumatic brain injury or stroke) or from a progressive neurodegenerative disease (e.g., Alzheimer's disease, advanced HIV infection, or brain tumor). An individual with a neurocognitive disorder may have problems understanding the nature of their actions or controlling their behavior, which can impair criminal responsibility. For example, an individual with frontotemporal dementia may become easily agitated and strike out at caregivers due to impairments to the frontal lobe, which controls judgment and behavioral inhibition.
- **Intellectual disability**: Intellectual disability (formerly termed mental retardation) is present from early childhood and exists on a continuum, from mild to profound. An individual with intellectual disability must display impaired intellectual skills, such as reasoning, judgment, and academic learning. They must also display impaired adaptive functioning, meaning the skills necessary to navigate daily life in a reasonably independent and competent manner (e.g., dressing, feeding, shopping, paying bills). An individual with intellectual disability may have difficulty interpreting the world around them or controlling their behavior in a manner that impairs criminal responsibility. For example, a severely intellectually disabled person may have sexual contact with a minor but have no ability to comprehend statutory rape as a prohibited behavior.

While the disorders just listed (particularly psychotic disorders) are by far the most common in successful insanity defenses, other diagnoses may result in relevant impairments less commonly. These include post-traumatic stress disorder (PTSD), dissociative identity disorder, impulse-control disorders, epilepsy, and others. Personality disorders (such as antisocial personality disorder, which is characterized by rule-breaking behavior) are almost never grounds for a criminal responsibility defense.

While some diagnoses are much more common than others in insanity acquittals, be aware that diagnosis alone is no guarantee of success. The *relationship* between the symptoms and the offense conduct is what matters, not the diagnosis. It is possible—indeed, common—for an individual to have genuine psychotic symptoms around the time of the offense yet fail to meet the strict criteria for the insanity defense. Research indicates that most illegal behavior by people with severe mental illness is committed for the same reasons as those *without* mental illness, such as anger, poor problem-solving skills, or desire for personal gain. Just a fraction of illegal behavior by people with severe mental illness occurs as a direct consequence of their symptoms.

For example, imagine an individual with known schizophrenia who strikes a family member, resulting in an assault charge. Is this person a good candidate for the insanity defense? That depends on what available evidence suggests about their mental state at the time of the offense. Evidence might suggest that the individual with schizophrenia became angry with their family member because of an ordinary disagreement and struck out as a result. This kind of reactive aggression occurs among people both with and without mental illness and does not suggest a lack of criminal responsibility, even if the person's symptoms include general problems with dysregulated behavior. On the other hand, evidence might suggest that the individual had a paranoid delusion that their family member was trying to kill them and struck out in perceived self-defense. The insanity defense is much more plausible in this case.

Voluntary Intoxication

Voluntary intoxication requires a special discussion. Certainly, an individual who is acutely intoxicated on drugs or alcohol may engage in illegal conduct without understanding the nature, character, or consequences of their behavior. Drugs and alcohol can produce effects very similar to those of severe mental illnesses, including hallucinations, delusions, disorganized behavior, and impaired cognition. Indeed, some of the most tragic cases we have seen involved defendants who harmed loved ones while under the influence of powerful intoxicants and then deeply regretted their actions once sober. However, as a matter of law, voluntary intoxication alone cannot qualify a person for a criminal responsibility defense because lawmakers do not wish to encourage substance use as an excuse for criminal behavior. On the other hand, a person who has developed a "settled" mental disorder because of longstanding substance use (e.g., Korsakoff syndrome from chronic alcohol use) would be eligible for a criminal responsibility defense.

What about a defendant who *both* has legitimate psychiatric symptoms *and* was acutely intoxicated at the time of the offense? This is a common circumstance, since mental illness and substance use problems often co-occur for a variety of complex reasons (e.g., shared genetic or environmental vulnerabilities, self-medication with substances). In these cases, voluntary intoxication is typically not an absolute bar to eligibility for the insanity defense. However, it can be difficult to disentangle the effects of mental illness from the effects of intoxication, so any criminal responsibility argument will necessarily be more speculative. As another variant, intoxication may trigger a psychotic episode that outlasts the effects of the intoxicant; this is termed substance-induced psychosis. A crime committed during a substance-induced psychosis is eligible for the insanity defense. The key question is whether the crime occurred *while* the person was still acutely intoxicated or *after* the effects of the intoxicant had subsided (but the psychotic symptoms persisted).

The Forensic Evaluation Process

To review, if (1) you suspect a client may have been severely mentally ill (most often psychotic) at the time of the offense, (2) there is a plausible relationship between their symptoms and the offense conduct, and (3) their behavior cannot be explained by voluntary intoxication alone, it may be worth investigating a criminal responsibility defense. Of course, at this stage, you may still be unsure whether your client is likely to meet the specific insanity defense criteria in your area of practice. A forensic mental health assessment can help clarify available evidence about your client's mental state at the time of the offense to determine whether an insanity defense is viable. In many states, a forensic evaluation is required to move forward with an insanity defense.

Self-Incrimination Concerns

It is critically important for defense attorneys to familiarize themselves with the rules governing disclosure of information obtained during the forensic assessment. In most states, the results of a forensic evaluation of insanity go directly (and exclusively) to defense counsel, and then the defense decides whether to present this information in court. In these states, there is little risk to the client in pursuing a forensic evaluation to assess criminal responsibility (aside from a delay in disposition of the case).

In a small minority of states (e.g., Alabama), the findings of a forensic evaluation of insanity ordered by the court for an indigent defendant are sent not only to defense counsel but also to the court. However, even in those states the report is typically not accessible to the prosecution unless the defendant formally raises an insanity defense. If a state were to make the report accessible to the prosecution in the absence of an insanity plea, the defense counsel should strongly object on the ground that doing so violates both the Fifth Amendment privilege against self-incrimination and the Sixth Amendment right to effective assistance of counsel. Some states seek to avoid these difficulties by redacting insanity reports to remove the defendant's statements about the offense unless and until the defense chooses to acknowledge them.

Relatedly, some states (e.g., Mississippi) allow or require an assessment of competency to stand trial *and* an assessment of sanity to be combined in a single document, which is then sent to parties outside of defense counsel. Further, some states (e.g., Wisconsin) allow the prosecution to call a sanity evaluator as a witness even if the defense does not—for example, when defense consulted the evaluator for consideration of an insanity defense, but the evaluator opined that the defendant did not qualify.

In the minority of states that expose insanity evaluations or reports to parties outside the defense, defense attorneys are in a bind and, as a result, may have a higher threshold for requesting a forensic evaluation of insanity. Thus, in all situations involving court-appointed mental health assessments, the attorney should clarify the rules in their jurisdiction governing disclosure of information derived from the evaluation. Of note, this problem arises only in cases involving indigent defendants who do not have resources to obtain an assessment on their own, entirely within the protection of the

Sixth Amendment. This is why legislatures and courts have increasingly protected indigent defendants from unwarranted disclosures in the absence of an insanity plea. Indeed, it is our view that insanity assessments sought by indigent defendants should also be protected by the Sixth Amendment and should be accessible to the court and the prosecution only if the defendant pleads insanity or otherwise puts their mental state in issue.

Retaining a Forensic Evaluator

Once you have decided to explore a criminal responsibility defense, the next step is to retain a forensic evaluator. In most jurisdictions, insanity evaluations can be performed only by licensed clinical psychologists (PhD or PsyD degrees) or psychiatrists (MD or DO degrees). While some states mandate some degree of forensic training or experience to conduct insanity evaluations, most states essentially have no "quality control" over forensic evaluators. That means it is the attorney's job to choose a qualified evaluator. Look for experience conducting insanity evaluations and specialized forensic training (e.g., postdoctoral fellowship in forensic psychology or psychiatry, board certification in forensic psychology). Recommendations from colleagues, state forensic boards, or forensic clinics may be helpful here.

When the defendant is indigent and has court-appointed counsel, the court will typically order (and pay for) the evaluation, although this will depend on state-specific norms. In the case of a privately retained evaluation, the attorney and evaluator should agree on fees in advance.

Once you have retained a forensic evaluator, you should have an initial call with the evaluator to describe the case, clarify expectations, and discuss logistics. This is also a time for the attorney to share important legal information the evaluator needs to know prior to the evaluation. For example, in the case of a *mens rea* defense, the parties should discuss the precise intent language of the charged offense, as the forensic evaluator will need to assess the defendant's ability to form that intent.

Gathering Records

Next, the defense attorney should gather relevant records for the forensic evaluator. In a forensic evaluation, third-party information is crucial and can make or break a criminal responsibility defense. Since the goal of a criminal responsibility evaluation is to retrospectively assess the defendant's mental state *at the time of the crime*, records from around that time are particularly important. For example, if the only evidence that a defendant was delusional at the time of the crime is their own self-report, that is weak evidence in favor of the insanity defense. However, if records document repeated psychiatric hospitalizations, and police reports, witness accounts, and body-worn camera footage all show the defendant acting erratically and speaking nonsensically about conspiracies, that is much stronger evidence in favor of the insanity defense.

While some states mandate that the prosecution provide limited information to the forensic evaluator (e.g., criminal history, description of the offense), the defense typically bears the onus of obtaining records and furnishing them to the forensic evaluator. The type of third-party information that is available and relevant will vary from case to case but may include the following:

- Police reports and other investigative materials (including audio or video footage, if available)
- Mental health records from throughout the defendant's life (e.g., therapy, medication, assessments, psychiatric hospitalizations)
- Jail records, including mental health and medical records (particularly if the defendant was incarcerated shortly before or after the offense)
- School records (particularly if the defendant is young or if intellectual disability is at issue)

In addition to these kinds of records, forensic evaluators will typically seek collateral interviews with family members, friends, treatment providers, employers, or others who know the defendant and can provide information about their life history, mental health symptoms, or behavior around the time of the offense. If needed, the defense attorney should help facilitate these interviews.

The Forensic Interview

After furnishing records, the next step is for the forensic evaluator to interview the defendant. Interviews typically last at least several hours and may require more than one meeting in complex cases. This is usually done in person but can also be done remotely in some circumstances. The defense attorney should help arrange the logistics of the interview (e.g., by communicating with the jail where the defendant is being held).

Attorneys may wonder how to prepare the defendant for the forensic interview. The best way to prepare the defendant is to explain the role of the forensic evaluator and details about the evaluation in advance so that your client has time to ask questions and get comfortable with the idea. You should emphasize that you want your client to be open and honest with the forensic evaluator, as this will ultimately be in your client's best interest. You should not coach your client to give any particular responses to the evaluator aside from their honest, full recollection of events. If your client is distrustful or paranoid, you may arrange a "warm hand-off" to introduce your client to the forensic evaluator in person. However, attorneys should not be present for the interview itself as the presence of a third party can skew results.

During the interview, the forensic evaluator will gather detailed information about the defendant's life history, covering areas such as family, school, work, medical history, mental health, substance use, relationships, and legal involvement. After obtaining a broad life history, the evaluator will assess in detail the time period surrounding the offense, including the defendant's account of the offense behavior. Again, while the defendant's account is important, it is only one source of information and will need to be supported by third-party evidence to put forward the strongest case for insanity.

What about cases in which a defendant claims they do not remember the offense at all? There are certainly legitimate mental health or medical conditions that can result in loss of memory of the offense. A defendant with a severe psychotic disorder or organic brain condition (e.g., dementia, traumatic brain injury) may have impaired memory of past events. Defendants who were dissociating at the time of the offense may also have impaired memory of events. Dissociation is an altered sense of the reality of one's surroundings or oneself, such as feeling detached from one's own mental processes or body or experiencing one's surroundings as unreal, distant, or distorted. Dissociation is often associated with trauma exposure and is typically viewed as an involuntary coping mechanism intended to protect the individual from overwhelming feelings of fear, pain, or distress. However, dissociation can also be associated with other mental health conditions, drugs, or medications.

If the defendant claims they cannot remember the offense, the forensic evaluation process is no different. As always, the degree of third-party corroboration (e.g., history of memory loss or dissociation documented in medical records or recounted by family members) will determine the strength of the evaluator's opinion about insanity.

Psychological Testing

The forensic evaluator may also conduct psychological testing while meeting with the defendant. There is no test to "prove" insanity or other kinds of impaired criminal responsibility. Any testing the forensic evaluator performs will neither prove nor disprove insanity directly but will be aimed at gathering evidence broadly relevant to criminal responsibility. While there exists one structured tool to help forensic evaluators assess the relevant domains of an insanity evaluation (the Rogers Criminal Responsibility Assessment Scales, or R-CRAS), it is rarely used. The most common types of psychological testing in insanity evaluations are as follows:

- **Tests assessing a wide range of psychological symptoms** (e.g., the Minnesota Multiphasic Personality Inventory-3, or MMPI-3; the Personality Assessment Inventory, or PAI). These kinds of tests compare the defendant's responses to those of large normative samples to assess areas of concern (e.g., psychotic experiences, mania) that are markedly different from the ways most people respond. These tests also have validity scales to assess if the defendant responded in an attentive, forthright manner.
- **Tests assessing intellectual ability or neuropsychological status** (e.g., the Wechsler Adult Intelligence Scales, 4th Edition, or WAIS-IV; the Wechsler Memory Scale, 4th Edition, or WMS-IV). These kinds of tests assess IQ or more narrow cognitive abilities such as memory, attention, or executive functioning. These tests are most relevant when there is a concern about intellectual disability or neurocognitive impairment.
- **Tests assessing feigning of cognitive impairment or psychological symptoms** (e.g., the Test of Memory Malingering, or TOMM; the Miller Forensic Assessment of Symptoms Test, or MFAST; the Structured Interview of Reported Symptoms, 2nd Edition, or SIRS-2). These kinds of tests use statistical techniques to assess whether the defendant is intentionally feigning poor memory or claiming bizarre or unlikely psychological symptoms.

Assessing Malingering

The forensic evaluator must assess the possibility that the defendant is feigning or exaggerating the claimed psychological symptoms. There is an obvious external motivation to feign symptoms in the context of an insanity evaluation. Beware of defendants who claim sudden, severe psychological symptoms that appeared for the first time during the offense with no documented history of mental illness. Of course, an individual may commit a crime because of a first psychotic episode, but even in these cases there is typically third-party evidence of prodromal symptoms (i.e., unusual behavior or perceptual disturbances that precede frank psychosis).

Likewise, beware of defendants who assert that the offense conduct was driven entirely by hallucinations or delusions (e.g., voices commanding them to commit the crime) but who do not show the kind of disorganized behavior or speech that typically accompanies such severe psychotic symptoms. Claims of improbable patterns of memory loss (e.g., defendants claiming to forget their own name or how to read) are also potential signs of feigning, particularly in the absence of corresponding impairments in daily living. As mentioned earlier, psychological testing can help clarify a defendant's response style if the evaluator suspects malingering.

After the Forensic Evaluation

The evaluator will integrate all strands of evidence (including records, the interview with the defendant, collateral interviews, testing results, and the malingering assessment) to form a final opinion about criminal responsibility. We strongly recommend that attorneys speak to the forensic evaluator *after* they have completed their evaluation but *before* they begin writing any report. This conversation allows time for the evaluator to describe their preliminary opinion and rationale and for the attorney to ask questions and clarify areas of confusion. This conversation may influence areas of emphasis in the report or determine whether a report is needed at all.

What If the Forensic Evaluator's Opinion Is Unfavorable?

If the forensic evaluator's opinion is unfavorable to a criminal responsibility defense, what happens next? Ideally, the forensic evaluator will "show their work," meaning they explain exactly why they do not believe your client meets the legal standard for insanity, utilizing all available evidence. If you understand and agree with their reasoning, that is likely the end of the road for a criminal responsibility defense, and you can turn your attention to representing your client in other ways. Remember that successful insanity defenses are rare, and that even defendants with legitimate, severe psychotic illness or other disorders will only rarely meet the strict criteria for the insanity defense. In the case of an unfavorable opinion, the attorney may not request a written report at all. However, we have known some defense attorneys to request a written report anyway, for the sake of documenting the defendant's life history and mental illness (e.g., to be used as mitigation at sentencing).

If you strongly disagree with the forensic evaluator's reasoning or suspect they did a shoddy job, you can seek a second opinion, although courts may be unwilling to fund a second evaluation. However, we would caution against "fishing" for a favorable opinion when available evidence is against it. While you may be able to find an evaluator, eventually, who will offer a favorable opinion, their opinion is unlikely to be convincing to a prosecutor, jury, or judge if the evidence and reasoning does not back it up. Further, in some states you are required to disclose that you sought multiple evaluations.

What If the Forensic Evaluator's Opinion Is Favorable?

Just because the forensic evaluator's opinion supports a criminal responsibility defense does not mean this route will be in your client's best interest or that your client will want to pursue this route. If the prosecutor does not agree to an uncontested insanity plea, you will still have to argue this defense at trial. Juries may be skeptical of insanity claims even when the evidence in favor is strong, and your client may be unwilling to take this risk. In our experience, defense attorneys often end up using favorable forensic opinions on criminal responsibility as leverage when negotiating a traditional plea bargain.

Further, there is a pervasive myth that a successful insanity defense is a "get out of jail free" card, meaning the defendant is immediately released and returned to the community. However, this could not be further from the truth. Insanity acquittees are committed to a psychiatric institution where they are held until a forensic review panel deems them appropriate to be released. While specific policies vary by state, release considerations usually include threat to public safety, risk of future criminal behavior, danger to self, current clinical functioning, release plan, and related issues. Often an insanity acquittee must pass through a graduated system of increasing freedoms and privileges (e.g., day passes, furloughs, probation-like requirements) before they are unconditionally released to the community. These requirements are more stringent than those governing civilly committed psychiatric patients.

In other words, while an insanity acquittee is not legally guilty of a crime, they are still subjected to significant curtailment of liberty. And the duration of this curtailment is indeterminate, as it depends on the individual's clinical progress and the judgment of a forensic review panel. Research indicates that the average length of hospitalization for an insanity acquittee is at least several years, while the average length of hospitalization for a civilly committed patient is around one month.

These realities can raise ethical issues for attorneys. Imagine a client who is an excellent candidate for the insanity defense, but who is charged with a misdemeanor or minor felony. That client might rationally prefer conviction and brief incarceration over an indeterminate hospitalization that could last years. On the other hand, an insanity acquittal might be a surer route to needed treatment for a client with severe, persistent mental illness, even if they are charged with only minor offenses. However, clients with schizophrenia or similar psychotic disorders may have poor insight into their illness and need for treatment, a condition known as anosognosia. Thus, clients may be resistant to an insanity defense as a direct result of their symptoms, even if you perceive that an insanity defense and hospitalization would be in their best interest in the long term.

These issues require clear communication with your client about the likely outcomes of different legal routes and their own goals and preferences. If you perceive that mental health symptoms are significantly interfering with your client's ability to rationally consider the pros and cons of various legal routes, you should request an evaluation for competency to stand trial. While practice varies, we recommend that attorneys do not pursue an insanity defense until their client is competent to stand trial. A client who is currently so mentally ill that they are unable to understand the proceedings against them or assist their attorney will not be capable of these important conversations about the risks and benefits of an insanity plea.

If you and your client decide to pursue a criminal responsibility defense, you should follow all statutory rules for notifying the prosecution. The prosecution may request its own independent forensic evaluation of your client, or they may request a second opinion of your evaluation (i.e., an independent expert who examines your expert's report and evaluation materials *without* meeting with your client). If the prosecution's expert agrees with your expert, that is very helpful to your case and may lead to an uncontested insanity plea or other agreement. If the prosecution's expert disagrees with your expert, you may face a "battle of the experts" in court. If your expert will be testifying in court, be sure to spend considerable time preparing them for testimony. Remember, though, that a forensic evaluator is intended to be a neutral and unbiased expert on whom the court can rely for impartial testimony. They are not on "your side" per se and will need to be transparent in their report and testimony about any contradictory evidence or areas of weakness in their opinion.

• • •

Lucy Guarnera is a licensed clinical psychologist and Assistant Professor of Psychiatry and Neurobehavioral Sciences at the Institute of Law, Psychiatry, and Public Policy (ILPPP) at the University of Virginia. She received her doctorate in clinical psychology from the University of Virginia. As a clinician, she completed a predoctoral internship focused on traumatic stress based at the Crime Victims Research and Treatment Center at the Medical University of South Carolina, as well as postdoctoral fellowships in forensic psychology and mental health law at the University of Virginia. She has conducted hundreds of forensic evaluations and testifies regularly as an expert witness. As a researcher, Dr. Guarnera seeks to improve the fairness and accuracy of the justice system, both by studying biased decision-making among forensic experts and by investigating the legal experiences of vulnerable individuals, such as adolescents and trauma victims. Dr. Guarnera's original research on the legal experiences of women who become pregnant from rape was honored with the Best Dissertation Award and multiple grants from the American Psychology-Law Society. She is an adjunct instructor in the University of Virginia Psychology Department and also co-coordinates the ILPPP's training program for forensic professionals, with a focus on children, adolescents, and the law. She lives in Charlottesville, Virginia, with her family.

Richard J. Bonnie is Harrison Foundation Professor of Medicine and Law Emeritus and Director Emeritus of the Institute of Law, Psychiatry, and Public Policy at the University of Virginia. He specializes in criminal law, mental health law, and public health law and has authored leading casebooks in these subjects. Professor Bonnie has been involved in public service throughout his career, including appointments as Secretary for the National Advisory Council on Drug Abuse (1976–1980) and Chair of Virginia's Commission on Mental Health Law Reform (2005–2011). He has served as an advisor to the American Psychiatric Association since 1979, receiving the Isaac Ray Award in 1998 and presidential commendations for service to American psychiatry in 2003 and 2016. He has also served on three MacArthur Foundation research networks, including, most recently, Law and Neuroscience. Professor Bonnie was elected to the National Academy of Medicine in 1991 and has chaired more than a dozen studies for the National Academies, including *Pain Management and the Opioid Epidemic* (2017) and *The Promise of Adolescence* (2019). He received the University of Virginia's highest honor, the Thomas Jefferson Award, in 2007.

Chapter

3

Mitigation

Marcia Shein

We live in the era of the vanishing trial. The vast majority of cases—state and federal, misdemeanor and felony—resolve in plea bargains. One of the reasons is that defendants prefer the certainty of a particular sentence or sentencing range rather than a potential conviction at trial, which all too often carries a significant "trial tax."

For people with mental disabilities, there is another reason for such a large number of pleas. The legal concepts of competency and insanity at the time of the act do not always serve them well. As the previous two chapters illustrated, competency is a very low standard, whereas insanity is a very high standard. Thus, in most cases where the accused has some sort of mental disability, that disability is used as a tool in mitigation.

The following chapter by criminal defense lawyer Marcia Shein is a comprehensive guide to using mental disabilities during sentencing. She discusses spotting the "red flags" if the client doesn't have a diagnosis, how to select an expert, and how to request that the court appoint an expert. Most importantly, throughout the chapter, attorney Shein details strategies to promote the argument that mental disabilities are not "an excuse for committing a crime or a defense, but rather, an explanation that invites compassion."

• • •

There are often subtle, and sometimes not so subtle, signs that your client may need a forensic mental health evaluation. Learning how to recognize those signs, weighing the pros and cons of the evaluation, and determining what steps are necessary to completing an evaluation are crucial parts of any effective criminal defense practice. This is true even if you are certain that your client is competent and that the mental health issues will not provide a complete defense to the crime (i.e., not guilty by reason of insanity). Potential mental health issues that do not have a direct effect on sentence exposure still could play a critical mitigating role. This is not an excuse for committing the crime or a defense, but rather an explanation that invites compassion. As an advocate at sentencing, understanding potential mental health issues and using those effectively can make a drastic difference in mitigation of sentencing and, in some cases, could even mean the difference between life and death.

We are all aware of the classic cases where mental health issues are used as mitigation at sentencing in death penalty cases. In these cases, it is common to have a mitigation specialist who conducts a complete background investigation and facilitates extensive mental health evaluations in order to build a case for a life in prison with parole or life in prison without parole as opposed to the death sentence.

Just because your client is not facing a possible death sentence and you may not have access to a mitigation specialist, however, does not mean that your client's mental health issues could not have a serious impact on the court and result in a shorter, or even probated, sentence. It is your job, as an advocate for your client at sentencing, to gather information and paint your client as a complete and multifaceted human, not just a faceless person accused of a crime. The more you can humanize your client to the court and show the court why your client deserves its compassion, the more likely your client is to receive a shorter sentence. It is not only the court that can be affected by the humanizing of your client; you can also use this information to try to convince the prosecutor to support your request for a lesser sentence in plea negotiations or a sentencing recommendation. In many criminal cases, the process of humanizing your client and asking for compassion involves examining mental health issues.

This chapter will examine how to recognize that your client may have a possible mental health issue, and although such a condition may not rise to the level of competency or insanity, it is nonetheless a significant factor for full and effective representation. Additionally, once you recognize a possible mental health issue, you must evaluate whether it might be helpful as a mitigating factor before sentencing and at sentencing; select a well-qualified expert to evaluate possible mental health issues; request court assistance, if necessary, in securing the evaluation; revisit whether the possible mental health issue might be helpful as a mitigating factor after the evaluation; and advocate for your client based on these issues.

How to Recognize Signs of a Possible Mental Health Issue

"Mr. Joel," an active and reserve military veteran, worked as a civil airplane mechanic for a military base. He had never been in trouble before. Suddenly, at the age of 50, he decided to set some fires in vacant houses. During the pendency of this state case, he sent over 150 letters to his attorney representing repetitive and disorganized thinking. This attorney did not see anything unusual about this behavior (!) but did get an evaluation done for competency. The evaluation came back noting Mr. Joel was competent to stand trial. What was missing however, was an understanding that although he was competent to stand trial, he was nonetheless mentally ill with several disorders. Thus, an evaluation related to this issue was needed but never sought.

While in state prison on the arson offense, Mr. Joel sent letters to several government agencies with threatening comments, trying to make the letters look like they came from people he wanted to get in trouble. He sent them from jail, but he was caught. The first case was a state case, but the serious nature of the second case made it a federal case. Indeed, the government requested a competency evaluation, and again he was found competent to stand trial. Finally, the federal attorney who also received some 200 letters from Mr. Joel in just a six-month period of time recognized that there was a serious mental health issue that needed a full evaluation for mitigation purposes. Two evaluations were completed, one from a psychiatrist and one from a psychologist, both finding significant mental health issues were contributing factors to Mr. Joel's conduct, which the multiple letters symbolized.

Competency is not a mitigation factor; rather, it is a procedural event to determine if a client can go to trial and assist his or her attorney in his or her own defense. Mental health conditions are mitigation questions that can be a valued tool in the defense attorney's toolbox for plea negotiations and sentencing mitigation. Recognizing this difference is critical to a successful outcome. Mr. Joel was given a much more lenient sentence in federal court than would otherwise have been given because the judge was provided with a plethora of information that assisted the court in finding that the mental health issues Mr. Joel was dealing with were a mitigating factor. The court also imposed conditions to help Mr. Joel deal with these problems once he was released. Recognizing the issue of mental health is not easy, but there are ways to be more aware of what to look for.

While sometimes your client's mental disability is apparent, either because he or she informs you of it or there is some clear outward manifestation, most often it will be much more subtle. The signs of a mental health issue vary widely, and can include anything from rapidly blinking eyes, to tics, to sluggish reactions, to extreme agitation, to the inability to complete a thought, to paranoia and delusions or hallucinations, to an entirely flat affect or as noted earlier, disorganized thinking manifested in obsessive writings. Look for information from others to determine if there has been a pattern of odd behavior. Some people may simply be odd, or act strangely in social situations. But that alone is not enough to say there is definitely a mental health issue that is directly affecting the criminal conduct or for mitigation purposes. So, how can you tell if it is time to have your client evaluated to determine if you can use a mental disability as a mitigating factor?

Unfortunately, just as a mental health issue does not fit neatly into a box, there is no clear-cut answer as to how you can determine when to have your client evaluated for a possible mental health issue. It comes down to experience, investigation, research, and sometimes just a gut feeling that needs to be further explored. For example, if you have a client who has never informed you that he or she has any mental health issues, and in fact denies them, but calls you repeatedly in a panicky rapid voice and continues to talk in repetitive circles, this should set off a red flag. If your client was charged with a crime that involves a situation where the client may have panicked, the red flags should be raised high. At this point, you should be asking yourself if your client has some sort of mental health issue that causes him or her to panic or overreact in situations that do not call for the type of response your client gave. Could that be what happened in the charged offense? Could you use this mental issue to help convince the court and/or the government that your client deserves leniency? There are mental health issues such as obsessive compulsive, bipolar, manic depressive and attention deficit disorders that can be perceived by just talking to your client. Attorneys should learn what some of the signs for these disorders are, and an easy Google search can help.

A good example of odd behavior is a case where the client drove off from a routine police stop for an alleged window tint violation. As a result of this conduct, he crashed his car and was eventually arrested, although he showed clear signs of a panic disorder when the police officers ran up to him with guns drawn. It turned out that he was shot by a police officer at a young age and even though it was an accident, the trauma remained an issue exacerbated by the officers' over response to a nonviolent traffic stop. The discovery of all of this occurred after a background review and referral to a psychologist who diagnosed post-traumatic stress disorder (PTSD).

In these scenarios, there is nothing to indicate that the possible mental illness would give rise to a defense of not guilty by reason of insanity. Nevertheless, these instances raise red flags and it is critical to take the time to determine if there is a mental health issue and, if so, if it can be used in a plea-bargaining effort or sentencing mitigation. This inquiry ideally will take place before trial so that you can give your client competent advice regarding both their underlying case and sentencing exposure.

Evaluating Whether the Possible Mental Health Issue Can Be Used in Mitigation

Not all clients will want to admit a possible mental health issue, even if it might aid their criminal case. This is especially true when an individual is incarcerated and may fear being singled out because of a mental issue. This is a real fear and one that you must acknowledge and consider when you set up the mental health evaluation in the facility. Further, not every case will benefit from the possibility of mental health issues, so you must weigh the pros and cons both before getting an evaluation and again after you receive the results from the evaluation if you decide to get one.

Once the red flags are raised you must investigate further. This could involve talking to family, asking about previous life experiences, asking about medications, and asking about traumas in your client's life history, where the seeds of mental health complications often begin. It is very important to get a complete background history of your client from others as well as the client themselves. As you are investigating, you also must be evaluating whether, assuming your client does have a mental health issue, it will be helpful as a mitigating circumstance. This inquiry necessarily considers what your client is charged with and how you can argue that mental health illness contributed to this charge. Does the potential mental health issue help explain why your client did what he or she did? Or does it make it more likely that your client will continue to commit crimes such as the one he or she is charged with? Can your client's mental health issue be controlled with proper treatment so that it is less likely that he or she will commit another crime? Or, even with proper treatment, is your client likely to commit another crime? The more you can link the mental illness with the crime and the more that you can show that treatment will help reduce the risk of recidivism, the stronger the mitigation argument.

In one case, a child pornography collector was determined to have an obsessive-compulsive disorder: The only reason he had so much child pornography in his home was because he had a collection obsession. The client would frequently just reorganize the videos and CDs and not look at them. It was also discovered that he had been abused as a child, a contributing factor to starting the collection in the first place. Though this did not negate the seriousness of the charges, it allowed the court to reduce the sentence that federal guidelines called for.

There are substantial options for mitigating the outcome of child pornography possession cases. Most of the people involved in these cases have been abused themselves or have other mental health issues. Discovering them is not easy, as many people are reluctant to speak about their own abuse. Once discovered, however, a full psychosexual evaluation can help on several levels. First, it can explain some of the background trauma in clinical terms, softening the appearance of the conduct itself. Second, the evaluation type can address, if favorable of course, the lack of recidivist tendencies if given proper treatment in lieu of long-term incarceration. Many courts have found significant mitigating factors associated with childhood pornography cases. Incorporated here are some significant sources of information on mitigating factors related to child pornography cases and mitigation applications.

Cases involving the possession and distribution of child pornography, as well as the production of child pornography, often require some kind of psychosexual evaluation to determine if there are any underlying issues that contributed to the offense conduct. Many of these offenders manifest their behavior due to their own past abuse or another mental health issue that needs to be discovered. These findings are not excuses for the criminal conduct but are mitigating factors. A recent case involving an 18-year-old required further evaluation to determine how and why this person began collecting and viewing child pornography when he was 15 years old. It is sad to say that the government knew about this conduct before the person turned 18, but waited until he turned 18 to charge him, thus putting him in an adult sentencing situation. The eventual evaluation showed no propensity for actual contact with an underage child. The evaluation also uncovered a deep-seated issue with an uncle who had fondled him in his early teens. The problem that arises in federal cases is that the guidelines are severe no matter what mitigating factors are evaluated. This places a heavy burden on the defense to find ways to encourage the courts to vary such harsh sentencing ranges under the guidelines. There are many cases that have defined variance factors in these types of cases to mitigate the sentencing outcome.

Traumatic Brain Injury and Post-Traumatic Stress Disorder

Traumatic brain injury (TBI) and post-traumatic stress disorder (PTSD) are two of the most significant brain and emotional injuries that can lead to serious mental health problems early or later in life. A key element of success in identifying these conditions is a full review of a client's background information. For example, were there any falls as a child or adult that caused a severe injury to the head or neck? What about activities such as soccer, football, and other sports where someone might have suffered numerous concussions? Military service can bring on both TBI and PTSD. TBI is the physical damage caused by the events leading up to the PTSD, while PTSD symptoms are due to the person's emotional condition. This combination is frequently seen in military personnel, especially those who are in combat-ready units, but not always. Both mental and physical health issues can be individual or related. Unfortunately, it is often hard to detect the damage caused by TBI development before a tragic event occurs, which can be criminal. Therefore, it is important to know the full background of the person involved. For PTSD or TBI, a full examination of any military service is important in finding out if something happened while serving the country, even if not in combat.

When someone suffers from either of these conditions, there are several options. One is to immediately get a neurological exam on the areas of the brain affected by the TBI. Second is to get a full psychosocial evaluation to determine what other mental health conditions may have developed as a result of TBI or PTSD. Remember that PTSD is not merely a military injury issue. PTSD can be caused by any set of circumstances in a person's life that deals with an emotional response to a traumatic event. Such events could be sexual assault as a child or adult, divorce when the client was a child, observing or being a victim of domestic abuse, traumatic injuries, or other events that severely affected a client's emotion well-being and normal life existence.

Many attorneys are not well-versed on taking down details of a person's life and history. In death penalty cases there are mitigation specialists, but for the average attorney, the mitigation effort starts at the door of the attorney's office due to cost concerns. Attorneys should develop an in-house form that sets out the main areas of a person's life, such as name; date of birth; where the client currently lives and has lived in the past; where the client grew up; history of medical conditions; serious injuries in life (such as sports injuries or car accidents); military service (including detailed notes about where the client served, for how long, and in what capacity); and if the client experienced any traumatic injuries or events while serving (this question can be adjusted to a person who has not been in the military as well). You can even include a list of symptoms or feelings people often experience that may have made a significant impression on the client (e.g., feelings of anxiety, low self-esteem, anger, frustration, fear, etc.).

To help develop your own background form to gather initial information that will help direct your services for mental health issues and mitigation, speak to sentencing mitigation specialists or work with a local psychologist or psychiatrist. This type of form can get you started on the road to discovering a client's TBI or PTSD or other mental health issues, which can be significant mitigating factors to a criminal event. An example of a form is included at the end of this chapter.

Selecting a Well-Qualified Expert

Assuming that there is a possibility of a mental health issue and that your client's mental health illness can be used in mitigation, your next step needs to be to approach your client regarding this topic. This is necessarily a very delicate inquiry. If your client admits to the mental health illness and has been under treatment, you will need to obtain the necessary waivers to speak with his or her doctors, determine if the doctors can qualify as experts in court, and determine if further evaluation or experts are needed.

If your client, however, denies having a mental health issue or has never been diagnosed, you must carefully explain that you want an evaluation to determine if you can play to the courts' and prosecutor's compassion and argue that the client's mental status is a condition that can be used to reduce his or her culpability and justify a lesser sentence. If your client absolutely refuses to participate in the evaluation, it will be very rare for a court to order him or her to do so because you are not raising a defense of insanity or an issue of competence to stand trial. You must clearly explain the downside and potential upside of having an evaluation. It may be necessary to have more than one conversation regarding this issue. If your client continues to refuse, make sure you document your client's refusal to protect yourself from future claims of ineffective assistance of counsel.

Assuming your client will consent to participating in the evaluation (or you believe the court will order one), the next step is to select a qualified mental health professional to discuss your concerns. The sort of expert you approach will vary depending on what sort of mental health issue you believe your client has—psychiatrist (usually for mental disorders), psychologist (usually for personality or behavioral disorders), neuropsychologist (usually for brain injuries, memory, language, or orientation issues). If you are unsure, ask a colleague or reach out to an expert to discuss your concerns. If the expert is not the proper expert, he or she may be able to point you in the right direction.

Once you have determined the type of expert needed and locate this expert, you will need to inform them of what your concerns are and why. You will need to discuss the evidence you have gathered to support these concerns, the nature of the charges, why you believe this mental health issue may be related in some way to those charges, and how you hope the expert can help. After this discussion you should know if the mental health expert believes, based on what you have told them, that your client may have a mental health issue that may have played some role in his or her decision to commit the crime, whether this mental health expert is qualified in the state or federal system where you are practicing, and if this mental health expert is willing to travel to the jail to perform an evaluation (assuming that your client is incarcerated).

Selecting a well-qualified mental health expert who is going to conduct a very thorough review, which necessarily includes the evidence and the evaluation, may also include speaking to family members, friends, or other witnesses. This is critical because this expert is going to be the one to explain to the court (and perhaps the prosecutor) why it should impose a lesser sentence based on your client's mental disability. This expert is going to have to highlight that this mental disability is not a weakness, but rather an issue that can be managed.

It is also important to recognize that the prosecutor will often want their own expert to do an evaluation. You will have to weigh this against what you know from your expert's opinion and whether such an evaluation would result in a similar outcome as your expert. Remember the prosecutor will be seeking an expert that likely will contradict yours, so find one who has good credentials and will be honest about the issues. Also, remind the prosecutor that any additional evaluation by them is not for competency or sanity but mitigation. See also Chapter 4, "Working with the Expert: From the Perspective of Experts" and Chapter 5, "Working with the Expert: Guidance for Lawyers."

Requesting Court Assistance in Securing the Evaluation

Of course, this mental health expert is going to want to be compensated for his or her time. If your client is not incarcerated and has the funds to pay for the evaluation, you can proceed right to the evaluation. If your client is indigent or incarcerated, you will need to involve the court. If your client is indigent, you will need to file an *ex parte* motion under seal for funds for the evaluation. If your client is incarcerated, you will need to file an *ex parte* motion under seal for an evaluation at the facility. In both motions, you will have to lay out why you believe there is a good faith basis that a mental health evaluation is necessary to provide a complete defense and, in many instances, identify in your motion whom you wish to secure to conduct the evaluation and the amount of time necessary.

If the court questions why the motion must be *ex parte* under seal, you can argue that a defendant who is not incarcerated and not indigent is able to secure an evaluation when his or her attorneys recommend one without disclosing it to the public or the prosecutor. Further, because a mental health evaluation is a health issue, the defendant has a right to privacy under the Health Insurance Portability and Accountability Act (HIPAA) and other medical record protections. Of course, this evaluation may become public if the defense ends up using it at sentencing. However, you can ask for it to be sealed yet provide the court and the prosecutor with a copy. After the court grants the motion for the evaluation, you will need to work with the facility to arrange for your expert to travel there and meet with your client for an appropriate amount of time.

Revisiting Whether the Possible Mental Health Issue Can Be Used in Mitigation

Once the evaluation takes place and you have the mental health expert's opinion, it is critical to revisit whether the assessment will support sentencing mitigation. In determining this, it is important to keep in mind that judges are humans and are not going to want to excuse criminal behavior. So, again, the closer the mental health expert has been able to link the cause of the crime to the mental disability and assure the court that there is viable means to manage and even treat the issue, the stronger the argument is to use the mental health evaluation in support of mitigation.

For example, if the evaluation reveals that your client suffers from mild depression or a common case of ADHD, the mental health evaluation may not help your mitigation argument, because the court and the prosecutor are not likely to excuse criminal behavior when your client is suffering from common, mild, and treatable mental health issues. If, however, the mental health expert says your client has PTSD that manifests as a panic disorder that causes them to overreact in stressful situations, and this is exactly the sort of crime your client was charged with, this could be powerful mitigating testimony. Or, if your client is suffering from a mental disorder that results in delusions and paranoia, but this disorder is entirely treatable with the appropriate drugs, and your client's actions were a result of this paranoia, this is extremely influential mitigating testimony. Or, if your client is suffering from a mental disorder and is self-medicating with illegal drugs, this could be significant mitigating testimony in a drug case.

In one case, "Mr. Peters" suffered from ADHD. He found that methamphetamine worked like Ritalin in calming his thoughts and behavior. He was arrested for possession of meth. An evaluation was conducted and presented to the court noting this condition. With the client's agreement, the court affirmed that the mental health condition was related to the criminal conduct, and the client agreed to get legal medication prescriptions in exchange for a reduced sentence.

It is critical not to forget the second portion of the evaluation—whether treatment can help ensure that this criminal behavior will not be repeated. Even if the court or prosecutor feels compassion for someone suffering from PTSD or paranoia or someone who is self-medicating, they are not likely going to feel comfortable probating your client's sentence without assurances that they won't panic again, stop taking medication and act out of paranoia, or start self-medicating once they return to society.

It is important that you secure an expert who can not only provide a diagnosis and treatment plan, but who can testify in broader terms regarding how someone with that particular mental health disorder sees the world and why he or she would act that way. Again, judges and government representatives are human beings, and many will look on someone who is different with suspicion and will be concerned that the mental disability is being used as an excuse for criminal behavior, or even feigned to try to avoid punishment. Your expert must help assuage these concerns with detailed testimony regarding both the mental disability in general and the specific diagnosis in your client's case, treatment options, and potential success of treatments. All of this will help humanize your client in the courts' and prosecutor's eyes.

Advocating for Your Client

While your expert is the one who will need to provide the assurance of treatability, this is also where you can put on your creative thinking cap. What kind of sentence can you create to give the court the assurance it needs? Can you ask for probation with mandated mental health visits? Can you ask for an order that requires that your client stays on their medication for the duration of the sentence? Can you ask for a sentence that mandates your client participate in in-house counseling or inpatient treatment for a specified duration?

If your client is not incarcerated, it will help your case if they are already seeking the treatment you are going to request. Post-offense rehabilitation is a significant mitigating factor, especially in drug cases where the offender has a substance use disorder (see Chapter 11). While you cannot force your client to seek treatment, you can explain to him or her that this will help show the court and the prosecutor that they are serious about treatment and will avoid future criminal episodes. If your client is incarcerated, it may help your case to research and contact facilities that will be available to treat them as soon as they are released.

You will know your expert's opinion and what it is based on before sentencing. You can choose to use the information or not, depending on what you find and what your expert says. It is often beneficial to prepare a detailed sentencing memorandum that outlines the mitigating evidence you want the court to hear and why your client deserves a more lenient sentence. This memorandum should paint a story in support of mitigation and start the process of humanizing your client to the court and the prosecutor before sentencing. For example, this memorandum could paint the story of a hard-working citizen, son, and brother, who was violently attacked and, as a result, suffers from severe untreated PTSD that results in him panicking in stressful situations. Unfortunately, a stressful situation occurred, and this person assaulted another in the midst of a panic attack. This person now understands that he has a severe but treatable disorder. The client is excited to receive treatment at a preselected facility that specializes in this sort of mental health disorder and the client is ready to reclaim his life. Therefore, a lengthy probated sentence that requires intensive mental health treatment would be appropriate to allow your client to seek treatment and assure the court and prosecutor they will complete this treatment. Another purpose of the sentencing memorandum is to allow the judge to come to sentencing prepared to ask any questions regarding the assurances they may need to impose a more lenient sentence.

There are some who have advocated for video sentencing memorandums or a combination of both written and video. The video represents a sort of "day in the life" of the defendant and can contain interviews with character references and family members that might not be able to attend the sentencing. This is something you will have to determine depending on your court and the judge in your case. Some think the video option is only for the wealthy, which can hurt your case. On the other hand, the written sentencing mitigation memorandum has become a permanent part of effective advocacy in criminal cases.

Understanding when and how to seek a mental health evaluation to determine if the potential issues can be used in mitigation at sentencing is not only good advocacy but also critical to provide effective assistance of counsel. Remember, the right to effective assistance of counsel extends to sentencing. And, just like representation at trial, it is necessary for counsel at sentencing to conduct an investigation or make a reasonable determination that an investigation is not necessary. Ignoring a mental health issue that could have a significant mitigating effect is ineffective.

IDENTIFYING DATA

Birth Name

First | Middle

Last

Maiden

Date of Birth

Month / Day / Year | Age

Aliases (other names you have used)

Race (White, Hispanic, Black, Native American, Asian, Other)

Social Security Number

___ - __ - ____

Citizenship

Legal Address

Street

City | State | Zip Code | Phone Number

Physical Identifications

Height (5' 10") | Weight (195) | Hair Color | Eye Color

Tattoos (location/description)

Scars/Marks (location/description)

Law Office of Marcia G. Shein
2392 North Decatur Road ♦ Decatur, GA 30033 ♦(404) 633-3797 ♦ Fax: (404) 633-7980

OFFENDER CHARACTERISTICS

Information Regarding Biological Parents

FATHER

First Name Last Name Age

City of Residence State Phone Number

Occupation/Employer City

Spouse's Name (if not your biological mother) Last Name Age

MOTHER

First Name Last Name Age

Your Mother's Maiden Name

City of Residence State Phone Number

Occupation/Employer City

Spouse's Name (if not your biological father) Last Name Age

Are either of your parents deceased: (if yes, note date, cause of death and your age)

Are your parents aware of your present federal prosecution: (if not, why)

Have either of your parents suffered from alcohol or drugs abuse: (if yes, explain)

Do either of your parents have a mental health diagnosis or treatment history: (if yes, explain)

Do either of your parents have a criminal history: (if yes, explain)

Law Office of Marcia G. Shein
2392 North Decatur Road ♦ Decatur, GA 30033 ♦(404) 633-3797 ♦ Fax: (404) 633-7980

Did you have a good relationship with your parents as a child:

____

____

____

Do you have a good relationship with your parents at the present time: (explain if answered yes or no - describe relationship)

____

____

____

____

How often do you contact or see your parents:

____

____

Siblings (include information regarding your brothers and sisters)

Name	City/State of Residence/ Phone Number	Occupation

Are any of your siblings deceased: (if yes, note date, age and cause of death)

____

Have any of your siblings ever abused alcohol or drugs: (if yes, explain)

____

____

Law Office of Marcia G. Shein
2392 North Decatur Road ♦ Decatur, GA 30033 ♦(404) 633-3797 ♦ Fax: (404) 633-7980

Do any of your siblings have any criminal history: (if yes, explain)

Do any of your siblings have any mental health diagnosis or treatment history: (if yes, explain)

Do you have a good relationship with your siblings: (explain if answered yes or no - describe relationship)

Formative Years

Are your parent's divorced: (if yes, explain - provide approximate year of divorce, your age, and custody information, if applicable)

Year_______________ Your Age____________

Who was granted physical custody______________________________

Describe your living arrangement following the divorce:

Were you ever abused as a child - physically, mentally, verbally, or sexually: (if yes, explain)

Are you currently a member of a gang or have you associated with gang members in the past: (If yes, explain)

Note any other relevant information pertaining to your formative years:

Marital/Relationship Information

Current Spouse/Significant Other

First Name | Last Name | Age

City of Residence (if different than yours) | State | Phone Number

Occupation/Employer | City

Date of Marriage | City or County | State

Years or Months

Length of relationship

Has your spouse ever abused alcohol or drugs: (if yes, explain)

Does your spouse have any criminal history: (if yes, explain)

Does your spouse have any mental health diagnosis or treatment history: (if yes, explain)

Describe your relationship with your spouse: (Note any periods of separation, reason for separation and any domestic abuse history.)

Prior Marriage(s) - Use last page, if extra space is needed.

Ex- Spouse - First Name | Last Name | Age

City of Residence | State | Phone Number

Date of Marriage (01/02/2006) | City or County | State

Year of Separation | Year of Divorce | Court / County Where Divorce Granted | State

Law Office of Marcia G. Shein
2392 North Decatur Road ♦ Decatur, GA 30033 ♦ (404) 633-3797 ♦ Fax: (404) 633-7980

Children

Name / Age	Other Parent	City / State of Residence	School / Occupation

Describe your relationship with your children: (Note - any criminal history, drug or alcohol abuse, physical or mental health concerns)

Do you have physical care custody of your children: (if no, describe what custody have, if any, and your children's living arraignments)

Are you ordered to pay child support: (if yes, when was the child support ordered, how much, name of court who ordered support)

Are you current with your child support: (if no, how much are you behind and when did you make your last payment)

Residency (List all prior cities of residence, birth to present, and whom you were living with at that time.)

City:______ State:______	From _____ To _____ Age _____ To _____	Other occupants: _____ ______
City:______ State:______	From _____ To _____ Age _____ To _____	Other occupants: _____ ______
City:______ State:______	From _____ To _____ Age _____ To _____	Other occupants: _____ ______
City:______ State:______	From _____ To _____ Age _____ To _____	Other occupants: _____ ______
City:______ State:______	From _____ To _____ Age _____ To _____	Other occupants: _____ ______
City:______ State:______	From _____ To _____ Age _____ To _____	Other occupants: _____ ______
City:______ State:______	From _____ To _____ Age _____ To _____	Other occupants: _____ ______

Describe your most recent living arraignment: (description of residence, rent or mortgage, with whom living, etc....)

____
____
____
____
____

If you were not born in the United States, please provide the date and location you first entered the United States and any other subsequent re-entries into the United States.

____
____

If you are a legal or permanent resident please advise and note date of citizenship.

____
____

Law Office of Marcia G. Shein
2392 North Decatur Road ♦ Decatur, GA 30033 ♦ (404) 633-3797 ♦ Fax: (404) 633-7980

Physical Health

Do you have any current health problems: (if yes, explain - Please include symptoms; date of diagnosis, surgery, or evaluation; physician; name of hospital or clinic, etc.) _____ _____ _____ _____ _____
Have you previously been treated for chronic illness or undergone major surgery: (if yes, explain - Please include date of diagnosis, surgery, or evaluation; physician; name of hospital or clinic, etc.) _____ _____ _____ _____
Are you taking any prescription or over-the-counter medications: (if yes, please list the name of the medication and what it is for, as well as who it was prescribed by and the date it was prescribed.) _____ _____ _____
Do you have a family physician: (if yes, provide doctor's name and address) _____ _____
Do you receive Social Security Disability income for any physical health condition(s): (if yes, for what condition, when did you start receiving SSI and how much do you receive) _____

Mental & Emotional Health

Are you currently being treated for any mental/emotional/psychiatric problems: (If yes, list any diagnosis, dates of diagnosis, doctor who diagnosed you, treatment information, and prescription medication.) _____ _____ _____ _____ _____

Law Office of Marcia G. Shein
2392 North Decatur Road ♦ Decatur, GA 30033 ♦(404) 633-3797 ♦ Fax: (404) 633-7980

Have you previously been treated for any mental/emotional/psychiatric problems: (If yes, list any diagnosis, dates of diagnosis, doctor who diagnosed you, doctors address, treatment information, and prescription medication.)

____

____

____

____

Have you ever contemplated or attempted suicide: (if yes, explain)

____

____

Substance Abuse History

Have you ever consumed **alcohol**? Yes / No

Age first began drinking ________ Age / date you last consumed alcohol ________________

Describe your alcohol consumption from when you first began until you last drank (type of alcohol how much alcohol per sitting, duration, cost to support habit).

____

____

____

Note any alcohol related arrests: ______________________________

Have you ever used **marijuana**? Yes / No

Age when first used ____________ Age and date last used ________________________

Describe your marijuana intake from when you first began until your last use (how much, how often, cost to support habit).

____

____

____

____

Note any marijuana related arrests: ______________________________

Have you ever used **methamphetamine**? Yes / No

Age when first used ____________ Age and date you last used ________________________

Describe your methamphetamine intake from when you first began until your last use (how much, how often, cost to support habit, how would you use this drug).

____

____

____

____

Note any methamphetamine related arrests: ______________________________

Law Office of Marcia G. Shein
2392 North Decatur Road ♦ Decatur, GA 30033 ♦ (404) 633-3797 ♦ Fax: (404) 633-7980

Have you ever used **cocaine/crack**? Yes / No

Age first began used ________________ Age and date you last used ____________________________

Describe your cocaine/crack intake from when you first began until your last use (how much, how often, cost to support habit, how would you use this drug).

____

____

____

____

Note any cocaine related arrests: ____

Have you ever used **heroin**? Yes / No

Age first began used ________________ Age and date you last used ____________________________

Describe your heroin intake from when you first began until your last use (how much, how often, cost to support habit, how would you use this drug).

____

____

____

____

Note any heroin related arrests: ____

Note any other drug history you have had (Barbiturates, Hallucinogens, Inhalants, etc.):

____

____

____

Substance Abuse Treatment (list all substance abuse treatment you have had in chronological order, starting with the most recent)

Dates & Type of Treatment	Treatment Provider/Address	Referral Source
Admit Date: ________ ☐ Inpatient ☐ Outpatient Discharge Date: ________	Name: ________ City: ________ State: ________	☐ Self ☐ Family ☐ Court ☐ Other ________ Were you successfully discharged from treatment: ☐ Yes ☐ No
Admit Date: ________ ☐ Inpatient ☐ Outpatient Discharge Date: ________	Name: ________ City: ________ State: ________	☐ Self ☐ Family ☐ Court ☐ Other ________ Were you successfully discharged from treatment: ☐ Yes ☐ No
Admit Date: ________ ☐ Inpatient ☐ Outpatient Discharge Date: ________	Name: ________ City: ________ State: ________	☐ Self ☐ Family ☐ Court ☐ Other ________ Were you successfully discharged from treatment: ☐ Yes ☐ No

Do you believe you could benefit from additional substance abuse treatment? Yes / No

Law Office of Marcia G. Shein
2392 North Decatur Road ♦ Decatur, GA 30033 ♦(404) 633-3797 ♦ Fax: (404) 633-7980

Education History (list in chronological order beginning with high school)

School: ______ ______ City: ______ State: ______	□ High School Diploma □ Bachelors Degree □ Masters Degree □ Other ______ Year of graduation: ______ If you did not graduate, why not: ______ ______ Last grade completed: ______
School: ______ ______ City: ______ State: ______	□ High School Diploma □ Bachelors Degree □ Masters Degree □ Other ______ Year of graduation: ______ If you did not graduate, why not: ______ ______ Last grade completed: ______
School: ______ ______ City: ______ State: ______	□ High School Diploma □ Bachelors Degree □ Masters Degree □ Other ______ Year of graduation: ______ If you did not graduate, why not: ______ ______ Last grade completed: ______

Have you been diagnosed with a Learning Disability (if yes, please describe):

______

______

Do you have a General Equivalency Diploma? Yes / No

Date of Completion ______ School / City / State ______

Employment History (include all employment for the past 10 years, list in chronological order, starting with the most recent)

Employer: ______ Address: ______ City/State: ______	Dates Employed: From ______ To ______ Salary: ______	Position Held: ______ Reason for Termination: ______ ______
Employer: ______ Address: ______ City/State: ______	Dates Employed: From ______ To ______ Salary: ______	Position Held: ______ Reason for Termination: ______ ______

Law Office of Marcia G. Shein
2392 North Decatur Road ♦ Decatur, GA 30033 ♦ (404) 633-3797 ♦ Fax: (404) 633-7980

Employer: ____ Address: ____ City/State: ____	Dates Employed: From ____ To ____ Salary: ____	Position Held: ____ Reason for Termination: ____ ____
Employer: ____ Address: ____ City/State: ____	Dates Employed: From ____ To ____ Salary: ____	Position Held: ____ Reason for Termination: ____ ____
Employer: ____ Address: ____ City/State: ____	Dates Employed: From ____ To ____ Salary: ____	Position Held: ____ Reason for Termination: ____ ____
Employer: ____ Address: ____ City/State: ____	Dates Employed: From ____ To ____ Salary: ____	Position Held: ____ Reason for Termination: ____ ____
Employer: ____ Address: ____ City/State: ____	Dates Employed: From ____ To ____ Salary: ____	Position Held: ____ Reason for Termination: ____ ____
Employer: ____ Address: ____ City/State: ____	Dates Employed: From ____ To ____ Salary: ____	Position Held: ____ Reason for Termination: ____ ____
Employer: ____ Address: ____ City/State: ____	Dates Employed: From ____ To ____ Salary: ____	Position Held: ____ Reason for Termination: ____ ____

Summarize any other employment not identified above:

____

____

____

____

____

____

____

____

____

____

____

Law Office of Marcia G. Shein
2392 North Decatur Road ♦ Decatur, GA 30033 ♦(404) 633-3797 ♦ Fax: (404) 633-7980

Military History

Were or are you in the military? Yes / No

Branch of Service: ______________________

Date Enlisted: ______________ Date Discharged: ______________

Type of Discharge: ______________________

Highest Rank: ______________ Rank at Separation: ______________

Describe any court martial or non-judicial punishments: ______________________

____

Describe any foreign or combat service: ______________________

____

Awards or Decorations received: ______________________

____

Specialized training or skills acquired: ______________________

____

Miscellaneous

Provide any other information that you think should be included in your Presentence Report (Including adoptive or foster parents, additional dependants, etc.):

____

____

____

____

____

____

____

____

____

____

____

____

____

____

____

____

____

____

____

Law Office of Marcia G. Shein
2392 North Decatur Road ♦ Decatur, GA 30033 ♦(404) 633-3797 ♦ Fax: (404) 633-7980

PARAOLE INFORMATION

1. Please provide detailed information of your history in prison since the alleged offense occurred (disciplinary actions & program completions):

2. Why you feel you should be released:

3. What you will be doing upon your release:

4. List or include any information pertaining to the Parole Board's review of your case including grid sheets, TPM dates, etc:

Law Office of Marcia G. Shein
2392 North Decatur Road ♦ Decatur, GA 30033 ♦(404) 633-3797 ♦ Fax: (404) 633-7980

LIST ALL PRIOR ARRESTS

Arrest Date	County, City, State	Charge(s)	Disposition, Sentence, & Date

Law Office of Marcia G. Shein
2392 North Decatur Road ♦ Decatur, GA 30033 ♦(404) 633-3797 ♦ Fax: (404) 633-7980

LIST ALL PRIOR ARRESTS

Arrest Date	County, City, State	Charge(s)	Disposition, Sentence, & Date

Law Office of Marcia G. Shein
2392 North Decatur Road ♦ Decatur, GA 30033 ♦(404) 633-3797 ♦ Fax: (404) 633-7980

• • •

Marcia G. Shein is a nationally recognized attorney in matters of federal trial, plea, sentencing mitigation, appellate, and post-conviction litigation. In addition to trial experience, she has consulted with some of the best federal criminal defense attorneys in the nation to help protect clients' sentencing and appeal mitigation rights. She has a master's degree in psychology from Nova University and was a family therapist before becoming an attorney. Attorney Shein is a life member of the National Association of Criminal Defense Lawyers and past president of the Georgia Association of Criminal Defense Lawyers. She has written numerous articles that have appeared in publications such as *The Champion*, *The Federal Lawyer*, and *The Georgia Defender* on topics such as the federal sentencing guidelines, mental health issues, and PTSD diagnosis and treatment. She has represented clients from Alaska to Maine and beyond U.S. borders in complicated federal criminal cases.

Ms. Shein has served as an adjunct instructor of legal and psychology courses for the Criminal Justice Programs for Broward Community College and Nova University in Florida, Troy State University in Alabama, and Kaplan University in Chicago. Ms. Shein's national office is located at 2392 North Decatur Road, Decatur, GA 30033. Her phone number is (404) 633-3797, and you can also find her on www.federalcriminallawcenter.com and www.federalappealslawyer.com.

Chapter

4

Working with the Expert: From the Perspective of Experts

Dr. Elliot Atkins and Joshua Shields

Much of what I've learned about representing people with mental disabilities I've learned from experts in my cases. I've peppered them with questions about their reports. I've read books and articles they've recommended and cited in their reports. I've listened to their war stories. I've asked them questions about their research. I've discussed cases in the news with them.

Aside from substantive knowledge, my experts have taught me a good deal about building a strong relationship with the mental health expert in my case as well as the appropriate customs and boundaries. For instance, what is the difference between a diagnostic report versus a report about future dangerousness, when is it appropriate for the family to communicate with the expert, and what should the expert include versus exclude in a report? Notwithstanding the fact that counsel may develop a strong relationship with an expert, and indeed, may use this expert in multiple cases, it must always be remembered that the expert is brought on to be an independent forensic expert, and this independence must be preserved. This is why selecting experts not only with superb credentials, but those with a reputation for integrity, is so important.

It is not enough to find a mental health expert, or even to find the perfect mental health expert for a given case. Rather, the challenge is to use that expert effectively and creatively. An expert should be brought in as early as possible and supplied with all relevant records. Indeed, because of the pandemic, experts are not only extremely busy with their forensic practices, but also with their clinical practices, if they have one. Thus, you need to have a firm commitment regarding when they can interview your client and produce a written report if appropriate. The expert should be available to speak with you about the reason for your referral and should confer with you after the interview and during the preparation of the report.

The following two chapters are meant to be read in concert. The first, by Dr. Elliott Atkins and Joshua Shields, describes the role of the expert in facilitating communication between counsel and the client as well as eliciting facts—sometimes intimate and embarrassing—which are important for effective representation. Moreover, the authors describe the essential components of a thorough evaluation, such as interviewing the client (sometimes multiple times), reviewing records, and interviewing collateral sources of information, such as family, teachers, and coworkers.

• • •

The public's awareness and interest in mental health has grown considerably in the past decade. Cultural artifacts focused on mental health and mental disabilities abound: literature, television shows, film, digital media, social media, and so on. This recent growth of media content often attempts to reveal the perspective of those who suffer from mental illness and portray the perspective of those who treat them.[1] Whether through an empathetic lens that seeks to educate or one of morbid curiosity (e.g., the rise of "true crime" podcasts), it isn't difficult to find people fervently discussing mental illness in their daily lives. Socio-political events,[2] global pandemics,[3] and the forms of media mentioned earlier[4] are all factors that have led to an

---

1. Latha K, Meena KS, Pravitha MR, Dasgupta M, Chaturvedi SK. *Effective Use of Social Media Platforms for Promotion of Mental Health Awareness.* J Educ Health Promot. 2020 May 28; 9:124.

2. Vargas T, Schiffman J, Lam PH, Kim A, Mittal VA. *Using Search Engine Data to Gauge Public Interest in Mental Health, Politics and Violence in the Context of Mass Shootings.* PLoS One. 2020 Aug 7;15(8).

3. Li C, Tan Q, Zou M, Zeng L, Kang M, Chen L. *Significantly Increased Public Interest in Major Depressive Disorder During the COVID-19 Pandemic: Insights From a Google Trends Analysis.* Cureus. 2022 Jan 14;14(1).

4. Latha K, Meena KS, Pravitha MR, Dasgupta M, Chaturvedi SK. *Effective Use of Social Media Platforms for Promotion of Mental Health Awareness.* J Educ Health Promot. 2020 May 28; 9:124.

increased awareness regarding the effects of mental health and how to treat those with mental health issues. While not universal, in the United States there is a trending societal shift in which mental disabilities, and those suffering from them, are viewed in a more compassionate and considerate manner.[5] Furthermore, the legal system has recently fallen under considerable scrutiny for perceived failings in dealing with inequality, including unequal treatment of those with mental disabilities. With these factors in mind, the importance of accurately identifying and understanding a client's mental disability has never been as powerful, or as important, as it is today.

Processing and conceptualizing the effects of a potential *lifetime* of mental disability with a client can be a daunting task. One must take into consideration how the defendant's mental illness or intellectual/developmental disability may have impacted their life prior to, during, and after the offense. It is in this domain that it is recommended the attorney employ a forensic mental health professional. This professional will investigate, conceptualize, and advise on the mental illness of the client, and how that conceptualization may be used in an effective defense for the client.

The Importance of Evaluation

Typically, a mental health professional is asked to evaluate the defendant in order to ascertain if, and to what extent, a mental disability is present. After evaluating, the professional may aid in conceptualizing how those issues may have affected the client. Their objective is to gain an understanding of the role that these issues may have played in the defendant's life prior to the offense, as well as the extent to which they may have influenced the criminal act itself and the circumstances surrounding it. Lastly, the evaluation can inform how the attorney interacts with the client, the type of strategy best suited to defend the client, and the client's understanding of their circumstances. In this way the evaluation provides an informed framework for understanding the client's past, present, and future.

Once this framework has been established, analysis of any past offenses and/or behavior can be used to define the history of the illness and its impact on the client's past. The mental health professional can aid in identifying patterns of behavior and associated or predisposing

5. Pescosolido BA, Halpern-Manners A, Luo L, Perry B. *Trends in Public Stigma of Mental Illness in the US, 1996-2018*. JAMA Netw Open. 2021;4(12).

factors influencing the behavior. Viewing and analyzing these findings through the perspective of the established framework can help interpret how these behaviors are related to the psychological issues of the client. Once patterns are established and the factors influencing the client's behavior analyzed, the professional may examine how these factors could have impacted the client, both before and during the offense. Factors that may have seemed insignificant before the evaluation may transform into important antecedents that help to establish a previously unseen primer for the client's state of mind and subsequent actions. The evaluation performed by the mental health professional provides a new lens through which the client's behaviors, beliefs, and motives can be examined more thoroughly and with greater insight.

The Attorney-Client Relationship

One of the most important ways that the evaluation and mental health professional can be of assistance is developing the attorney-client relationship. The professional may serve as a facilitator between counsel and defendant by helping to develop overall communication strategies that lead to honest and effective collaboration. For example, if not approached with care, some disorders (e.g., borderline, paranoid, or narcissistic personality disorders) could contribute to potentially devastating results in the establishment of a healthy attorney-client relationship. The mental health professional's assistance allows the team to gain insight into particular areas of vulnerability that may need to be approached with increased consideration and care. The mental health professional may also assist in tactfully engaging the client when working through these vulnerable areas, aiming to avoid possible rupture in the relationship. However, it is worth noting that when working with clients with severe personality disorders, relationship rupture may be unavoidable. Luckily, with the skill and guidance of a mental health professional, repair of that rupture can lead to an even stronger collaborative attorney-client relationship.[6] An example for consideration:

> An attorney began working with a new client with borderline personality disorder (BPD). After several relatively unremarkable meetings, the

6. King-Casas, B., Sharp, C., Lomax-Bream, L., Lohrenz, T., Fonagy, P., & Montague, P. R. (2008). *The Rupture and Repair of Cooperation in Borderline Personality Disorder*. Science (New York, N.Y.), *321*(5890), 806–810.

attorney was forced to cancel a meeting last minute due to a family emergency. When the attorney next met with the client, the client immediately berated the attorney, criticized their judgment, and threatened to fire the attorney, even going so far as to suggest that the attorney was colluding against the client. The attorney contacted a forensic mental health professional, who in conducting an evaluation, consulting with the attorney, and discussing the incident, identified that the client's diagnosis of BPD likely predisposed them to feelings of rejection or betrayal.

Through a diagnostically informed lens, the mental health professional uncovers that prior to the argument the client felt they "weren't a priority" for the attorney and believed the attorney had fabricated an excuse to avoid meeting with the client. The client felt it was inevitable that the attorney would develop a dislike and subsequent avoidance of the client, and that the missed appointment was the first sign of this assured animosity. These beliefs and actions were congruent with the client's lifetime of experiences, often self-fulfilling prophecies in which the client's own behaviors drove people away.

The mental health professional met with the attorney and formulated a strategy of communication and messaging to repair the rupture. In the mental health professional's perspective, this was not a setback, but an opportunity. The attorney and mental health professional collaborated to demonstrate to the client that the attorney was working in the best interest of the client, was not abandoning them, and was prioritizing the client and their needs (to a healthy and professional degree).

Most importantly, the willingness to engage the client in reparative work such as this demonstrated the attorney's resolve to support the client, contradicting the client's preconceived beliefs and feelings of perceived animosity. Typically, in this client's life, most relationship ruptures resulted in the termination of that relationship, reinforcing the maladaptive beliefs and actions the client habitually used to respond to possible abandonment or rejection. It is in this way, through repairing the rupture, the attorney created a truly supportive relationship that led to honest and effective collaboration moving forward.

Communication and Collaboration

The forensic professional may assist the attorney in working collaboratively with the client in a variety of ways. As previously stated, the professional can aid in fostering the attorney-client relationship, yet a strong attorney-client relationship and willingness to collaborate does not always yield effective communication or useful information. In this sense, the professional will have the information-gathering skills, as well as the training, most lawyers simply don't have. The professional will have the ability to elicit sensitive, embarrassing, and often humiliating evidence that the defendant may have never disclosed if not for the skills of the mental health professional. To be effective, the forensic mental health professional must remain cognizant of the defendant's potential resistance to providing information and/or making decisions in his or her best interest. Many defendants are severely impaired in ways that make effective communication difficult: They may have mental illnesses or personality disorders that make them highly distrustful or impair their reasoning and perception of reality, or they may have other cognitive impairments and/or intellectual/developmental disabilities that affect their judgment and understanding. The mental health professional will be able to nimbly navigate these impairments, conveying a sense of understanding and unconditional positive regard that allows the client to disclose the details and information necessary for the attorney to best serve the client. For example:

> An attorney working with a client begins informally assessing the client's ability to understand the legal proceedings and requirements for effective collaboration with counsel. During their first meeting the attorney notes that the client seems defensive, often replying with single-word answers or "I don't care." The attorney, in an attempt to demonstrate their own competence and "win" the client over, lays out a well-constructed plan to defend the client. The attorney explains each step and asks the client for feedback between each step. The client responds with a simple "Whatever you say." The attorney, sensing the client is growing impatient, rushes through the remainder of the plan and receives the client's consent for representation.
>
> A few days later, the attorney hears back that based on correspondence, the client had fundamentally misunderstood the content of their conversations. Furthermore, the client has concerns about "why" the attorney was taking the steps they agreed upon, prompting ethical concerns around informed consent.

The previous example demonstrates that often individuals with an intellectual or developmental disability are likely to present with challenging behaviors or psychiatric disorders that make collaboration difficult.[7]

---

7. Marrus, N., & Hall, L. (2017). Intellectual disability and language disorder. *Child and Adolescent Psychiatric Clinics of North America*, *26*(3), 539–554.

The client in the example demonstrates a perceived defensiveness and irritability that likely developed through a difficulty understanding what was being communicated to them and what was expected of them. This was worsened by the attorney "rushing" through some of the communication, and it is likely that the client was unable to give informed consent since they were not able to understand what they were consenting to. The attorney perceived the client as impatient and annoyed, while in reality they were confused and overwhelmed. A mental health professional would be able to identify any intellectual/developmental disability and utilize skills and techniques to ensure comprehension and effective communication between attorney and client.

In addition to effective communication, the mental health professional can help discern the accuracy of statements. Some clients suffer from disorders or impairments that drive them to make statements or claims that may not be true, even so far as claiming certainty where there realistically is none, or taking responsibility for actions they did not take part in.[8] The mental health professional can help analyze the information gained from the client to assure accuracy and truthfulness. Furthermore, if the client is being dishonest, misleading, or unintentionally providing inaccurate information due to their mental health, the professional can strategize effective ways to gather more accurate information and evidence. Additionally, some clients may not be able to accurately perceive reality or provide accurate reports of their own experiences.

The mental health professional can support the attorney in understanding how and why the client's mental status may be impacting their communication. This guidance is informed by the initial evaluation, but often requires more continuous support by the professional. This suggests that the evaluation is a pivotal first step in working with clients with mental disability, however, it may not be sufficient to best serve the client throughout the legal process. The following scenario demonstrates the challenge of relying on an evaluation without continued support, as well as the necessity of professional support in ongoing communication:

> An attorney is working with a client who has a limited criminal record and no history of violence. While discussing their past before the committed offense, the client informs the attorney that they are responsible

---

8. Redlich, A.D., Summers, A. & Hoover, S. (2010). *Self-Reported False Confessions and False Guilty Pleas Among Offenders with Mental Illness.* Law Hum Behav 34, 79–90.

"for horrible things happening," including a fire later deemed arson that occurred during their youth. The attorney, concerned over what they heard, reviews the records and the forensic evaluation and finds that the report contains a diagnosis of an anxiety disorder (obsessive compulsive disorder, or OCD) and depression.

Returning to the client, the attorney attempts to ascertain the reality of whether or not the client was truly responsible for the arson. The attorney, having had experience representing clients with mental disabilities, begins to investigate "how certain" the client is that they were responsible for the fire; perhaps they claimed responsibility in a less than literal sense? The client responds that they are "9 out of 10 certain" they alone were responsible for the fire. After investigating the arson itself, the attorney finds concrete evidence that it was impossible for the client to have had any role in the arson, yet their confession remains.

The attorney revisits the evaluation searching for something to explain this apparent contradiction. With no psychotic disorders or illness that in their experience could explain the client's reports, the attorney struggles to understand how and why the client continues to make these claims. Luckily, the attorney reaches out to a forensic mental health professional who joins the team and provides assistance. After revisiting the evaluation report, the professional identifies that these claims may be explained by the client's diagnosis of OCD. The professional considers the connection between the claims and the diagnosis, and subsequently meets with the client to clarify.

After some discussion, the mental health professional is able to ascertain the following: The client has an obsessive fear of "harm to others." Furthermore, they inaccurately perceive their own impact pertaining to events that affect others negatively. Through questioning, the professional identifies that the client has a subtype of OCD called "OCD with poor insight." The professional discovers that the fire in question destroyed the residence of a peer with whom the client had been involved in social conflict. The client remembered after a particularly difficult conflict with the peer "wishing something bad would happen to them." It was days later that the fire destroyed the residence.

With the client's limited ability to challenge their anxiety, the fire occurring after their "wish" was analogous to arson. The professional, with the diagnosis in mind, works with the client and attorney to create a strategy to extract accurate information from the client that allows the attorney to focus on the evidence and more effectively discern fact from distorted claims.

As stated previously, processing and conceptualizing a lifetime of psychological and mental health history is a daunting task. The mental health professional will be crucial in identifying and analyzing useful sources of information. In addition to serving as a substrate for the evaluation, information regarding a defendant's life and mental health history will likely be helpful throughout the entirety of the legal process. The mental health professional should ask the attorney for all available records necessary to formulate their opinion for the evaluation and remainder of the legal process. The professional may need to guide the attorney in the acquisition of the required records, keeping in mind the fact that the requests for additional records are likely to be forthcoming as the evaluation progresses. Such records are often extensive and some may require a subpoena. In addition to school records, medical records, and military records, the consulting professional would want to have a complete set of the criminal investigation reports, witness statements, the defendant's statement, the indictment, presentence investigation reports, sentencing memorandum, the defendant's juvenile and adult criminal history, case files related to previous convictions, jail records for both the current and prior periods of incarceration, records of any prior court-ordered mental health evaluations, and so on.

As it would be extremely rare for all of the significant events in a defendant's life to have been fully documented and available for review, the expert should also convey the importance of personally interviewing collateral sources of information, such as family, previous employers, and teachers, who may shed light on the defendant's personal characteristics as well as their observations of his or her social and emotional functioning. Information and documentation conceptualizing and detailing the defendant's history of mental health will likely be the first opportunity for counsel to provide the prosecution with humanizing information about the defendant—information that distinguishes the client from the prosecutor's preconceived perceptions of the offender. As the stigmas associated with mental health diagnoses erode with cultural awareness, the ability for the attorney to humanize the client becomes increasingly important. The attorney and mental health professional should collaborate on the construction of the client's narrative—a narrative that details the history of the client's struggles with mental health and its effect on their life. The narrative should describe the ways in which mental health issues have created barriers in accessing education, employment, meaningful and healthy relationships, adequate and preventative medical and psychological care, and any other components needed to build a healthy life. All of this should explain how mental health issues impacted the client's healthy development as well as treatment by others.

Conclusion

Hopefully, the importance of a comprehensive look into a client's developmental past, recent history, and present psychological conditions has been made evident throughout this chapter. The use of a mental health professional can be beneficial to all stages of the legal process. Navigating the seemingly infinite nuances of the client's mental health history, present and past diagnoses, and current psychological state is a task well-suited to the forensic mental health professional.

Through conceptualization, support in communication, fostering and strengthening the attorney-client relationship, as well as effective collaboration, the professional can support the attorney in providing the most effective defense for their client. The mental health professional serves as the guide, directing the attorney through the often maze-like corridors of the client's mind and psychological history. It is the professional's job to illuminate previously unseen paths, connecting rooms and corridors that seemed inaccessible, opening doors that seemed to, at first glance, be permanently shut. The professional can help the attorney understand the contents of those rooms, uncover the patterns of the paths leading from one room to the next, and even interpret the methodology of how and why the paths were created. Ultimately, it is up to the attorney to use the information, knowledge, and content of their exploration in the manner they find most advantageous. Yet it seems clear that much of this exploration won't be as fruitful, nor the maze itself as thoroughly understood, without the guidance and expertise of the forensic mental health professional.

• • •

Dr. Elliot L. Atkins is a clinical, forensic, and consulting psychologist who has been in clinical practice since 1977 and has worked in the forensic arena since 1980. Dr. Atkins has been admitted as an expert witness before state and federal courts in both the criminal and civil arenas. He has been called upon by attorneys from across the country to address issues related to substance abuse and addiction, professional malpractice, criminal state-of-mind defenses, sentencing, and the assessment of both perpetrators and victims of sexual abuse. He has recently provided consultation to defense counsel in multiple high-profile civil and criminal institutional child sexual abuse cases. He has also been retained by both the prosecution and the defense as a trial consultant in sexual abuse cases by the United States Air Force's Judge Advocate General's Corps.

Dr. Atkins coauthored two chapters ("Capacity to Waive *Miranda* Rights" and "Sentencing") in the *Handbook of Forensic Assessment: Psychological and Psychiatric Perspectives* (Wiley, 2011). He has also coauthored a chapter on death penalty mitigation in the *Handbook of Forensic Psychology and Forensic Sociology* (Springer, 2013). In 2014, he prepared an amicus brief and testified on the constitutionality of polygraphing paroled sex offenders. He has been an adjunct clinical assistant professor at Widener University and has provided clinical supervision for the doctoral internship programs at both Hahnemann and Drexel universities. He has been a consultant to municipal, state, and federal agencies and legislative bodies on the issue of substance abuse and rehabilitation.

Dr. Atkins has published articles and presented continuing legal education workshops on topics related to the insanity defense, neonaticide, borderline personality disorder, sentencing, and the collaboration of clinicians and attorneys regarding the issue of professional boundary violations. For the past two decades he has chaired the American College of Forensic Psychology's Forensic Skills panel of attorneys and forensic psychologists as they address professional and ethical issues confronting forensic mental health practitioners. In 2020, he authored a chapter in the first edition of this book on working with defendants that are on the autism spectrum. More recently, he coauthored a chapter on remote combat stress ("Remote Combat Exposure and Moral Injury from Drone Operations: The Cost of a New Form of Warfare") in *Preventing and Treating the Invisible Wounds of War* (Oxford University Press, 2023). Dr. Atkins can be reached at elliotatkins@msn.com and his website is http://www.elliotatkins.com.

Joshua N. Shields, MSEd, obtained his BA in psychology from Franklin and Marshall College, and his MSEd in school and mental health counseling from the University of Pennsylvania—Graduate School of Education. Since 2018 he has worked in PHIICAPS (Philadelphia

Intensive In-Home Child and Adolescent Psychiatric Services) through Penn Medicine. In addition, alongside Doug Clapp, LMFT, and Emily Becker-Haimes, PhD, Josh co-founded an exploratory program that provides intensive exposure-based treatment for Medicaid-eligible youth and families affected by OCD and/or anxiety disorders. Through this program he has provided therapeutic services across home, school, and community settings. Josh previously worked using principles of ABA (applied behavioral analysis) in school, community, and inpatient settings as a certified crisis interventionist. He has plans to pursue a PhD in clinical psychology and a future career in forensic psychology. He can be reached at Joshua.N.Shields@gmail.com.

Chapter

5

Working with the Expert: Guidance for Lawyers

Jeffrey E. Thoma and Dale Watson

The following chapter by veteran criminal defense lawyer Jeffrey E. Thoma and Dr. Dale Watson is virtually the same chapter that appeared in the first edition of this book. The reason for this is simple: The guidance they provide about building a strong relationship with the client, selecting the right expert, qualifying your expert to testify, and cross-examining opposing counsel's expert is timeless.

• • •

Selecting an Expert

Before ever getting to the critical stage of selecting an expert, there is one fundamental principle that underlies not just this aspect of your case but is paramount in all aspects of your case before any other. You must patiently, carefully, and sincerely build your relationship with your client. Without this crucial step, much or all of what you attempt will fail. Without a relationship with the client based on mutual trust and understanding (sometimes only to the extent either of you can), the client's relationship with both you and the expert may be doomed from the start, and the efforts of both you and the expert will be inefficient at best and disastrous at worst.

Selecting the right expert for a criminal defense case is based on experience, just as we make many of our decisions in life. In this instance, the experience may be based on the particular expert's work on a case or situation strikingly similar to your client's or might be driven by your own experience of gaining trust in this expert. You may even have a colleague or acquaintance who has vast knowledge and experience in the subject matter or situation and the wisdom to help guide you through this process. Gut instinct, or simply coming across a name associated with a specific expertise, is not the proper method for arriving at such a crucial decision in your client's case.

Cost should not be a deciding factor, nor even a barrier in this decision. In almost all jurisdictions, courts recognize the right to experts' services, including mental health experts, even when counsel is retained by the client's family when the client is indigent.

Another factor in the decision to select the proper expert for your case is based on the expert's recognition that any work he or she is doing for your client is utterly and completely confidential. While you may go into this process believing that this factor is a given, you might be very surprised to know that the confidentiality necessary to criminal defense is not practiced in areas of expertise necessarily, and in particular, scientific evidence in general. The need for publishing and critically analyzing other experts' theories, methods, and formulas lends scientists to a different understanding of confidentiality than we as criminal defense lawyers enjoy.

In an alarming number of situations, it has been found that experts do not necessarily understand their fiduciary obligations to work in confidence. Therefore, counsel has a duty to make sure their expert does, and this should be addressed in the retention letter. Such a letter should include at least the following provisos:

- Written communication labeled "confidential" to ensure that employees and staff know this is *always* the case regarding information about your case. If the other side contacts them, then all staff, and particularly the expert, must respond: "I cannot help you."
- Remind them that they cannot and should not under any circumstances rely on the expressions of others who say that it is okay to talk to them.
- Confidentiality is not time-limited.
- This case should never be part of a presentation at a professional conference or the subject of an article.

In addition to these provisos, case law has held that there are specific minimums in retention letters:

- Written confirmation of the confidential nature of the relationship
- Correspondence must be labeled "WORK PRODUCT COMMUNICATIONS"

Once you have retained your expert, you *must* provide your expert with *all* necessary data. It is simply ineffective assistance of counsel not to do so. This does not necessarily mean that your expert must read every shred of documentation in your matter. Conversely, this means that you must consider the length and breadth of examination and cross-examination, and not leave to chance that they might be unfamiliar with information a fact finder might utilize to consider them unreliable based on their perspective that your expert is not thorough enough in delivering their opinions. Thus, do not be "penny-wise and pound foolish" by withholding data that might reasonably be asked about in cross-examination.

Avoiding Expert Bias

A crucial consideration in avoiding even the appearance of expert bias is to always ensure the expert has the requisite information about the facts and the case to render a valid, unbiased opinion. For example, regarding mental health experts, often the prosecution attempts to admit a quick, uninformed opinion. We will discuss this later in the chapter, but our position can be greatly solidified by meeting the relevant professional standards. Regarding mental health evidence, these criteria are essential for this purpose:

- Obtaining and reviewing basic medical, military, and school records, as well as other relevant records.
- Obtaining and reviewing relevant police, eyewitness, and defense reports.
- Interviewing family members, close friends, or other relevant people.
- Conducting an independent battery of psychological and/or neuropsychological tests.
- Interviewing the accused over time.
- Critically reviewing previous mental health reports and raw data.

Be wary of any "expert" who does not follow these proscribed minimum criterions, and make certain in advance that the expert you select not only is aware of these standards but also has always adhered to them. Failure to do so, even in a past case, might be very relevant to the expert's ability to be qualified, due to cross-examination issues that might prevail over their specific expertise and following of correct protocols in the case at bar.

Qualifying Experts and Overcoming Exclusion

Pursuant to Evidence Code Section 801(a), expert testimony is admissible on "a subject that is sufficiently beyond the common experience that the opinion of the expert would assist the trier of fact." For a half century, the standard of admissibility was based on the landmark case *Frye v. United States*.[1] This created a formidable barrier to new or novel scientific evidence: that it must have received "general acceptance in the particular field to which it belongs." Then in the 1970s, several state courts began to weigh in with more specific guidelines, including accuracy, lack of standards in a particular field, and the time and impact on a jury.

Finally, the United States Supreme Court weighed in with the landmark *Daubert v. Merrell Dow Pharmaceuticals, Inc.* decision in 1993. Since the 1970s, individual states have determined their own standards in these cases, either *Frye*, *Daubert*, or, in the case of California, some combination of *Frye* and their very own case, *People v. Kelly*,[1] regarding novel scientific techniques.

Under *Daubert*,[2] to serve as a basis for testimony in federal court, a theory or technique must be empirically validated. This means that the theory must be published and thoroughly subjected to peer review and counterarguments before being considered properly vetted. Later, in *Kumho Tire Co, Ltd. v. Carmichael*,[3] our nation's highest court ruled that a *Daubert*-style reliability requirement applies to every type of expert testimony, including soft science and even nonscientific expertise. Thus, a proponent must be prepared to exhibit that this validation process has been met.

1. People v. Kelly, 17 Cal.3d 24 (1976).
2. Daubert v. Merrell Dow Pharmaceuticals, Inc., 509 U.S. 579 (1993).
3. Kumho Tire Co, Ltd. v. Carmichael, 526 U.S. 137 (1999)

Under Evidence Code Subdivision 801(b), there are three permissible sources for the expert's case-specific information once validation is either proven, stipulated to, or assumed. This statute refers to information (1) "personally known to the witness," (2) hypothetically assumed facts, and (3) hearsay reports not otherwise excluded by law. The proponent must know when each of these will be most effective in his or her individual case, or which might be available.

Ask yourself: (1) Has the theory or technique been tested? (2) Has there been peer review and publication? (3) Is there a known potential rate of error and standards of the technique? (4) Is it generally accepted in the field? By considering these issues beforehand, the proponent should be able to adeptly admit his or her expert's opinion on a given issue either without objection or by overcoming one.

Challenging and Cross-Examining Opposing Counsel's Expert

The most critical consideration in your challenge to the opposing expert is your pretrial and in limine work in the area of discovery. There is an exception to every rule, but regarding this aspect, we cannot think of one. The rule is this: *Never* rely on informal discovery, or even boilerplate discovery letters and motions. You must explicitly request, first by letter, and then in formal motions, both pretrial and in limine, and when, as in most cases, you are not completely cognizant of every aspect of the expert's background, opinions, and the scope of their testimony, always add a request for any and all *other* relevant information that is either related or subject to their obligations under *Brady v. Maryland*,[4] to provide any and all information that could be considered exculpatory either in your case or as related to your client. You should also consult *General Electric v. Joiner*,[5] concerning the trial court's exclusion of an expert witness whose opinion strayed from supporting studies.

4. Brady v. Maryland, 373 U.S. 83 (1963).
5. General Electric v. Joiner, 522 U.S. 136 (1997).

To this end, make certain that you adhere to these basic guidelines:

- File the motion even if you think you have any and all discovery (because you may not).
- Challenge the expert and/or expertise under state and federal rules.
- Even if qualified, limit the testimony to demonstrated expertise of the witness and only to conclusions for which you have discovery.
- Get bench notes of any evaluations (do *not* accept conclusions).
- Get the protocols of the laboratory.
- Get proficiency testing done of the laboratory and the technician involved. (Remember: The gold standard in proficiency testing is "double-blind" proficiency testing, where neither the laboratory nor the technician is aware that the items are involved in said testing.)
- Get the error rates for both the specific technician and the entire laboratory or company.
- Demand and receive certifications and licenses of the laboratory and technician.

The trial judge should exclude proffered expert opinions if the subject of the inquiry is one of such common knowledge that people of ordinary education could reach a conclusion as intelligently as the witness. Even if the subject matter is appropriate for an expert opinion, you may object as to whether the proponent has laid a foundation for the opinion, whether the witness qualifies as an expert, and whether the witness's major premise is reliable. If before trial you realize that you may have to object at trial, consider filing an in limine motion. This is an excellent vehicle for focusing the judge's attention on the specific areas you are challenging, as well as assisting to make a record for a petition for writ or an appeal on an issue that is paramount to the defense of your case.

There are currently four grounds to exclude expert testimony. It is highly recommended that you find as many as are applicable. As with most principles in criminal law, the cumulative effect of several grounds together will be stronger than any individual one:

1. Evidence Code Section 801—Data Basis: Must be based on matter, that is, of a type that reasonably may be relied on by an expert in forming an opinion on the subject which his or her testimony relates, unless such expert is precluded by law from using such matter as a basis for his or her opinion.

2. Evidence Code Section 802—Reasoning: The court may require that a witness *before* testifying in the form of an opinion be first examined concerning the matter on which his or her opinion is based.
3. The trial court may find the opinion is otherwise precluded by constitutional, statutory, or decisional law (more prejudicial than probative, common knowledge, or usurps jury function).
4. Relevant to *all* types of expert testimony, not just scientific/forensic, and not limited to new or novel techniques.

Another reason for utilizing this in limine opportunity is that at trial, foundational objections to expert opinion are technically premature until the proponent asks the ultimate question regarding the expert's opinion which usurps jury function. Without having raised the objection in limine, even if the judge ultimately rules the opinion inadmissible, the jury may have already been exposed to a substantial amount of prejudicial testimony. Unringing that bell has been the quandary and contemplation of many losing advocates. Avoid this.

The benefits of in limine challenges are many:

- Opening up settlement opportunities by making the prosecutor and court work.
- Limiting/excluding damaging evidence.
- Educating and preparing the trier of fact for a more focused attack and presentation of your case.
- Meeting your constitutional obligation to challenge government expert testimony.

Conclusion

Our message here should be very clear: The most important aspect of either working with or opposing expert testimony is meeting the requirement of knowledge and vast preparation of the specific and general area of expertise, the client, and your case. As Professor Edward J. Imwinkelried, one of our nation's foremost authorities on scientific and forensic evidence explained:

> The effective litigator is much more than a legal technician. A legal technician knows only what his or her client's rights are. By contrast, an effective litigator also has a strategic and tactical sense, enabling him or her to

answer the tougher questions: whether to exercise those rights and, if so, how best to do so. As the common saying among business consultants goes, "Intelligence comes a dime a dozen. Good judgement is what is really rare."

Following our recommendations and using good judgment are equally crucial. Be prepared, confident, and adept.

• • •

Jeffrey E. Thoma is criminal defense attorney in private practice who has been licensed in California and Nevada for over 35 years. He previously served as the public defender for Solano County and Mendocino County, California; as a deputy public defender in San Diego, Orange, and Santa Cruz counties in California, and Clark County, Nevada; and as a deputy district attorney in Humboldt County, California.

He has appeared before the United States, California, and Nevada Supreme Courts. He is an acknowledged national expert on DNA evidence, having served as a commissioner on the U.S. Commission on the Future of DNA Evidence from 1996 to 2001. He has conducted over 250 jury trials, including several capital trials, and hundreds of forensic admissibility hearings and has been published many times statewide and nationally on forensic and other relevant issues.

Mr. Thoma has been on the faculty of the National College of Capital Voir Dire in Boulder, Colorado; the Death Penalty College at Santa Clara University; and the Capital Case Seminar in Monterey, California, and served as cochair of the National Association of Criminal Defense Lawyers' (NACDL) Death Penalty Committee.

He previously taught evidence at the University of Hawaii School of Law and trial practice at University of California at Davis School of Law. He teaches each year at the Annual Hawaii State Public Defender Seminar, served as a faculty consultant for the National Drug Court Institute, and has been the coordinator and chair of NACDL's Annual Forensic Program in Las Vegas, Nevada, since its inception over ten years ago.

Mr. Thoma has previously served two full terms (six years) on the Board of Directors of NACDL and is a past president of California Attorneys for Criminal Justice (2015). He can be reached at jetlaw@sbcglobal.net.

Dr. Dale Watson is a clinical and forensic neuropsychologist. Dr. Watson received his MA from John F. Kennedy University and his PhD from California School of Professional Psychology, both in clinical psychology. He is currently in private practice in Pinole, California, and a consultant to Neurobehavioral Cognitive Services, a transitional living and brain injury recovery program in Dixon, California. He has extensive experience in the evaluation and treatment of traumatic brain injuries. He is also a frequent consultant to attorneys regarding the interface between neurocognitive dysfunction and criminal law. He has made numerous national presentations on neuropsychology and the evaluation of intellectual abilities and deficits, including developmental disabilities in capital litigation. He has testified in state courts in California, Washington, Oklahoma, and Montana, as well as in various federal courts.

Dr. Watson was formerly an adjunct faculty member at the Wright Institute, an American Psychological Association accredited graduate psychology program. His current research interests include the neuropsychological correlates of violent behavior and the stability of intelligence. His publications include a contributed chapter, titled "Disaster Trauma in Cognitive Behavioral Strategies," in *Crisis Intervention*, edited by Frank M. Dattillio and Arthur Freeman (The Guilford Press; 2007). Dr. Watson can be reached at watson.dale@comcast.net.

Chapter

6

Assessment of Malingering for Criminal Defendants with Mental Disabilities

Richard Rogers, Kamar Y. Tazi, and Eric Y. Drogin

After reading the following chapter on malingering, even the most experienced criminal defense lawyer will surely say "I can't believe I knew so little about malingering. In fact, I can't believe I had so many misconceptions about malingering!"

Just as the colloquial definitions for competency and sanity do not always match the legal definitions for those terms, so too, the concept of malingering in the forensic context is often misunderstood. The authors of this chapter—Richard Rogers, Kamar Y. Tazi, and Eric Y. Drogin—have written a valuable guide for malingering. They explain the differences between malingering versus feigning, as well as discuss dissimulation and factitious disorders. They analyze the DSM-5's potential indicators, discussing their weaknesses, as well as the risk of misclassification and overclassification. They detail six major misconceptions about malingering. And they shed light on various detection strategies.

Should the prosecutor, or even your own expert, conclude or even suggest that your client is malingering, the authors suggest that you add an expert specifically qualified in malingering to your toolkit. As they note, malingering is a term too often used and too inaccurately applied.

• • •

Determinations of malingering represent a pivotal issue in many criminal forensic cases. Even a single forensic report of malingering may be sufficient to override volumes of clinical data that corroborate a genuine history of mental disorders. This chapter addresses important conceptual issues that inform counsel's understanding of malingering and related response styles. For example, malingering is not a "diagnosis" with formal inclusion and exclusion criteria. Instead, it is merely a definition, with possible indicators that have questionable value. Likely as a result, forensic practitioners are sometimes influenced by their own misconceptions and biases to reach unwarranted conclusions about malingering. As a foundation for accurate classifications of malingering, readers are introduced to research-based detection strategies for malingering. This foundation is valuable and necessary preparation for consulting with experts on the often very technical aspects of malingering determinations.

Malingering (i.e., the intentional fabrication or gross exaggeration of symptoms motivated by external gain) is of critical importance for criminal attorneys. For example, a defendant may elect to malinger during an insanity evaluation to avoid decades of incarceration. Attorneys on both sides of the bar want to ensure that forensic practitioners conduct fair and comprehensive evaluations of malingering. This chapter carefully distinguishes malingering from feigning: Both share the faked symptoms/impairment, but feigning omits external motivation from its definition. The chapter is conceptualized as a primer for attorneys on how to address malingering in criminal cases. They need to be especially knowledgeable about fundamental misconceptions about malingering. For instance, some forensic practitioners—unintentionally or not—manifest a malingering bias, as a result of which they look closely for any data about malingering, but ignore other findings to the contrary (e.g., evidence of a genuine mental disorder).

This chapter is organized in three sections. The first section introduces conceptualizations of malingering and provides important distinctions between this and other response styles. Given the complexities in establishing criteria for malingering, the second section addresses key issues and corrects some highly consequential misconceptions about malingering. The final substantive section provides a practical foundation about detection strategies that are designed to identify feigned mental disorders.

The Determination of Malingering

To set the stage, malingering is *not a diagnosis*. Rather than having a formal diagnosis, the *Diagnostic and Statistical Manual of Mental Disorders*, now in its fifth edition with a Text Revision (DSM-5-TR; American Psychiatric Association, 2022), has for decades relegated malingering to simply one of its many "V codes," which are described as "other conditions that may be a focus of clinical attention" (p. 821). As such, malingering does not have any formal inclusion criteria (i.e., what is required for its determination) or any formal exclusion criteria (i.e., what would preclude its determination).

Consistently since 1980, the DSM's determination of malingering has relied only on its description and four potential indicators. As good news, the DSM-5-TR (American Psychiatric Association, 2022) and many earlier editions offer a thoughtful and widely accepted description of malingering: "The essential feature of malingering is the intentional production of false or grossly exaggerated physical or psychological symptoms, motivated by external incentives" (p. 835). Three important features stand out in this description. First, the malingering presentation is intentionally produced. Second, the magnitude of the malingering must be large, involving either an entire fabrication or gross exaggeration in the clinical presentation (e.g., symptoms and psychological impairment). Third, the motivation for malingering must be established; guesswork about real or imagined incentives does not qualify. The opportunity to fake a mental or physical disorder for unwarranted rewards may be present in many circumstances but is seldom acted on. As an extreme example, death row inmates might malinger a psychotic or other severe disorder to postpone their execution, potentially a life-preserving incentive. However, anecdotal evidence suggests that very few do and that, perhaps, a similarly small number do the opposite, categorically denying their mental disorders. Nonetheless, a subset of neuropsychologists has wrongly equated supposed incentives with established motivation for malingering (see *Diagnostic Criteria for Malingered Neurocognitive Dysfunction*; Slick et al., 1999 and Sherman et al., 2020).

The bad news about the DSM-5-TR involves its potential indicators for malingering. According to Rogers (2021, p. 296), these indicators were "doomed to failure from the onset because they confused common characteristics with distinguishing characteristics." What is the crucial difference? *Common characteristics*—such as opposable thumbs—are shared by most persons but cannot be used to distinguish between categories, such as malingering from genuine responding. In contrast, *distinguishing characteristics* are specifically designed to differentiate between categories (e.g., response styles). For example, persons with genuine mental disorders almost never create their own words (i.e., technically known as "neologisms") or hear nonexistent voices (i.e., hallucinations) in multiple languages. Some malingerers with blatantly fake psychotic presentations may endorse and elaborate upon such symptoms. As distinguishing characteristics, such items differentiate malingerers from genuine responders.

The four DSM-5-TR potential indicators are paraphrased next in italics. Each enumerated point provides a brief commentary regarding common versus distinguishing characteristics.

1. *Forensic context of the evaluation.* All persons evaluated in the context of a contested legal issue meet this potential indicator. This is a common characteristic.
2. *Marked discrepancies between claimed stress or disability and objective findings.* A major problem is that most objective findings are comparatively general and not necessarily related to malingering. With that caveat, this potential indicator is more aligned with distinguishing than common characteristics. Notice, however, that the direction of the discrepancies is unfortunately not specified. A person denying any mental disorders could paradoxically be categorized by this indicator as malingering.
3. *Lack of cooperation with assessment and noncompliance with treatment.* This potential indicator is written ambiguously and seems to imply that both uncooperativeness and noncompliance are required, but this makes little sense when only an evaluation is being conducted. As subsequently explained, this indicator is a distinguishing characteristic, but in the *opposite direction than malingering.*
4. *Antisocial personality disorder (APD).* Antisocial backgrounds are predictably common among persons involved in criminal forensic evaluations. Findings between antisocial personality and malingering are inconsistent, with some (e.g., Kucharski et al., 2012) finding more frequent evidence of malingering for those with APD, but others

(e.g., Pierson et al., 2011) finding no difference when compared to persons without APD. Thus, this potential indicator—especially in criminal forensic cases—is much more aligned with a common characteristic than a distinguishing characteristic.

The lack of cooperation in a forensic context deserves further comment. In the only published archival study of forensic inpatients, Rogers (1990) compared the lack of cooperation by malingerers directly to other patients. Clearly, uncooperativeness was most common in non-malingering patients. When comparing rates of uncooperativeness, less than 10 percent were malingerers, but 91.5 percent were categorized as non-malingering patients. This potential indicator is a distinguishing characteristic, but it is a polar opposite to the DSM-5-TR formulation; uncooperativeness is most often found in non-malingering patients. Guidance concerning DSM-5-TR is provided in Insight #1.

INSIGHT #1: Forensic practitioners applying the DSM-5-TR potential indicators are likely to misclassify many examinees as malingering when this is not the case. To make a compelling case, you need your own malingering expert to address the weaknesses of this approach and underscore the very real risks of misclassifications.

For malingering, criminal attorneys on both sides of the bar might well be alarmed at the conceptual failures and serious inaccuracies of the DSM-5-TR potential indicators. By definition, common characteristics will markedly over-classify malingering when it is not the case. Moreover, the one distinguishing characteristic—lack of cooperation—works entirely in the opposite direction, further contributing to the over-classification of malingering. In light of these findings, DSM-5-TR potential indicators should definitely be avoided. Attorneys need to be prepared to address this matter vigorously.

Differential Diagnoses and Other Response Styles

Importantly, malingering is not the only explanation in forensic and clinical settings for the intentional or unintentional overreporting of symptoms and impairments. Many cases do not appear to be forthright, but no clear deceptive pattern is observed. The accurate term for such cases is *dissimulation*, which is characterized by some general misrepresentation of symptoms and clinical features that is clearly different from malingering and feigning. In addition, other persons may feign a mental disorder, but in the absence of any established motivation. They may be diagnosed with *factitious disorders*. This alternative to malingering is often overlooked by forensic practitioners.

Some examinees may respond inconsistently on psychological tests for a variety of reasons, including intrusive symptoms of mental disorders, lack of attention, and deficient reading ability for grasping the instructions and content of certain written measures. This lack of sustained effort, attention, or skill can be misinterpreted as malingering. On written tests in particular, an inconsistent response pattern often results—by chance alone—in elevated scores on feigning indicators. In such instances, the examinee's incapacity to complete the measure consistently may be misconstrued as an intentional, fraudulent attempt to appear mentally disordered. Attorneys always need to inquire about inconsistent responding as a potential alternative to feigning.

While malingering was previously defined and discussed, feigning was not. *Feigning* (Rogers, 2008, 2018) shares the first half of the malingering definition with respect to the purposeful fabrication or gross exaggeration of symptoms (psychological, cognitive, or physical). With gross exaggeration, the focus is sometimes on impairment such as claiming an incapacity to function. However, the crucial distinction is that feigning makes no determination of an examinee's motivations, which is the second key component of malingering.

Fundamental Issues and Misconceptions about Malingering

Legal and mental health professionals alike may be vulnerable to intuitively appealing yet fundamentally inaccurate misconceptions about malingering and feigning. Six fundamental misconceptions about malingering are selected for explanation and discussion. For ready reference, each of the six misconceptions is enumerated.

Misperception #1: There Are Tests for "Malingering" Per Se

On first reading, this assertion about tests of malingering being nonexistent appears entirely untenable. After all, several psychological measures include some form of the word "malingering" in their titles, such as the Structured Inventory of Malingered Symptomatology and the widely used Test of Memory Malingering. Moreover, literature searches find dozens of articles citing a "malingering" test or scale.

Rogers (2021) questioned whether a test of malingering would ever be possible: "No measure has been developed, or likely will be developed, to capture the often-complex motivations underlying decisions to malinger." Consider the decision to malinger in favor of supporting an insanity defense. As illustrated by Rogers, this consideration might include the following three questions:

1. What would be the likely consequences of unsuccessful (i.e., detected by the forensic practitioner) malingering? In criminal matters, these answers might include an almost certain conviction and very limited opportunity for plea bargaining.
2. What would be the chances that successful (i.e., undetected) malingering will result in being found not guilty by reason of insanity (NGRI)? Most insanity defenses are unsuccessful. Being informed by counsel that the odds strongly favor a conviction over NGRI may render the choice of malingered insanity very undesirable.
3. More situationally, what would be the examinee's appraisal of the forensic practitioner, including expertise for the assessment of malingering? It would be naïve of forensic practitioners to assume evaluations are entirely unidirectional rather than bidirectional. The presence of a seemingly gullible practitioner may by itself substantially increase the odds of malingering.

Examinees are not limited to these considerations. They may also be influenced by stigma about mental disorders, or by a clear preference in living conditions (e.g., medium-security prison vs. maximum-security hospital). Moreover, for those examinees with long-term perspectives, sentencing typically has clearly defined outcomes (e.g., specified years of incarceration). In contrast, NGRI verdicts for violent felonies are often indeterminate without any quantifiable end point (e.g., an eventual release from a maximum-security hospital to another secure facility).

Thus, scales of overstated pathology should properly be considered as *feigning* measures rather than malingering. Counsel may fully appreciate why some forensic practitioners may opt for the term "malingering" as a shortcut to avoid any detailed examination of an examinee's motivation. With patient but detailed questioning—informally or via cross-examination—criminal lawyers may expose the underlying weakness of this flawed extrapolation by forensic practitioners in the interest of full and unbiased assessment of response styles that will serve justice.

Misperception #2: The Presence of Malingering Precludes Genuine Disorders

This fundamental misconception is often not explicitly articulated, but it is readily observable in clinical records and other documentation. For instance, progress notes for a particular forensic inpatient may frequently document signs and symptoms of a serious mental disorder. Once malingering is determined, however, no psychological issues are considered genuine and worthy of including in the clinical record. One author of the current chapter, Richard Rogers, recently experienced a striking example of this complete disavowal. An intake was conducted by a staff psychiatrist for a forensic patient documenting prominent delusions on the day of admission. Several hours later, a more senior psychiatrist—totally disregarding the earlier intake—hastily determined that the same patient was malingering. No symptoms were reported for the ensuing weeks of hospitalization. Instead, all clinical issues were attributed to malingering with the patient being described in pejorative terms (e.g., "uncooperative," "evasive," and "guarded").

This simplistic dichotomization (i.e., all malingered or all genuine) ignores more nuanced—and likely more accurate—conclusions. As a common example, detained criminal defendants may grossly exaggerate sleeping issues in hopes of securing unwarranted medication (i.e., malingering) but still have genuine mood issues (e.g., major depression) and enduring personality features (e.g., narcissistic and antisocial traits). The example involving sleeping medication is particularly instructive because it demonstrates a multifaceted perspective to deception. In some correctional facilities, administrative policies explicitly prohibit prescriptions of sleeping medications—even in well-documented cases—to eliminate their potential misuse (Vitacco & Rogers, 2015). Thus, selective manipulations by offenders and categorical denials of medication needs by health care staff may represent different but related facets of deception.

Counsel may need to collaborate with more experienced colleagues in order to dislodge polarized conclusions in cases involving malingering that conclude that all symptoms and clinical characteristics must be feigned. For inpatient determinations, it may be helpful to review with one's own expert notes from those in different mental health disciplines to dispute the "total feigning" hypothesis.

Misperception #3: Sole Reliance on a Single Measure Is Sufficient to Establish Malingering

Rogers (2021) applied the poker metaphor of "going all-in" to illustrate how some forensic practitioners rely solely on a single measure for the complex determinations of malingering. As noted by Rogers, however, practitioners are betting on an examinee's future and not their own. High volume expectations often occur in forensic centers where practitioners are pressed to complete three or more forensic assessments each week, regardless of their complexities. What can sometimes be the consequence of such unrelenting pressures? Assessments of malingering may be pared down to a deficient level. Perhaps a medical analogy would be helpful. Would you want a family member to undergo surgery for a brain tumor removal based only on bloodwork confirming the presence of a mass, without additional scans or testing to confirm the type of tumor and likelihood of success?

The substitution of screens (e.g., the bloodwork) for comprehensive assessments is particularly relevant to deficient determinations of malingering given the serious legal implications at hand. In our forensic practices, it is unfortunately common to see the Miller Forensic Assessment of Symptoms Test (M-FAST), a brief screen, being used as the only standardized measure to confirm feigned mental disorders. As background, the M-FAST is a 26-item, true-false screen that is easily administered in 2 to 3 minutes. It was expressly designed to identify *possible* cases of feigning. It is clearly an excellent screen (Detullio et al., 2019), but it is definitely not a substitute for a comprehensive assessment of malingering.

Misperception #4: Malingering Is a Static Response Style

Malingering is a dynamic response to an often-challenging situation, which the examinee likely construes as high stakes (i.e., having much to gain or much to lose). On this point, malingering rarely occurs for a misdemeanor where probation or community service may be the most likely legal sanctions. Contrastingly, malingering may be considered for a larger (but still relatively small) proportion of examinees who are faced with high-stakes consequences that can be either negative (e.g., decades of incarceration) or positive (e.g., a large monetary reward in a fraudulent personal injury case).

Counsel should be aware that some forensic practitioners may wrongly assume "once a malingerer, always a malingerer" (Rogers, 2018). As a case in point, one of the current authors, Richard Rogers, consulted on an insanity case in which the defendant had malingered as a juvenile offender and then again on current adult charges. One consultant on the case characterized this as a "pattern" of malingering. However, this "pattern" appeared to have missed several decades of non-malingering involving minimal contact with both mental health and law enforcement.

In summary, forensic practitioners can be questioned about patterns of malingering as well as concomitant patterns of non-malingering. Sometimes, analogies can be helpful. Most persons including forensic practitioners have occasional sleeping problems, but relatively few have chronic and severe insomnia. Such a commonplace example may be informally helpful to illustrate what is technically known as the "fundamental attribution error." This occurs when persons wrongly assume that occasional behaviors—often viewed very negatively—reflect stable personality characteristics rather than situational responses. Isolated efforts to malinger represent a prime opportunity for a fundamental attribution error.

Misperception #5: One-Sided or Biased Reports on Malingering Are Sufficient

Feigning indicators for many forensic cases produce mixed results. Such results can be placed in one of three broadly conceptualized categories: feigned, questionable, and genuine. "Questionable" constitutes a middle ground that cannot be accurately classified as feigned or genuine. On most feigning scales, questionable would be higher than most genuine cases but lower than seen with most feigning cases. Some forensic practitioners have the tendency to lump questionable results with feigning. It is best that questionable findings be clearly identified and not used as evidence of feigning.

Evidence of one-sided reports is clearly observable when forensic practitioners entirely omit findings in the genuine range on feigning indicators. Instead of being balanced in their reporting, they focus entirely on evidence of feigning. Such selective reporting can be viewed as a *malingering bias* that, similar to confirmation bias, looks only for evidence of feigning and ignores contrary findings.

Malingering (e.g., overreporting) can be viewed as the polar opposite of defensiveness (e.g., underreporting). Why does this matter? High scores on scales of defensiveness should also raise serious questions about whether a particular examinee is feigning. This and other response patterns are clarified in Insight #2. Mixed presentations are typically more frequent than the other three clearly defined classifications. Some experts may assert their objectivity and then conclude that all indicators point to malingering. In such instances, counterexamples (e.g., feigning scales in the normal range or elevated defensive scales) may raise questions regarding a practitioner's bias as well as credibility.

INSIGHT #2: Clear and Mixed Classifications

- Clearly Feigning: Consistently high scores on feigning and low scores on defensiveness
- Clearly Defensive or Minimizing: Consistently high scores on defensiveness and low scores on feigning
- Clearly Genuine: Consistently low scores on defensiveness and low scores on feigning
- Mixed: Other combinations

Misperception #6: There Is No Middle Ground between Feigning and Genuine Responding

All measurements—including psychological measurements—have some level of imprecision to them. Obviously, cutoff scores for feigning are imperfect and include measurement error; thus, a result close to the cutoff score for feigning or other classifications may well be considered "too close to call" (Rogers, 2021). This point parallels the "questionable" designation described previously in Misperception #5. Consulting experts of psychological assessments are likely needed because addressing measurement errors can become complex and full of jargon.

Some forensic practitioners may downplay the importance of measurement errors in their forensic reports and testimony. Therefore, it is important to note that the Supreme Court of the United States in *Hall v. Florida* (572 U.S. 701 (2014)) affirmed that measurement error must explicitly be considered when making decisions that involve the IQ scores of defendants in capital cases. This affirmation was directly based on an amicus brief authored by the American Psychological Association. The brief also covers psychiatrists, being cosigned by both the American Psychiatric Association and the American Academy of Psychiatry and the Law. Importantly, the amicus brief stated that the consideration of measurement errors was standard practice within these professions. As a result, criminal attorneys may wish to question the omission of measurement errors of feigning measures based on standard practices.

Detection Strategies for Feigned Mental Disorders

Forensic practitioners should go far beyond their hunches and intuitions when making determinations of malingering. Over the last four decades, detection strategies have gradually been developed to differentiate feigned disorders from genuine mental disorders. What are detection strategies? They consist of two key components: a sound conceptualization and rigorous validation (i.e., research proving their accuracy). Let's take as an example the overreporting of contradictory symptoms for the same time period. For example, can hopelessness and euphoria overlap for days? Patterns of overreporting contradictory symptom pairs could be seen as evidence of feigned mental disorders, if other response styles, such as acquiescence (i.e., saying "yes" to most questions) could be ruled out. Interestingly, contradictory or incongruent symptom pairs are generally not emphasized as a detection strategy out of understandable concerns that feigners could identify them because of their obvious implausibility.

Rigorous validation is needed to avoid "lucky mistakes" where a single finding appears to be accurate but cannot be replicated. For sufficient rigor, the detection strategy needs to be studied multiple times and under different conditions (e.g., feigned psychosis and feigned depression) with the same measure. For further rigor, the detection strategy should also be tested across different feigning measures using the same detection strategy.

With the assistance of experts in malingering, attorneys can learn to identify overreliance on samples of convenience. Let's say you are developing a measure of feigned psychosis with several detection strategies. This measure is administered to undergraduates who take it honestly and then fake psychosis. What went seriously wrong? Virtually none of the undergraduates are actively psychotic. Therefore, the crucial differentiation (i.e., feigned psychosis vs. genuine psychosis) was never addressed.

Generally, detection strategies for feigned mental disorders fall into one of two general categories: either "unlikely" or "amplified" presentations by those fabricating and exaggerating their clinical presentations (Rogers et al., 2005). Unlikely detection strategies use improbable symptoms and clinical features as evidence of feigning. By their presence alone, a small cluster of unlikely responses may signify feigned mental disorders. In direct contrast, amplified detection strategies are a matter of degree (see Insight #3). In other words, many persons might report a perceptual disturbance such as hearing one's name being called in a crowded place. While this can often actually occur on an occasional basis, some feigners may markedly exaggerate its frequency (e.g., daily) and their subsequent emotional reaction (e.g., experiencing terror). Thus, amplified strategies identify feigning by the unexpected large magnitude of the reported symptoms.

INSIGHT #3: Unlikely vs. Amplified Detection Strategies

- Unlikely Strategies: Detection strategies addressing the likelihood and presence of symptom(s) presentations
- Amplified Strategies: Detection strategies addressing the quality (frequency, severity) of reported symptoms

---

Unlikely Detection Strategies

Scales for unlikely detection strategies often require careful consideration in their item development so as to clearly capture the unlikely content without becoming transparently absurd, thus alerting examinees to the presence of bogus test items. Four unlikely detection strategies (see Rogers, 2018) are featured here:

1. *Rare symptoms*: Some symptoms and clinical features are clearly observed in clinical populations whose members are responding candidly; however, they only occur infrequently when tested across diagnostically diverse sample. Neologisms—previously described—occur infrequently even when the inpatient sample focuses on persons diagnosed with schizophrenia.

2. *Improbable symptoms*: Feigning items for this strategy go far beyond rare symptoms because they are virtually never observed in clinical populations. The reason is typically their fantastical or implausibly bizarre content. Consider the following: "It seems unreal to me, but the left side of my face is gradually shrinking for no apparent reason." Ruling out strokes and other medical conditions, the implausibly bizarre content is a hallmark of improbable symptoms.
3. *Symptom combinations*: Some symptom pairs are commonly observed in clinical populations but infrequently reported at the same time. The major advantage of this approach is that feigners are usually unable to discern unlikely symptom pairs. Even with concerted coaching, few feigners are apt to be successful. Most symptom combinations are conceptually based on which symptoms are rarely paired together (e.g., Structured Interview of Reported Symptoms, 2nd Edition; SIRS-2). Rogers et al. (2014) used research to distinguish bogus pairs for which feigners might unwittingly endorse both items. On the Structured Inventory of Malingered Symptoms (SIMS), a bogus pair included the following content: (a) an inability to express emotions and (b) food not tasting the same as in the past. Out of hundreds of combinations, feigners will most likely become lost even if they were taught the underlying detection strategy for symptom combinations.
4. *Spurious patterns of psychopathology*: Spurious patterns follow a similar pattern to symptom combinations but focus on combinations of scales and subscales rather than infrequent item pairs. To date, spurious patterns have only been applied to the Personality Assessment Inventory (Morey, 2007), which is widely used in forensic evaluations. For instance, some feigners—when compared to large clinical samples—substantially overplay their symptoms of impulsiveness in contrast to thoughts of grandiosity about themselves.

Criminal law practitioners will appreciate the depth and range of unlikely detection strategies, even from this brief summary. Knowing this, defense counsel may wish to advise their clients against feigning or exaggerating their clinical presentations, which may seriously backfire. In contrast, prosecutors may focus on forensic practitioners and test their knowledge of unlikely detection strategies via cross-examination.

Amplified Detection Strategies

Amplified strategies address the magnitude and intensity of clinical presentations. Rather than the careful construction of item content accomplished with unlikely strategies, amplified detection strategies examine patterns of responding. For example, "indiscriminant[1] symptom endorsement" (see number 1 in the following list) occurs when examinees endorse a large majority (e.g., > 75 percent) in a list of symptoms and features covering a broad range of mental disorders. More in-depth coverage is provided by Rogers (2018), and four amplified strategies are featured here:

1. *Indiscriminant symptom endorsement*: Using what is sometimes referred to colloquially as the "kitchen sink" approach, some feigners endorse most symptoms and features available, describing each as highly personally distressful. This strategy works the best when examinees are presented with a wide-ranging list of symptoms and features—either orally or in writing—so they do not need to generate their own list.
2. *Symptom severity*: This strategy focuses of the intensity of reported symptoms. Some feigners report most symptoms at the highest possible level. This strategy works best when the range of ratings addresses distress (e.g., unbearable) or its negative effects (e.g., extreme impairment). Readers can easily see how severity and indiscriminant endorsements, while conceptually separate, may go hand in hand.
3. *Reported versus observed symptoms*: This valuable but underutilized strategy is most easily applied to structured interviews where an examinee's report is compared to the practitioner's observations. Discrepancies alone are not indicative of feigning. Instead, feigning is sometimes observed with a one-directional pattern, with reported difficulties by the examinee not being observed in the forensic assessment. Occasionally, feigners substantially worsen the questioned behavior. For example, if asked about suspiciousness, the examinee may begin to glance furtively around the room. Ruling out suggestibility, this worsening is clearly aligned with feigning.

---

1. "Indiscriminant symptom endorsement" occurs when examinees claim most or all of the psychological problems suggested to them in an interview or test, in order to make themselves look as impaired as possible, and typically without any apparent attempt to establish the presence of a specific mental health condition. See Rogers (2018).

4. *Erroneous stereotypes*: This detection strategy capitalizes on common misconceptions about psychoses or other serious mental disorders. Feigners often use whatever ideas they have—whether accurate or false—to inform their fabrications. Thus, false stereotypes represent an effective strategy for feigned mental disorders. The most salient example involved the MMPI-2 (Minnesota Multiphasic Personality Inventory). Unfortunately, it is no longer available for the MMPI-3, but research is underway to rectify this oversight.

Like unlikely strategies, amplified strategies cover an array of feigned presentations with indiscriminant endorsement and symptom severity being salient examples. They are supplemented by more intricate approaches such as observational discrepancies (number 3), which requires feigners to not only respond to the question but to have insight into how their behavior may be perceived. Of these four amplified strategies, erroneous stereotypes pose formidable challenges for many malingerers who cannot alter what they do not know (i.e., false stereotypes).

Concluding Thoughts

In closing, this chapter provides attorneys with a practically oriented framework for understanding such key terms as *malingering* and *feigning* as they relate to forensic practice. In particular, it strongly emphasizes how motivation must be established for malingering to be present, exemplified by various reasons in an insanity case, for decisions to malinger or not to malinger. Despite their advanced knowledge and impressive credentials, it is our experience that many, perhaps the majority, of forensic practitioners are susceptible to the fundamental malingering misconceptions. It is our aspiration that attorneys can directly address these fallacies in experts and also themselves.

Attorneys need to have a working grasp of detection strategies and the pivotal role of these strategies in determining feigned mental disorders. With dozens of feigning scales and reams of scholarly and practice-based articles, it would be understandably easy for attorneys to become overwhelmed with technical data. Instead, this chapter is written to build a foundation concerning unlikely and amplified detection strategies, to facilitate meaningful professional communications with malingering specialists.

Insight #4 differentiates the general skills of most forensic practitioners from the advanced competencies of malingering specialists. Without any official designation, malingering specialists are often identified by referrals from forensic psychologists and psychiatrists. Often, senior counsel with decades of experience in criminal cases constitute a rich source of referrals. Ideally, malingering specialists will have a scientist-practitioner background that integrates research on feigned mental disorders with their extensive forensic experiences that include expert testimony in criminal cases where malingering and feigning play a central role.

INSIGHT #4: Assessments of Malingering as a Forensic Specialty

- Most forensic practitioners have a general working knowledge for the evaluation of feigning and its relationship to malingering.
- In contested (i.e., practitioners reaching different conclusions) and complex cases, criminal attorneys should consider retaining forensic practitioners specializing in malingering and feigned mental disorders.

• • •

Richard Rogers, PhD, ABPP, is a Regents Professor of Psychology at the University of North Texas (https://psychology.unt.edu/node/faculty/richard-rogers). He has expertise in malingering and other response styles and consults on forensic cases nationally. In criminal cases, he has evaluated malingering on far-ranging issues, such as trial competency, criminal responsibility, and even competency to be executed. Dr. Rogers continues as an editor and lead author of multiple chapters in the award-winning book *Clinical Assessment of Malingering and Deception* (Guilford Publications), now in its fourth edition. Dr. Rogers is also the principal author of the Structured Interview of Reported Symptoms (SIRS) and its second edition (SIRS-2), which have been used extensively in criminal forensic cases investigating malingering and related response styles. Dr. Rogers is nationally recognized for his contributions to forensic psychology and psychiatry by the American Psychiatric Association, the American Academy of Forensic Psychology, and the American Academy of Psychiatry and the Law. In 2011, Dr. Rogers became only the third psychologist in the history of the American Psychological Association (APA) to receive APA awards for Distinguished Professional Contributions to both applied research and public policy.

Kamar Tazi is a third-year doctoral student in clinical psychology at the University of North Texas, working closely under the mentorship of Dr. Rogers. Her program of study focuses on clinical psychology with a specialization in forensic psychology. Her research broadly focuses on forensic assessments and factors (e.g., intellectual functioning) underlying legal decision-making in underserved populations. Several scholarly projects, including this chapter, are devoted to malingering and other response styles in forensic populations. In striving for a rewarding academic career, Ms. Tazi is deeply committed to the specialty of forensic psychology and currently serves in a key leadership role as the Chair of the American Psychology-Law Society Student Committee.

Eric Y. Drogin, JD, PhD, ABPP, is a fellow of the American Psychological Association, a fellow of the American Academy of Forensic Psychology, and a diplomate and former president of the American Board of Forensic Psychology. He currently holds faculty appointments with Harvard Medical School, the Harvard Mass General Brigham Forensic Psychiatry Fellowship, the Brigham and Women's Hospital (BWH) Harvard Medical School Psychiatry Residency Training Program, and the Beth Israel Deaconess Medical Center (BIDMC) Harvard Psychiatry Residency Training Program. He is the affiliated lead of psycholegal studies for the Psychiatry, Law, and Society Program at BWH and participates in the Forensic Psychiatry Service at BIDMC and the Program in Psychiatry and the Law at Massachusetts Mental Health Center. Dr. Drogin is a life fellow of the American Bar Foundation and a former chair of the American Bar Association's Section of Science and Technology Law. His multidisciplinary practice encompasses mental health law, expert witness testimony, and trial consultation.

Complete citations are available from the authors upon request.

Chapter

7

Testing

Jemour Maddux and Ira K. Packer

Watch a judge, prosecutor, or another criminal defense lawyer read a psychological evaluation. When many, if not most, reach the testing section, they either skip over it or look for the "bottom line" number. After all, many attorneys went to law school precisely because we wanted to avoid math.

This chapter by Dr. Jemour Maddux and Dr. Ira Packer is a valuable primer on how to understand the numbers and deal with core concepts of various testing instruments—instruments which are often called the "gold standard." The authors explain terms such as reliability, interrater reliability, and validity. They caution attorneys about the security obligations psychologists have regarding the administration of tests. The authors emphasize that notwithstanding the importance of various testing instruments, they are only one factor in understanding the complexity of a client's behavior.

• • •

The birth of psychology as an applied science is often associated with World War I and the administration of psychological testing to help in the selection of soldiers. Scores of professionals from various mental health disciplines provide treatment services, such as social workers, psychiatrists, licensed professional counselors, life coaches, and others. However, psychological testing is typically considered to be a service that uniquely falls within the purview of licensed psychologists. Psychological testing plays an important role for the public in a number of domains, including assisting in determining whether a child is entitled to individualized educational services and informing a variety of medical and psychological treatment decisions. It also serves a crucial role in criminal proceedings regarding competency, responsibility, delinquency, and other issues.

This chapter will provide an introductory overview of measurement science as well as psychological tests and instruments appropriate for use in criminal proceedings. Tests that are commonly used in one jurisdiction may not be frequently used in others, and summarizing every test and instrument that could arise in a criminal case is beyond the scope of this chapter. However, it is helpful to know the names and uses of some "gold standard tests," which is a problematic but often used term. This chapter will identify psychological tests and instruments that criminal defense attorneys may encounter in their work. Some of these measures are part of categories of instrumentation defined by how and/or what they assess, which will also be illustrated.

It is important to understand the actual meaning of scores on psychological tests, for example the meaning of a particular score on a standardized psychological test of a defendant. This chapter will help the reader understand this as well as the limitations of psychological tests and instruments that are used during forensic mental health assessments. It will also introduce terminology a criminal defense lawyer will likely encounter when presented with expert opinions based upon data from psychological tests and instruments.

It is important to keep in mind that the information in this chapter is introductory, limited, and written for attorneys seeking a deeper understanding of testing instruments. Entire books are dedicated to the instrumentation used by psychologists to assist the court in criminal cases. Therefore, readers are encouraged to consult the relevant sources listed in the Suggested Works section at the end of this book to deepen their understanding of these important issues as well as many other topics. When selecting these sources, particular consideration was given to those that are accessible and comprehensible for non-psychologists.

What Is a Psychological Test?

You have probably seen clickbait for psychological tests and quizzes claiming to reveal the real you or promising to uncover your typology. They are often free, readily available to the public, and capable of being scored and interpreted without training. Now, compare these tests to the SAT or GED—tests that are carefully protected, securely managed, and privately scored. When it comes to psychological tests and instruments that are used in criminal proceedings, they have more in common with the SAT, for example, in terms of accessibility, security, and the high-stakes decisions supported by these tests. Understanding elements of test construction and measurement science helps to differentiate between the caliber of tests presented in courts versus social media and dating apps.

Test Construction

Specific methods are used to scientifically develop test questions and to ascertain the meaning of test responses. Such methods are key to the construction of reliable and valid psychological tests and instruments. For lawyers, the term *reliable* is synonymous with what psychologists call *valid*. However, for psychologists, a measure's reliability refers to its consistency.

Reliability

If a test is reliable, "Beth" should not get a vastly different score on Friday than she got on the same test two days prior if other factors and circumstances remain the same. This psychometric property is called *test–retest reliability*. Also, provided that other factors and circumstances remain the same, "Bob's" score should not significantly change if the same psychological test were administered and/or scored by different examiners, which is called *interrater reliability*. When similar items on a psychological test yield comparable information about an examinee, then the items are likely measuring the same thing, which is a desired form of consistency called *internal reliability*.

Validity

In addition to ensuring the reliability of a psychological measure, validity is key during the test construction process. There are several types of validity. If a psychological test is valid, the measure is assessing its intended target or construct (i.e., *construct validity*). If a psychological test were constructed to assess depression, then it would be promising if high scorers on this new instrument also tended to score high on other published tests of depression (i.e., *convergent validity*) and low on existing measures of resilience or hyperactivity (i.e., *discriminant validity*).

In order to explain the concept of *criterion validity*, imagine we are constructing a self-report test of hopelessness. Bob completes the test and produces a very high score. By looking at Bob's scores on a criterion from the past, such as psychiatric hospitalizations, we can explore the retrospective validity of our new measure. Similarly, by looking at his scores on a current and related criterion, such as collateral ratings from others, we can ascertain the concurrent validity of our new measure. If we designed this measure to predict future suicide attempts, we can assess predictive validity by following up with high scorers after three months to see if their scores were indeed associated with frequency of suicide attempts.

Psychological test construction requires subject matter expertise, statistical knowledge, and access to large samples of people to assess a prospective measure's reliability and validity, which are collectively described as psychometric properties. These properties are commonly communicated in terms of statistical coefficients ranging from zero to one (bad to good). In terms of what is acceptable, it really depends. Some have argued test-retest and interrater reliability should be at least 0.80, and a 0.70 alpha coefficient is the conventionally accepted minimum for internal reliability. These statistical analyses can vary and be difficult to understand. You can find further information in the sources listed in the Suggested Works section for this chapter.

Standardizations, Norms, and Comparison Groups

What if a test developer working at a rural psychiatric hospital where Beth was admitted just relied upon Beth and nine other patients—all white women in their 50s—to analyze a prospective measure's psychometric properties: Would this be an appropriate psychological test to assess an urban Asian male defendant in his 20s who allegedly offended during his second consecutive deployment to Afghanistan? Absolutely not! The small sample size, demographic differences, and population dissimilarity (i.e., racial and gender differences, as well as military versus civilian) would substantially limit what we can know about this examinee for the purpose of his or her criminal case. In such a case, the validity and relevance of the test results would be questionable. For the same reason, it would be difficult to justify the appropriateness of testing an adult Gen Zer with a measure constructed using a normative sample from the late 1980s, especially if a newer edition of the measure is available with updated norms. These concerns are becoming increasingly important to consider and address as the United States becomes a more diverse nation. According to census data, less than half of U.S. children under 15 are non-Hispanic White.

It is important to note that our score(s) on standardized tests are simply indicating something about our responses relative to the comparison group(s) used to standardize the measure, and psychologists are recommended to clearly communicate this fact. If a test taker's demographics or unique population (e.g., prison inmates) is not represented in the test's comparison group(s), then the psychological evaluation should acknowledge the limitations associated with relying upon such a test for that examinee, as well as the psychologist's efforts to address the limitations.

A psychological test can yield valuable information about examinees' responses to test questions as a function of a measure's comparison groups. However, the test results must be interpreted in the context of other factors as well, in order to make clinical determinations about people (not responses). For example, imagine a defendant who scored high on a scale used to assess feigned mental health symptoms. The psychologist must consider other factors to clinically determine if this is an examinee who is crying out for help, struggling to comprehend written tests, engaging in malingering, and/or experiencing severe psychopathology. There are several possible explanations for producing such responses. Assessing for information that is consistent with and inconsistent with these hypotheses is complex but important.

Qualified Users and Security Obligations

Again, psychological tests used in criminal proceedings are generally inaccessible to the public for purchase. Test publishers sell psychological measures and are responsible for ensuring purchasers have the appropriate qualifications to possess, administer, and interpret the instruments they are seeking. Some instruments require a professional license, degree, or certificate, and suitable experience and training in administering, scoring, and interpreting them. Some instruments can only be obtained by those who have completed coursework in measurement science and a bachelor's degree in psychology or a similar field. Other instruments are unavailable to those without advanced degrees that require training in psychological testing, such as doctoral-level psychologists.

A licensed doctoral-level psychologist will ordinarily have the user qualifications to purchase any psychological test, including neuropsychological and forensic assessment instruments. Board certification in neuropsychology or forensic psychology is not required in order to be qualified to administer such measures. While board certification is an indication of a psychologist's proficiency in the specialty, psychologists without this credential could have acquired a wealth of knowledge, experience, and training in psychologically testing defendants in criminal proceedings. However, careful vetting of your potential expert is recommended to determine this qualification.

User qualifications also work to protect the integrity of these tests. Imagine if a test designed to assess poor effort on cognitive testing were leaked. Consider the potential impact of such a leak on criminal proceedings. Due to test security issues, psychologists are guided by ethics and their contracts with test developers to keep test materials secure. Test materials include manuals, questions, books, and objects. This does not include test data, such as true/false endorsements and other information written by the examiner or examinee. In a criminal proceeding, psychologists ordinarily release raw test data to opposing experts who are qualified when requested. However, concerning the protection of test materials, psychologists should be guided by applicable guidelines, rules, law, and the needs of the court.

For example, in response to your requests for test materials, psychologists may ask for test items and responses to be omitted from pleadings and filings, or sealing this information if it must be included. Psychologists may or may not request the exclusion of quotes and descriptions of test questions and responses from opinions, recommendations, fact findings, reports, and conclusions. On some tests, the responses elicited may not individually hold a significant degree of relevance to the proceedings and could jeopardize the security of test items if included.

However, on tests such as the MacArthur Competence Assessment Tool–Criminal Adjudication (MacCAT-CA), a psychologist may opt to include the examinee's responses to demonstrate poor understanding or reasoning. Taken together, lawyers should expect psychologists to exercise professional judgment around these issues while striving to balance competing demands upon them. Lastly, if ordered to release test materials, psychologists will often request an order of protection that specifies the following: (1) no copying of test materials or sharing them with nonparties; (2) materials are to be given back to the psychologist when the matter is finished; and (3) omission of the materials from the public record or sealing that portion of the record, such as testimony regarding test items.

This partially explains why a lawyer's request to observe psychological testing might be met with resistance by a psychologist. Psychologists have obligations to test publishers, ethical obligations, and perhaps concerns about whether defense counsel will share test questions and coach future clients. Also, particularly in neuropsychology, psychologists have expressed concerns about the impact of third-party observers on examinee performance in addition to distraction and deliberate interference by attorneys. That said, in multiple states, attorneys are entitled to observe evaluations of their clients. The experienced psychologist will know this and have a reasonable set of ground rules for third-party observers to follow in order to address some of these risks, including exclusion from the testing portions of the evaluation.

Categories of Instrumentation and Related Criminal Proceedings

The following tests and instruments are commonly used by psychologists in criminal proceedings. Many of these tests are further discussed in other chapters, so specifics about their psychometric properties are not provided here. However, they are offered to illustrate the types or categories of instrumentation applied by experts in these proceedings. These instruments can be conveniently grouped by what they assess, such as personality, intelligence, or feigning. They can also be distinguished and categorized by their relationships with specific forensic questions. Also, some instruments are more like structured interview guides than tests. These instruments help psychologists generate opinions regarding the severity and/or imminence of risk, for example, in a way that is reliable and valid. Again, this is not an exhaustive list and some of these tests may not be in regular use by experts in particular jurisdictions. However, they have all been mentioned in major texts (i.e., treatises in the field) regarding forensic practice.

Ability Assessment Instruments

Standardized tests of intelligence or other cognitive abilities and educational achievement are often categorized as ability assessment instruments. This category also includes measures of adaptive functioning, such as the Vineland Adaptive Behavior Scales, 3rd Edition. When a diagnosis of intellectual disability or a lack of sophistication or maturity is relevant (e.g., *Atkins* and juvenile waiver cases, respectively), then a psychologist could administer a Wechsler Intelligence Scale for Children, 5th Edition (WISC-V) or a Wechsler Adult Intelligence Scale, 4th Edition (WAIS-IV). Depending on the underlying condition, ability assessment could also be relevant to the evaluation of competency, false or involuntary confession, and *Miranda* waiver. If there is a concern about an examinee's ability to read written testing, or if eligibility for special education is relevant (e.g., juvenile transfer cases), then psychologists may administer the Wide Range Achievement Test, 5th Edition (WRAT-5) or a similar test of reading, spelling, math, and other academic skills.

Neuropsychological Testing Instruments

These are standardized measures of cognitive, verbal, motor, visuospatial, learning, problem-solving, memory, and other abilities. Such tests are used in the assessment of brain disorders as well as cognitive and behavioral dysfunction. They include the Halstead–Reitan Battery (e.g., the Trail Making Test and the Category Test), the Wisconsin Card Sorting Test, the Bender Visual-Motor Gestalt Test, 2nd Edition (Bender-Gestalt II), the Wechsler Memory Scale, 4th Edition (WMS-IV), the Conners Continuous Performance Test, 3rd Edition (Conners CPT-3), California Verbal Learning Test, 3rd Edition, and others. Depending on the jurisdiction and case-specific facts (e.g., suspected brain disorder or ADHD), such assessments can offer useful data in competency, responsibility, mitigation, risk assessment, false confession, *Miranda*, and diversion cases.

Objective Multiscale Personality Assessment Instruments

Objective personality assessment refers to the collection of testing data in response to objective true/false questions. In comparison, some projective tests (e.g., House-Tree-Person or the Thematic Apperception Test) elicit test takers' responses to ambiguous information. However, the use of such instruments by forensic psychologists has declined over the years and they have been criticized regarding their psychometric properties. That said, the Rorschach Inkblot Test is a projective instrument for which there continues to be a lively debate about its appropriateness for some aspects of evaluations requested during criminal proceedings. For example, if there is a need to thoroughly investigate a potential thought disorder in a guarded test taker, the projective nature and psychometric properties of the Rorschach may support its appropriate inclusion within a battery of other psychological tests.

The most-used objective measures of psychopathology and personality functioning are the Minnesota Multiphasic Personality Inventory-3 (MMPI-3) and the Personality Assessment Inventory (PAI). These standardized self-report instruments assess for a variety of psychological problems, such as depression, anxiety, psychosis, substance use issues, and trauma, as well as personality issues associated with antisocial, borderline, and other personality disorders. Both measures have multiple scales to assess response style, which is critical in most criminal proceedings. Both tests have been extensively studied and this research includes investigations using correctional and forensic populations. The normative groups used to standardize these measures are demographically diverse.

Psychologists also have objective multiscale instruments that are condition-specific at their disposal. For example, if trauma is at issue, a psychologist may consider administering the Trauma Symptom Inventory, 2nd Edition (TSI-2). For minors, the Trauma Symptom Checklist for Children (TSCC) could be appropriate. Also, the Clinician-Administered PTSD Scale for DSM-5 (CAPS-5) is an example of a structured interviewing instrument for trauma assessment.

Forensic Assessment Instruments

The term "forensic assessment instrument" was coined in 1986 by Thomas Grisso to describe tests that directly measure psycholegal elements and abilities at issue in a particular proceeding. For example, in competency proceedings, a psychologist may deploy the MacArthur Competence Assessment Tool–Criminal Adjudication (MacCAT-CA), which presents a vignette and then a variety of items to assess the examinee's understanding and reasoning, as well as awareness of the examinee's own circumstances. Other instruments used by psychologists for competence evaluations include the following:

- Evaluation of Competency to Stand Trial-Revised (ECST-R)
- Fitness Interview Test-Revised (FIT-R)
- Competence Assessment for Standing Trial for Defendants with Intellectual Disability (CAST-ID), formerly known as the CAST-MR
- Interdisciplinary Fitness Interview-Revised (IFI-R)

Compared to the MacCAT-CA, some of the instruments noted earlier make greater use of structured interviewing. Others are better at addressing psychopathology, decision-making in response to pleas, and examinee consideration of trial strategies. Still others focus on targeting particular considerations in assessing specific populations, such as those with intellectual disabilities.

It should be noted that while these tests are helpful, they do not provide mechanical decision-making about competence. In other words, none of these measures are to be used as stand-alone methods for unilaterally controlling psychologists' opinions, as scores on these instruments do not equate with a finding of competence or incompetence. Rather, they are tools to aid in that determination, to be incorporated with other data. The same is true for the Rogers Criminal Responsibility Assessment Scales (R-CRAS), which are designed to assist in the evaluation of criminal responsibility. Likewise, the Gudjonsson Suggestibility Scales (GSS), which are appropriately used in *Miranda* and false or involuntary confession cases, should also be used in conjunction with other sources of information.

Actuarial Instruments

Some instruments mechanically classify a defendant's risk simply based on what is statistically known about certain risk factors (e.g., prior convictions) and future behavior, such as violence. These instruments inform psychologists' communication of risk. They provide mechanically derived findings regarding the categorization of risk apart from psychologists' professional judgments. These actuarial instruments have been developed for assessing sexual risk, such as the STATIC-99R, the STATIC-2002R, and the Sex Offender Risk Appraisal Guide (SORAG). Other tests have been developed to aid in the assessment of general violence risk, such as the Violence Risk Appraisal Guide-Revised (VRAG-R) and the Classification of Violence Risk (COVR), although psychologists should ensure that the individual being evaluated is comparable to the population on which these tools have been normed.

Structured Professional Judgment Instruments

Actuarial instruments, as just described, are touted for overcoming the limitations of estimating risk solely based on unguided clinical judgment. However, when properly structured, clinical judgment can effectively be used to estimate risk in a way that permits sensible adjustments based upon the unique characteristics of the person being evaluated. Structured professional judgment (SPJ) instruments have been developed to estimate risk of violence across various domains such as: adult violence (e.g., HCR-20, Version 3); domestic violence (e.g., Spousal Assault Risk Assessment Guide, SARA); sex offending (e.g., Sexual Violence Risk–20, Version 2); juvenile violence (e.g., Structured Assessment of Violence Risk in Youth, SAVRY); juvenile sophistication and maturity (e.g., Risk-Sophistication-Treatment Inventory, RSTI); and juvenile sex offending (e.g., Estimate of Risk of Adolescent Sexual Offense Recidivism, Version 2, ERASOR).

Mental Status Examinations

While formal instruments are available (e.g., Mini-Mental State Examination, 2nd Edition, MMSE-2, or the Montreal Cognitive Assessment, MOCA), the mental status examination (MSE) generally refers to a semi-structured assessment of current functioning. Across all evaluations conducted by psychologists for criminal court cases, it is quite common to find an MSE. The MSE generally consists of observations and questions to capture the defendant's psychological status, such as physical appearance, posture, grooming, activity level, ambulatory status, facial expression, alertness, vision, hearing, other basic sensory and motor function.

Much of the data captured to complete an MSE is observed by the psychologist during the evaluation. Speech (e.g., volume, pace, intonation, and clarity), disposition, interpersonal style, mood, and affect are examples. Affect refers to the quality of a test taker's immediate emotional expression. Psychologists typically note the range, intensity, variability, and other affective qualities. Mood and anxiety symptoms are also part of the MSE. Memory, abstract reasoning, and other cognitive abilities are often sampled through questions like those on ability assessment measures. For example, an examinee could be asked to count backwards from 100 by sevens or to describe how two seemingly unrelated things are alike. Regarding thought process, psychologists carefully observe whether the test taker's thinking was goal-directed, tangential, based in reality, indicative of psychosis, or marked by preoccupations, for example.

During the MSE, careful attention is given to the level of consistency between the examinee's presentation and self-reported issues. Inconsistencies are likely to be analyzed in the contexts of varying hypotheses, such as malingering. Sometimes a structured clinical interview for mental disorders (e.g., Structured Clinical Interview for DSM-5, SCID-5) will also appear if a diagnosable condition is salient to the case for which the evaluation was sought. Incorporating such an instrument may increase reliability, decrease the potential role of bias, and reduce the chances of overlooking diagnostic possibilities. When warranted, psychologists may also incorporate structured clinical interviews for specific issues, like trauma, with the Clinician Administered PTSD Scale for DSM-5 (CAPS-5). Some unstructured clinical interviewing will typically be needed in these cases, but the instruments described thus far can certainly complement the multiple methods and sources of information psychologists seek and rely upon to optimize the reliability of their opinions.

Symptom Validity, Response Style, Effort, and Malingering Instruments

It is almost always the case that defendants with a sufficient level of functioning will have the clarity to realize how the outcome of their psychological evaluation could benefit them. This awareness incentivizes efforts to control examination findings through impression management, such as exaggerating problems, making up symptoms, or putting forth poor effort on ability assessments. Given these incentives, psychologists typically administer tests or utilize psychological instruments to assess response style, effort, and feigning. As noted earlier, some multiscale instruments include validity scales that capture this data, such as the PAI and MMPI-3. There are also instruments to assess for feigned mental health symptoms, such as the Structured Inventory of Malingered Symptomatology (SIMS) and the Miller Forensic Assessment Test (M-FAST). Concerns that arise on any of these tests may prompt psychologists to further assess for dissimulation with the Structured Interview of Reported Symptoms, 2nd Edition (SIRS-2).

In some instances, malingered mental health issues are not the concern, but rather intentionally poor effort on ability assessment is deserving of greater attention in the evaluation process. In these instances, psychologists may use the Validity Indicator Profile (VIP), the Green's Word Memory Test, or the Test of Memory Malingering (TOMM). When response style is being assessed in the context of competence to stand trial, the Inventory of Legal Knowledge (ILK), which was designed for this very purpose, may be used.

Some Final Thoughts

As noted earlier, it is important to ensure that any psychological tests employed have been normed on the appropriate racial, ethnic, gender, and age groups. That said, attorneys should also be aware of how this concept could theoretically be misapplied, such as relying upon race norming in support of a defendant's eligibility for capital punishment during an *Atkins* hearing.

At the risk of getting too technical, the Flynn effect is certain to crop up at some point in an attorney's career, perhaps sooner rather than later. The Flynn effect refers to an observed rise in how well people across the world are performing on intelligence tests. Suppose an intelligence test was standardized and released for publication in 1990. Ten years later, a psychologist uses the measure to assess a defendant. Due to the Flynn effect, that defendant's score might be three points higher than what the defendant would have scored if data were collected from around the nation in 2000 for re-standardization purposes. Also, if a 90 or 95 percent confidence interval is written in the psychologist's report, alongside a range of scores, then the evaluator is communicating that the odds of the examinee's true score falling within this specified range is either 90 or 95 percent. If a case can turn on a three-point difference, then perhaps this brief discussion of these complex issues will prove to be of assistance.

For more information on psychological testing, the American Psychological Association (APA) released guidelines in 2020 describing aspirational best practices in this area. While the document is not specific to forensic psychology, its contents are applicable to forensic practice. Also, the *Standards for Educational and Psychological Testing* is an APA policy that sets forth critical guidance regarding the construction, evaluation, and use of psychological tests, amongst other pertinent topics.

Culture and language are also of critical importance in conducting psychological testing for criminal court cases. If an examinee does not speak English, having a lay interpreter translate the written materials would not be appropriate. A variety of tests have published language translations and a great degree of care goes into producing them in an effort to preserve the measure's psychometric properties for non-English speakers. Ideally defendants should be offered the chance to be assessed in their native language. In addition to practice guidelines on culture, APA has published practice guidelines on *Assessment and Intervention with Persons with Disabilities*, which became association policy in 2022. These guidelines collectively offer a wealth of information for psychologists as well as stakeholders concerning testing best practices for an evolving and increasingly diverse practice landscape.

Summary

Given the interests of society, concern for victims of crime, and the rights of defendants with mental disabilities, psychological testing can be of vital importance in criminal proceedings. That said, psychological testing is not always required to answer referral questions, and its necessity to address the psycholegal questions should dictate decisions about its administration.

Psychological testing uniquely falls within the purview of licensed psychologists irrespective of whether they identify as forensic, clinical, or neuropsychological specialists. While this chapter is about testing, it also describes categories of psychological instruments—a term that is often used interchangeably with psychological tests. Also, the role of a thoughtfully undertaken and sufficiently detailed and comprehensive MSE is generally part and parcel with psychological test administration. While generally structured to some extent, this too is not a test per se.

As a recap, reliability means consistency in measurement science. Validity refers to the extent you are measuring what you desire or claim to measure. There are multiple forms of reliability as well as validity that support the rigor of a test, and ultimately its proper admissibility as a basis for expert testimony. However, it is important to keep in mind the critical role of comparison groups in interpreting what a particular test result means. Psychologists are acculturated in their training to place a high priority on the security of psychological testing. Therefore, when bringing psychological science inside the culture of the criminal court where transparency is paramount, experts may exhibit resistance to the cooperation you are seeking as an attorney—much of which can be resolved with a protective order and a coherent set of ground rules for third-party observers to the forensic evaluation process.

• • •

Jemour A. Maddux, PsyD, ABPP, is a postdoctoral instructor in forensic psychology and core faculty in the Doctor of Psychology Program at William Paterson University of New Jersey. His research surrounds the convergence of trauma and justice. Dr. Maddux is the past president of the New York State Psychological Association's Forensic Division, and he served two terms on the board of directors for the American Professional Society on the Abuse of Children (APSAC), initiating its Commission for Racial Justice in Child Maltreatment. Dr. Maddux has also consulted for the New Jersey Institute for Social Justice. He coedited the text *Assessing Trauma in Forensic Contexts* and has provided editorial leadership for Springer's *Psychological Injury and Law*, Oxford's *Best Practices in Forensic Mental Health Assessments*, and the American Psychology-Law Society's interdisciplinary book series through APA Books.

Dr. Maddux served as the elected 2023 Chair of the American Psychological Association (APA)'s Committee on Professional Practice and Standards. He has contributed to the development of various policy statements, amicus briefs, and practice guidelines for the APA and APSAC. He chaired the task force that developed APSAC's *Practice Guidelines for Forensic Mental Health Evaluations When Child Maltreatment Is at Issue*. He was appointed to the six-member work group that revised APA's *Guidelines for Child Custody Evaluations in Family Law Proceedings*. He was also appointed to the seven-member work group revising APA's *Guidelines for Psychological Evaluations in Child Protection Matters*.

Dr. Maddux is a licensed psychologist in Michigan, New York, and New Jersey, in addition to practicing under the Psychology Interjurisdictional Compact (PSYPACT). He is a fellow of the American Academy of Forensic Psychology. He is also board certified in forensic psychology by the American Board of Professional Psychology (ABPP). He specializes in forensic assessment of ability, risk, and psychological injury in family, civil, sentencing, and law enforcement cases. Maddux is currently under contract with APA Publishing to write *Psychological Evaluation of Children in Personal Injury Lawsuits*, a pioneering book on this subject. He can be reached at jm@rule702.com and https://rule702.com/.

Ira K. Packer, PhD, Professor Emeritus of Psychiatry at the University of Massachusetts Medical School (UMMS), received his BA in psychology from Columbia University and his PhD in psychology from the University of Pennsylvania. He has authored or coauthored over 50 articles and chapters, as well as two books: *Evaluation of Criminal Responsibility* and *Specialty Competencies in Forensic Psychology* (with Tom Grisso, PhD). Dr. Packer has over 40 years of experience providing and supervising forensic evaluations, with an emphasis on competence to stand trial, criminal responsibility, and violence risk assessment. In addition to his clinical forensic work, Dr. Packer has extensive experience managing forensic mental health programs and providing consultation on forensic systems nationally.

Dr. Packer served as Assistant Commissioner for Forensic Services for the Massachusetts Department of Mental Health (DMH), and also directed Forensic Evaluation Services at Bridgewater State Hospital (the maximum-security forensic facility for men), as well as at Worcester Recovery Center and Hospital (a DMH facility for both men and women), and the court clinics in western Massachusetts. From 1999 to 2001 he chaired the Designated Forensic Professional Training and Certification Committee, which is responsible for oversight of the training and certification of forensic psychologists and psychiatrists in Massachusetts. He also directed the highly respected UMMS Postdoctoral Fellowship Program in Forensic Psychology.

Dr. Packer served nationally as the president of the American Board of Forensic Psychology, president of the American Academy of Forensic Psychology, and president of the Council of Specialties in Professional Psychology. Along with colleagues, he has provided forensic consultation services to a number of jurisdictions across the country, with an emphasis on improving the systems for evaluation and care of individuals referred for competence to stand trial evaluations and restoration. These jurisdictions include Washington State, Alabama, Colorado, New York, and Los Angeles County.

Chapter

8

Neuroimaging

Stephen G. Cobb

The introduction to this chapter in the 2018 edition stated that neuroimaging is the "new frontier in criminal defense." As this substantially updated chapter by criminal defense lawyer Stephen G. Cobb shows, although neuroimaging has become more prevalent, substantial obstacles like funding and resistance by judges remain. Specifically, neuroimaging is expensive, and for defendants in custody, the costs of transportation and security in addition to the actual cost of the procedure, make it prohibitive. Beyond that, most insurance companies will not cover the expenses. Moreover, in a political climate where scientific discoveries are often greeted with skepticism, judges may deem neuroimaging unpersuasive, if not inadmissible.

This chapter provides a guide to neuroimaging, explaining what it is, what to request, and how to strategically use the results in the contexts of competency, sanity, and mitigation. Attorney Cobb discusses at length the difference between the use of the diagnostic evaluation for treatment versus forensic purposes, namely regarding the issues of motivational language and proprietary supplements. He provides suggestions for working with the doctors performing the neuroimaging, including that the attorneys themselves have their own neuroimaging experts, in order give a more detailed and authentic description of the procedure to the client.

• • •

There are three practical uses of neuroimaging when defending people with disabilities: competency, not guilty by reason of insanity, and mitigation of sentence. The laws of each jurisdiction will determine whether and how this evidence may be used to defend people with disabilities in court, but in all cases this evidence may be used in negotiations for mitigation of sentence.

What Is Neuroimaging?

There are several types of neuroimaging that may be used for diagnostic evaluations of the human brain. There is functional imaging such as SPECT, PET, and fMRI. There is structural imaging such as CT and MRI. Simply put, neuroimaging uses nuclear medicine to take a picture (such as CR or MRI) or video (such as with fMRI) of the brain. These images are then read by advanced neuroimaging physicians who analyze the operational effectiveness of the different parts of the brain. This information is used along with a detailed behavioral analysis in order to diagnose various types of disorders of the brain and to prepare a healthy brain treatment plan.

The type of neuroimaging I have used for criminal case negotiations and presentation of evidence since 2005 is single-photon emission computed tomography, or SPECT. Brain imaging can provide powerful visual evidence for receptive prosecutors, judges, and even juries.

Obtaining Patient-Defendant Neuroimages

The practical considerations regarding patient-defendant imaging and analysis revolve around two main issues: funding and whether your client is on bond or not. Funding the neuroimaging evaluation is virtually impossible if your client is not on bond unless the trial judge grants a motion for a furlough. Your client or their family will be unlikely to afford the exorbitant cost to transport someone who is incarcerated. They will have to pay for multiple law enforcement officers' salaries, lodging, and all of their other travel expenses, as well as pay for custody, often in a different state or jurisdiction.

Another funding obstacle is the insurance industry. Insurance companies will not pay for psychiatric brain imaging and claim it is "experimental." This is a difficult position to maintain in the face of increasing proof of efficacy and many in the medical community express skepticism that the "experimental" designation is sincere. Accordingly, the reality is that your client's insurance company will not pay for the diagnostic evaluation.

As of this writing, a high-quality series of SPECT scans will cost over $5,000 and travel expenses must be considered unless your client lives near a major city. Diagnostic evaluations take two to three days. CT and MRI can be obtained in one relatively short appointment on a single day.

To obtain the neuroimages for a diagnostic evaluation, a multi-day medical appointment is made with a provider. Patient-defendants go to the clinic no less than twice and sometimes more. At the clinic, doctors and their staff have a protocol to perform two sets of brain images over a two- to three-day period. One set will be produced while the brain is actively working and concentrating on a task, and the second will be taken while the brain is resting.

Although you and your client will be given the option to have only one set of scans produced for analysis rather than two, this is not advised. Over the last 17 years, I have seen several cases where a patient-defendant's brain showed far more problems with one set of images than the other. When comparing the patient-defendant's images to images of healthy brains (adjusted for age and gender), you might have one scan that looks slightly abnormal while the other looks much worse. Since you never know which set of scans will look better or worse, two sets are strongly advised.

For each set of SPECT scans, the patient-defendant will have a basic saline drip line placed into a vein at the clinic. For both resting and concentration scans, a skilled medical technician will inject the radioisotope Tc-99 into the saline drip line at the right time for the image to form. Tc-99 has about as much radiation as a third of an X-ray.

The image for the SPECT brain scan is produced shortly after the radioisotope is injected. After the rest period or concentration task has concluded, the patient-defendant is taken to a specialized medical device. Your client will lie on a surface with their head gently but securely fastened to the surface to prevent movement. Three rotating heads circle the head for approximately 19 minutes. A total of eight concentration scans and eight resting scans are produced as neuroimages for a total of 16 images. These images will be compared to images of healthy brains within the same age range and gender.

Trained psychiatric specialists use these scans for their findings and final report. Each report contains two main sections: diagnosis and treatment recommendations. Most patient-defendants receive a 20- to 25-page report with personalized treatment recommendations.

Use a Well-Established Medical Clinic

The most valid criticism against the psychiatric use of neuroimaging is that there are far too many studies with small sample sizes. You may be lucky enough to have a neuroimaging clinic right next to your office, but there is a magnitude of difference when your expert has a database of 600 images versus close to 1 million.

Most clinics do not have large psychiatric databases with hundreds of thousands of scans. This can result in multiple issues for the practitioner, but the biggest challenge is credibility of analysis. For this reason, I have used Amen Clinics since 2005. As a national provider, they have multiple clinics across the country and most importantly, a giant database approaching 1 million scanned images. They produce excellent reports and produce results when other treatment providers have failed. Their website at www.amenclinics.com can provide the full list of locations. From my practice area, all clients have to plan on travel and lodging. If your client lives near a large urban area with a clinic, this will shave hundreds if not thousands of dollars off of the cost.

Use of the Diagnostic Evaluation for Forensic Purposes versus Treatment Purposes

Diagnostic evaluations written for patient-defendants have two problems with easy remedies: motivational commentary and the use of proprietary supplements.

Motivational Commentary

While appropriate in a medical setting focused upon diagnosis and treatment, motivational language is not suitable for legal purposes, is distracting, and can be dangerous for credibility. Comb the report carefully and maintain contact with the psychiatrist to ensure the report is written correctly for criminal case purposes. Your jurisdiction and practice experience will guide you as to how the report needs to be written.

Proprietary Supplements

Proprietary supplements have a history and a reason, but you can be assured opposing counsel will attempt to make it look like the clinic financially operates on supplement sales to patient-defendants. First the reason for proprietary supplements and then how to handle them.

The reason brain clinics often prescribe essential nutrients is simple: Most people have terrible diets filled with foods and liquids that damage the human body. The damage to the brain is detectable with the images clinicians produce. Frankly, this should surprise no one. Doctors are routinely treating patients for preventable illnesses ranging from diabetes to high blood pressure only to find their patients continue to add massive quantities of sugar and salt to their diets.

Thus, it should come as no surprise that clinicians are routinely finding brain problems where essential brain nutrients are far below levels needed for healthy brain function. In some cases, the absence of essential nutrients is so severe that medication alone will have significantly reduced efficacy. This nutritional deficit creates a second problem: When prescribing nutritional supplementation, what will a majority of your clients do?

They will buy the cheapest supplements they can find without any way to know if the product purchased can even be absorbed by the body. Thus, the problem with low-cost supplements is lack of sufficient, bioavailable nutritional supplementation. For example, for years we were told by the dairy industry that "milk does a body good" only to learn the calcium in milk products is largely unavailable. The human body is simply unable to extract very much calcium from cow's milk.

Cheap, over-the-counter yet heavily marketed nutritional supplements will claim some version of "100 mg of X" on the label, yet your client has no way of knowing what percentage of that 100 milligrams can be absorbed and used by the human body. Worse, many are marketed as "100 mg of X, Y, and Z."

Fish oils are the number one nutritional recommendation I've seen over the last decade and a half, and will be used as an example. Specific types of fish oils are only one set of multiple supplements your patient-defendant will be prescribed. When attempting to purchase them, your client is confronted online and in the store with an array of products that look nothing like what the doctor prescribed. Many think they are on target with their treatment plan when in reality the discount supplements may actually provide only a fraction of the brain supplementation needed for a therapeutic result.

Bioavailable, prescription *medication* is comparatively easy to prescribe compared to a nutritional supplement prescription. Prescription medication comes with disclaimers, cautions, and warnings. Most over-the-counter nutritional supplements come with marketing hype right on the label. As a result, Amen Clinics (and many other treatment providers) created their own set of pharmaceutical-grade supplements that will be referenced in brain SPECT reports. For patient-defendants, this makes restoring brain health much easier, but also gives your courtroom opponent an attack point if your expert needs to take the stand.

The solution to the problem is fairly simple: Ask the diagnostic psychiatrist to provide a report that focuses on the *individual* supplements regardless of brand, why they are needed, and what they do. An easy-to-follow treatment plan for a client is not the same as a forensic report for legal purposes. A prescription for generic, medical-grade EPA/DHA fish oil supplements along with why the supplementation is needed is far more useful than proprietary supplements that give your opponent an opportunity to attack the diagnostic psychiatrist as having an interest in selling supplements. It's as simple as contacting the doctor prior to the evaluation to ensure the report is for legal purposes instead of patient education and motivation.

Evidentiary Issues Related to Admissibility

The first question I had in 2005 when first using neuroimaging in a criminal case was whether it was admissible for competency, insanity, or mitigation. This is also the number one question I am asked about by other lawyers. The answer is surprisingly simple: Treat it like any other type of scientific evidence. There are no major problems with getting relevant brain image and medical analysis evidence submitted.

Advanced neuroscience itself is complicated, but not any more so for practitioners skilled with other scientific evidence such as blood, breath, or urine test evidence. As you educate yourself over time, you will develop a great understanding of how to explain the evidence to prosecutors, judges, and juries. Neuroimaging analysis is easy-to-understand visual evidence. Just a glancing at a healthy set of images compared to an unhealthy set produced by your client is enough for the viewer to instantly see the two sets look different. Visual comparisons between healthy and client sets of images are often dramatic. Simply use the normal evidentiary and procedural rules in your jurisdiction for scientific evidence in the courtroom and good professional judgment when releasing brain imaging reports for settlement negotiations.

One note of caution: In addition to collecting a proper medical release and filing under seal, you may want to inoculate the evidence under your jurisdiction's civil and criminal procedure rules. Make any initial release for settlement negotiations subject to your jurisdiction's "settlement negotiation" exclusion from trial.

Determination of Competence

The most common practitioner critique of neuroimaging with regard to competency is "Why do we need it?" After all, competency and insanity are well-established legal doctrines specific to your practice jurisdiction.

Competency is normally determined by a legal finding after forensic psychologists and psychiatrists have examined the patient-defendant and rendered either reports or testimony. The normal routine is to use indirect methods to observe brain function as manifested by behavior. This is a nice way to say that opinion witnesses with doctorates are making an educated guess. The practical equivalent is an emergency room physician forgoing an X-ray for a broken bone and relying on a series of questions instead.

As a practical matter, your client with a competency issue is usually not on bond. For the small percentage where competency issues were ignored or arise later and the client is out on bond, there is value in using neuroimaging. This being said, how do you normally handle a competency issue when some of the expert witnesses disagree? Cross-examination. Your expert has visual evidence as shown in Figure 8.1.

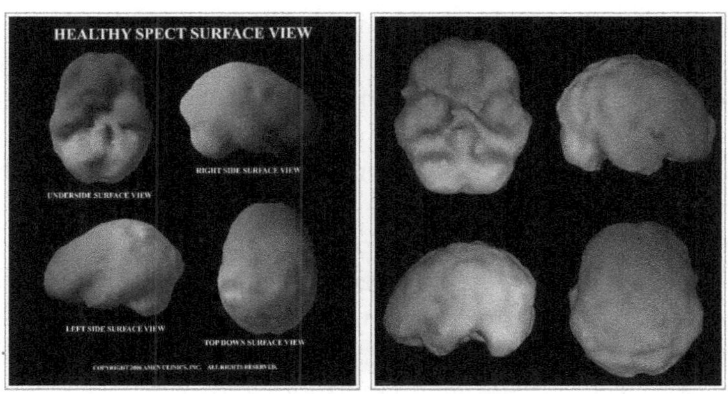

FIGURE 8.1 Healthy images on the left, unhealthy patient-defendant images on the right.

Opposing counsel's competency expert is not qualified to render an opinion about brain imaging. The witness can see the two sets of images in Figure 8.1 look different yet cannot read the scan and explain what those differences mean:

> **Q:** Can you point out for the court the left temporal lobe on each set of images and explain to the court what those differences between sets of images mean?
>
> **A:** Uh … no.

Your usual cross-examination techniques will produce one of the largest sets of "I don't know" answers and deer-in-headlights expressions you have ever seen. Opposing counsel's forensic expert can often tell you what a sub-organ of the brain does, but they are unable to explain anything about the image in front of them. This is your opportunity to demonstrate a lack of competence and credibility to the fact finder. In contrast, your expert can easily explain the function of a sub-organ as it relates to human behavior far better than traditional forensic experts who never tie specific sub-organs to behavior. In a contested competency proceeding, this may make the difference.

Not Guilty by Reason of Insanity (NGI), Guilt/Innocence Phase

Insanity as a legal doctrine is specific to your jurisdiction. Indeed, there are some with no insanity defense. (See Chapter 2, "Criminal Responsibility.") In most jurisdictions, the insanity defense is an outdated relic of law created hundreds of years ago. The reason I say "outdated" so bluntly is simply because the science underpinning the various legal doctrines about insanity are out of date by over two centuries. Nevertheless, we have to use the legal tools available to us. As earlier, a similar question: How is insanity determined?

In my practice jurisdiction, the prosecutor, the defense, and the court can each ask to have a forensic mental health expert appointed by the trial court. Privately retained experts (now called "opinion witnesses" in Florida) are also available. However, these psychologists and psychiatrists almost never get neuroimaging evaluations and, as with incompetency, neuroimaging can make the difference. Let's walk through an insanity case step by step using the traditional methods and with neuroimaging.

A person is arrested and taken to jail. At first appearance the day following the arrest (often by video), bond and bond conditions will be determined. In Florida, Pretrial Release Services wakes everyone up before the crack of dawn for a bail bond screening. They ask a series of questions and compare it to other data and produce a report with bail bond recommendations for the judge according to a point system. As I am making final edits to this chapter, a client is in a local psychiatric hospital because Pretrial Release Services noticed Jane Doe may not actually be the historical Jesus Christ as claimed. The client is clearly incompetent and a danger to self and others.

Thus, the first warning you may have that your client is in need of mental health services may be from a first appearance screening. If sanity is later presented as a legal issue to examine after the client regains competency, you are more likely to be able to establish insanity at the time of the offense if you can tie abnormal behavior to the date and time of arrest. Our default practice is to gather everything we can from first appearance proceedings during the discovery process. If your jurisdiction is a preliminary hearing jurisdiction without favorable discovery procedural rules, this task may be more difficult.

If incompetent, there can be no sanity evaluation unless and until the patient-defendant has been restored to competency. After restoration of competency, the traditional approach has been indirect examination methods by a forensic psychologist or psychiatrist. The evaluation may be done confidentially and then later released with a notice of reliance upon an insanity defense. Opposing counsel will look for the expert most likely to produce a report with a finding of sanity and, if there is a split of opinion, the court can appoint a third and final forensic expert.

This is the single most important practice tip I can give you regarding insanity trials: Waive a jury trial. Move for a bench trial instead. This is a partial transcript from a trial where the state had no chance of winning:

> **Trial judge:** State, do you object to the doctor's report finding the defendant insane at the time of the offense?
>
> **Assistant state attorney:** No, your Honor.
>
> **Trial judge:** Okay, I'm going to find the defendant not guilty by reason of insanity and schedule a commitment hearing on …

This was easily the shortest trial of my career. Most insanity trials take many months to prepare, yet under a minute to complete if you waive a jury. But what about contested cases?

You already know what will happen in a jury trial: The prosecutor will show the jury every awful photograph and other piece of evidence designed to produce an emotional conviction instead of a lawful verdict of not guilty by reason of insanity. A brain image is a powerful piece of visual and logical evidence. Assume your opponent's evidence to be admitted is not for logical reasoning purposes but so that logic of your science is overwhelmed by emotions of fear and anger.

A juror might be thinking "Oh, my God! That could be my child!" An experienced trial judge is more likely to be thinking "That's about what I expected, I've seen worse." This is likely to be each juror's only experience with mental health issues in the criminal justice system. Your trial judge has handled hundreds. Any shock value left your trial judge a long time ago and their mindset is more like "just another day at the office."

Science Skepticism in NGI Cases

In my first edition chapter for this book, the science was looked upon favorably by most judges even if they did not rule for my client. However, since then politically induced science skepticism has exploded due to the politicization of public health. Although difficult to fathom, practitioners have to factor in the reality of science politicalization on the bench and in the jury box. Many are opposed to knowledge, facts, and logical reasoning and favor "belief." This often presents as "I know, because I believe." In my view, this only reaffirms the value of a bench trial instead of a jury trial, yet we now have science skeptics on the bench like never before.

We have literally seen judges devalue brain imaging evidence simply because it conflicts with deeply held religious and political beliefs. While such denialism has always been a part of using neuroscience in the courtroom due to the novel nature of an unfamiliar technology, politically driven science skepticism is very different and impervious to reason. As an experienced practitioner, you already know that the truth does not matter in a criminal proceeding: A jury votes and a judge rules based upon what each *believes* to be true.

Accordingly, detecting science skepticism is critical. This is like the standard "know your judge" research practitioners already perform. For example, you already must know which misdemeanor criminal traffic court trial judge gives jail time for a first-offense DUI if there is a child in the car and which judge does not, but routinely gives first-offense jail time if there is an accident.

As part of the strategic calculation, we use brain images in front of some judges and definitely not in front of others. For science-hostile judges, we still have the brain imaging diagnostic evaluations performed but we give them to the trial judge's favorite mental health expert instead of the court. The trial judge's favorite expert almost never gets this type of information and none I have worked with has criticized the science behind neuroimaging. In fact, they appreciate the extra diagnostic material to render a more accurate report.

Although conspiracy theories have been around forever, social media, politicians, and media bubbles have acted as accelerants to the endorsement of nonsensical beliefs. Be aware that both judges and jurors can come across as rational, intelligent people while harboring counter-factual beliefs. At the current time, practitioners should *presume* science skepticism unless it has been proven otherwise. Most trial judges are appointed for political reasons, and fealty to counter factual belief systems is a requirement for consideration in many jurisdictions. You want judges who are focused on factual evidence and logical conclusions, not wondering if the medical equipment was "rigged by Big Tech" or asking themselves if the neuroimaging evidence is merely proof of "sin."

After a finding of verdict, there is a hearing to determine whether the patient-defendant will be (1) committed to the state forensic mental health system, (2) released into the community but required to follow a treatment plan with six-month reports given to the court, or (3) released into the community with no requirements.

NGI Commitment Hearings: Begin with the End in Mind

After a finding of NGI in misdemeanor court, there is no commitment hearing and the patient-defendant is released into the community. The trial judge has no other choice. However, in felony court the judge has three options. Although the options that follow are based on the state of Florida where I practice, the principles are applicable to other jurisdictions. Let's examine each in more detail.

Option #1: Commitment to the Forensic Mental Health System

If it is held to be the "least restrictive alternative," the patient-defendant can be committed. Every six months, a report for the court is produced, and if an outpatient treatment plan has been created and is appropriate, the patient-defendant is released by the state and required to follow a treatment plan. If the patient-defendant does not follow the plan, they can be taken into custody and returned to the forensic medical system.

NGI should result in treatment and humane release when the patient-defendant is stabilized. However, many practitioners refuse to use NGI defenses and their reasoning is sound: In some jurisdictions the forensic mental health system is both a dumping ground and a political football where patient-defendants go in but never come out. As bizarre and cruel as it sounds, a jail or prison sentence for a marginally competent client may be a better choice than a life sentence in a deliberately underfunded forensic mental health facility from which they will never return.

Option #2: Release According to an Outpatient Treatment Plan

This is the most common outcome we aim to achieve. Your experts from a quality neuroimaging clinic are far more likely to get any treatment and medication cocktails correct on the first try because they are using advanced scientific equipment for diagnosis instead of educated guesses. There will be patient-defendant-specific recommendations, which may include further medical testing, targeted nutritional supplementation, counseling, self-education, biofeedback, and numerous modern treatment modalities.

If this is potentially obtainable, the sooner the patient-defendant is evaluated and starts treatment, the better. Judges are far more impressed by a laundry list of treatment modalities that were implemented several months prior to a commitment hearing after an NGI finding. Have your client do everything recommended, and produce doctor's appointment receipts and other evidence of compliance. We have had far more success with using the diagnostic evaluation's treatment plan over time than cases where the client went to the clinic and did nothing.

Option #3: Release with No Requirement for Outpatient Treatment

This is what happens if the patient-defendant no longer needs treatment. Although Option 3 is mandatory in misdemeanor cases, it is extremely rare in felony cases. In three decades, this has only happened one time in a felony case: The pandemic lengthened the case's time cycle significantly prior to trial. During that time, a family member carefully monitored the patient-defendant, there was perfect compliance with the Amen Clinics diagnostic evaluation and treatment plan, and the patient-defendant no longer needed treatment.

If this long-shot result is sought, then compliance is even more critical. All of us have heard defendants promise the sun, moon, and stars at a sentencing hearing. All of us have also seen that such appeals routinely fail to move the needle.

Negotiations and Mitigation of Sentence

Negotiations and mitigation grounds in mental health cases are jurisdiction specific. In some cases, you will use them quickly with the prosecutor for charge bargaining. In others, you may need to present testimony to a judge for a sentencing hearing.

Florida state cases are prosecuted by assistant state attorneys who normally file "Information of Indictments" rather than present evidence to a grand jury. They have varying levels of discretion regarding everything from charge bargaining to sentencing policy. Most Florida state court judges ratify plea and sentencing agreements negotiated by the parties. However, Florida has a specific legal ground for a departure from point-based minimum sentencing, which I use frequently: "The defendant requires specialized treatment for a mental disorder that is unrelated to substance abuse or addiction, or for a physical disability, and the defendant is amenable to treatment."

When it is possible to move the needle with brain imaging settlement negotiations, a properly prepared diagnostic evaluation and treatment plan is critical. The longer the patient-defendant has been compliant with treatment, the better. When using this type of evidence during negotiations or a sentencing hearing, these basic elements from the sentencing statute and corresponding procedural rule will be in the prosecutor's mind:

- Does the defendant really have a mental disorder or physical disability, or are they faking it?

- Does the defendant really need specialized treatment or can they get treatment in prison?
- Is this really behavior from drugs and alcohol, which disqualifies this departure ground?

When your courtroom adversary is looking at brain images instead of an evaluation from the forensic experts they normally use, at a minimum they can literally see the state has a problem with denying a physical disability of the brain. With a traditional, non-imaging mental health case they never see these things and rely on the prosecution's favorite forensic expert.

Your jurisdiction may have similar procedures or vastly different. The key is to be flexible. If you choose to negotiate, give the prosecutor time to process the information when they look at the images for the first time. They have doubt and they have curiosity. Ask: "Is there a part of you that is wondering if this explains why people keep breaking the law?" They do not have to answer. A part of them will be wondering.

Remember also that science skepticism may be a problem with your prosecutor: Despite the evidence, they may find it conflicts with deeply held beliefs. I cannot overemphasize the impact of pandemic politics and the explosion of science skepticism within the criminal justice system.

Government-Sponsored Mental Health and Drug Treatment Programs

Although this is beyond the scope of the chapter to some degree, negotiations often involve faith-based treatments. Scholarly articles, research papers, and numerous books give a clear picture of the dangers posed by faith-based treatments. They will help fewer than one in ten of your clients while harming many. The only redeeming quality of faith-based mental health treatment is the socialization factor with others dealing with substance abuse issues.

Resist all attempts to impose faith-based treatments and programs during negotiations and during sentencing hearings. If you want your client to violate probation, commit new law violations, return to illegal drug use, and a whole host of other negative outcomes, send them to a faith-based treatment program instead and avoid neuroscience entirely.

Government treatment programs based on Alcoholics Anonymous (AA) have startlingly high failure rates, like AA itself. Yet science-hostile politicians brag about the Florida drug court program and tout the high completion rates as a success. Completion of the program is rarely effective, yet this is hidden by a convenient failure to fund post-completion effectiveness studies.

In reality, politicians already know drug court is a massive failure, but that conflicts with their beliefs. They were often elected by a political constituency that wants to hear that faith-based treatment is effective. When the treatment fails after drug court has concluded, relapse is the fault of your client. Think about this carefully: You break a bone, the doctor prescribes whatever your broken bone needs, the treatment fails, and the doctor blames you for the bone not healing. You have followed the ineffective treatment plan perfectly, yet somehow the failed treatment is your fault. This "blame the patient" game makes no logical sense. This is happening in Florida's drug court program every day. Most drug court graduates do not remain abstinent.

Without an accurate diagnostic evaluation including neuroimaging, faith-based treatment programs both public and private harm more people than they help. This has to be handled delicately with your client and their family when deep religiosity is a long-term fundamental value. Amen Clinics has handled this extremely well. For example, your client's diagnostic evaluation *will* take your client's faith into consideration. There are some cases where faith-based treatment is even specifically recommended as part of a multi-modal treatment plan. In these cases, faith-based treatment should be followed along with all other recommendations. If the people who know what they are talking about are recommending faith-based treatment as part of a comprehensive treatment plan, listen to them and encourage you client to implement all treatment modalities the clinic recommends. If you are not vigilant, many will implement only part of the recommendations and potentially damage their legal position.

One of my clients was treated for alcohol abuse disorder with high doses of the anti-psychotic medication Seroquel. He lost all desire to drink and has not reoffended for over a decade. Others have been specifically recommended for 12-step programs in addition to other healthy brain treatment modalities.

Generally, resist the "rush to treatment" from frustrated family members who want relief from dysfunctional behavior yesterday. They often clamor for your client to do an expensive stint in faith-based rehab at the start of the case. This is a bomb in the case that may go off any moment.

Instead, your default with dysfunctional but competent clients who are not a danger to themselves or others should be the same as when you handle a legal case: Diagnose first, prescribe a course of treatment second. You wouldn't file a motion to dismiss without gathering evidence first. Our doctorates are in law, rarely in psychology or psychiatry. Accordingly, send your client to a brain clinic first.

Difficult Clients Resistant to Evaluation and Treatment

Many years ago, a couple of parents wanted me to see their son in the jail for a felony charge. They knew something was wrong with him mentally but their son for whatever reason was in denial. He refused to seek any help. He knew what he needed. The parents had clued me into his denial mechanisms during the initial consultation, so I deliberately did not have a legal services contract prepared for the jail visit. Instead, I spoke with the parents afterward:

> **Attorney:** He doesn't want to get an evaluation and does not think he needs treatment. Therefore …
>
> **Mom:** Oh my God, (Sigh) we'll go ahead and bond him out and retain you.
>
> **Attorney:** No. Let him sit in jail. If he wants my help, he will agree to get the diagnostic evaluation and follow the treatment plan. If you want my help, you will agree to go off of his bond if he fails to follow through with treatment.

There is no guarantee it will work every time, but this has proven to be a very effective method.

The key with dealing with difficult clients is to recognize their brain literally is not functioning correctly and that the abuse they sometimes babble is a symptom of mental illness. This key does unlock every mind. You still have to occasionally fire a client or cut off their family member due to bad behavior. Personally, I draw the line with death threats.

Both the client and the patient-defendant's family must have a clear understanding that the goal is to solve the legal problem and any brain problem at the same time. Experience has taught me that clients and their family members present separate problems and can be difficult to deal with in any case.

If the client does not appear to be competent, you have already learned that it is a waste of time to listen to babble. Document your file and perform the next task. If you don't want the patient-defendant or the family calling you constantly to ask countless irrelevant questions outside of your influence or control, take the time to educate them about the legal process, what you can do and what you cannot. Let them know there will be long periods of silence where the answer to "What's going on in the case?" is "Nothing, we are waiting due to time limits and scheduling." Many parents and other relatives with an interest in how their family member's case will turn out also have mental health issues yet can function on a day-to-day basis.

Additionally, you probably know about client stress in legal cases due to years of experience. Criminal cases are a top ten life stressor for clients. The more serious the case, the more serious the stress. We send every client and their involved family members specific instructions to follow in order to manage stress including books, audios, videos, therapy, and even neuroimaging diagnostic evaluations and treatment plans.

Many patient-defendants have been given multiple medications that did not work and have often already been to court-ordered treatment programs and classes that were not effective. When your patient-defendant has experienced multiple treatment failures, they and their loved ones are often skeptical. Ten minutes in court for violation of probation proceedings is enough time to see why: Not only is the victim of an ineffective treatment plan told they are a failure, they are punished for it.

Educate Yourself, Your Patient-Defendant and Family

Change Your Brain, Change Your Life by Dr. Daniel Amen is a great starting point for self-education on this subject. Unlike this chapter, the book is filled with multiple sets of brain images along with an explanation regarding what the scientists see in the images.

Consider spending time with the imaging clinic you choose and consider having your own brain imaged. Is dementia in your future? SPECT brain imaging can give someone up to a decade and a half of advance warning before any symptoms are present. Medical benefits aside, you will be able to describe the procedure in vivid detail to your client and their family. As you put the necessary time in to learn about neuroimaging and what the images mean for doctors, you will understand the science better. You will be able to use a library of brain images when discussing the case with your client, the prosecutor, or the court.

Personally, I didn't think I needed one in 2006 but got one anyway. As a result of that experience, I can explain the medical procedure to clients and their family in great detail. I even altered my daily nutritional load from a "sports" focused supplement protocol to a "healthy brain" combination. The difference in sports performance was unexpected, and the results were a dramatic improvement.

For your client, one of the most important things they will learn is that they are neither broken nor evil. They have a brain problem like someone might have a cold, color blindness, or some other medical condition. Begin with the end of the legal case in mind and demonstrate with brain images how this approach is different. Explain the process at the clinic. This is unlike any previous attempt at diagnosis and treatment. In almost every case you will encounter, this is the first time treatment has not meant blame.

The time I have spent with Drs. Daniel Amen, Jay Faber, Nelson Bennett, and many others has proven to be incredibly valuable. During a casual conversation I learned they use imaging to determine which medication among several should be used for a specific brain pattern. Psychiatrists who have been denied the wealth of information brain imaging provides are forced to use their best professional judgment, much like healers used for thousands of years before the invention of the X-ray machine.

Your patient-defendant's traditionally trained psychiatrist almost never has neuroimaging to help determine medication type or dosage due to the insurance industry's refusal to recognize that brain imaging has gone mainstream for diagnosing various disabilities of the brain. This results in a much higher risk of prescribing a medication that is more likely to cause a negative outcome.

With imaging, determining the correct medication is a major step forward when dealing with treatment-resistant clients, giving them hope that this time they are likely to be successful. Most of the time, their treatment failures have been attributed and internalized as moral failures. This is not only ineffective, but in many cases it is harmful. I have many stories of someone on a powerful brain medication who had a dangerous adverse reaction resulting in violent behavior, arrest, and prosecution. If you have practiced exclusively in criminal law for more than five years, you do as well.

Someone is literally taking the wrong prescription medication as you are reading this sentence right now. The doctor had the greatest of intentions yet the absence of needed technology. In many cases, your newfound knowledge in this area can change the lives of your clients for the better. How you apply this knowledge will determine whether you do.

• • •

Stephen G. Cobb has practiced criminal law exclusively since 1990. He founded the Cobb Law Firm in 1997 and the Florida Bar first certified him as a criminal law trial specialist in 2002. He began using SPECT brain imaging for negotiation and mitigation of sentence in 2005. His work was discussed in Kevin Davis's groundbreaking book *The Brain Defense: Murder in Manhattan and the Dawn of Neuroscience in America's Courtrooms*. In 2017, Mr. Cobb published the first of a series for the general public titled *Florida Criminal Law*. A life member of the Florida Association of Criminal Defense Lawyers and the National Association of Criminal Defense Lawyers, Mr. Cobb handles criminal cases ranging from driving under the influence to capital murder. He has handled more SPECT brain imaging cases involving criminal law than any attorney in the world. He can be reached at Stephen@cobblawfirm.com and his website is http://www.cobblawfirm.com.

Chapter

9

Structured Violence and Sexual Risk Assessment

Ryan C. W. Hall

A risk assessment is a vital component of any forensic evaluation. Even if a diagnostic report does a comprehensive job of describing the accused's mental disabilities, and even if that report explains the nexus between the disability and the alleged conduct, most prosecutors after reading such a report will legitimately ask, "But will they do this again?" Although no instrument can predict with 100 percent accuracy, a risk assessment may describe why, with the appropriate management and accommodations, the accused's risk of reoffending is minimal.

This chapter by Dr. Ryan C. W. Hall is a guide to the responsible use of risk assessments by lawyers, prosecutors, and criminal defense lawyers. As he cautions, risk assessments are only one factor in trying to gain insight into possible future conduct. Beyond that, risk assessment instruments themselves have some limitations. Some may be normed on a population far different than your client. Some are only as credible as the information gathered. For example, if an instrument is based largely on self-disclosure by the client or omits vital facts, the results will be inherently skewed. (Or, as Dr. Hall notes, "garbage in, garbage out.") Finally, the balancing of static versus dynamic factors is largely subjective. Nonetheless, risk assessments are intended to be structured and to the extent possible, objective and standardized. They should be neither accepted as foolproof nor rejected as without merit.

• • •

Behavioral risk assessments, of which violence and sexual recidivism assessments are specific subsets, are an important, but at times controversial, topic in legal and mental health fields. Often, one's personal views on an individual's responsibility, free will, and capacity for change may influence whether one believes that a risk assessment has utility or how much weight these assessments should have in influencing legal decisions (e.g., bond amount, conditional release status, civil placement for sexual offenders) (Monahan et al. 2020). In general, violence is a complex issue that is often influenced by multiple factors (see Table 9.1), some of which can change (i.e., dynamic factors) and others that are historical or unchanging (i.e., static factors) (Buchanan et al. 2012; Hall & Iannuzzi 2023).

Which factors should be looked at? Do certain factors "cancel each other out" (e.g., early age of first arrest is generally a negative factor, but living ten years since then with no incidents can be positive)? Can all factors even be quantitated or accounted for? Is a factor applicable to a real-world population or just the normative sample? These are often questions that come up and are debated when looking at risk assessment (Buchanan et al. 2012).

This chapter will try to familiarize the reader with aspects of the risk violence assessment process and discuss the pros and cons of the process. Given that new instruments and studies come out frequently, that there can be substantial variations in training between evaluators, and certain jurisdictions may favor one style of assessment or instrument over another. Thus, it is not possible to cover all instruments (see Table 9.2) and aspects of this process (Buchanan et al. 2012). This chapter will discuss broad principles, with some specific examples, such as the Historical Clinical Risk Management-20 (HCR-20) and the Static-99, discussed in more depth.

Table 9.1 Factors Involved with Violence

Biology
Social
Economic
Political
Health (e.g. traumatic brain injury, delirium, medications)
Developmental life experience
Substance use
Environmental factors and exposures

Sources: Volavka 1999, Siever 2008

Table 9.2 General Examples of Instruments

The Classification of Violence Risk (COVR): Guided structured interview that estimates the risk that a person hospitalized for mental disorder will be violent to others.
Psychopathy Checklist (PCL, or the Hare Psychopathy Checklist): Assessment checklist to be completed based on a semi-structured interview along with a review of ancillary information to determine personality traits that have some cross validity for violence.
Historical Clinical Risk Management-20 (HCR-20, the most recent version is 3): One of the most commonly used assessments that is based on the Structured Professional Judgement model that uses 20 question areas related to past and current behaviors to assess future risk.
Static-99 (current version is Static-99R): One of the most commonly used instruments for assessment of sexual offending based on ten questions. Information can be obtained from historical documents or in-person interview. Developed from the separate instruments of the Rapid Risk Assessment for Sexual Recidivism (RRASOR) and Structured Anchored Clinical Judgement (SAC-J-MIN).
Violence Risk Appraisal Guide (VRAG): 12-item actuarial risk assessment instrument for the prediction of violent recidivism.
Sexual Offender Violence Risk Appraisal Guide (SORAG): 14-item actuarial scale designed to predict violent hands-on sexual recidivism among individuals who have already committed a hands-on offense.
Statistical Information about Recidivism Scale (SIR): Developed as part of the Parole Decision-Making Project, the SIR scale is a statistical model of significant factors that contribute to recidivism patterns in large groups of offenders.
This is not an all-inclusive list and many of these may have revisions or variations in versions.

Sources: Nuffield 1989; Monahan et al. 2006; Buchanan et al. 2012; Douglas et al. 2013; no author 2022d; no author 2022e

Why Have a Structured Approach to Risk Violence Assessments?

Clinicians have been trying to develop a structured way to evaluate violence for at least the last 50 years (Monahan et al. 2020) (see Table 9.3). Although there may be limitations in structured assessments, the general thought process is that having a uniform approach will result in less subjective and unfounded opinions overall (Buchanan et al. 2012).

For an abstract example, consider a scene from the 2011 movie *Moneyball*, which depicted baseball scouts determining if a player was going to be good or not based on factors that had nothing to do with

Table 9.3 General Elements of a Clinical or Forensic Risk Assessment

- Identify risk factors
- Identify protective factors
- Assess overall risk of violence based on risk factors and protective factors
- Document the assessment
- Use the information gathered to determine the risk level, treatment plan, and preventative interventions

Source: Adapted from Vanderpool 2016

baseball, such as the car the player drove or the physical qualities of the partner they were dating (e.g., dating a physically attractive partner meant the player had self-confidence and would likely perform well under the pressure of Major League Baseball). The "professional opinion" of these grizzled scouts came across as very subjective, lacking in foundation, and subject to random change (e.g., if a person had a new, more attractive partner, would they suddenly be a better player?). Although there may be something to be said for having "gut instincts" or subjective opinions based on experience, it is generally seen as preferable to have a more structured approach when predicting future behavior (Buchanan et al. 2012). This is even more so when legal concerns are being addressed since the opinions need to withstand the adversarial system of court (e.g., Daubert challenge or whichever standard is applicable in a jurisdiction) (Hall et al. 2011). Ideally, risk violence opinions need to be consistent across a multitude of cases and have reproducibility and objectivity while still allowing for consideration of unique factors or circumstances.

With that stated, there may be somewhat of a sliding scale on how structured an approach is used based on the training of the evaluator, resources available at time of the assessment, and time allocated for the evaluation process (Buchanan et al. 2012, Scott & Resnick 2017). For some evaluators, a structured assessment will be a detailed history-taking approach and review of available records, with certain factors always being assessed based on their training; for some, it may be more of a focus on actuarial instruments; and for others, it will be a combination of both approaches.

Many structured interviews and actuarial assessments will look at past behaviors, such as prior violence, prior arrests, and age when these incidents occurred. They will also take into account past and current behaviors, such as drug or alcohol use and abuse, ability to maintain long-term stable relationships (work and personal), or the likelihood of engaging in risk-taking behavior that may be a marker for impulsivity. Present circumstances, such as current age and degree of engagement in treatment, speak to current maturity, insight, and personal growth and stability. A significant factor that has been identified in multiple studies is compliance with treatment. One of the most famous studies to address this is the MacArthur study, which found that individuals with mental illness who were compliant with mental health treatment (psychotherapy and/or medications) were at the same risk of engaging in violent behavior as the baseline population where they were living (Hall & Friedman 2013). Additional environmental factors may be looked at, such as access to weapons, stability of housing, and influence of friends or significant others. Some assessments will also look at personality factors, such as narcissistic and antisocial traits.

Benefits of Structured Instruments

The benefit of a structured approach is that it is consistent and theoretically reproducible. The evaluator should be able to identify the specific factors they are weighing and be able to justify why they were assessed as such. Many of the structured instruments are subjected to ongoing research and validity updating. In addition, many instruments recommend training before performing, which should help improve interrater reliability. Statistical information, such as degree of correlation, standard deviation, risk of error, and interrater reliability, can be determined and are often maintained by the instrument's publisher. Many of these instruments have also been translated and validated for different languages, although it does need to be noted that language and culture do not necessarily correlate 100 percent. For example, a French language version of an instrument may be used, but there could be significant cultural differences that affect interpretation or applicability between French Canadians, Parisians, and Haitians. For this reason, many of these instruments have been studied based on language, as well as the cultural aspects of different geographic regions (Fujii et al. 2005).

In addition to consistency, the structured approach also allows for stratification of risk, with many actuarial instruments concluding with a statement of percentage of risk or categorization level of risk, such as very low, low, moderate, or high risk. No structured risk violence assessment, just like no evaluator, can predict the future or claim that an individual will 100 percent offend or not offend again in the future (Buchanan 2012). If an evaluator states either extreme position, this should raise flags in the legal system. Many of these instruments have been studied for a period of years, if not decades, and some can even define for how long an assessment of future risk is good (five years, ten years, etc.; Doren 2004, Baudin 2021).

Structured assessments are often developed based on a specific population, which can be seen as a positive or a negative. It is not the instrument's fault if an evaluator uses it in the wrong context or misrepresents the results. As somewhat of a humorous example, the author of this chapter once overheard a colleague joke that their risk of becoming a sexual offender had decreased since they had been in a stable relationship for three years (a question assessed on some sexual offender instruments). Another colleague with a dry sense of humor suggested the individual should not boast about such an accomplishment unless they mean to reveal more about their past than they meant to. It was pointed out that that factor had been shown to be statistically valid for individuals who had already committed a hands-on sexual crime and should not necessarily be generalized to a population that had not offended previously. This is why many of the instruments have manuals that clearly denote which populations or situations the instrument is appropriate for.

In general, mental health professionals' abilities to assess violence risk have been improving over the last 50 years, in large part attributable to these more structured assessment approaches (Buchanan et al 2012).

Potential Problems or Limitations with Structured Risk Violence Assessments

It needs to be remembered that a lot of risk assessments are based on actuarial statistical data and conclusions. This means they will be more accurate when applied to a large population that is similar to the normed population of the instrument, but may not accurately reflect the individual involved in every legal case, situation, or issue (Hall & Iannuzzi 2023).

A key question to ask (if the information is known) is what is the correlation value for the instruments? This is often statistically represented by the Pearson correlation coefficient "r" value. Although there are many factors that go into determining correlations and definitions of strength, such as when a correlation is a weak correlation versus a strong correlation (e.g., differences between scientific fields, nature of the question being studied), an approximate guide for interpretation is little to no correlation ($r < 0.25$), weak correlation ($0.25 < r < 0.5$), moderate correlation ($0.5 < r < 0.75$), and strong correlation ($r > 0.75$) (Zach 2021). In general, many of these instruments have r values below or around 0.75, which may need to be acknowledged and its significance described to the triers of fact.

Many of these instruments look at large monolithic blocks or groups, such as "sexual offenders," even though the individual before the court may fall into a subset of offenders. For example, although it is generally agreed that the risk of sexual reoffending decreases with time, the subgroup for which it decreases the most is nonconsensual rape offenders (Hall & Hall 2007). This is thought, in part, to be due to loss of physical strength with age, which is often required for a nonconsensual rape. Offenses against children, which often rely more on "tend and befriend" techniques and not physical strength, also decline with age, but not as much when compared to a rapist. This may lead to an occurrence where the structured instruments, although applied appropriately to a "sexual offender," may not take into account some of the specific factors for the case in front of the court. It also needs to be noted (CITI.org):

> [h]ow both researchers and the public perceive risk is a matter for consideration. There seems to be a general tendency for people to over-estimate the probability of something happening if the outcomes are severe. Conversely, we tend to underestimate the likelihood of events with less severe outcomes.

Therefore, when looking at instruments that examine criminal recidivism, there is often a propensity for people to assume that extreme felonies will be the reason for the recidivism, when in actuality many of these instruments were normed on all types of behavior, including re-arrest for misdemeanors. So, sometimes it is important to clarify exactly what level of event (minor, severe, or both) the instrument norming was based on. For example, when looking at sexual offending, was the instrument normed or validated off research based on self-report, re-arrest but no conviction, probation violation, conviction for new sexual crime, or new conviction for generic criminal act (Hall & Hall 2007)?

Many of these instruments have been normed or standardized on criminal populations or inpatient psychiatric patients (Buchanan et al.

2012; Hogan 2016). This may make them more relevant for making decisions related to criminal release decisions (e.g., parole, probation, sentencing) or hospital release, but they may not apply as well to civil cases (e.g., custody evaluation, security clearances, fitness for duty) where there is not necessarily a preexisting criminal record or past psychiatric hospitalization. The population that many of these instruments have been normed on are also usually more severely ill individuals or the most recalcitrant antisocial examples since they have already ended up in a locked-door location for their own safety or the safety of others (Buchanan et al. 2012).

In addition, many of these samples have been comprised mostly of 18- to 45-year-old males, which raises questions about the applicability to females and the extremely young and old (Friedman et al. 2013; Sorrentino et al. 2016). Some of the original populations studied may not have included a diverse or representative racial, ethic, or cultural sampling (e.g., they may have overrepresented populations from lower socioeconomic groups or countries with traditionally more homogeneous populations, such as Canada). As mentioned earlier, some of these limitations have been addressed with additional validity studies, but these usually occur with smaller populations, have potential variations in study design from the original work for the instruments, and have not necessarily been independently replicated themselves.

As stated before, these instruments cannot predict the future and at times may be prone to overprediction due to concerns related to base rates (i.e., not adequately knowing the frequency at which an event occurs for the population at large) (Buchanan et al. 2012). As noted in the American Psychiatric Association's psychiatric risk violence assessment resource document (Buchanan et al. 2012):

> While research will continue to advance, the pervasive influence of base rates means that, at the base rates of violence seen in most clinical settings and for the foreseeable future, technique will be available to identify those who will act violently that will not simultaneously identify a large number of people who would not.

For more of a real-world example, many governmental organizations have tried to put together screening profiles for a school shooter. Multiple risk factors have been suggested, such as poor grades, change in behavior, and the presence of disciplinary problems. As noted by Regehr et al. (2017):

> Per both the National Research Council study and the U.S. Federal Bureau of Investigation's (FBI) National Center for the Analysis of Violent Crime:

> there is no accurate way to develop a profile of a school shooter and no checklist of danger signs pointing to the next perpetrator of lethal violence in an educational environment. Further, the potential predictive factors are so common that it would be impossible to avoid over-prediction by simply considering warning signs.

Part of the problem in predicting who will become a school shooter is that it is a relatively rare event, which makes it difficult to study (Hall & Friedman 2013). Even events that occur more frequently, such as suicides or homicides, are still considered rare events due to the large percentage of the population who do not engage in these actions. For this reason, risk violence assessments need to be done in a judicious manner on a limited population base to try to ensure that the instruments are being used in a manner similar to which they were normed.

Even when an individual has undergone significant psychological testing or actuarial assessments, the degree of future predictiveness may be limited due to new or changing factors in the person's life. A classic example is the case of Lisa Nowak. (*This case should be seen primarily as a teaching point and not a direct comment on any individuals involved.*) Miss Nowak was an individual who had attended the U.S. Naval Academy and later became a NASA astronaut. Based on her pedigree and record, this would be an individual who would be expected to do well with stress, perform well in hostile environments, have little to no static risk factors (e.g., no arrests, no psychiatric hospitalizations), and be in control of her emotions in general. She likely went through multiple challenges while attending the Naval Academy and underwent psychological screening to be accepted into the astronaut corps. (*The exact instruments used are not known since selection process is somewhat proprietary in terms of specific instruments NASA uses.*) Therefore, when she was arrested for allegedly attempting to abduct a romantic rival, it was a shocking occurrence (Moore 2009; Couwels 2009). No one predicted that the suspected dynamic factor of a romantic rivalry would have led to her arrest. It also should be noted that she was not part of the population that most of these instruments were normed on or validated for if a risk violence assessment instrument was used by NASA prior to her arrest.

At times, a problem with risk violence assessments is whether or not the instruments have enough accurate information to make a conclusion. In short, it is the classic dilemma of "garbage information in, garbage assessment out." For example, the author of this chapter experienced a specific case where there was a concern that a patient brought into the hospital for a psychosis (which resolved quickly with treatment) was a risk in general, and specifically to a particular family member based on their situation and statements made around the time of admission. Given the treatment team's concerns, the individual was kept longer than usual for observation; records were requested, but not received at the time of discharge; supervised discharge plans were made; and Tarasoff warnings (to the police and potential victims) were issued.

Given behavior on the unit (the person was overheard making veiled threats on phone calls, stealing food, and bullying other patients), there was concern about antisocial behavior unrelated to the individual's mental illness (e.g., behavior not caused by or driven by the psychosis). An official independent risk violence assessment was ordered prior to the individual being discharged, which utilized structured assessment instruments. The ultimate conclusion was that the individual was low risk for future violence since psychotic symptoms resolved, no clearly documented history of substance use disorder existed (even though it was suspected), and the individual had minimal historical information, such as past violent actions and legal trouble. After discharge, the individual, unfortunately, did go and harm the family member. During the follow-up investigation, it was learned that information that was available and provided was not factually accurate. So, although many risk assessment instruments provide structure for an evaluation, there may be limitations on the accuracy of their predictions if they are based on faulty or limited data.

Stories like this are also why risk violence assessments should be seen as one of many factors or tools used by a mental health professional to reach a final conclusion (Buchanan et al. 2012). In the particular case discussed, the treatment team acknowledged the standardized instruments conclusions, but put more weight into their clinical judgment when delaying the discharge and trying to take additional steps to reduce risk since other factors seemed to be more relevant (e.g., the veiled threats and bullying, which they directly witnessed). For these reasons, many of the possible problems or limitations of risk violence assessment are highlighted by this anecdotal case example.

An additional problem with risk violence assessments is the risk of the outlying individual or, put another way, how to balance static risk factors (unchangeable events like age of first arrest) with dynamic factors (changeable factors like current age and compliance with treatment). Although some instruments do take into account both static and dynamic factors, it can still be a challenge. For example, this could be a person who has legitimately changed due to therapy, gained maturity with age, or just learned from negative past experiences even though they have strong static risk factors. On the reverse, an individual may have few, if any, static factors, but has recently received a head injury, which greatly impacts their current functioning, impulsivity, and behavior, which puts them at future risk. Another concern is the individual who may currently have very good dynamic factors (e.g., no recent violent acting out or substance use), but is in a controlled or monitored environment (e.g., probation, parole, hospital, or prison) and could potentially revert back to their old ways once they are in a less-supervised environment or an environment with triggers that led to problems in the past (e.g., drugs). In this scenario, the static factors are actually still a significant issue. These examples are often where reasonable experts may weigh factors differently and arrive at different opinions even if a structured approach or instrument is used. These are also the types of situations where the old adage "the best predictor of future behavior is past behavior" may be applied differently.

It needs to be remembered, and potentially pointed out to the trier of fact, that most of these instruments will give a prediction level. So, just because someone is "low risk," it has to be remembered that is not the same as "no risk." It is also true that somebody who is at high risk is not necessarily guaranteed to commit a crime in the future. At this time, there is no definitive structured risk assessment instrument (Large & Ryan 2015, Fazel et al. 2012, Buchanan et al. 2012).

The HCR-20

The Historical Clinical Risk Management-20 (HCR-20) was first published in 1995 and is currently on its third version, which was published in 2013 (Douglas et al. 2013). The HCR-20 has been translated into 20 languages, has been studied or used in 35 countries, and is generally seen as one of the most commonly used risk violence assessment tools (HCR-20.com 2022). It is considered a structured professional judgment (SPJ) approach, which, to oversimplify, is a mixture of the actuarial method with clinical judgment and guidelines affecting the weight applied to the factors (Hart et al. 2017). The evaluator obtains information from the person and reviews records and other collateral sources when available.

In addition, the Hare Psychopathy Checklist (PCL) is part of the HCR-20. The PCL was originally developed as a clinical tool and has been incorporated more into the legal realm. It will be noted that the Hare's usage in the legal realm is controversial at times, with many supporters and detractors frequently publishing and testifying on its strengths and weaknesses in court.

The HCR-20 assessment is frequently used in forensic and treatment settings involving individuals 18 years old and older. The HCR-20 was designed to help mental health professionals meaningfully develop formulations of violence risk, build appropriate risk management plans, and communicate perceived risk more clearly. It is not meant to be a standalone instrument and does not cover all risk factors. It is part of a whole evaluation (HCR-20.com 2022). This instrument can be used longitudinally and can be readministered multiple times due to assessing dynamic factors, as well as static factors.

The questions in the HCR-20 focus on three domains: historical, clinical, and risk management (Encyclopedia.com 2022) (Table 9.4). Each question is scored on a 0 to 3 scale: 0 (not present), 1 (possible/less serious), or 3 (definite/serious). Based on these factors, the HCR-20 will stratify risk of violence as a low, moderate, or high probability.

Table 9.4 General Factors Assessed in HCR-20

Historical	Clinical	Risk management
• Past violent events • Age at first violent incident • Relationship instability • Employment problems • Substance use problems • Major mental illness diagnosis • Psychopathy • Early maladjustment • Personality disorder • Failure to respond to clinical supervision or treatment (noncompliance)	• Lack of insight • Negative attitudes • Active symptoms of mental illness • Impulsivity • Treatment responsiveness	• Plans lack feasibility • Exposure to destabilizers • Lack of personal support • Refusal or resistance to attend counseling sessions or take medications • Stress

This instrument is copyrighted so the table does not list exact wording or provide score criteria.

Static-99

The Static-99, as the name implies, is based on 10 "static" factors that actuarially assess the risk of an individual sexually offending again (California Megan's Law 2022, SAARNA.org 2022) (Table 9.5). The "99" in the name refers to the year 1999, when the instrument was first developed and released. Most of the questions are scored as either 0 or 1 point, although some questions can have higher point values (e.g., multiple prior sexual offenses may earn a score as high as 3). The instrument was originally developed in Canada and the office of Public Safety Canada holds the copyright to the instrument and the manuals. The original instrument was normed on three sexual offender populations in Canada, with an additional validity study group out of Great Britain being used. Like many instruments, the Static-99 has been updated, with the most recent version being the Static-99R released in 2012 by Karl Hanson, PhD, and David Thornton, PhD (SAARNA.org 2022). The Static-99R coding manual was further redefined in 2016. The Static-99R is the most widely used sexual risk recidivism instrument in the world. Just like the HCR-20, the instrument has been translated and validated in many different languages and cultures.

The population upon which the instrument was originally developed was hands-on convicted male offenders, those found not guilty by reason of insanity, or those who were convicted on a nonsexual act who had engaged in hands-on crimes against children and nonconsenting adults. The Static-99R is not appropriated for individuals who have just committed a

Table 9.5 Static-99R General Factors Assessed

- Age
- Time lived with partner
- Index nonsexual violence conviction
- Prior nonsexual violence conviction
- Prior sexual offenses (greater the number, greater the score)
- Prior sentencing dates
- Conviction for non-contact sexual offense
- Unrelated victims
- Stranger victims
- Gender of victims

This instrument is copyrighted so the table does not list exact wording or provide specific scoring criteria.

sex crime with a consenting partner (e.g., prostitution, sex in public location with consenting partner, "consensual" statutory rape where both individuals are close to the same age) or non-hands-on offenses, such as possession of pornography. The instrument also cannot be used to determine guilt or innocence, just the likelihood of reoffense. The instrument is best used for individuals who are in custody or within a close period of custody. If an individual has been at liberty for ten years, the Static-99R may not be as beneficial. If not all information is available, the Static-99R should be marked as incomplete because the missing information could result in a higher score if it was available. The Static-99R is not valid for females and individuals under the age of 18 at this time (California Megan's Law 2022).

The following statement should be interpreted with caution since new studies or special subpopulation analyses may come out after this chapter is published, but generally speaking, many of the validating studies and meta-analysis studies on the Static-99 have found it to have a "moderate" to "large" correlation for prediction of sexual, violent, or general recidivism (Stephens 2018).

Conclusion

Risk assessment is a field of study that is continuously growing and changing. Structured interviews and instruments are tools for providing a more reproducible and objective approach to answering questions frequently found in the legal and clinical realms. With that said, it needs to be noted that these tools and approaches are not foolproof and cannot give definitive answers. They need to be used by people who have been trained on the instruments and know when to use them, when not to use them, and their limitations. When and how to use these tools needs to be examined on a case-by-case basis to ensure they are not misused and that findings are not applied in an inappropriate manner.

Although there may be controversy at times in the use of these instruments and in the general ability of mental health professionals to predict future behavior and actions, it does not change the fact that mental health practitioners are frequently called upon in many court jurisdictions to do so. As noted in the Supreme Court case *Barefoot v. Estelle*, the courts will likely continue to look at mental health professionals to provide some degree of knowledge on the topic of risk assessment. As written by Justice Byron White:

> The suggestion that no [mental health professional's] testimony may be presented with respect to a defendant's future dangerousness is somewhat

> like asking us to disinvent the wheel . . . and if it is not impossible for even a lay person sensibly to arrive at that conclusion (committing further crimes), it makes little sense, if any, to submit that [mental health professional], out of the entire universe of persons who might have an opinion on the issue, would know so little about the subject that they should not be permitted to testify. . . . at least as of now, that the adversary process [can] be trusted to sort out the reliable from the unreliable evidence and opinion about future dangerousness, particularly when the convicted felon has the opportunity to present his own side of the case.

• • •

Dr. Ryan C. W. Hall graduated Phi Beta Kappa with honors with a double major in biology and psychology from Johns Hopkins University. He completed his medical training at Georgetown University School of Medicine and did an internal medicine internship at Johns Hopkins University. He completed his psychiatric residency in the Department of Psychiatry and Behavioral Sciences at Johns Hopkins and a forensic psychiatry fellowship at the Case Western Reserve School of Medicine. Dr. Hall has been practicing psychiatry in central Florida since 2008.

Dr. Hall has served as president for the Florida Psychiatric Society, Southern Psychiatric Association, and the Physicians Society of Central Florida. In 2019, he was selected to be part of the Florida Medical Association Delegation at the American Medical Association's House of Delegates, which is responsible for determining national policies for the organization. Dr. Hall has written numerous peer-reviewed journal publications and multiple textbook chapters on topics varying from psychopharmacology, psychotherapy, forensic issues, and societal concerns. He also serves on the American Academy of Psychiatry and the Law's Newsletter and Journal Editorial Board.

Dr. Hall serves as an affiliate associate professor for the University of South Florida's Department of Psychiatry in Tampa, Florida, as well as an associate professor of psychiatry for the Department of Medical Education at the University of Central Florida College of Medicine in Orlando, Florida. Dr. Hall is also an adjunct faculty member at the Barry University Dwayne O. Andreas School of Law in Orlando, Florida. Dr. Hall's email is dr.rcwhall@live.com and his website is www.drryanhall.com.

Complete citations are available from the author upon request.

Chapter

10

False Confessions and *Miranda* Waivers

William C. Follette, Richard A. Leo, and Deborah Davis[1]

This chapter by professors William C. Follette, Richard Leo, and Deborah Davis is an update of the version that appeared in the first edition of this book. The chapter contains some developments in the laws governing interrogations and a new section about compliance with the Americans with Disabilities Act (ADA). It remains a valuable guide for explaining why people with various kinds of mental disabilities are vulnerable to making false confessions; the role prescription drugs and self-medicating practices have on various kinds of mental disabilities; identifying and challenging false confessions; and working with experts for purposes of suppressing a false confession or diffusing the power of a false confession on a jury.

It would be wonderful to say that during the approximately five years since the first edition was published, false confessions have ceased. However, despite some changes in policy and increasing public awareness, false confessions still occur. Moreover, the steady stream of individuals who are exonerated shows that much work is still to be done in terms of righting the wrongs of the past.

• • •

1. We thank Sara Murphy, a recent graduate of Maurice A. Deane School of Law at Hofstra University, for her excellent research and editorial assistance with this chapter.

Each day across America hundreds, if not thousands, of people with mental disabilities come in contact with our legal system. Individuals with mental illness are more likely to provoke the attention of law enforcement or the broader legal system at some point in their lives. They may be homeless and violate laws unintentionally or by necessity. They may simply behave strangely and cause fearful others to contact police. They face competence or commitment hearings and hearings to establish legal guardians. For countless reasons they face involvement with law enforcement and legal proceedings at a higher rate than their normally functioning peers. And when they do, they face the many stereotypes and prejudices held by the public and many professionals. They may be simply disliked and suffer harsher outcomes for that reason. A recent study, for example, revealed that a major mental illness was associated with a 50 percent increase in the odds of a jail sentence for misdemeanor arrestees. Or they may be considered more likely to commit crimes, or to be violent, and viewed as more likely guilty when accused.

There is another way in which people with mental disabilities can be at a disadvantage: They can be more likely to be arrested by police and interrogated. Once interrogated, they can be more vulnerable to confession, including false confession. This specific disadvantage is the focus of our chapter. We begin with brief discussion of the larger problem of interrogation-induced false confessions. Next, we discuss the reasons why people with mental disabilities might suffer increased risk of interrogation—even if they are innocent. Then we briefly review how interrogations are conducted, why they are effective in eliciting confessions, and the processes through which they can elicit false confessions. In this context, we discuss what makes individuals more vulnerable to interrogation tactics, and therefore at increased risk of coerced, involuntary, or false confession. Next, we describe how a selection of some of the hundreds of mental disorders and vulnerabilities described by the classification system for mental disorders in the United States could multiply the potential effectiveness of interrogation tactics. Lastly, we briefly describe how attorneys can make use of confession scholars to explain to courts and jurors that coerced or false confessions do occur, how and why they sometimes occur, and who is vulnerable.

The Problem of False Confession

No other evidence is as persuasive to juries as a confession. No other is harder to explain or discount. Studies have shown that when a false confession is presented to juries, they convict the false confessor 73 to 88 percent of the time. Most jurors are skeptical that false confessions occur, especially in serious crimes, because they perceive that to confess to a crime that one did not commit is highly counterintuitive, irrational, and self-destructive.

Beginning in the late 1800s social scientists and legal scholars have documented a growing tide of cases where false confessions have prominently contributed to the convictions of innocent persons. Innocent persons offered full false confessions, some complete with weeping and physical reenactment of terrible crimes. They were convicted by jurors who failed to recognize that their confessions were false. Only later, sometimes decades later, they were proven innocent. Today, there are many published individual and aggregated case studies of proven false confessions, many of them leading to wrongful conviction and incarceration. Additionally, two prominent organizations, the Innocence Project (innocenceproject.org) and the National Registry of Exonerations (https://www.law.umich.edu/special/exoneration/Pages/about.aspx) maintain websites reporting exonerations of the wrongfully convicted and specifying the role of various types of misleading evidence presented against the person in trial. All of these sources reveal a prominent role of false confession in provoking wrongful convictions. False confessions have been documented for terrible crimes such as murder of one's own mother, father, sister, or child; rape and other assaults; and many others—crimes to which intuition tells us people will simply not falsely confess. Yet they do!

These studies of real-life false confessors have also attempted to identify special populations that might be especially prone to falsely confess. Several categories of persons are overrepresented in samples of false confessors compared to their representation within the population interrogated. For example, even though juveniles represent a small proportion of those interrogated, they represent a much larger proportion of proven false confessors. The same is true for individuals with mental illness or low IQ. This has led to substantial research asking such questions as: What are the forces of influence in interrogation to which one might succumb and involuntarily or falsely confess? What personal resources are needed to resist interrogative influence? Which necessary resources are compromised in these special populations? Although our focus is on people with mental disabilities, many sources of vulnerability apply to other vulnerable populations. Before discussing these issues, we turn to the nature of interrogation and the kinds of influences brought to bear on suspects.

Pressures of the Interrogation: What Are They and How Do They Work?

The first goal of an interrogator is to question the suspect freely. To accomplish this and other goals, it is best not to raise resistance in the suspect to being questioned or to the interrogator. The interrogator may attempt to question the suspect without informing them that they are suspected of the crime. Sometimes police ask people to come in for an interview to "help them" with the investigation, with no clarification about whether the person is actually a suspect or merely someone providing "helpful" information. This strategy also helps avoid the necessity of administering *Miranda* warnings that might make clear one's status as a suspect and raise unwanted resistance. These are only required if the suspect is under arrest or would reasonably not feel free to refuse questioning. In many cases an interrogator can successfully proceed from the seemingly friendly "helping with the investigation" phase of questioning into a long accusatory interrogation that results in a confession before *Miranda* rights are brought up.

Many influences lead to failure to invoke rights. Among these are misunderstanding of the true purpose of the interview or of one's status as a suspect; beliefs among many that if police want to talk to you, you must do so; failure to appreciate the significant risks associated with police questioning; and effects of interrogators' direct expressions of pleasure or displeasure in response to the suspect's choices. Many suspects fundamentally misunderstand the *Miranda* warnings themselves, and this is more likely among the young or mentally compromised. Many, particularly innocent suspects, believe that they will benefit from the conversation and demonstrate their innocence. And many (perhaps accurately) believe that refusal to talk to police will at least create more suspicion, and potentially evoke displeasure or reprisal. Many are simply unwilling to defy the obvious wishes of the police. Almost none understand what will happen in interrogation, and the risk they run of self-incrimination and great harm to their cases posed by the forces of influence in the interrogation.

Perhaps most importantly, brief administration of *Miranda* rights sometimes takes place in the context of interrogations spanning hours and even days. The entirety of interrogation can be thought of as an extended "anti-*Miranda*" message to the effect that *not* talking to police will be held against you, and full confession will work to your benefit in a court of law and elsewhere. How can the brief messages of *Miranda* stand against the elaborate and repetitive messages of interrogation that directly contradict them?

The Interrogation

Interrogation Is Deceptive

It must be understood that interrogation is a fundamentally deceptive[2] and guilt-presumptive process designed for one goal: to persuade the suspect to confess with the detail and specific admissions needed to support the charges in question. The interrogator will misrepresent such things as his or her own goals and orientation toward the suspect; the interrogator's own power and control over the suspect's outcomes; the true purpose of questioning; the options available to suspect and the consequences of those choices; the nature of the case evidence; and much more. These deceptions are carried out to convince the suspect that confession is a good choice that will result in superior legal outcomes to denial. This is clearly summarized in one of the most prominent investigator's training manuals:

> Psychologically speaking, a successful interrogation is analogous to selling a resident of the Yukon air conditioning in January; for a suspect to acknowledge a criminal act involving negative consequences requires that the suspect believe a confession is in his best interest.[3]

Many suspects are, indeed, convinced. The interrogation convinces them that confession may be without serious consequences or will result in better outcomes than denial. As we discuss later, the social skills and general knowledge (and the emotion regulation needed to use them in the situation of interrogation) necessary to see through these deceptions are important sources of resistance to interrogative influence, and their lack an important source of vulnerability.

---

2. Given the deceptive nature of interrogation, there is a trend toward developing legislation to ban deception during the police interrogation of juveniles. So far five states (Illinois, Oregon, Utah, Delaware, and California) have taken this step.

3. Brian C Jayne & Joseph P Buckley. The Investigator Anthology: A Compilation of Articles and Essays About the Reid Technique of Interviewing and Interrogation, p. 207 (John E. Reid and Associates, 1999).

Interrogation Is Distressing

One often enters interrogation knowing that one has been, or is likely to be, accused of a crime. Either way, once the interrogation begins, the detective will accuse the person of the crime, persist in those accusations, and call the person a liar unless they admit to what the interrogator insists the person has done. Though most interrogations last one hour or less, others last many hours or extend across days. Others are repeated on a number of different days. The person may or may not be offered nourishment, toilet facilities, breaks, cigarettes, or other comforts, and may be already distressed by grief or other emotions, fatigue, sleep deprivation, illness, intoxication, or other factors before entering interrogation.

It is not surprising that many false confessors do so in order to escape the stressors of the interrogation. This is most likely to occur when the person is already distressed when the interrogation begins (and therefore finds it harder to tolerate additional distress), when the interrogation is particularly aversive or long, when the suspect cannot manage his or her distress or emotions well, when they are particularly impulsive, and when they do not truly understand the actual consequences of confession. All of these conditions (except the nature of the interrogation itself) are more prevalent among people with mental disabilities, as we discuss later.

Interrogations Are Conducted by Powerful Authorities Demanding Compliance

Interrogation is an interaction between two persons of asymmetrical power, in which the interrogator is perceived as possessing considerable power over the suspect and his or her ultimate legal outcomes (and interrogators work to promote this perception), while the suspect has no power to affect those of the interrogator. Most citizens view police as authorities who must be obeyed. If not, the person will face the peril of negative consequences. It takes personal strength to resist a very insistent authority who demands a specific behavior. In interrogation, some of this strength can come from absolute knowledge that one is innocent, or that the consequences of confession are dire. Some of it comes from personal willingness to engage in a conflictual interaction with the interrogator or interrogators and to endure their displeasure and other negative reactions to denial, sometimes over very long periods of time. Some suspects cannot tolerate the distress of any interaction with the interrogator and simply comply.

They "go along to get along." This may be viewed as a subcategory of distress-induced confession. But it may also occur without substantial distress, and sometimes very quickly before distress builds, as a result of a lifetime tendency to defer to others, particularly the more powerful.

Confession through this pathway is most likely to occur when the person doesn't understand or give weight to the actual consequences of confession, when the person is particularly fearful of police (e.g., illegal immigrants or other minorities, people with mental disabilities, or others with an aversive history with police), when the interrogator behaves in a particularly threatening manner, when the person has personality characteristics associated with conflict avoidance or insecurity, or when the person has a life history involving dependence (particularly dependence on dangerous others) or deference to authority (such as the young or those in the military). Some of these vulnerabilities are predictably associated with mental illness and are also more prevalent among the young or those with low IQ.

Other Pathways to Confession

We discussed three primary pathways to confession: (1) becoming convinced that it is in one's best long-term interests, (2) confessing to escape immediate distress, and (3) confessing through compliance with authority. A few others are also worth mentioning.

In some cases, interrogators persuade innocent suspects that they must have committed the crime despite no memory of having done so. The interrogator may present arguments or seemingly overwhelming evidence that convinces the innocent suspect of the possibility of his or her own guilt. When the person has reason to doubt his or her own memories this becomes more likely. This can occur when the person was intoxicated and doesn't remember at all or doesn't remember clearly. It can also occur among individuals with mental illness who distrust the reliability of their memories, or their ability to distinguish the real from imagination or hallucination.

Although this type of confession is still interrogation-induced (often in a particularly vulnerable person), other confessions are due to outside influences. These can come from family or friends, alleged co-perpetrators and others. Some may misguidedly encourage confession, and others may encourage the suspect to take responsibility to protect himself or herself (or the suspect might do this for his own reasons). Some are particularly susceptible to influence from others on whom they depend for survival, advice, or otherwise.

Psychological and Maturational Processes Relevant to Interrogation

Resisting the pressure of an interrogation and succumbing to the demand to explain (confess) requires physical, cognitive, and psychological self-regulatory processes that interrogation procedures are designed to undermine.

Executive Functioning and Self-Regulation

Executive functioning describes the ability to manage one's thoughts, emotions, and behaviors in order to achieve a goal. These skills include control of thinking, attending to relevant information (and ignoring distractions), retrieving relevant information from memory, and analyzing all relevant information to select and plan the pursuit of appropriate goals. They include control of behavior, or executing goal-related plans and suppressing impulses that might interfere with achieving those goals. These skills also include controlling the emotions necessary to control cognition and behavior, and to avoid succumbing to distress-induced impulses.

The development of executive functioning involves neurological maturation, environmental stimulation, and experience. Current magnetic resonance imaging (MRI) studies investigating the neurodevelopment of executive functioning identify the primary brain structure of interest as the prefrontal cortex, with emerging findings that the cerebellum and the corpus callosum play roles in the brain's participation in developing executive functioning. Evidence indicates that the prefrontal cortex is still developing until about age 25. Prior to that age, it is doubtful that there is optimal executive functioning. This partially accounts for why police interrogation practices are more likely to influence teenagers (as opposed to adults) to falsely confess. (See Chapter 12, "Youthful Offenders.")

Simply having developed mature brain structures does not assure good judgment or goal-directed behavior. Impoverished early life experiences may also impede the development of executive functioning. Children in low-income families, particularly from single-parent families, have less-developed executive functioning than children from higher-income families. It is not known how malleable executive functions are with additional development and environmental changes. Of particular relevance here, of course, executive functioning is particularly poor in many people with mental disabilities.

Delay (Temporal) Discounting

Choice behavior frequently focuses on a discounting function that reflects choices between a behavior leading to a smaller-sooner (SS) reinforcer or a larger-later (LL) one. In the real world that question might be posed as: Would you rather have $100 now or $4,000 20 years from now? Researchers have identified differences between children by leaving a marshmallow in front of them and saying, "If you don't eat that now, I'll be back in ten minutes and you can have two of them." Differences in these characteristics are detectable in very young children.

In older adults this same type of choice behavior takes the form of "Shall I have this desert now or skip it in order to lose weight in the future?" Smokers, alcohol abusers, drug abusers, and people with type II diabetes frequently go for the smaller-sooner choice across different kinds of reinforcers. This delay discounting (choosing the SS outcome) is sufficiently robust to be considered a personality trait by many researchers.

Figure 10.1 shows the difference between people on such a task with more impulsive (those preferring the SS) people following the dashed line with the steeper initial slope. Whatever is plotted on the X-axis is colloquially called the nuisance variable (one that might discourage waiting for the LL reward). Time is one such variable, while mounting distress might be another.

Another way to consider how a confession is elicited over time is shown in Figure 10.2. The solid line presents the value of not confessing, and the dotted line the value of confessing. The payoff for not confessing is at some unknown future point in time and evaluated without experiencing the increasing levels of distractors from reaching that goal. In interrogations, the strength of nuisance (distressing) variables are increasing, and terminating the aversive properties of the interrogation has a value that is more immediately available as shown by the dotted line. The events in an interrogation are designed to place impediments in the way of the suspect so they come to perceive that benefits of confessing (SS) outweigh benefits of denial (LL).

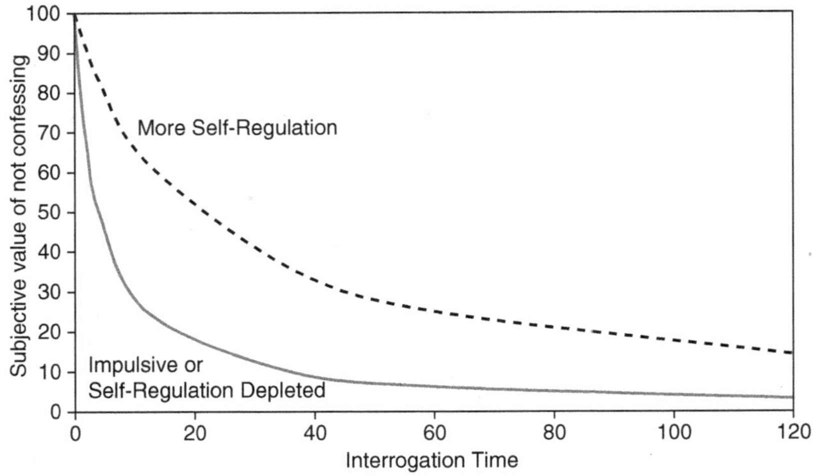

FIGURE 10.1 Delay discounting. (Note: Delay discounting indicates the degree to which stressors discount the value of larger but later occurring outcomes, in this case not confessing.)

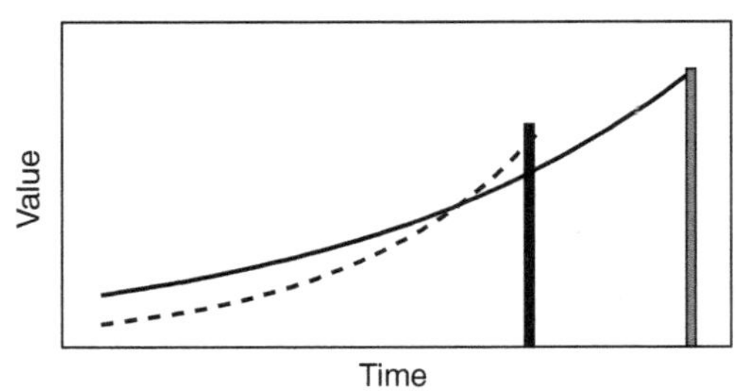

FIGURE 10.2 Changeover to confession. (Note: The value of not confessing (gray bar) initially (Time 1) has high reinforcement value. As interrogation is more aversive over time, the value of the formerly rejected option of terminating the interrogation by confessing comes to exceed that of not confessing as indicated by the black bar.)

Vulnerabilities to False Confessions

Individuals with mental disabilities are at greater risk for false confession in response to interrogation. We first highlight mechanisms that affect the risk of false confession for virtually anyone. Next, we indicate mechanisms making these factors more potent for people with mental disabilities.

Distress Tolerance

Interrogation is generally structured to increase anxiety anytime one asserts his or her innocence and reduce that anxiety whenever one shows an inclination to move toward confession. Distress can build over time with repeated accusations, insistence on law enforcement's accounts, increasing fatigue, and so on, such that the level of distress can become overwhelming to suspects. Distress tolerance is necessary to resist confessing.

Emotion Regulation

Interrogations challenge the ability to regulate one's emotions. Emotion regulation permits sufficient range and flexibility in emotional responding to have useful spontaneous reactions when appropriate but moderate those reactions in ways that benefit the individual. One must also regulate emotions effectively to be able to manage distress, think clearly, and control impulses. There are wide individual differences between people, families, regions of the country, and cultures as to what constitutes appropriate emotion regulation.

Mental Disabilities and False Confessions

People who demonstrate signs of mental illness are 67 times more likely to be arrested than those who do not. Most arrests are for misdemeanors, but some are for more serious crimes. If interrogated, it is uncertain how often individuals with mental illness falsely confess, but there is every reason to suspect they are at greater risk. According to the National Registry of Exonerations, of the exonerees with reported mental illness or intellectual disability, 72 percent had confessed.

To serve as a framework for considering how mental illnesses might increase the likelihood of false or coerced confessions, Table 10.1 presents some attributes that help an interviewee to withstand interrogation pressures toward confession.

Factors Influencing Likelihood of Confession

Escape

Behaviorally, escape is emitting a behavior, in this case confessing, that terminates an aversive state of affairs. Whereas interrogation tactics are

Table 10.1 Personal Resources That Help Mitigate Likelihood of Coerced Confession

Protective Cognitive Skills
• Understanding
• Receptive/expressive communication skills
• Reality monitoring
• Memory
• Conceptual skills
• Sense of self
Affective Skills
• Appropriate affect
• Emotion regulation
• Distress tolerance
Conative Abilities
• Well-developed executive functioning
• Volition to gain larger-later goal
Physiological Preparedness
• Neurophysiological maturity
• Rested, nourished
• No medical or drug vulnerabilities

primarily designed to convince suspects that confession is a good idea, these tactics can be highly aversive, as can the environment and circumstances in which the interrogation takes place. Suspects may confess simply to escape, not recognizing that they can do so by invoking their rights instead.

Avoidance

Avoidance is emitting a behavior that prevents the occurrence of an aversive consequence. Confessing is presented as a way of explaining what happened in such a way as to avoid the most severe consequences.

Pleasing the Interrogator

Often the interrogator presents himself or herself as wanting to understand what happened so that they might be an effective advocate for the suspect. In several conditions, pleasing an authority figure who is thought to be on the suspect's side becomes reinforcing in itself.

Cognitive Skills Deficits

As classified in the current version of the *Diagnostic and Statistical Manual of Mental Disorders*, 5th edition (DSM-5), several disorders involve impairments of cognitive abilities that vary across a continuum from mild to severe and that can be heavily influenced by context. These deficits can include comprehension, discrimination of reality, memory, expressive and receptive information processing and communication deficits, impulsivity, and combinations of each. If one doesn't understand what is being said, remember the facts with clarity, reason with them effectively, and is not effectively expressing oneself, one is more vulnerable.

Conative Deficits

Conative deficits refer to those regarding the desire or volition to perform a goal-oriented action. In some severe mental disorders, lack of volition is a pronounced symptom. For example, schizophrenia symptoms can include apathy and avolition (a decrease or lack of self-initiated purposeful behavior). In aversive or prolonged interrogations, those with conative deficits may simply give up rather than exert the effort and will to defend their innocence.

Arousal Control Deficits

For many high-stakes tasks there is an optimal level of arousal that maximizes performance. Too little arousal results in lapses in concentration, inadequate preparation, or an inadequate marshalling of resources. Too much arousal interferes with performance because it interferes with cognitive processing or leads to physiological arousal that can detract from accomplishing the task at hand. Several mental disorders can result in suboptimal attention and arousal that could compromise performance in an interrogation setting.

Legal and Illegal Drug Effects

Many drugs affect cognitive, conative, and physiological processes that might compromise thinking or exacerbate distress during interrogation.

Prescription drugs addressing physical or mental conditions can have both intended effects and side effects and may interact with other drugs to produce such effects. These, as well as illegal substance use (or withdrawal), can affect memory, fatigue, and other physical discomfort, volition, restlessness, and involuntary motor movements, walking difficulties, dry mouth, blurred vision, and many others.

Personality Characteristics

Personality disorders (discussed later) are characterized by a significant impairment in one's sense of self and interpersonal functioning. The former refers to such things as the capacity for self-reflection, knowing one's own internal standards of behavior for self-regulation, empathy, and comparison to others, among other features. Because the interrogation process is a highly charged, highly consequential interpersonal interaction that directly challenges one's sense of self and often reality, significant social skills and self-confidence are needed to resist such challenges. Some disorders can promote confession through effects on compliance and others through effects on suggestibility.

Being Picked Up by Police

If one were not arrested in the first place, false or coerced confessions would not occur. Each arrest puts one at risk to confess. Thus, any group of individuals at increased risk of arrest, as are individuals with mental illness, are particularly vulnerable.

Youth

Simply being young is not a mental illness (though some parents of teenagers may beg to differ). However, adolescents—especially minority and homeless adolescent—are frequently stopped and questioned. If arrested, they are about three times more likely to confess than adults, with the likelihood of confession increasing as age decreases. Resisting interrogations requires considerable self-regulation and well-developed executive functioning. Neurobiological immaturity, lack of relevant knowledge, and inexperience all place young individuals at greater risk of interrogation-induced confession.

Odd Behavior and Serious Mental Illness

Serious mental illness (SMI) has several different definitions depending on its use in federal policy, political advocacy, or state legal contexts. For our discussion, SMI refers to a mental disorder resulting in obvious signs of dysfunction subjecting the person to enhanced attention by the public or law enforcement. Public displays of psychological dysfunction are often frightening or off-putting to people, leading to arrest. Odd or eccentric behavior, delusions, and hallucinations acted on in public make people anxious and fearful. Such behavior, especially near the location of a crime, may lead to contact with the police, misunderstandings, and subsequent arrest. In turn, each arrest involving interrogation places one at risk of false confession.

Adding to the risk, detectives may engage in a pre-interrogation interview designed to assess the suspect's likely guilt (if a firm opinion is not already held), and to gather relevant information—sometimes before the suspect becomes aware that they are, indeed, a suspect. Common interrogation trainers and manuals teach detectives to believe that they can detect, with a high degree of accuracy, suspects who are guilty with a pre-interview set of questions and observations. This is done, in part, to minimize the risk of false confessions by restricting interrogation to only guilty suspects—a great idea if only the strategies for detecting guilt were valid. Research on detection of deception has clearly shown that the clues interrogators are taught to use are not highly diagnostic of deception. These include signs of arousal and anxiety that can occur due to the stressful situation, for example. Some known false confessors were targeted and interrogated because they displayed "inappropriate" affect such as flat affect in the face of the death of a loved one, or seemingly unjustified hysteria. Some studies have indicated that those who display unexpected or strange behavior are more likely to be judged deceptive. Thus, it can be expected that some individuals with mental illness will be targeted as suspects and subjected to interrogation because they display cues of the anxiety inherent to many disorders, behave unusually, or show flattened or exaggerated affect.

Vulnerabilities for Specific Mental Disorders

Mental disorders and factors related to their development and treatment place individuals at higher risk of confession. It is important to emphasize that there is significant variability between people within and between each category. We are talking about people as individuals, not diagnoses. Similarly, there are people who don't meet the necessary criteria for a diagnostic label, but still show elements of one or more categories. One of the features of DSM-5 is the recognition that disorders vary along a spectrum.

Each new version of the DSM adds, subtracts, redefines, and reorganizes the nomenclature of mental disorders with questionable reliability and validity. It is not possible to describe vulnerabilities to the interrogation process for each of the hundreds of individual diagnoses. However, it is instructive to describe some of the major diagnostic categories and indicate what processes and characteristics of those within each category might make them more vulnerable to interrogative influence.

Intellectual Disabilities

The DSM-5 places intellectual disabilities under a broader category of neurodevelopmental disorders. A federal statute has required replacing the term "mental retardation" with "intellectual disability." The degree of intellectual disability is determined by the level of adaptive functioning one exhibits rather than an IQ score. The classification of intellectual disabilities includes mild, moderate, severe, and profound. Individuals in the latter two categories require support for almost all activities of daily living and are therefore usually supervised. Individuals with mild or moderate levels of intellectual disability can function without constant supervision.

Awareness of the boundary between legal and illegal behavior may vary considerably between these populations. Executive functioning, cognition, memory, and communication are often compromised, as is understanding of risks in social situations. They are at risk for being socially manipulated and commonly exhibit significant gullibility. Ability to recognize the many deceptions of interrogation, understanding of *Miranda* rights, and understanding of the true implications of confession decrease as intellectual disability becomes more significant. Being less certain of oneself, the person is more suggestible, and may either be convinced that confession is wise, or even that they may have committed a crime, though they are innocent.

Persons with intellectual disabilities often have difficulties understanding social norms and dealing with social ambiguity. It is common to manage social stress by agreeing with and pleasing others. Although this may be adaptive in many social situations, it is certainly not adaptive in an interrogation setting, where the person may falsely confess through compliance. Agreement in the context of *Miranda* warnings can also be simple compliance. Neither interrogators, attorneys, nor jurors should assume when an interrogator asks, "Do you understand what I just said?" that a "yes" response should be taken literally. To the extent interrogators make use of closed-ended (e.g., yes-no) questions, rather than open-ended questions (requiring the respondent to formulate an answer or explain) the true meaning of the response is more suspect. In short, this is a highly vulnerable population.

Attention Deficit Hyperactivity Disorder

Another disorder under the larger category of neurodevelopmental disorders is attention deficit hyperactivity disorder (ADHD). ADHD is often thought of as a diagnosis related only to children, but it can persist into adulthood. The very name of the disorder implies the vulnerabilities to the interrogation process. Common features of this diagnosis are the inability to sustain attention on a specific task (in this case maintaining innocence and thinking through what one is being told) and succumbing to the strong tendency to exhibit impulsive behavior (i.e., confession to escape). Correlates of this diagnosis include low frustration tolerance, problems with memory, and impaired executive functioning. Again, given the interrogator's continued insistence on guilt and confession, and the building pressure on the suspect to escape the aversive situation, this population can be predisposed to impulsive responding and escape behavior (i.e., confessing).

Schizophrenia Spectrum and Other Psychotic Disorders

Individuals who manifest particularly bizarre behavior are more likely to get the attention of the public and police. The specific clinical diagnosis in this class of disorders generally depends on the duration and severity of symptoms. The term "positive symptoms" refers to readily observable signs of abnormality. These include hallucinations, delusions, and disorganized thinking as manifested primarily by bizarre speech or abnormal motor behavior. The other class of symptoms of schizophrenia is called "negative symptoms" primarily because they are associated with the absence of important adaptive behaviors including diminished emotional expression, both verbal and nonverbal, and avolition. If in an active phase of the disorder, every aspect of self-regulation may be compromised (i.e., control of cognition, emotion, and behavioral impulse).

Medication Effects

Medications are almost always prescribed for schizophrenia spectrum disorders. These medications are major tranquilizers, and patients often complain of impairment in their ability to concentrate. Side effects include sedation, mood changes, changes in bladder and bowel habits, dry mouth, confusion, tremors, restlessness, tardive dyskinesia (involuntary movements of the face, tongue, lips, or extremities), and other unsettling effects. Other drugs, such as anticholinergics, are given to counteract some of those side effects but also produce side effects of their own. Polydipsia, excessive intake of water that can lead to poorer cognitive functioning and even death, can also occur. We mention this because excessive thirst can add to distress during an interrogation.

A newer generation of antipsychotics began to appear in the 1990s that had less risk for tardive dyskinesia. The new drugs were thought to more effectively treat some symptoms than the original antipsychotic tranquilizers. Although these drugs do have a somewhat lower risk of tardive dyskinesia, they nevertheless produce unpleasant side effects of their own. Additionally, some are associated with metabolic syndrome and the development of diabetes.

The point of listing medications and their effects is to underscore the fact that it is not only the primary disorder that exacerbates the aversive impact of interrogation or vulnerability to interrogative influence. So too can the medications used to treat those problems. Withholding sleep, nourishment, water, access to a lavatory, the ability to walk around, or prolonged interrogations may all contribute to creating conditions experienced as more distressing to those with some mental disorders, in part because of drug effects.

Bipolar I Disorder

There are three types of bipolar disorder (bipolar I, bipolar II, and cyclothymic disorder). Bipolar I requires at least one manic episode. A major depressive episode may also occur. A manic episode requires a period of mood disturbance and increased energy or activity. Mood may be elevated, irritable, expansive, or grandiose. There is frequently a decreased need for sleep, easy distractibility, pressured speech, flight of ideas, or racing thoughts. During a manic episode one may engage in activities that have a high potential for aversive consequences, such as spending large amounts of money with little to show for it or indiscriminate high-risk sexual behavior. One may engage in highly goal-directed behavior such as writing a book or creating an invention, the quality of which the person may severely overestimate. During severe manic episodes it is frequently difficult to discriminate between bipolar disorder, schizophrenia, or drug-induced psychosis. Some individuals find these episodes to be quite enjoyable, while others can be very irritable and paranoid. In either case, self-regulation is severely compromised. As with schizophrenia, cognitive process of all kinds necessary to understand the interrogation and its consequences can be compromised, as can impulsivity.

Medication Effects

Many of the same medication practices for schizophrenia are used in the treatment of bipolar I disorder, with the same side effects. Lithium is also used to treat bipolar disorder. Its side effects include drowsiness, tremors, dry mouth, and thirst, among others. In addition, antiseizure medications such as divalproex sodium are given as mood stabilizers and can cause a host of unpleasant side effects. As with schizophrenia, patients with bipolar I disorder frequently have to continue maintenance doses of these medications. The aversive side effects of these medications, even in the absence of a manic episode, could make any interrogation a more distressing process.

Electroconvulsive Treatment

One controversial treatment for schizophrenia, depression, and bipolar disorder is electroconvulsive treatment (ECT). There are vastly different practices across psychiatrists, hospitals, and regions within the country regarding how often ECT is used, for which disorders, the frequency and spacing of treatments, the length of convulsions, whether they are uni- or bilateral, and so on. The degree and duration of memory effects are debated, but some people receiving this treatment have short-term effects while others can have profound memory impairments of long duration. To the degree that disorientation and memory are affected, executive functioning can be compromised. Moreover, if the person loses memory for any relevant evidence for the crime in question, this can increase vulnerability to suggestion from others who appear to have more extensive or accurate knowledge and to false confession.

Bipolar II Disorder

Bipolar II disorder requires a hypomanic episode. For simplicity, we can think of a hypomanic episode as having similar symptoms to a manic episode though lesser in degree and number as well as less impairment in functioning. Often people with bipolar II experience hypomanic episodes as productive and enjoyable and rarely seek treatment. With respect to interrogation vulnerability, the primary symptom of concern is increased impulsivity.

Cyclothymic Disorder

Cyclothymic disorder is described as the third and more mild form of bipolar disorder, characterized by frequent mood swings of hypomanic and depressive symptoms. Treatments for cyclothymic disorder are often comprised of medication and talk therapy.

Major Depressive Disorder

There are several varieties of depressive disorders, with major depressive disorder being the most severe. A diagnosis of major depressive disorder requires a change in level of functioning accompanied by either depressed mood or loss of interest or pleasure (anhedonia). Symptoms are quite varied. For example, people can have insomnia or hypersomnia, increased or decreased appetite, weight loss or gain. Most relevant for interrogations are decreases in ability to think or concentrate. People experiencing a major depressive episode can be indecisive and lack motivation. Clinically, patients experience worthlessness, guilt, and negative views about themselves, the future, and the world. During interrogations, persons with major depressive disorder are likely to feel depleted of self-regulation skills and of motivation. A person must care about what happens (not going to jail, for example) to resist a confession that might have serious consequences, but depression can involve lack of concern for the future.

Medication Effects

Newer antidepressant medications have two benefits over older medications. First, the potential for a lethal overdose is substantially less than for older antidepressants. The second, more controversial, claim is that they may have a faster onset of action to reduce depressive symptoms. The effectiveness of these medications is the subject of considerable debate. But side effects pertinent to interrogation include drowsiness, insomnia, dry mouth, and sometimes increased anxiety. The pharmaceutical industry recently advocated adding some of the same major tranquilizers used in treatment of schizophrenia and bipolar disorder for those who do not respond to the current antidepressant medications. Few data support increased efficacy, but those taking these drugs suffer the additional side effects.

These newer major tranquilizers can produce a metabolic syndrome that includes significant weight gain and the development of type II diabetes. During the course of prolonged interrogation, blood glucose levels may change significantly and affect cognitive functioning. Diabetes can also cause changes in drinking and urination needs that can make longer interrogations more aversive and escape more attractive.

Anxiety Disorders

Some features of these disorders tend to vary across the lifespan, but fear or anxiety is prominent among them. In some instances, the fears are more specific, such as fears of negative social evaluations. Such fears can enhance the effectiveness of social reinforcements during interrogation contingent on whether the person is denying (e.g., resulting in accusations of lying, threats, or nonverbal disapproval) or progressing toward admission (e.g., resulting in praise for "being honest" or "taking responsibility").

In generalized anxiety disorder, the fear and worry are less focal and address multiple issues. As mentioned earlier, performance tasks generally have an optimal level of arousal. Anxiety disorders, by definition, entail some compromised functioning because of fear, worry, or anxiety. Add the many stressors of interrogation to this existing anxiety and the person may experience sufficient distress to confess to escape, notwithstanding the perceived importance of resisting. If not, the anxiety can increase susceptibility to persuasion that confession is best because the person can no longer think clearly and recognize the flaws in the interrogator's arguments.

Medication Effects

If drugs are used in these disorders, they are generally the newer generation of antidepressants that are thought to work through different pathways. Because they are the same drugs, they have similar side effects. Other drugs in the sedative-hypnotics class include benzodiazepines (e.g., diazepam and alprazolam) that can produce memory impairment, confusion, and addiction.

Drug and Alcohol Intoxication

The influence of intoxication or withdrawal during interrogation appears simple. Intoxication impairs attention, memory, concentration, and communication and leads to disinhibition and focus on immediate rewards. Opioids or stimulants can affect those processes as well. Discomfort due to nausea or withdrawal would be expected to increase the aversive properties of interrogation and increase the likelihood of confession to escape.

Personality Characteristics

The DSM-5 defines personality disorders as enduring patterns of behavior and experience that deviate markedly from expectations within the individual's culture. The behavior is pervasive and inflexible, with a young onset, and leads to distress and impairment. The DSM-5 describes ten personality disorders that are grouped in three broader clusters. Again, any characteristic of the suspect that exacerbates the effectiveness of demands on the individual to act against their actual better interests is relevant.

Cluster A includes disorders characterized by odd or eccentric behavior, of which *schizotypal personality disorder* is one. Features of schizotypal personality disorder include cognitive impairment and reduced capacity for close relationships. Information processing is often impaired, and expression is odd in a variety of ways. Some have argued that this configuration of cognitions and behaviors is on a continuum with schizophrenia. Thus, the ability to separate facts from interrogator-supplied narratives is likely to be compromised. Social interactions are frequently impaired and odd or unusual thinking apparent, so information processing would likely be compromised. The person may seem suspicious and become subject to interrogation just because of odd behaviors.

Cluster B is characterized by dramatic, emotional, erratic behavior. Persons diagnosed with or showing features of *borderline personality disorder* have severe deficits in emotion regulation and executive functioning. They engage in highly reactive behavior to stressors and are often impulsive and dramatic. The origin of borderline personality, like most disorders that evolve over time, is debated (recent research surrounding borderline personality disorder has identified a neural signature associated with the disorder, known as the rostromedial prefrontal cortex). However, one frequently encountered element in the history of people with this diagnosis is that of unstable and intense interactions starting early in life.

One common report is that of childhood molestation and feelings of threat. People with this history often develop close, intense relationships that are characterized by initial over-idealization followed by disappointment and devaluation. Often these relationships are also abusive or exploitive in some way, but they are highly preferred to being alone without someone who could be at all protective. Because of the history of not being able to trust or feel safe around people who should signal safety, seeking safe relationships remains important throughout adolescence and adulthood. One might well expect the stress of interrogation to produce highly reactive emotional responding, impulsive decisions, compromised goal-directed behavior, and ultimately seeking the safety and approval offered by the interrogator if the person confesses (versus disapproval, threats of punishment, etc.). Again, the emotional drama characteristic of such persons may, in some cases, have led to suspicion and their involvement in interrogation.

Cluster C personality disorders are described as being in the anxious, fearful cluster. *Avoidant personality disorder* is in cluster C. People with this diagnosis are characterized by a sense of inadequacy, fear of disapproval or criticism, sensitivity to rejection, avoidance of relationships if there is risk of being disliked, and a personal sense of ineptitude. People with these tendencies could find it difficult to actively disagree with an interrogator who offers escape or avoidance of negative evaluations contingent on confession.

Each of the other personality disorders describes characteristics that anyone can display. Those who don't meet the diagnostic criteria can still manifest the same proclivities, but much less often and with more sensitivity and flexibility to one's current context. Anyone being interrogated can be worried about being judged, be sensitive to criticism, and want to seek safety and minimize risks. Personality disorders show these behaviors at high rates, across inappropriate circumstances, and with less regard to whether they are functioning in their long-term best interests.

Medications

Treatment recommendations for personality disorders do not generally include pharmacotherapy. Nevertheless, it is common to see medication prescribed for symptom reduction or management. This is especially the case for borderline personality disorder, where patients may be treated with many medications at one time. It is important to get a medication history for those with any personality disorder diagnosis. Keep in mind that besides medications used to treatment mental disorders, other medical conditions may be treated by drugs that have effects that can compromise behavior in an interrogation setting.

Suggestibility

Suggestibility refers, essentially, to susceptibility to influence. Much of our previous discuss of mental illness has addressed characteristics associated with suggestibility. One form of suggestibility involves adoption of suggested information. For example, suggestibility has been defined by Dr. Elizabeth Loftus and colleagues as the degree to which one incorporates information provided after an event into his or her recollection of that event. Dr. Gisli Gudjonsson and colleagues consider suggestibility to mean acceptance of messages communicated during questioning in ways that affect subsequent behavior.

A second form of suggestibility involves compliance with suggestions for behavior. Interrogation is full of suggestions that can exert undue influence on the suggestible. That is, suggestion consists of anything that suggests either what is correct (e.g., what information is correct or what behavior is appropriate) or anything that suggests what the interrogator would *prefer* the suspect to say or do. The person may succumb to such suggestions by coming to believe what the interrogator says is true (regarding the wisdom of confession or the suspect's role in the crime), by guessing what is true based on the interrogators' suggestions, or by simply offering responses the interrogators' behaviors have led the suspect to expect will result in more positive interrogator responses. The more suggestible the person, the more likely they are to succumb to suggestion in these ways.

The degree to which one is suggestible is influenced by the degree to which the person has knowledge contradicting what the interrogator suggests is true, the person's willingness to engage in conflictual interactions with the interrogator, and the person's confidence in himself or herself. In turn, these things depend on many individual characteristics, such as youth, intellectual disability, mental illness, and personal history.

What Is the Attorney to Do?

Surveys have revealed that approximately one-third of the public believe that false confessions do not occur at all. Those who agree that false confessions do sometimes occur nevertheless misunderstand the nature of police interrogation, the reasons why false confessions occur, and who is vulnerable. Increasingly, testimony by confession scholars on the conditions that give rise to false or coerced confessions has met Daubert standards and been allowed in trial or suppression hearings to provide understanding of these issues. Therefore, it is important to seek expert consultation to determine the degree to which coercive procedures occurred in an interrogation (for suppression hearings) and whether factors associated with false confessions are present, and if so, to assist in the development of motions to suppress or trial strategy. If confessions are admitted into the proceedings, the confession scholar can educate the jury on the persuasion and influence processes that can produce false confessions, and the personal and situational factors that can increase personal vulnerability. (See Chapters 4 and 5 on working with experts.)

There are generally two types of experts whom attorneys will use to challenge false confession evidence: (1) social and cognitive psychologists who specialize in the study of how and why psychological police interrogation methods can and sometimes do move innocent suspects from denial to admission, and (2) clinical psychologists who measure adult suggestibility, compliance and other personality traits, and mental illness or disabilities. These assessments can inform judgments of the voluntariness of any statements the person makes in the context in which they were made. They are also used to assess the vulnerability of the person to false confession, in the context of the circumstances of the interrogation. In most jurisdictions, judges permit social and cognitive psychologists to testify both generally as educational experts (about the phenomenon of false confessions, the psychology of police interrogation, psychological coercion, specific interrogation techniques, risk factors for false confession, indicia of unreliability, etc.) as well as to apply their expertise to the facts of the case at hand, while other trial judges only allow social and cognitive psychologists to testify generally as educational experts. Clinical psychologists administer tests and testify about the defendant's personality traits and characteristics.

In addition to seeking experts, lawyers need to ensure that clients with disabilities are aware of the accommodations they are entitled to under the American Disabilities Act (ADA), which law enforcement agencies are mandated to provide. On July 26, 2023, ADA.gov issued guidance that criminal justice agencies must make reasonable modifications to policies, practices, and procedures where needed. Examples include handcuffing a deaf individual in front of the body so that they may communicate using sign language or writing and having someone with an intellectual disability repeat back each sentence of their *Miranda* rights in their own words to ensure that these rights are understood.

What Does the Consultant Need?

The expert should have information pertaining to: (1) the nature of the crime and accusations against the suspect; (2) the condition of the suspect going into the interrogation; (3) a life history, and possibly psychological evaluation of the suspect; (4) a recording and transcript of the interrogation; (5) police reports; (6) preliminary hearing and grand jury transcripts; (7) psychological and psychiatric records and reports; (8) the written statement, admission, and confession; and (9) the relationship of the evidence to the content of the confession. The nature of the evidence the expert needs will depend in part on the nature of the task and whether the testimony is for a pretrial suppression hearing, a jury trial, or postconviction proceeding. It will also depend somewhat on whether the expert is to offer general educational only, or both that and case-specific testimony.

Ideally, there will be recordings of the interrogation and all other interactions between the suspect and police, such that what actually occurred during the interrogation will not be disputed. Where available, recordings or transcripts of the interrogation will generally allow one to determine what interrogation techniques were used and whether the interrogators contaminated the suspect with nonpublic case facts. Courts vary on whether expert witnesses are allowed to refer to actual transcripts to demonstrate the presence of specific behaviors, or whether the defense must do so after the expert testified. Recordings are also useful to assess the emotional condition of the suspect, indicators of hopelessness and submission, or the demeanor of the interrogator.

If police failed to record the entire interrogation, the expert should ask the suspect to write down everything they remember occurring during the interrogation in as much detail and narrative sequence as possible. The expert should also interview the suspect on tape about his or her memory of what occurred during the interrogation. Although memory is incomplete and selective, the suspect can at least report on his or her memory of what occurred during the interrogation, what was said, in what order, and what they were thinking during the interrogation. The expert should also request to interview on tape any police interrogators or witnesses present during the unrecorded interrogation and seek to get their best recollection of who said what to whom and in what order.

Beyond interrogation tactics, other characteristics of the interrogation procedures are also important and can be revealed by recordings. Lengthy interrogation and deprivation of food, water, bathroom breaks, or access to medication can all serve to deplete the resources necessary to resist interrogative influences. It is also helpful to know how interrogators were trained and by what organization. Interrogators may not actually know what specific interrogation procedures they were taught, as police departments sometimes do what they describe as their own training, even though they are actually training common techniques, such as the Reid method. The attorney may also bring information about the interrogator's training out on cross-examination of the detective by asking whether they did or did not do certain things during the interrogation (describing the details of what was done rather than the standard name of the tactics). The detective may deny using a particular technique by name, but admit to the same technique when asked whether they said or did a specific thing.

The expert will also need to look at the confession statement itself in the context of the interrogation. Whether permitted to testify about the specifics of the case or not, the expert can point out things useful for the attorney. For example, one can note instances in which the content of the confession has been first suggested by the interrogator, or that content could be easily guessed based on what interrogators have said, and is therefore not indicative of guilty knowledge on the part of the suspect. Some experts will want to see all the case evidence to do an active comparison between the content of the confession and the case facts. False confessions are more likely to have glaring inconsistencies with the evidence because the person is confessing, at least in some degree by guessing, to something they did not actually do. This is not always the case, however, since the police may have contaminated the suspect by feeding him or her information, showing him or her crime scene photos, or taking him or her to the crime scene for a "reenactment" of the crime. Or the suspect may have been present, but not involved, and therefore have some accurate knowledge.

The expert may also want detailed information about the suspect. Depending on the circumstances of the case, judges and juries may be more responsive to evidence of individual vulnerabilities than to evidence of the coercive nature of interrogation tactics. Thus, it is important to present evidence of any vulnerabilities that may exist, though false confessions can still occur in their absence. It may also be important for the expert to have a detailed understanding of the developmental and life history of the accused along with any relevant medical and psychiatric information. The life history information may be important in evaluating how particular interrogation tactics could have affected the suspect. For example, if one had a history of child abuse, it may be that techniques that imply safer outcomes if the person were to confess would have particular influence. Likewise, if the suspect showed a history of marginal adaptive living and cognitive flexibility, the importance of misleading statements by interrogators might be more salient. Social and occupational histories can also shed light on the cognitive and adaptive functioning of the accused.

The physical and emotional condition of the suspect at the time surrounding the interrogation may also be important. How distressed was the person going into the interrogation due to crime relevant (e.g., grief or fear) or crime irrelevant (e.g., job-related) stressors? Greater preexisting distress leads to less tolerance of additional distress and quicker vulnerability to confession just to escape. Was the person fatigued, sleep deprived, or sick? All physical and emotional distress can promote distress intolerance and self-regulation failure.

The defense theory of the crime is often useful to the expert since a discussion of the theory may lead to identification of other suspect vulnerabilities or potentially external influences on reactions during interrogation. In particular, in some instances false confessions may occur due to forces outside the interrogation. The person may have confessed to protect others or due to pressures from family, friends, or others. For example, in some cases parents may be coercive secondary interrogators who refuse to believe their children, accuse them of lying, and even threaten them with severe consequences of denying or failing to talk to police. Thus, it is crucial to understand the full social circumstances facing the suspect and pressuring him or her toward a confession.

Conclusion

Interrogation tactics can elicit false confessions regardless of the mental status of a suspect. But there is no doubt that many mental disorders place suspects at greater risk confessing (even falsely) against their own best interests. As illustrated by our discussion, it is important for those who defend such at-risk defendants to become aware of direct effects of the risk factor as well as those of prescription drugs or self-medicating practices the person may be using to address the primary disorder or complaint.

These must be considered in light of the basic processes that increase a person's suggestibility, or vulnerability to interrogative influence. These include factors that compromise relevant knowledge and memories or the ability to think clearly and evaluate information and arguments from the interrogator. That is, how might the characteristic in question impair the person's ability to realistically evaluate his or her actual involvement in the crime and assess the consequences of confession versus denial?

Other characteristics might impair the ability to resist the demands of a powerful authority. That is, how might the characteristic affect social motives and skills, self-confidence in one's views, fears of the interrogator, or expected reactions to denial? Does the person have a history that involves dependence and the need to please others to survive or prosper? Still others might entail decreased tolerance for distress. That is, how might the characteristic relate to the person's ability to manage impulses and emotion, suppress impulsive behavior, and control his or her behavior to pursue the most important goals?

A final consideration for the evaluation of vulnerability is the person's general self-efficacy for his or her own defense. That is, does the person feel confident, given who they are and what resources they can muster, that they can successfully defend themselves against the allegations in question? If not, this hopelessness will leave them more vulnerable to persuasion that confession will produce the best outcome. Many things that can affect such feelings are problematic for people with mental disabilities, such as the self-confidence and self-esteem underlying the belief that others will believe in their innocence; the solid memories that tell them they are innocent; the financial and social resources to support their defense; and knowledge of how to pursue their defense.

Whether considering a client's characteristics such as youth, race, prior offenses, poverty, or any other personal characteristic, the lawyer should consider the impact of all of these sources of vulnerability, and perhaps seek the assistance of an expert to explain the importance of such vulnerabilities to judges and juries.

• • •

Dr. William C. Follette received his PhD in clinical psychology from the University of Washington with additional specialty training in research design and quantitative psychology. Dr. Follette is professor emeritus in the Department of Psychology at the University of Nevada, Reno. He has served as a member of multiple grant review panels for the National Institutes of Health. Additionally, he has been a participant in several scientific conferences sponsored by the National Institutes of Health. Dr. Follette has more than 200 academic papers, book chapters, and presentations at professional conferences. Among his varied research interests are the study of training of complex social interactions, investigating the mechanisms of change in psychotherapy, and the application of behavioral principles to understand adaptive and maladaptive behavior. Dr. Follette can be reached at follette@unr.edu.

Richard A. Leo, PhD, JD, is the Hamill Family Professor of Law and Psychology at the University of San Francisco School of Law. He is one of the leading experts in the world on police interrogation practices, psychological coercion, false confessions, and the wrongful conviction of the innocent.

Dr. Leo has authored more than 100 articles in leading scientific and legal journals as well as several books, including the multiple award-winning *Police Interrogation and American Justice* (Harvard University Press, 2008); *The Wrong Guys: Murder, False Confessions and the Norfolk Four* (New Press, 2008; with Tom Wells); and *Confessions of Guilt: From Torture to Miranda and Beyond* (Oxford University Press, 2012; with George C. Thomas III).

Dr. Leo has won numerous individual and career achievement awards for research excellence and distinction. Dr. Leo has been the recipient of Soros and Guggenheim fellowships, as well as a fellowship from the Center for the Advanced Study in the Behavioral Sciences at Stanford University. In 2016, the *Wall Street Journal* named him as one of the 25 law professors most cited by appellate courts in the United States. His publications have been translated into multiple languages and downloaded almost 70,000 times on the Social Science Research Network (SSRN). Dr. Leo has been featured and quoted in hundreds of stories in the national print and electronic media, and his research has been cited by numerous appellate courts, including the U.S. Supreme Court. He is regularly invited to lecture and present training sessions to lawyers, judges, police, forensic psychologists, and other criminal justice professionals. Dr. Leo is also often called to advise and assist practicing attorneys and has served as a litigation consultant and expert witness in hundreds of criminal and civil cases. Dr. Leo can be reached at rleo@jrcsf.com.

Deborah Davis is professor of psychology at the University of Nevada, Reno, and a member of the faculty of the National Judicial College. She has published widely in the areas of witness memory, police interrogation and confessions, communicating and understanding sexual intentions, and others. She worked for more than 20 years as a trial consultant, has testified as an expert witness in close to 200 trials, and is a frequent speaker at Continuing Legal Education (CLE) seminars across the country. Professor Davis can be reached at debdavis@unr.edu.

Complete citations are available from the authors upon request.

Chapter

11

Substance Use Disorder

Dr. Carol J. Weiss

Criminal defense lawyers school ourselves about substance use disorder (SUD). We familiarize ourselves about the availability of drug courts and rehabilitation programs. We know that our clients may very well relapse. We know that many clients self-medicate. Some of this we know simply because we must; after all, people with substance use disorder constitute a large portion of our jail and prison population. But our knowledge can be often just enough to get by.

This chapter by Dr. Carol J. Weiss of Cornell Weill Hospital is a guide to the neurobiologic-psychosocial aspects of substance use disorder. As she correctly notes: "The structure and expectations of the legal system do not necessarily align with the structure and expectations of someone with SUD."

The criminal legal system is founded on responsibility. As such, people with SUD who are charged with crimes are entangled in a world where they are criticized for moral failings or the inability to Just Say No. It is not that simple. Moreover, people with mental disabilities who have co-occurring SUD may be more susceptible to substance use, or the symptoms of substance use may mimic mental illness. The criminal defense lawyer must understand the complexities of addiction and remission, be able to navigate those complexities when working with the client, and work for an appropriate resolution in a legal system that is often intolerant.

• • •

Substance use disorders (SUDs) have come to be understood as biologic disorders, replacing earlier beliefs of moral weakness. Although it is important to appreciate the full bio-psychosocial aspects of this chronic, relapsing, treatable condition, the neurobiology of individuals with substance use disorder likely underlies their behavior more significantly than psychology and socioeconomic variables. The perpetuation of addiction can be described as a repeating cycle with three stages: (1) binge/intoxication, (2) withdrawal/negative affect, and (3) preoccupation/anticipation (craving). This relentless cycle can compromise a client's capacity to be collaborative and productively engage with their legal representation.

Understanding the role of biology in SUD is key to managing interactions and expectations with this population. Appreciation of the biologic and sociologic determinants of the behaviors associated with SUD can help generate compassion and patience. The structure and expectations of the legal system do not necessarily align with the structure and expectations of someone with SUD. Hopefully, this chapter can help the criminal defense attorney recognize the inevitability of such misalignment, tolerate the misalignment without resentment, and find ways to facilitate translations between the two structures. This chapter will provide a review of basic, relevant concepts of SUD, followed by practical suggestions for behavioral management of this population.

Epidemiology

Estimates of the prevalence of SUD among sentenced and incarcerated individuals vary, but all confirm a high incidence. Based on a 2017 U.S. Department of Justice report (Bronson, 2017):

> 58% of state prisoners and 63% of sentenced jail inmates met the *Diagnostic and Statistical Manual of Mental Disorders*, Fourth Edition (DSM-IV) criteria for drug dependence or abuse during 2007–2009. In comparison, according to the 2007–2009 National Survey on Drug Use and Health (NSDUH), approximately 5% of the total general population age 18 or older met the DSM-IV criteria for drug dependence or abuse during this period.

Lifetime drug use among the incarcerated populations was unchanged from 2002 to 2009: 40 percent of prisoners and jail inmates used drugs at the time of the offense for which they were currently incarcerated, and 21 percent of sentenced people in state prisons and local jails were incarcerated for crimes committed to obtain drugs or money for drugs. Almost 40 percent of people locked up for property crimes and 14 percent of those incarcerated for violent crimes reported that they had committed their most serious offense for drug-related reasons.

A 2010 report from the National Center on Addiction and Substance abuse (CASA, 2010) estimates 85 percent of the 2006 prison population had an active SUD or were incarcerated for a crime involving drugs or drug use. They further report that in 2006, alcohol and other drugs were involved in 78 percent of violent crimes, 83 percent of property crimes, and 77 percent of public order, immigration or weapons offenses, and probation or parole violations. Alcohol was implicated in the incarceration of more than half of all inmates in America. Illicit substances were implicated in three-fourths of incarcerations.

Looking at drug offenders, as opposed to those diagnosed with SUD, according to a report of the 2012 U.S. prison population (Taxy, 2015), drug offenders comprise 52 percent of the federal prison population, and 99.5 percent of drug offenders in federal prison were serving sentences for drug trafficking. The number of federally sentenced prisoners in the Federal Bureau of Prisons increased 84 percent between fiscal year 1998 and 2012. The number of drug offenders in federal prison grew 63 percent during this time, and 42 percent of the growth in the federally sentenced population was attributed to an increase in the number of drug offenders. Sentence length for this subpopulation was the greatest source of federal prison population growth.

Surprisingly, more recent epidemiologic assessments of SUDs in the U.S. prison population are lacking. One 2016 report of county jail inmates revealed 87 percent of inmates met criteria for any DSM-5 SUD (Proctor et al., 2019). Two more recent large meta-analyses of SUD and mental illness in the international prison population utilize U.S. prison data prior to 2009 (Baranyi et al., 2022; Fazel et al., 2017).

Diagnosis

According to the *Diagnostic and Statistical Manual of the American Psychiatric Association*, 5th edition (DSM-5) (APA, 2013), substance use disorder (SUD) is distinguished from substance use, not by quantity, but by four core concepts:

1. Loss of control in limiting intake of the substance, i.e., failed attempts to decrease or stop use (criteria 1 and 2)

2. Mental preoccupation with obtaining and using the substance (criteria 3 and 4)
3. Continued use despite adverse social, occupational, or medical consequences (criteria 5 through 9)
4. Physiologic tolerance and withdrawal (criteria 10 and 11, not present for all substances)

DSM-5 Criteria for Substance Use Disorders

A. A problematic pattern of substance use leading to clinically significant impairment or distress, as manifested by at least two of the following, occurring within a 12-month period:

1. The substance is often taken in larger amounts or over a longer period than was intended.

2. There is a persistent desire or unsuccessful efforts to cut down or control substance use.

3. A great deal of time is spent in activities necessary to obtain the substance, use the substance, or recover from its effects.

4. Craving, or a strong desire or urge to use the substance.

5. Recurrent substance use resulting in a failure to fulfill major role obligations at work, school, or home.

6. Continued substance use despite having persistent or recurrent social or interpersonal problems caused by or exacerbated by the effects of the substance.

7. Important social, occupational, or recreational activities are given up or reduced because of substance use.

8. Recurrent substance use in situations in which it is physically hazardous.

9. Substance use is continued despite knowledge of having a persistent or recurrent physical or psychological problem that is likely to have been caused or exacerbated by the substance.

10. Tolerance, as defined by either of the following:

a. A need for markedly increased amounts of the substance to achieve intoxication or desired effect.

b. A markedly diminished effect with continued use of the same amount of the substance.

11. Withdrawal, as manifested by either of the following (does not apply to PCP, hallucinogens, and inhalants):

a. The characteristic withdrawal syndrome (specific to each substance)

b. The substance, or a closely related one, is taken to relieve or avoid withdrawal symptoms.

B. Specify severity:
 1. Mild: presence of 2–3 symptoms
 2. Moderate: presence of 4–5 symptoms
 3. Severe: presence of 6 or more symptoms

C. Specify:
 1. Early remission: ≥3 to <12 months without meeting substance use disorders criteria (except craving)
 2. Sustained remission: ≥12 months without meeting substance use disorders criteria (except craving)

Neurophysiology

Although many variables may contribute to the initiation of substance use (e.g., curiosity, availability, or peer pressure), once the substance use passes a certain threshold, continuation of use becomes a biologic imperative, or "addiction." The acute and long-term neuroadaptive changes in the brain that accompany substance use underlie the chronic, relapsing aspect of this disorder.

The manifest behaviors of SUD have specific neurophysiologic loci and mechanisms. The relationship of substance use behavioral phenomenology and neurophysiology is continuing to evolve. Four core behaviors are central to the addiction cycle (Koob & Volkow, 2010):

- **Impulsivity**: An inability to resist urges, deficits in delaying gratification, and unreflective decision-making. It is a tendency to act without foresight or regard for consequences and to prioritize immediate rewards over long-term goals. (This behavior is described in DSM-5 criteria 1 and 2.)
- **Positive reinforcement**: The process by which presentation of a stimulus (e.g., the drug) increases the probability of a response (e.g., non-dependent drug taking).
- **Negative reinforcement**: The process by which removal of an aversive stimulus (e.g., the negative emotional and/or physical state of drug withdrawal) increases the probability of a response (e.g., dependence-induced drug taking, criteria 10 and 11).
- **Compulsivity**: Repetitive behaviors in the face of adverse consequences, and repetitive behaviors that are inappropriate to a particular situation. People suffering from compulsions often recognize that the behaviors are harmful, but they nonetheless feel compelled

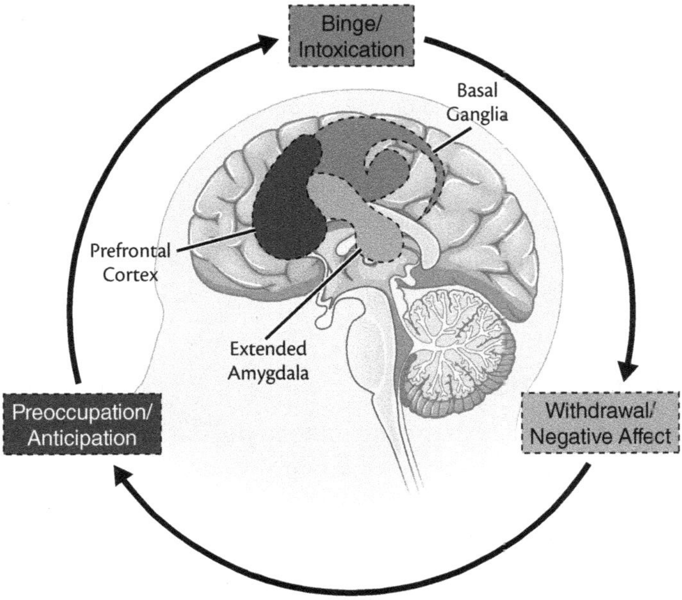

FIGURE 11.1 The three stages of the addiction cycle and the brain regions associated with them. (U.S. Department of Health and Human Services, 2016.)

to perform them. Doing so reduces tension, stress, or anxiety. (This behavior is described in DSM-5 criteria 5 through 9.)

The biologic perpetuation of SUD is summarized by a three-part model: (1) binge/intoxication, (2) withdrawal/negative affect, and (3) preoccupation/anticipation (craving). The neuro-anatomical location and processes underlying these behaviors are summarized in Figure 11.1.

The Reward Pathway (Basal Ganglia)

Many organisms, including humans, engage in behaviors that are rewarded by pleasurable feelings; the pleasurable feelings provide positive reinforcement so that the behavior is repeated. "Natural rewards" such as food, water, sex, and nurturing, are required for the survival of the species. The identification of the brain pathway that is responsible for reinforcing rewarding behaviors solidified the biologic understanding of addictive behaviors.

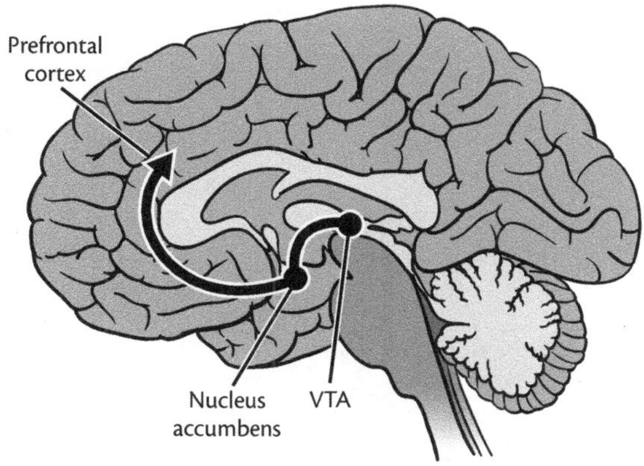

FIGURE 11.2 The reward pathway: basal ganglia (nucleus accumbens and ventral tegmental area) and prefrontal cortex.

For narrative purposes, the following description is a simplification of the reward pathway. The primary brain region of the reward pathway (Figure 11.2) is the basal ganglia, consisting of the nucleus accumbens (NAC) and ventral tegmental area (VTA). The prefrontal cortex is involved in all three stages of the addiction cycle (Figure 11.2). The primary neurotransmitter of this pathway is dopamine. Neurons in the VTA release dopamine to the NAC. Other portions of the brain and other neurotransmitters are involved, but these serve as the foundation of the reward pathway.

The animal model of the reward pathway was identified by implanting an electrode in a rat brain. An electrode implanted in the nucleus accumbens of a rat's brain will stimulate the rat to repeatedly press a lever to get more stimulation. Electrodes placed in other brain regions did not stimulate such lever-pressing behavior. Accompanying stimulation of the nucleus accumbens, an increase in the neurotransmitter dopamine can be measured in the rat brain. If dopamine release is blocked, the rat will not continue to press the lever (Figure 11.3).

When the reward circuit is activated by a pleasurable experience, dopamine is released. The downstream effect of this release causes changes in neural connectivity that make it easier to repeat the behavior (reinforcement). Drugs produce much larger surges of dopamine than those released from natural pleasurable activities. These large surges of

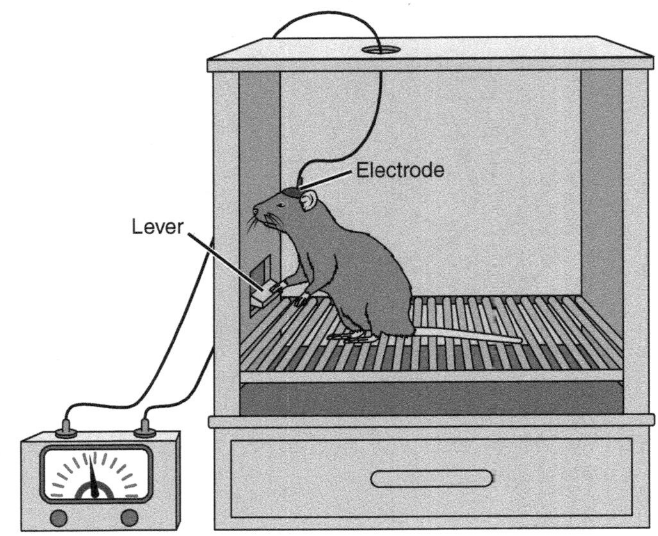

FIGURE 11.3 Identification of reward circuitry in animal model.

dopamine "teach" or "hijack" the brain to seek drugs at the expense of other, healthier goals. Cues linked to drug use can trigger cravings (NIDA, 2020).

Withdrawal/Negative Affect (Extended Amygdala)

Physiologic withdrawal from some substances (e.g., alcohol and sedatives) is life threatening; for other substances (e.g., opioids), withdrawal can be physically excruciating. The human organism is driven to avoid such withdrawal states as much as it is driven to avoid suffocation. Stressful feelings like anxiety and irritability can accompany cessation of drug use and trigger the drive to resume use. Over time, this withdrawal circuit becomes increasingly sensitized such that any stress can become a drug-associated cue and trigger the drive to resume use.

Preoccupation/Anticipation/Craving (Prefrontal Cortex)

Craving and compulsive use (defined as "use despite adverse social, occupational, or medical consequences"), even with substances that do not have severe physiologic withdrawal (e.g., cannabis or inhalants) are behaviors driven by biology. The prefrontal cortex, the last part of the brain to mature and develop, enables humans to exert self-control over impulses. The dysregulation and increased sensitivity of the reward circuit and extended amygdala, described earlier, can shift the balance in the brain away from the prefrontal cortex, decreasing its ability to control impulses. Effectively, during the craving stage, the prefrontal cortex can be considered temporarily "offline."

The three-part system has alternatively been described as two competing systems: the impulsive or limbic system (basal ganglia and extended amygdala) and the executive system (prefrontal cortex). A hyperactive impulsive system weakens or overwhelms the executive system, leading to poor or unreflective decision-making, deficits in learning from past mistakes, and difficulty choosing delayed rewards over immediate ones. These behaviors will be further reviewed later in this chapter.

Impulsivity: Biology or Behavior, State or Trait

A core behavior, or "deficit," in SUD is impulsivity; as already defined, impulsivity is an inability to resist urges, deficits in delaying gratification, and unreflective decision-making. It is a tendency to act without foresight or regard for consequences and to prioritize immediate rewards over long-term goals.

Impulsivity can be understood from both neurologic and behavioral perspectives. A core behavior in SUD, impulsivity is also a feature of other neurologic states frequently encountered among criminal defendants, such as attention deficit disorder, brain injury (e.g., traumatic brain injury), or inadequate brain development (e.g., youth). Lesions specific to the prefrontal cortex or amygdala also lead to impairments in decision-making.

The field of behavioral economics has provided a valuable understanding of potential behavioral mechanisms that influence impulsivity and the relative valence of rewards. A key behavioral concept relevant to SUD is temporal discounting (also called delay discounting or time discounting). Temporal discounting refers to the preference or cognitive bias for immediate rewards given a choice between smaller immediate and larger delayed rewards, also called smaller sooner (SS) and larger later (LL). Studies of temporal discounting measure the choice between two rewards separated in time. For example, if an individual chose a reward of $800 now as opposed to $1,000 in a month, the individual making the choice discounted the amount of money by 20 percent in a month period (Bickel et al., 2006).

The cognitive bias of temporal discounting can be a trait (innate characteristic), state (situational behavior), or both. Animal models and studies in humans demonstrate that greater time discounting reflects a vulnerability to conditions such as drug dependence (including nicotine) and obesity. This supports the trait concept. For example, in a study of opioid-dependent individuals and non-addicted control participants, given the choice between money available immediately or after a delay, opioid dependent individuals discounted significantly more than controls (Madden et al., 1997). However, in another study, ex-addicts discount the future less than current addicts and, in some cases, are not different than controls (Bickel et al., 1999). This supports the state concept. In sum, temporal discounting can be (1) an innate vulnerability predisposing the individual to addiction, (2) a cognitive mindset that occurs during addiction, even for rewards unrelated to drug use, or (3) a mindset only in conditions where there is an absence of sufficient resources for immediate needs (e.g., when a substance user is trying to prevent withdrawal or other adverse states).

Poverty and starvation are other settings in which there is an absence of sufficient resources and where time discounting is evident. In such settings, time discounting is not necessarily a measure of impulsivity, but a reasoned, sensible choice. In this context, the individual selects the SS reward because delay actually devalues or cheapens the LL reward. For example, if starvation now precludes you from getting the later nourishment, food now is indeed more valuable than food later. Time preference, rather than time discounting, refers to circumstances when delay actually devalues the LL reward. Time preference is adaptive in settings of scarce resources and would not be considered a measure of impulsivity. Individuals with active SUD manifest behaviors similar to individuals with specific neurologic deficits or individuals in settings of scarce resources. For many, the experience of living with SUD is like living in a perpetual state of urgency.

Behavioral economics and neurobiology converge in the field of neuro-economics, which examines brain function in decision-making and choice. For example, one study (Bechara, 2005) tested the hypothesis of the two competing systems, the impulsive or limbic system (basal ganglia and extended amygdala) and the executive system (prefrontal cortex), by asking participants without SUD to perform a temporal discounting task during an fMRI scan. fMRI measures increased blood flow reflecting increased brain activation. According to the study, "The results showed greater activity in limbic areas for choices that included an immediate reward and, conversely, greater activity in frontal and parietal regions when participants chose the later reward."

Relapse

Not everyone exposed to reinforcing ("addictive") substances develops SUD. Numerous risk factors contribute to the evolution from intermittent or controlled use to compulsive use.

- Biologic risk factors: genetic vulnerability, duration of use, potency of drug
- Psychologic risk factors: trauma, persistent stress, co-occurring psychiatric illness ("self-medication")
- Social risk factors: environment, poverty, wealth, peer pressure, easy access

On occasion, the court considers the "relapse risk" of a defendant to be a relevant factor in the disposition of the case, and they request a "risk assessment" from the substance use consultant or expert. Given that substance use disorder and other compulsive behavioral disorders are considered chronic brain diseases, affecting reward, motivation, and memory (Volkow & Li, 2004), any individual with such disorders is at risk for relapse.[1]

Definitions of relapse vary widely. From a cognitive-behavioral perspective, relapse can be defined as "a setback that occurs during the behavior change process, such that progress toward the initiation or maintenance of a behavior change goal (e.g., abstinence from drug use) is interrupted by a reversion to the target behavior" (Hendershot et al., 2011). From a biological perspective, the decrease in natural reward function (basal ganglia) and increase in stress sensitivity (extended amygdala) are hypothesized

---

1. Relapse risk is one of the six dimensions utilized in the American Society of Addiction Medicine treatment placement criteria. *The ASAM Criteria: Treatment Criteria for Addictive, Substance-Related, and Co-Occurring Conditions*. (Mee-Lee D, Fishman MJ, Gastfriend DR, Miller MM, eds., 3rd ed., The Change Companies, 2013). For this dimension, the clinician "assesses readiness for relapse prevention services, identifies what worked to achieve previous periods of sobriety, and, in early stages of treatment, raises consciousness of consequences of continued use."

to persist in protracted abstinence and contribute to the motivation to relapse and re-escalate compulsive drug use (Volkow et al., 2016). From both perspectives, "relapse is best conceptualized as a dynamic, ongoing process rather than a discrete or terminal event" (Hendershot et al., 2011).

According to the DSM-5, an individual who has not engaged in addictive behavior for 12 months or more meets criteria for SUD in remission. However, numerous longitudinal studies evaluate remission in terms of longer periods of time, from five years to decades (Vaillant, 1996; Trim et al., 2013; McLellan et al., 2008; Skipper et al., 2009; Krampe et al., 2006; Schuckit & Smith, 2011).

"Relapse risk" is an extremely complex topic, dependent on numerous variables, including but not limited to, definition of relapse, individual neurobiology (Koob & Volkow, 2016; Volkow et al., 2016; Sinha, 2011); family history (Chassin et al., 2004); demographics, including gender (Potenza et al., 2012; Hyman et al., 2008); psychological traits (Fisher et al., 1998; Miller, 1991); attitudes and beliefs (Marlatt & Gordon, 1985); comorbid psychiatric disorders or factors, such as trauma (Hyman et al., 2008), stress (Enoch, 2011; Sinha, 2001), depression, and anxiety; substance(s) used; and available psychosocial and treatment support (Trim et al., 2013). Consequently, applying relapse studies to any one individual, in an attempt to "predict" relapse risk or cite "relapse rate" is unreliable, an oversimplification, and not advised for forensic contexts. Nonetheless, relapse risk can be mitigated by evidence-based treatment (Hendershot et al., 2011), psychosocial support, and monitoring (DuPont & Humphreys, 2011).

Co-occurring Psychiatric Disorders

There is a striking degree of psychiatric comorbidity with SUD. Approximately 50 percent of individuals with SUD have co-occurring mental illness. Conversely, of those diagnosed with mental illness, 50 percent also have SUD (Compton et al., 2007). Because the symptoms of SUD may mimic other psychiatric disorders, confirmation of a psychiatric diagnosis should occur in the absence of an active SUD. For example, symptoms that appear to be panic or anxiety disorder may actually be manifestations of the withdrawal state in sedative or alcohol use disorder, which is characterized by anxiety and panic. Depression may be a symptom of opioid withdrawal.

To provide a system to clarify this diagnostic dilemma, a distinction is made between primary and secondary psychiatric disorders. If an individual appears to have symptoms consistent with depression, but only in the context of drug use, that person may be said to have secondary depression (i.e., depression secondary to substance use). If the person had symptoms of depression before the onset of SUD or during periods of extended abstinence, they likely have primary depression.

The distinction between primary and secondary disorders also applies to personality disorders. According to Gendel (2006), "A personality disorder diagnosis should not be made solely on the basis of behaviors that are related to intoxication or withdrawal or arise as part of the process of sustaining a dependency. Practically, years of substance dependence are often associated with behavior that appear to be personality disorders but that resolve after a period of extended abstinence." A notable example of this distinction occurs with the diagnosis of antisocial personality disorder (ASPD). The DSM-5 criteria for this disorder are:

1. A pervasive pattern of disregard for and violation of the rights of others, since age 15 years, as indicated by three (or more) of the following:
    a. Failure to conform to social norms concerning lawful behaviors, such as performing acts that are grounds for arrest.
    b. Deceitfulness, repeated lying, use of aliases, or conning others for pleasure or personal profit.
    c. Impulsivity or failure to plan.
    d. Irritability and aggressiveness, often with physical fights or assaults.
    e. Reckless disregard for the safety of self or others.
    f. Consistent irresponsibility, failure to sustain consistent work behavior, or honor monetary obligations.
    g. Lack of remorse, being indifferent to or rationalizing having hurt, mistreated, or stolen from another person.
2. The individual is at least age 18 years.
3. Evidence of conduct disorder typically with onset before age 15 years.
4. The occurrence of antisocial behavior is not exclusively during schizophrenia or bipolar disorder.

If a person engages in these behaviors or manifests these traits only while actively misusing substances, and not during a period of extended abstinence, ASPD would not be an appropriate diagnosis. Those behaviors were situational, and not innate or enduring traits (Gendel, 2006). However, ASPD can be diagnosed if substance use is co-occurring, especially if the core feature of lack of remorse is present and predated substance use.

One of the more common and overlooked SUD comorbidities is trauma and post-traumatic stress disorder (PTSD). According to Farley (2004), "Trauma history increases risk for drug and alcohol use. Sexual assault, childhood sexual abuse, physical assault, and partner violence are each associated with drug and alcohol abuse and dependence. Compared to individuals without SUD, those with SUD report more traumatic events. Among those seeking treatment for SUD, 42–95% report histories of trauma."

Individuals who have experienced trauma can manifest a myriad of behaviors that can mimic other diagnoses, such as bipolar disorder, attention deficit hyperactivity disorder (ADHD), borderline personality disorder, or histrionic personality disorder. As with SUD, these behaviors and other manifestations of behavioral dysregulation can remit with appropriate trauma-focused treatments.

Social and Environmental Factors

As previously demonstrated, there are clear neuro-biologic, neuroeconomic, and psychiatric determinants of behaviors characteristic of individuals with SUD. Some social and socioeconomic variables are worth mentioning. Social and environmental risk factors for drug initiation, drug use perpetuation, and relapse include poverty, wealth, peer pressure, and easy access. According to McLellan and colleagues (2000):

> Repeated pairing of a person (drug-using friend), place (corner bar), thing (paycheck), or an emotional state (anger, depression) with drug use can lead to rapid and entrenched learning or conditioning. Thus, previously drug-dependent individuals who have been abstinent for long periods may encounter a person, place, or thing that previously was associated with their drug use, producing significant physiologic reactions such as withdrawal-like symptoms and profound subjective desire or craving for the drug.

"People, places, and things" is a common phrase of Alcoholics Anonymous referring to triggers associated with substance use.

Individuals with SUD often have lived in an environment where they have been marginalized and stigmatized (Volkow, 2020). Understandably, they have come to mistrust and avoid certain institutions from which they are disenfranchised, especially medical and legal institutions. Navigating both institutions requires a great deal of frustration tolerance and an ability to value LL rewards over SS ones. Understanding these deficits among individuals with SUD can help principals in the medical and legal systems partner more easily with these clients.

Responsibility

The biological understanding of SUD is an important rejoinder to the stigmatizing notions of SUD as a moral weakness or character flaw. This perspective touches upon the philosophical and forensic issues of volition (e.g., voluntariness, choice, and will) and responsibility. Although these neurologic alterations result in a "profound alteration in the nature of choice and decision-making about drug seeking and drug using, and the consequences of addictive drug use" (Gendel, 2006), these alterations do not erase responsibility.

The relationship between the neurologic changes of SUD and the concept of choice is clearly elaborated by one legal scholar (Bonnie, 2002). Free will may be heavily influenced by these neurologic changes, but there is a difference between the impulsive and compulsive behavior of SUD and the behavior associated with Parkinson's disease, Alzheimer's disease, or seizure disorder, where there is no volitional component. According to Bonnie, the neurologic changes in the substance user explain why the drive to use is so great that it is *unlikely* to be resisted. The voluntariness of drug seeking is limited or altered, resulting in an "impairment of volition," but this does not equate to involuntary behavior. "Limited volition and lack of volition are fundamentally different. Limited or impaired volition involves a hard choice rather than no choice."

This choice is most explicit in the phenomenon of relapse. The likelihood of relapse, although a central component of the biologic model, can be reduced by certain measures, embodied in the principles of the relapse prevention model, defined as "skills based treatments that emphasize cognitive behavioral skills building and coping responses" (Marlatt & Gordon, 1985; Hendershot et al., 2011). Another treatment tool that underscores the capacity for choice is contingency management, which is based on principles of operant conditioning and helps build sobriety by offering rewards for positive behavioral change. Negative reinforcement, in the form of deterrents or "leverage," are also effective in highly motivated populations such as physicians (DuPont & Skipper, 2012), attorneys (ABA, 2019), pilots (HIMS, 2019), or parents in high-conflict custody litigation (Weiss, 2021).

The notion of choice and responsibility is captured in one of the many aphorisms of Alcoholics Anonymous: "You are not responsible for your disease, but you are responsible for your recovery."

Management of Behavior

Much like individuals coping with starvation or war, individuals with SUD have a biologic imperative to sustain survival at any cost. This behavior may appear impulsive or "antisocial," but it is best understood in its biologic context. Stabilizing a client's biological needs is an essential prerequisite for optimal interaction and case management. If the client is acutely intoxicated or, more likely, in withdrawal, every attempt should be made to rectify that situation, usually with medical attention. Opiate-dependent individuals should be administered methadone or buprenorphine; sedative- or alcohol-dependent individuals will require medical monitoring and management to prevent a seizure. Much behavior that is described as oppositional, aggressive, or "sociopathic" can actually be manifestations of withdrawal.

Protracted periods of such biological need can generate a habitual or entrained cognitive mindset of immediate gratification. For some, delayed gratification is a mere abstraction without much meaning. The criminal defense attorney could present his or her objectives to the client by clearly, and without condescension, making distinctions between short- and long-term goals. They can inquire about which immediate needs must be gratified before delayed goals can be considered.

As previously described, stress, which is practically unavoidable in legal contexts, is a precipitant for use and relapse. Treatment can be an effective source of stress management. Clients should be encouraged to pursue treatment as a means to help them endure their legal course. Of course, where there is access to drug courts, treatment can also be an alternative to incarceration.

Substance users are not accustomed to being treated with respect and may not be accustomed to showing respect for others. Protracted periods of stigmatization and disempowerment may lead to a defensive bravado or compensatory sense of entitlement. Any manifestation of compassion or respect from the criminal defense attorney will go a long way. Remarks such as "What were you thinking?" or "Where did you think that would end up?" should be replaced with an understanding of biologic needs, temporal discounting, and years of disenfranchisement.

Showing interest and curiosity about areas where the client has expertise can be disarming and bonding. If there is sufficient time, asking detailed, nonjudgmental questions about their drug use history, procurement, effects, attempts to quit, and so on can show respect for knowledge about a topic where they have greater expertise than their attorney. In spirit, this may address the experience of imbalance between the "less than" defendant and "authoritarian" attorney, thereby increasing the potential for collaboration.

The preceding suggestions address the biology, psychology, and sociology of individuals with SUD. Understanding the relevance of these variables can help both the attorney generate compassion and patience and the client feel respected and engage collaboratively.

• • •

Carol J. Weiss, MD, is clinical associate professor of psychiatry and clinical associate professor of psychiatry in medicine at Weill Cornell Medical College. She has served in a forensic capacity as an expert witness, substance use evaluator, or neutral monitor, primarily in matrimonial matters, from 1994 to the present. She is the author of "Protocol Design and Implementation for Monitoring Parental Substance Use in Child Custody Litigation" in *Family Court Review* (July 2021).

Dr. Weiss attended Johns Hopkins University Medical College and completed a two-year fellowship in addiction psychiatry at Cornell University Medical College, after which she spent nine years working in the AIDS field. She is the current associate medical director of the Center for Trauma and Addiction at Weill Cornell Medical College and former associate medical director of Headstrong Project, a nationwide program providing free mental health care to post-9/11 veterans with PTSD. She is member at large of the board of directors of the American Academy of Addiction Psychiatry; is triple-board-certified in psychiatry, addiction psychiatry, and addiction medicine; and has been in private practice since 1989. She has consistently been listed in numerous Castle Connolly Top Doctors Guides from 1996 to 2022. Dr. Weiss may be reached at Cjw2001@med.cornell.edu.

Complete citations are available from the author upon request.

Chapter

12

Youthful Offenders

Jay Blitzman

You may wonder, "What is a chapter about youthful offenders doing in a book about representing people with mental disabilities?" The answer is twofold: First, to the degree that mental disabilities are brain-based and the adolescent brain is still developing, thus lacking maturity when it comes to issues like self-regulation and long-term thinking, it is vital that criminal defense lawyers are aware of the particular characteristics of this population; and second, a disproportionately high number of youth involved in the criminal legal system have behavioral issues and have suffered trauma.

The author of this chapter, retired Juvenile Court Judge Jay Blitzman, provides a valuable guide for advocating for youthful offenders. Not only does he discuss the implications of the growing body of knowledge concerning brain development and the impact of trauma on young people, but he details the implications of recent U.S. Supreme Court rulings regarding youthful offenders and strategies for effective advocacy.

For too long, the criminal legal system has given scant attention to the plight of youthful offenders. This has allowed incredible abuses such as those exposed in the podcast "The Kids of Rutherford County." Research and writing by scholars like Judge Blitzman should increase the quality of representation for youth, thus preventing flagrant violations of constitutional rights and at the same time, meaningfully intervening in young lives. As such, all of us will benefit.

• • •

In the introduction to this chapter in the first edition of this book (where it was called "Juveniles"), editor Elizabeth Kelley noted, "If you are representing a youth, you are not simply representing a small adult." Attorneys representing youth are obligated to familiarize themselves with the science that supports this assertion by connecting developmental research to personal and family narratives. Relying in large part on brain imaging studies amplifying psychological and developmental research regarding the maturational arc of adolescence, the U.S. Supreme Court has abolished the juvenile death penalty,[1] juvenile life without parole in non-capital cases,[2] mandatory juvenile life without parole in murder cases,[3] and ruled that the chronological reality of age is an important consideration in custodial statements attributed to children.[4] Youth and children are accountable but in a constitutional sense they are different than adults. Applying this precept to practice is the new frontier. It is time to revisit issues such competency to stand trial, specific intent and mens rea, joint venture, transfer to criminal court, mandatory sentencing, sex offender registration, and zero tolerance constructs in schools. Critical policy questions such as the minimum and maximum age of juvenile court jurisdiction and life without parole are also implicated. Navigating this landscape entails an understanding of adolescent development.

An important 2019 Judge Baker Guidance Center report, *Promoting Positive Outcomes for Justice-Involved Youth: Implications for Policy Systems and Practice*, notes that "[a]dolescence is largely a cultural and societal construct that also has clear developmental benchmarks typically referring to the period of time between childhood and adulthood."[5] Adolescent development is a dynamic construct, occurring simultaneously and often inconsistently across multiple developmental domains which include cognitive, emotional social, moral, and racial-cultural domains.[6] Social context is also very important. The sociologist Urie Bronfenbrenner has observed that we all live in social nests. This is especially true for adolescents. Consideration of the social context that affects many court-involved youth

1. Roper v. Simmons, 543 U.S. 551 (2005).
2. Graham v. Florida, 560 U.S. 48 (2010).
3. Miller v. Alabama, 567 U.S. 460 (2021).
4. J.D.B. v. North Carolina, 564 U.S. 261 (2011).
5. Robert Kinscherff, PhD et al., *Promoting Positive Outcomes for Justice-Involved Youth: Implications for Policy, Systems and Practice*, at 8, Judge Baker Children's Center (February 2019).
6. *Id.*

is important. Many live in segregated neighborhoods, attending schools with environments featuring high degrees of surveillance from both police and child systems.

It is necessary to consider issues affecting youth through a developmental lens and to understand the socioeconomic realities they encounter. Youth development is a psychodynamic process which occurs in a complex intermingling of biological, familial, community, and social influences. Our increased understanding of the adolescent brain has influenced how we think about juvenile justice and the supports and services we provide to justice-involved youth. The Supreme Court decisions in the cited cases reflect the recognition that adolescents, because of their relatively immature brains, are not consistently capable of the same reasoning capabilities as adults, especially when with peers or in emotionally charged "hot cognition" situations.[7]

Adverse Child Experiences and Trauma

Practitioners must also educate themselves about the social context of their clients' lives. This type of framing is helpful in beginning to more adequately address issues such as adverse child experiences and racial trauma. All youth experience adversity and most experience at least one traumatic event in their lifetimes. Not all adverse experiences result in trauma, and not all traumatized youth end up in the juvenile justice system. However, higher rates of adversity than the general population resulting in trauma are more often experienced by youth of color and other minority groups. More than 75 percent of justice-involved youth have experienced traumatic victimization, and 93 percent of children in detention facilities report exposure to adverse experiences.[8]

Adverse childhood experiences (ACEs) research examines potentially traumatizing events that may have negative and long-lasting effects on behavioral health and development. Adverse childhood events include exposure to trauma, abuse, neglect, community violence, domestic violence, and family instability. The research reveals that more than 50 percent of the general population has at least one adverse childhood experience, and

7. *Id.* at 6.
8. Judge Baker Guidance Report, *id.*

25 percent experience more than two. ACEs scores for court-involved youth are dramatically higher.

The *Diagnostic and Statistical Manual*, 5th edition (DSM-5) published by the American Psychiatric Association defines trauma as exposure to actual or threatened death, serious injury, or sexual violence. Traumatic experiences can adversely affect brain development. The amygdala, the area of the brain specializing in processing fearful or threatening stimuli, acts as a first responder to stress. The thalamus functions as a gatekeeper to the amygdala in processing information about perceiving and reacting to past threats. Child exposure to trauma can result in exaggerated amygdala responses for detecting and processing emotional information. This process is directly related to impulsivity, hypervigilance, and fight or flight reactions. It also makes it much more difficult for youth have who experienced trauma to self-regulate.[9] Complex trauma, which is trauma that occurs frequently and repetitively, and racial trauma exacerbate these issues. The incidence of post-traumatic stress disorder (PTSD) is eight times higher for children in the juvenile legal system.[10] The damage to the brain delays the developmental trajectory but need not be permanent, which underlines the importance of prosocial support for children and youth.

A 2013 study of children and adolescents seen by Massachusetts Juvenile Court clinicians found that over 50 percent had experienced emotional neglect, 40 percent had experienced physical abuse, and 15 percent had experienced sexual abuse.[11] In addition, the experience of the court system can by itself constitute a traumatic event. Out-of-home child welfare placement and juvenile detention can dramatically exacerbate post-traumatic symptoms for children who have prior ACEs. The clear message here for practitioners and judges is that detention is to be reserved for palpable public safety cases and that child welfare placement is a last resort.

Many young people are dually involved in the child welfare system because of abuse and neglect petitions filed against their families or because of status offense cases. In Massachusetts, for example, a review of data between 2010 and 2012 reveals that 72 percent of youth committed to the state's youth correction authority, the Department of Youth

9. *See e.g.*, Julie Rosenthal, *Understanding Psychological Trauma*, Pathways, PSYO, Portland, Oregon, Aug. 20, 2022.

10. Julian Ford et al., *Trauma and Youth in the Juvenile Justice System*, Nat'l Ctr for Mental Health and Juv. Just. 1,1 2007.

11. Judge Baker Children's Center, *supra* fn. 5.

Services (DYS), had been involved with the state's child protection agency, the Department of Children and Families (DCF).[12] Of that number over half were involved with DCF at age five or younger, at rates of racial and ethnic disparity that parallel those seen in the juvenile system, contributing to what Harvard historian Jill Lepore characterizes as a child version of the carceral state—a birth to prison pipeline.[13] Kate Lowenstein, the multisystem project director of the Massachusetts Citizens for Juvenile Justice (CFJJ) reports that 70 percent of black male youth in Massachusetts live in families against whom DCF has filed allegations of neglect. Given subjective perceptions of what constitutes neglect, critics such as Dorothy Roberts have raised the issue of racial bias in analogizing patterns of neglect allegations to racial profiling seen in abuse of stop-and-frisk practices in the criminal context.[14]

Environmental factors are directly related to whom we see in our child welfare and juvenile regulatory systems. Issues of class and race are implicated, as disproportionately high numbers of youth who become court-involved are black and brown and live in segregated neighborhoods with inadequate community-based public health and mental health services. These neighborhoods are also subjected to high rates of police and child welfare surveillance. Youth who become court-involved have high rates of adverse childhood experiences, trauma, environmental stress, and behavioral health issues. Considerable research has shown that youth with mental health conditions and substance use disorders are disproportionately represented in the juvenile justice system. It is estimated that justice-involved youth have diagnosable behavioral health needs at least two to three times higher than rates among all youth. A 2006 National Center for Mental Health and Juvenile Justice (NCMHJJ) study found that 70 percent of justice-involved youth met the criteria for at least one mental disorder and more than half met criteria for two.[15]

---

12. Jill Lepore, *Baby Doe: A History of Political Tragedy*, New Yorker (Feb. 2016).

13. *Baby Doe*, *id.*

14. Kate Lowenstein, author of *The Trauma to Prison Pipeline*, CFJJ (2018) during lecture to this author's "Cradle to Prison Pipeline" class, Boston College Law School (April 2022); Dorothy Roberts, *Torn Apart: How the Child Welfare System Destroys Black Families—and How Abolition Can Build a Better World*, Barnes & Noble (April 2022).

15. Judge Baker Children's Center, *supra* fn. 5 at 5.

Positive Youth Development and Holistic Representation

Positive youth development (PYD) is a strength-based asset-driven model that proceeds from the premise that each child "can" if we give them the tools to do so. PYD focuses on a youth's talents, strengths, interests, and future potential.[16] This approach recognizes that working with youth everyone is exposed to risk and adversities, but that healthy development can be promoted by building on strengths and resiliency factors. PYD holds that every youth has potential strengths that can be built upon to offset risk factors and emphasizes developing youth as leaders, participants, and active decision-makers in their lives. This philosophy is directly related to the importance of client engagement, empowerment, and being heard. "Nothing about me without me" should be the credo in juvenile and child welfare proceedings.

Every attorney and every juvenile or family court judge should reread the seminal *In Re Gault* case from 1967, in which the Supreme Court established the right to counsel for indigent youth during bench trials.[17] The case is notable in bringing a degree of due process into juvenile proceedings, which had formerly disdained the adversarial process, as well as exposing an inglorious history of focusing on so-called well-intended therapeutic interventions. Justice Fortas opined that as far as the juvenile is concerned, a more therapeutic approach is the essential of fundamental fairness, which of course is synonymous with due process.[18] He critiqued the parens patriae philosophy, which had rationalized practices in the pre-*Gault* world as a Latin phrase of dubious origin and ancestry used to justify exclusion of the juvenile from the constitutional scheme.

PYD reflects an ecological approach, recognizing that youth development is influenced by multiple systems and contexts, ranging from peers and families, schools, neighborhoods, and communities to governmental policies. The Youth Advocacy Division (YAD) of the Massachusetts state public defender system has incorporated PYD practices into

---

16. Richard M. Lerner, Michael D. Wiatrowski, Megan Kiely Mueller, Christopher M. Napolitano, Kristina L. Schmid, and Anita Pritchard, *A Vision for the American Juvenile Justice System: The Positive Youth Development Perspective*, in Juvenile Justice: Advancing Research, Policy, and Practice, eds. Francine T. Sherman and Francine Jacobs (John Wiley & Sons, Hoboken, NJ, 2011).

17. 387 U.S. 1 (1967).

18. *Id.* at 26.

their representation of all clients. YAD attorneys employ a client-directed model of advocacy that is holistic in nature. YAD evolved from the Roxbury Youth Advocacy Project, a community-based public defender unit that featured a multidisciplinary staff that included social workers, a community liaison, educational advocacy specialists, and a psychologist.[19]

The Youth Advocacy Project was committed to developing a contextual or holistic model of legal representation that included lawyers representing clients in all legal and disciplinary matters in which they were involved. Dealing with one attorney instead of multiple attorneys helps develop trust, an essential component of a productive client-attorney relationship. It is also helpful in understanding and humanizing your client. Building a relationship with a client takes time and will entail multiple meetings. Sometimes it is preferrable to meet in a client's home or in a community setting. You earn trust by engaging in client-directed advocacy and being sensitive to the realities of their circumstances. There is a misconception that attorneys who represent youth are social workers. Lawyers do have a counseling function, but that function derives from the primary obligation of client-directed advocacy.

If your client is facing a school disciplinary hearing, it is wise to represent the adolescent at that hearing. This is especially so if the school disciplinary hearing is related to the alleged delinquency or criminal offense. Some states, including Massachusetts, will reimburse court-appointed attorneys who defend clients in school disciplinary hearings that are related to the delinquency cases they have been appointed on. YAD attorneys have the benefit of an Education Law Project that focuses on this issue. Educational continuity is a critically important component of positive youth development and combatting the school-to-prison pipeline. A 2012 study, *Arrested Futures* (ACLU-CFJJ), indicates that students who do not graduate high school are five to eight times more likely to later enter the juvenile or criminal system. These numbers soar for youth with disabilities and for youth who identify as LGBTQ.

A 2021 national study[20] shows the magnitude of the intersection of disability and race. This research demonstrates how special education has

19. The first director of the Roxbury Youth Advocacy Project is the author of this chapter. The deputy director was Joshua Dohan, who recently retired as the director of the Youth Advocacy Division.

20. Danile Losen et al., *Disabling Inequity: Urgent Need for Race-Conscious Remedies* (Civil Rights Remedies Project, UCLA, 2021).

unfortunately been used in some school districts as a disciplinary tool, which fuels the school-to-prison pipeline by disproportionately characterizing black and brown children as behavior problems and then placing them in separate classrooms and alternative schools.[21] This sad reality exacerbates the fact that ever since the 1999 Columbine school shooting, over two-thirds of students suspended from school are black or brown. Attorneys should marshal data and research connected to individual narratives to address barriers facing all students, including those with disabilities and unmet or misdiagnosed special education needs and youth who identify as LGBTQ.

Representing children and youth requires more than understanding juvenile and criminal law; it requires understanding the worlds and systems families and their children inhabit. Finding out about a client's individual education plan, involvement with any state agency, and any diagnostic evaluations are invaluable tools in developing a psychosocial history of a client and their family. As trust is established, having parents and guardians sign releases of information to gather such information is necessary to understand multi-systemic involvement and cognitive functioning. Family history is very relevant as well. In a juvenile murder case that I was appointed to, I learned that my client's expressive language order reflected a family pattern. I would not have been aware of this without investigation and preparation and the assistance of my expert in the case, Thomas Grisso. This issue was important in litigating the motion to suppress of statements, given that Massachusetts employs an interested model in juvenile *Miranda* analysis that requires a showing that both the interested adult and the adolescent have made knowing and intelligent waivers of their right to remain silent.

An important component of the PYD model is encouraging child-serving agencies and responsible adults to engage in the practices. "Accountability" is a two-way street. PYD envisions systemic change that focuses on healthy development. The Massachusetts DYS has embraced the model in helping youth maintain educational continuity and community connection and proactively helping with community reentry. Recently retired DYS Commissioner Peter Forbes indicates that almost 60 percent of youth who are discharged from DYS voluntarily work with the agency's Youth Engaged

---

21. *See e.g.*, Daniel Losen & Gary Orfield, *Racial Inequity in Special Education* (Harvard University Press, 2002).

in Services (YES) program. A major factor in reducing technical probation violations (violations for violating conditions other new reoffending) is attributable to the Commission of Probation embracing the PYD model. This is consistent with efforts to reconceptualize probation officers as youth development officers as is being attempted in Los Angeles.[22]

Brain Development and the Legal System

Research has shown that childhood and adolescence is a period of significant brain development. As neural pathways become more efficient, brain gray matter diminishes as neuronal connections are pruned back. During adolescence, usually starting by age 14, the prefrontal cortex, which helps regulate and govern behavior (so-called executive functioning), is still developing. As a result, youth may demonstrate impeded judgment and decision-making, making them more likely to exhibit risky or impulsive behaviors. Impulsivity, failure to fully appreciate consequences of actions, and lack of cognitive development are factors that the Supreme Court has referenced. In striking down mandatory juvenile sentences without parole in *Miller v. Alabama*, the court explicitly noted adolescents' tendency toward immaturity, impetuosity, and irresponsibility. By early adulthood, perhaps around the age of 20, youth demonstrate advanced capacity for decision-making, yet they are not fully mature cognitively until their mid-twenties.[23]

The context of adolescent decision-making is also of critical importance. The quality of decisions and conduct after time for reflection and deliberation may approximate or even surpass those of adults. In his dissent in *Roper*, Justice Scalia argued that juveniles should be treated as adults, citing as an example the mature minor doctrine, which allowed for judicial bypass in medical decision-making involving abortion decisions. However, "hot cognition" circumstances that characterize much of the conduct involving youth that leads to court involvement implicate more reactive, impulsive, and peer-related behavior. Teens and late teens are the age group that is at the heart of spikes in car crashes (as reflected in car insurance rates), unintended pregnancies, drownings, attempted suicides, non-fatal self-inflicted injuries, and drug use and dependence, all

22. Haywood Burns Institute, *Los Angeles County: Youth Justice Reimagined* (Oct. 2020).
23. *Supra*, Judge Baker Guidance Center Report. at 8.

owing in no small part to the stage of adolescent brain development that emphasizes stimulation and immediacy while de-emphasizing self-control and executive function. A 16-year-old with an IQ of 160 is still a 16-year-old. This reality is illustrated by a story shared by one of my colleagues. When he confronted his Mensa-level son, who had been suspended from school after spontaneously jumping into a fight in the school cafeteria, my friend asked his son, "What were you thinking?" The son, now calm and composed hours after the event, wittily replied, "Father, you are assuming a fact not in evidence."

An invaluable primer in navigating this complicated landscape is a report published in January 2022 by the Center for Law Brain and Behavior (CLBB).[24] The document reflects the latest research and developmental neuroscience concerning adolescence, late adolescence, and emerging young adulthood. It is a must-read for attorneys who represent young people in all contexts. For purposes of its discussion, the report uses the following terms to describe young people of different ages: (1) *juveniles*: broadly persons between 13–17; (2) *early adolescents*: persons aged 10–13; (3) *middle adolescents*: persons aged 14–17; (4) *late adolescents* (some use the term *late teens* for this cohort): persons aged 18–21; and (5) *young adults:* persons aged 22–25. The report includes an extensive discussion of juvenile sentences without parole and provides guidance on practice and policy issues in other domains. It also includes an analysis of the age-crime curve, that is, the process of natural desistance and its application in critically important domains, including transfer to adult court, juvenile life without parole, life without parole, and mitigation in all contexts.

While it might seem counterintuitive, serious offending at young ages has limited prognostic value regarding future criminality. Psychological developmental experts such as Laurence Steinberg and Robert Kinscherff are educating judges, juries, and parole boards all across the country about the age-crime curve, desistance that occurs with maturation, and the reality that there are really no significant developmental differences between 17- and 18-year-old youth. There is no basis in science to draw a bright line ending juvenile court jurisdiction at 18.

---

24. Center for Law, Brain, and Behavior at Massachusetts General Hospital, *The Science of Late Adolescence: A Guide for Judges, Attorneys, and Policy Makers* (January 27, 2022), available at https://clbb.mgh.harvard.edu/white-paper-on-the-science-of-late-adolescence (accessed April 9, 2024).

In *Jones v. Mississippi*, the Supreme Court held that sentencing a juvenile to life without parole does not require a specific finding of "permanently incorrigible." The Court also declined to provide guidance regarding consideration of the so-called *Miller* factors, which the Court had previously determined to be relevant in the rare or uncommon circumstances when a juvenile life without parole determination would be appropriate. The five factors were a juvenile's age and immaturity; family and home environment; circumstances of the offense; that the youth might have been charged with a lesser offense if not for the incompetencies associated with youth, such as inability to deal with police or assist his or her attorneys; and the possibility of rehabilitation, including the role the juvenile had in the offense and the role of peers. The *Jones v. Mississippi* holding entailed a finding that discretionary decision-making permitting a sentencing court consider age and *Miller* factors if the court chose to do so sufficed. The decision almost certainly signals the end of further expansion of Supreme Court Eighth Amendment protections for juveniles. In abolishing mandatory juvenile life without parole, *Miller* had noted that such sentences should be uncommon because of the great difficulty noted in *Roper* and *Graham* of distinguishing between the juvenile offender whose crime reflects unfortunate yet transient immaturity, and the rare juvenile whose crime and conduct reflects irreparable corruption.

Miller allowed for the possibility of juvenile life without parole, but strongly suggested that sentencing decisions consider the factors previously discussed and consider how children are different than adults and how those differences counsel against irrevocable sentencing to a lifetime in prison. *Montgomery v. Louisiana*,[25] which applied *Miller* retroactively, suggested that it was impermissible to impose a juvenile life without parole sentence unless that person was the rare individual who exhibits such irretrievable depravity that rehabilitation is not possible. Advocates who had hoped this message would resonate in *Jones* now fear that with juvenile life without parole decisions being based on discretion, that "justice by geography" will result in inequitable outcomes and will exacerbate racial and ethnic disparities.

However, the post-*Jones* landscape may not be as bleak as some believe. The *Jones* case permits each state to make its own determination regarding the issue of juvenile life without parole, including the right to abolish the

25. 577 U.S. 190 (2016).

practice entirely. Simply stated, the Supreme Court sets the ground floor, but each jurisdiction can set their own ceiling. As noted in the CLBB report, the legal framework established in previous Supreme Court cases has been incorporated to varying degrees by some states in their statutory and case law and "offers at least the possibility for a more robust application of *Miller*." The focus of the *Miller* court on the concept of "transient immaturity" also offers a way of asserting protection of young offenders in individual cases at the trial and sentencing phases and upon appellate review. The CLBB report also notes that this type of framing may also encourage prosecutors that the *Miller* approach remains viable for pursuing expansion of categorical protections to age 18 and beyond, and perhaps for raising the age of full criminal responsibility by raising the age range of juvenile court jurisdiction.

Recognizing the realities of transient immaturity and incorporating developmental science and research into practice will have beneficial results. This type of framing may also encourage prosecutors to consider research-based diversion and community-based intervention programs as alternatives to traditional charging decisions and sentencing recommendations. If science and research are applied to practice, states may also reconsider transfer hearing models and mandatory sentencing. An example of this occurred in 2014, when the Iowa State Supreme Court abolished mandatory sentences for juveniles who had been transferred to their criminal system.[26] In addition to applying this research to inform the scope of *Miller* hearings, the CLBB report's conclusion that there is not scientific justification to draw a bright line of juvenile court jurisdiction at 18 may inspire states to revitalize raise-the-age bills.

While some states allow for extended youthful offender jurisdiction, to date only Vermont has explicitly raised the age by phasing in 18- to 20-year-old adolescents over a three-year period.[27] Examples of states that have extended juvenile court jurisdiction to a new age for enumerated offenses include California (CA Welfare and Institution Code 707(b), extending jurisdiction to age 25) and Utah (Utah Code Section 80-6-605, extending jurisdiction to age 25 for certain felonies committed by youth 14 and older). Massachusetts has enacted a youthful offender law that extends juvenile court jurisdiction to age 21 and allows for jury trials of 12 persons for alleged offenses by youth 14 and older who have been charged

26. State v. Lyle, 854 N.W. 2d 378 (2014).
27. VT. Stat. Ann. Tit. 33 secs. 5102, 5103, 5104 (West 2020).

with crimes that threaten or result in the infliction of serious bodily harm (G.L. c. 119, sec. 58). The Washington D.C. Comprehensive Youth Justice Act makes a person eligible for parole for any crime after serving a minimum term of 15 years, if they were between the ages of 18–25 at the time of their offenses. While this law does not pertain to youth below the age of 18, it recognizes "the diminished culpability of juveniles and persons under the age of 25 and recognizes the hallmarks of youth, including immaturity, impetuosity, and the failure to appreciate consequences" (601, D.C. Official Code Sec. 403.03). On the front end of the system, states should also rethink the minimum age of juvenile court jurisdiction given the developmental research that indicates that many who are 15 and younger may present serious issues concerning the cognitive capacity to be competent to stand trial.[28]

A report from the National Juvenile Justice Network, *Raising the Minimum Age for Prosecuting Children*, notes that as of January 21, 2021, over half the states in the U.S. had no minimum age of juvenile court jurisdiction.[29] In the juvenile justice-by-geography world, there is great variability regarding this subject. New Hampshire sets the minimum age at 13; Massachusetts at 12 for all cases; California, Utah, and Delaware for enumerated offenses; Nebraska at 11; and 15 states at age 10. Two states, North Carolina and Washington, have set the age at 12. This patchwork quilt is contrasted by European guidelines and the UN Convention on the Rights of the Child, which recommend that the minimum age of court jurisdiction should be 14. The ABA passed a resolution in August of 2021 urging all jurisdictions to raise the minimum age to 14 (ABA Res. 505). Justice by geography is also reflected in different ages and statutory schemes set by states regarding determination of transfer of children and adolescents to criminal court. This subject is directly related to competency to stand trial (CST), a topic that was thoughtfully addressed by Dr. Antoinette Kavanaugh in the first edition of this book (Chapter 8, "Juveniles," pp. 135–136) and the discussion of whether children and preteens have factual and rational understanding of court process and can communicate effectively with their attorneys as required by *Dusky v. U.S.*[30]

---

28. See e.g., Thomas Grisso, Laurence Steinberg, Jennifer Woolard, and Elizabeth Cauffman, *Juvenile Competence to Stand Trial: A Comparison of Adolescents' Capacities as Trial Defendants* (Law and Human Behavior, Sept. 2003)

29. National Juvenile Justice Network, *Raising the Minimum Age for Prosecuting Children* (January 22, 2020).

30. 362 U.S. 402 (1960).

I have written about the importance of the mantra Let's Follow the Science[31] in discussing the imperative of using data, research, and evidence-based practice. The importance of applying developmental research and science to policy and practice is supported by the growing evidence that promoting community-based programming in lieu of traditional carceral isolation models is a better model in supporting positive youth development and the socially connective tissue of family and neighborhood while reducing recidivism at significantly less cost. This perspective is reflected in a study commissioned by the Office of Juvenile Justice and Delinquency Prevention (OJJDP), *Reforming Juvenile Justice: A Developmental Approach*.[32] The traditional juvenile justice model of "heavy reliance on containment and control removes youth from their families, peer groups, and neighborhoods, the social context of their future lives."[33] "In general, multi-faceted community-based interventions show greater reductions in arrested than institutional programs."[34]

In discussing recidivism and the age-crime curve, the CLBB report notes that the highest rate of offending occurs in the late teen years, peaking at around age 19 or 20, after which criminal offending declines precipitously. One of the most consistent findings in developmental research concerns the age-crime curve. The report corroborates and confirms the findings of Edward Mulvey's seminal *Pathways to Desistance* study.[35] The natural desistance that comes with maturation and becoming older is perhaps the most effective crime prevention treatment we have. The process is accelerated if accompanied by implementation of polices that promote positive youth development and include a nurturing adult or adults. In this context, an attorney who has developed a trusting relationship with a client qualifies as a nurturing adult. An example of natural desistance as an effective treatment concerns adolescent sex offending. According to experts such as Frank DiCataldo, the most effective treatment in this context is maturation, as reflected in exceedingly low recidivism rates for children and adolescents.[36] Given the malleability of adolescent personality,

31. Jay Blitzman, *Let's Follow the Science on Late Adolescence*, 37(3) Crim. Just. (2022).

32. Richard Bonnie et al., National Research Council 2013 (Committee on Assessing Juvenile justice, Division of Behavioral and Social Sciences and Education, Washington D.C.).

33. *Id.* at 3.

34. *Id.*

35. Edward P. Mulvey, Carol A. Schubert, and Alex Piquero, *Pathways to Desistance* (OJJDP, 2015).

36. Frank DiCataldo, *The Perversion of Youth* (New York University Press, 2019).

DiCataldo's research questions the use of relapse-reduction models used for adults and the need for juvenile sex offender registration.

In terms of policy, the CLBB report suggests that given lower recidivism rates in more rehabilitative juvenile systems, it might make sense to treat late teens or late adolescents in the juvenile court or develop more rehabilitative criminal models, as has occurred in Europe. In Massachusetts for example, the recidivism rate for youth leaving the state's DYS system is approximately 25 percent, as contrasted to over twice that number in the criminal district courts. National Center for State Court data indicates that within three years, people leaving Massachusetts jails and prison will be rearraigned.[37]

The evidence that there are no developmental differences between a 17-year-old and an 18-year-old was reflected by the Washington State Supreme Court's decision to extend the scope of *Miller* hearings to include youth accused of murder between the ages of 18–20.[38] The state of Michigan took a similar position on July 28, 2022, in extending *Miller* hearings in that state to include 18-year-old youths.[39] On January 11, 2024, the Massachusetts Supreme Judicial Court went where no court or state has gone before in abolishing life without parole for 18- to 20-year-old individuals who had committed murder. The Washington and Michigan decisions abolished mandatory life without parole but still allow for discretionary life without parole sentencing decisions. The Massachusetts decision paralleled what Massachusetts had done for youth under the age of 18 in *Commonwealth v. Diatchenko* (2013). The Massachusetts Supreme Judicial Court relied on its interpretation of cruel and unusual punishment. This decision signals a potential sea change and is perhaps the most robust application of applying an appropriate developmental lens to issues regarding late teens and emerging adults. The case also has implications for other issues, including the range and scope of juvenile court jurisdiction, transfer, and mandatory sentencing.

---

37. *MA DOC Three-Year Recidivism Rates: 2016 Release Cohort*, Mass. Exec. Off. of Pub. Safety & Sec., https://www.mass.gov/doc/three-year-recidivism-rates-2016-release-cohort/download; *Justice Reinvestment in Massachusetts: Third Presentation* (July 18, 2016), https://csgjusticecenter.org/publications/justice-reinvestment-in-massachusetts-third-presentation/.

38. *In re Personal Restraint of Kurtis William Monschke*, No. 96772-5 (Wash.) consolidated with *In re Personal Restraint of Dwayne Earl Bartholomew*, No. 96733-33, https://www.courts.wa.gov/opinions/pdf/967735.pdf.

39. People v. Parks, Docket. No. 162086.

J.D.B. v. North Carolina

In *J.D.B. v. North Carolina*, the Supreme Court applied the chronological fact of age to juvenile *Miranda* analysis regarding the issue of custodial detention in the context of a 13-year-old child questioned by police and educators in school. In the first edition of this book, Dr. Kavanaugh thoughtfully reviewed the literature of Thomas Grisso and others indicating that generally, 15-year-old youth do not understand their *Miranda* rights as well as older youth. She also cited data indicating that 84 percent of youth in the justice system between ages 13–17 displayed at least ten misconceptions related to the adversarial nature of interrogations. These findings are related to the abstract concepts and polysyllabic language contained in the *Miranda* warnings.

Concerns about whether statements attributed to children and youth are made knowingly and voluntarily are exacerbated by questionable law enforcement tactics related to minimization of consequences and using misinformation during interrogations. It is also important to note the interplay in the *J.D.B.* case of law enforcement and school personnel. While a school official has not been traditionally seen as a state actor who is obligated to provide *Miranda* warnings, the landscape changes appreciably if a police officer is involved in directing or participating in the interview. This issue is also related to school-based searches, where the traditional standard of reasonable suspicion to conduct a school-based search[40] may be elevated to a probable cause standard if a school resource officer or law enforcement officer is involved.

J.D.B. may also have wider implications. How do you apply the traditional requirement of whether "a reasonable person" would perceive they are in custody to a 13-year-old? The case discusses age as a factor in the objective calculus of custodial detention, but is a reasonable 13-year-old an oxymoron? Advocates are exploring ways to develop arguments that apply developmental research to support a "reasonable juvenile" or "reasonable adolescent" construct. This thinking is relevant in attacking the legal orthodoxy concerning the ability to form intent in multiple contexts and could affect issues such as felony murder, joint venture, and the ability to form specific intent.

---

40. T.L.O. v. New Jersey (469 U.S. 1985).

Animating the Narrative

Thinking thematically about theory of the case and storytelling are important tools for any lawyer. In this context, in addition to mastery of the facts of the case, an attorney has to know how to illuminate their client's story. This maxim is particularly important in addressing the nature of an alleged offender as well as the nature of the offense and connecting developmental research to individual narratives. As has been discussed, neuroscientists and developmental researchers have taught us that the brain is developing until age 25 or beyond. Adverse child experiences and trauma may prolong this maturational process. But science is probabilistic. How do you animate your client's story and ensure that fact finders consider the nature of the alleged offender as well as the nature of the alleged offense? This entails connecting the research to individual history and the use of experts.

Virtually every state has some form of indigent court cost act or mechanism to have your client evaluated. Ex parte motions for indigent clients are recommended in lieu of court-ordered forensic evaluation to avoid burden shifting. Seeking funds for social workers for purposes of psychosocial assessments is also important. This type of assistance is relevant in all realms, including pretrial preparation, transfer hearings, raising competency to stand trial and criminal responsibility issues, motions to suppress, specific intent cases, as well as in sentencing and mitigation.

Trial lawyers must connect the developmental research to the realities of their cases. In some instances, it may be necessary to proffer multiple experts. Courts are reluctant to permit an expert to opine about the propensities of an individual unless he or she has interviewed and evaluated the client. An expert can educate the tribunal about the science of adolescent development and general information regarding the age-crime curve, natural desistance, and hot and cold cognition, but a second expert who has interviewed the client and conducted objective and projective testing may be necessary in order to introduce salient information concerning an individual client. The admissibility and scope of expert testimony will be informed by motions in limine and appellate decisions regarding the line between expert assistance and ultimate issue. For example, in *Massachusetts v. Okoro* (SJC MA 2015), an expert called to testify in an effort to mitigate the specific intent required to sustain a second-degree murder conviction was limited to testifying about the cognitive capacities of the adolescent he had evaluated. However, he was precluded from testifying more generally about propensities and capabilities of adolescents more globally.

Adolescence is a time of experiment and change. Personality is still malleable and developing. We all grow and change, especially children and adolescents, which supports Bryan Stevenson's observation that each one of us is more than the worst thing that we have ever done. Dramatists know how to tell this story. When I discuss this concept, I often invoke the parole hearing depicted in the movie *Shawshank Redemption*. In the film, Red, played by Morgan Freeman, after serving 40 years of a life sentence is asked whether he feels as if he has been rehabilitated. He responds that "There's not a day goes by that I don't feel regret … I look back on the way I was then: a young, stupid kid who committed that terrible crime. I want to try and talk some sense to him, tell him the way things are. But I can't. That kid's long gone, and this old man is all that's left. I got to live with that…." I discussed this movie with inmates at M.C.I. Concord in Massachusetts in March of 2020, shortly before the institution was closed to visitors because of the pandemic. I was speaking at a restorative justice session that was attended by about 65 inmates. A significant percentage were doing life for murder, some had committed their crimes when they were 18 or older, and some had been behind the walls for many years. When I asked the group if they had seen the film, virtually every hand was raised, and I knew what their favorite scene was. Each one of us has a story to tell. Advocates are needed to share these narratives in order for all of us to live in a world of balanced and proportionate accountability and equity.

The fragility of this moment and issues related to justice by geography were underscored by a recent Washington Supreme Court case, the same court that, as previously noted, had extended the scope of *Miller* hearings in the state to include the 18- to 20-year-old age group. In a 5–4 opinion on September 8, 2022, a year after holding that virtual life sentences (a sentence beyond the average life span before parole eligibility) were questionable, the court upheld a 61-year sentence for two first-degree murders committed by the defendant at age 17.[41] The court had previously seemed to have held no juvenile offender could receive a sentence of 46 years or longer. Each state designs the contours of its own system. Nevada has determined that juveniles who have committed murders are parole

41. Washington v. Anderson (No. 97890-5, Wash. Sept. 8, 2022).

eligible at age 15. In Nebraska the age is 40.[42] Now more than ever, there is a need to apply a developmentally appropriate lens to these issues.

• • •

Hon. Jay D. Blitzman (retired) served as the First Justice of the Massachusetts Middlesex Juvenile Court. Prior to his judicial appointment he was a public defender who was a cofounder and the first director of the Roxbury Youth Advocacy Project, an interdisciplinary public defender's unit that was the template for the creation of the statewide Massachusetts Youth Advocacy Division. He was also a cofounder of Citizens for Juvenile Justice (CFJJ). Since his judicial retirement, he has consulted for the Sixth Amendment Center (6AC), served as the interim executive director of Massachusetts Advocates for Children (MAC), and serves MAC as an emeritus policy advisor.

Jay consults on juvenile, criminal, and child welfare issues; mentors attorneys; and holds teaching positions at Harvard Law School (trial advocacy), Northeastern Law School (juvenile law) and Boston College Law School (the cradle-to-prison pipeline). Jay is also on the faculty at the Center for Law, Brain, and Behavior focusing on late teen and emerging adult issues (CLBB–MGH and Harvard Medical School). He also was an affiliate of the Boston University Center for Antiracist Research. Jay writes and presents frequently on a wide array of issues related to advancing equity and deconstructing the cradle to prison pipeline.

Jay's recent publications include *Let's Follow the Science on Late Adolescence* (ABA Criminal Justice, 2022), *Shutting Down the School to Prison Pipeline* (ABA Human Rights, 2021), *Open The Doors* (*Mass. L. Rev.* 2021), *Justice for Some: A Tale of Two Americas* (Civic Right Institute Juvenile Justice Update, 2020), and *Deconstructing the School to Prison Pipeline* (*BBA Journal*, 2018), as well as chapters in the ABA's annual publication *The State of Criminal Justice* beginning in 2018 through 2024. *Commonwealth Magazine* has published a series of Jay's opinion pieces on subjects including deconstructing the cradle-to-prison pipeline, raising the age of juvenile court jurisdiction, removing police from schools, expanding expungement, and opening the doors to closed juvenile court sessions.

---

42. Josh Rovner, *Juvenile Life Without Parole: An Overview*, Sentencing Project Policy Brief (May 24, 2021).

Judge Blitzman serves on the boards of directors of Discovering Justice and the Massachusetts Mental Health Advisory Committee, and is a member of the advisory boards of Citizens for Juvenile Justice (CFJJ), United Teen Equality Center, a youth empowerment organization based in Lowell, Massachusetts and Northeastern Law School's Cradle to Prison and *Salus Populi* (Social Determinants of Public Health). Jay is also a fellow of Massachusetts Advocates for Justice, working with More Than Words (MTW). In 2023, he was the first recipient of CFJJ's Youth Juvenile Justice Icon award and also received the 2019 ABA Livingston Hall Juvenile Justice Award. Other recognition includes being the first person to receive the MBA Juvenile and Child Welfare Section Award, the 2023 Boston College Law School Holland Lifetime Achievement Award, the Lowell 100 Award, the Judge Paul Chernoff Servants of Justice Award, and the Rebecca Pries Adolescent Consultation Services Indispensable Friend Award. Massachusetts' public defender system annually presents the Jay Blitzman Award for Youth Advocacy.

Complete citations are available from the author upon request.

Chapter

13

Mental Health Courts and Other Diversion Options

Katherine Bujak and Jeffrey Berman

There are approximately 4,000 problem-solving courts in the United States. Of that number, approximately 450 call themselves mental health or behavioral health courts. As the United States grapples with strategies to deal with people with mental disabilities who are charged with crimes, problem-solving courts of various sorts are frequently praised as one of the many solutions to a complex societal problem.

The following chapter by criminal defense lawyers Katherine Bujak and Jeffery Berman is an invaluable guide to mental health courts. Mental health courts, as described by attorneys Bujak and Berman, are far more than a diversionary option for the client with a mental disability. Indeed, mental health courts require an understanding of who the client is, if that particular court is a good fit for the client, if the client can succeed in a mental health court, and what the advantages and potential dangers are. The chapter discusses possible ethical issues for the criminal defense lawyer representing someone in a problem-solving court, such as the lawyer's role as a member of the team and the right of a client against self-incrimination.

Additionally, the chapter serves as an introduction to other kinds of problem-solving courts such as community courts, drug courts, reentry courts, and sex trafficking courts. These courts, because of the nature of the population they serve, encompass mental health issues, and may serve as another option for a client who would benefit from a diversionary option. Problem-solving courts have existed for over 30 years. As such, there is now a good deal of data, both objective and observational, about their effectiveness. The chapter acknowledges some of the shortcomings of problem-solving courts, such as the fact that they may exclude certain categories of offenders and that prosecutors may serve as gatekeepers. The chapter concludes by embracing the successes of problem-solving courts and arguing for wider support and expansion, with a clarion call for criminal defense lawyers to quell fear-mongering by educating other members of the Bar as well as the general public.

• • •

Criminal courts across the United States are reckoning with the reality that punishment-driven prosecution, and the expansion of the carceral system, do *not* increase public safety. Research overwhelmingly proves that the harm inflicted by mass incarceration vastly outweighs the harm caused by the criminal behavior alleged, not only for the individual accused, but for society as a whole. Incarceration has been proven to *increase* recidivism, whereas successful diversion *reduces* future criminal legal involvement by half. Incarceration is also fundamentally more expensive and less cost-effective than the use of problem-solving courts. Not only does it cost significantly more to imprison than to treat, the use of diversion actually grows quarterly employment rates by almost 50% over a decade.

Importantly, incarceration and mental illness, cognitive disabilities, and substance use disorders have also had a historically disparate impact on Black, Indigenous, and People of Color; those who face issues of poverty and homelessness; and those who identify as LGBTQIA. This racial, economic, and discriminatory injustice to historically disempowered members of our communities is diminished by the use of specialized courts that directly address the underlying issues that precipitate these groups' overrepresentation in the criminal legal system.

Criminal court systems across the country were overwhelmed with increased arrests and detainees even prior to global pandemic interruptions. Such backlogs caused serious issues of capacity in the courts. Diverting cases wherein the accused is deemed to pose little risk or where the charges are less serious is a proven and effective way to conserve court resources for the most serious cases. Our criminal legal system is evolving so that those involved now have options other than mandatory jail or prison when eligible for diversion from the carceral system to a problem-solving court. Currently there are diversion courts in all 50 states.

We discuss mental health courts as well as other diversion options in a book about representing clients with mental disabilities in light of the science as to the root causes of "criminality." Approximately one in five Americans have symptoms and/or diagnoses of a mental health condition, and too many do not have access to or receive meaningful, if any, treatment. This number is expected to rise as the effects of the still-ongoing COVID-19 pandemic are fully appreciated. Clinicians anticipate the creation of new, or exacerbation of already-existing, mental health issues due to anxiety, depression, or trauma from fear of—or infection with—the virus, as well as cognitive issues due to physiological damage in addition to the effect of the individual and collective grief over lives, livelihood, and lifestyles lost due to the pandemic.

Significantly, in many states, jails and prisons house more people with mental illness than psychiatric hospitals. Yet the largely inadequate treatment received in carceral settings, combined with widespread violence and drug use there, serve to inflict further harm and exacerbate these illnesses. Thus, when a person is released from incarceration, it is not only after estrangement from their community and services, but with the trauma of the incarceration itself, the stigma and collateral consequences of convictions, and frequently without the benefits of reentry support such as housing or programming in place.

Immense voids exist in addressing mental and physical health, education, housing, fair employment, the ongoing harms of discrimination and racism, and generational poverty in our communities. Substantial reductions in funding for social services, public health, and mental health were already problematic pre-pandemic; the situation is even more dire now. The result is poor mental and physical health outcomes, as well as greater risk of involvement with the criminal legal system. As most criminal behavior is now understood to be a consequence of systemic failures, diversion courts seek to focus on filling these critical gaps in societal care to tend to the individual and protect public safety.

What Are Problem-Solving Courts?

Also known as diversion or specialized courts, problem-solving courts generally work by having dedicated courtrooms and a docket tailored to whatever problem the court is tasked with "solving." They endeavor to address specific societal lapses, public safety, due process, and the individual needs of the accused (and where applicable, the complainant), through "therapeutic jurisprudence."

Most of these courts are structured with a model of collaboration of an interdisciplinary team, including judges, lawyers, clinicians, and peer specialists. Treatment is individualized to address what brought the accused before the court, while public safety is safeguarded through screening and eligibility criteria (and where relevant, ensuring the needs and wishes of a complainant are met). Unlike traditional criminal court practice where a judge rarely reviews a case once the sentence is imposed, in most diversion courts sentences are deferred and the court retains oversight and jurisdiction over the accused.

In general, a specialized court requires accountability of the client throughout via intensive monitoring; placement in programming when clinically recommended; open communication in court between the judge, prosecutor, defense attorney, clinicians, and the client about progress or setbacks; and a system of graduated sanctions and incentives. The goal is for the participant to emerge from their involvement with the criminal legal system with little to no barriers to reentry, an improved quality of life, and without conditions leading to reoffending. This is all ultimately to the benefit of the community as a whole. Specific diversion courts differ in mechanics depending on what issues they seek to "solve" and will be discussed later in further detail.

We focus primarily on mental health and drug courts here, but also discuss other diversion options such as community court, youth courts, and sex trafficking courts. While not purely diversionary, we also examine the specialty courts of domestic violence courts, sex offender courts, and parole reentry courts, which follow problem-solving court models. A review of veterans court will be not be discussed here, but will be in the following chapter (Chapter 14, "Veterans Courts").

Mental Health Courts

Mental health courts were initially created to address the high rates of mental illness among incarcerated populations. They were also developed with the understanding that continuing to impose jail and prison on people with mental disabilities, rather than offering treatment, is inhumane. It leaves the urgent needs of individuals unmet, and the resultant recidivism ultimately works to the detriment of public safety. In practice, these specialty courts tend to focus on rehabilitating and treating the accused, improving their outcomes by addressing any potential barriers to community reengagement, and ameliorating their quality of life. Mental health courts vary somewhat from state to state but most have the same basic dynamics of ascertaining whether diversion is a good fit for a specific client, having an interdisciplinary and highly supervised approach, interfacing between all stakeholders, and a system of graduated sanctions and rewards, culminating in the graduation of a client when they have fulfilled their mandate or termination from participation if they do not.

Not every client will be a suitable fit for mental health court. Lawyers must first consider whether their client is eligible for a treatment-based disposition. Most states require mental health court participants to be at least 18 years old, charged with a felony, and have a diagnosed "serious mental illness." Mental health courts typically require a nexus between the applicant's diagnosis and their involvement with the criminal legal system. Clients generally must enter a knowing and voluntary plea, show insight into their mental health condition, and be open to treatment. In most jurisdictions, there is also the requirement that the local district attorney's office consent to the client's participation.

While many mental health courts exclude "violent" felonies, there is a greater push for charge inclusiveness. This is based on the successes of courts that admit those and studies that show that participants with violent charges are just as successful in treatment as those with nonviolent charges. Many mental health courts have evolved to follow the evidence-based practice of assessing charges and criminal histories on a case-by-case basis. Additionally, more misdemeanor mental health courts currently exist. "Serious mental illness" is often construed to mean conditions such as depression, anxiety, bipolar disorder, schizoaffective disorder, and schizophrenia. However, many mental health courts are refining their practices in expanding what diagnoses make a client eligible. As such, a greater spectrum of mental illnesses as well as intellectual and cognitive disabilities are acceptable diagnoses in some jurisdictions. Clients currently deemed incapacitated are not considered able to enter a knowing and voluntary plea, and thus cannot participate unless and until they are restored to competency. Clients with brain injuries rendering them not fit to proceed to trial are similarly disqualified. Additionally, a client's mandated "treatment" may vary depending on their assessed needs and likely includes medication if prescribed.

Advocacy for clients with mental illness and cognitive or other issues often requires overcoming existing stigma of and prejudice against such conditions. When the prosecutor or judge seeks to thwart a client's eligibility based on "violence" or concerns for public safety, lawyers should highlight salient changes in circumstance, such as when the client's current status differs from that of the time when the violent acts were alleged. For example, you can contextualize that the "violence" was a result of a trauma response, or a self-medicating drug-induced psychosis, or a lack of stability at the time of the incident, and that your client is currently stable due to medication, housing, and treatment needs being met. You may also contend that previously your client was estranged from their supports but they are now intact, or if from an older case in their history, that the client has "aged-out," and so on. Lawyers can also use data-driven research about the lack of sufficient mental health treatment in the carceral system, share information as to how incarceration is more dangerous for clients with mental health or cognitive issues, and disseminate the truth that people with mental illness are rarely the perpetrators but rather more likely the victims of violent crimes. In this way the court or prosecutor can be assured that the public safety risk is far outweighed by the public safety harm done by barring the client from mental health court. You can also cite social science studies showing that society suffers when clients with mental health and cognitive issues have their challenges exacerbated while incarcerated; experience more trauma from the carceral experience; and then are released back into the community without stable housing, treatment options, and community resources in place.

Importantly, advocates referring clients with mental disabilities to mental health courts should be intentional with the language they use, and always endeavor to use "person-first language." For example, instead of saying "My client *is* mentally ill," say "My client *has* bipolar disorder" (a good way to remember this is that one would never say "My client *is* a heart condition"). Attorneys should also eradicate derogatory words for clients with those challenges from their vocabulary. This is not about political correctness, but rather effective assistance of counsel. When we respect our client's humanity, we set the tone for other court players to take the same approach, and in so doing improve chances of attaining a better outcome for the client.

Lawyers who represent clients with mental disabilities should have at least a basic comprehension of such issues to effectively assist clients with mental health challenges. We should educate ourselves about this in the same way that we do about immigration issues for clients who are noncitizens, or about collateral consequences of criminal convictions to a client's civil rights. We will then be able to immediately assess whether our client has a mental illness or cognitive or intellectual disability that would make them eligible for a mental-health-based diversion, and know when to bring in a specialist or clinician. Sometimes courts provide defense counsel with a prescreening letter documenting substance use or mental, intellectual, or cognitive disabilities at intake. When that is not available, clues may be found in a client's behavior, affect, or appearance during their interview; their responses to targeted inquiries about whether they have prior psychiatric hospitalizations, are prescribed psychotropic medication, or have clinicians, doctors, or therapists whom they see on an ongoing basis; and notations on their criminal history showing their discharge to forensic hospitals during incarceration or dismissals due to their lack of mental fitness in states with those practices.

In general, be aware that certain diagnoses present specific challenges in communicating with clients. It is helpful to memorialize conversations in writing, and expect that you will need to redirect a client's attention, repeat information, exercise patience and compassionate listening, and not take things personally when your client is very ill. Notably, at times, practitioners will need to request accommodation for clients with these issues under the American with Disabilities Act (ADA). Some clients will need longer adjournments between court dates to avoid unnecessarily retraumatizing them, or to ensure noninterruption of treatment services. Some clients will need morning-only calendar calls when their condition includes a state of confusion, anxiety, aggression, or the inability to follow directions that occurs in the late afternoon and through the night, also known as "sundowning." Similarly, the effects of medication can dictate when would be the best time to have someone appear in court; for example, with methadone, there is a period when people "nod off." Clients with complex trauma or post-traumatic stress disorder might need permission to wait in the hallway on court dates, or to sit in such a way so their back is against a wall as opposed to a place of ingress or egress to avoid triggering panic attacks or hypervigilance. Importantly, if a client is incarcerated, you must ensure they receive mental health assessment and medical attention, and in jurisdictions with specialized housing for clients needing a higher level of mental health care, request that the judge order this.

It is necessary to know the difference between carceral housing options in the locality in which you practice, and if your client is not incapacitated, to ensure their voice is heard with respect to this. If your client is suicidal, and has expressed overt and specific plans to die by suicide, it is incumbent upon the attorney to request suicide watch. Such placements are far more restrictive than other jail or prison housing, and you must also explain this to your client. It is also crucial to manage your client's expectations and keep them informed as to what will happen on a given court date. In many jurisdictions, the process from intake to commencing treatment by a mental health court can be very lengthy, so ensure your client is aware of this. Moreover, participation in most mental health courts ranges from six months to two years, and your client should be informed of this at the outset. It can also be daunting for a client with these issues to be in court generally, and sometimes it helps to describe the layout and explain the mechanics and procedure of the court process in detail.

When representing a client with mental health, cognitive, or intellectual challenges, attorneys should also have them assessed by clinical experts such as social workers, psychologists, and psychiatrists. This is helpful especially when your client does not have a current working diagnosis as needed for referral to the mental health specialty court. When your client permits, seek information from collateral sources such as family and friends, and any agency or hospital that might have a client's educational, medical, psychiatric, and other records. To that end, lawyers should ensure the client signs a Health Insurance Portability and Accountability Act (HIPAA) waiver as soon as possible to facilitate access. Attorneys are always bound by rules of confidentiality and cannot share information without client consent. Also, if a client is incapacitated, their signature on a HIPAA waiver can be challenged as not knowing and involuntary. Moreover, unless a danger to themselves, attorneys must be careful of the ethical quagmire of putting a client's mental health at issue if the client does not authorize this.

In localities where the prosecutor is the gatekeeper for mental health court, it is also important to educate them about your client's diagnosis as soon as practicable following intake to avoid unnecessary delays in getting them processed and referred. Where the court alone is empowered to make the decision, it should be made aware at the earliest opportunity. Providing psychosocial reports or psychological evaluations prepared by a clinical expert is an extremely helpful tool for enlightening others.

Most often, the prosecutor or court requires your client to be screened before allowing them to participate in mental health court. This could take the form of an interview by a prosecutor's office, and additionally through forensic assessment ordered by the judge. Mental health courts routinely require clients to sign waivers of confidentiality, so this must be explained to your client. Additionally, it is essential to prepare your client to discuss prior issues, events, and trauma with strangers. Your client should know to be forthright about their mental health issue, show an openness to treatment (including medication, if prescribed), and understand that besides assessing their treatment needs, the evaluator will also be trying to discern whether they pose a danger to themselves or others. Clients should be prepared to respond to questions from those screening them, who may seek assurances as to whether they would remain on medication and in treatment, and, if there was prior noncompliance, how they could trust that this time would be different. The client will also be asked about the instant case and should be prepared to take responsibility. Unless they have no memory due to disassociation or psychosis, advise your client that the honest answer is the best response. Finally, some screeners ask questions typical of job interviews, such as where the client sees themselves in five or ten years. You do not want your client to appear too coached or to have canned replies, but you do want them to be prepared in light of the fact that depending on their diagnosis, unexpected stress may trigger other psychological distress leading to their appearing uncooperative or belligerent to the screeners. Endeavor to appear at this evaluation with your client to safeguard your client from harm and ensure the process goes smoothly. When sensitive topics are broached during the assessment, be mindful of whether your client is being retraumatized. If this occurs, request a break, that the interview be resumed on another day, or whether your client can provide this information differently. For example, if in a psychosocial report or medical or other records, offer that, or request that you ask the questions to elicit the information they seek.

Attorneys should also equip their clients for direct communication with the judge, prosecutor, and clinical staff in court. While advocates must always be mindful of their ethical duties to protect their client from self-incrimination at all stages of the criminal legal process, they will routinely be required to interface with other stakeholders on the record as a condition of their participation in this specialized court. It is helpful for lawyers to preview what your client might say prior to their addressing the court, prosecutor, or clinicians. Especially when a client is still being stabilized, their right to be heard in the manner in which they wish to express themselves must be balanced with your protecting their right to not incriminate themselves or endanger their termination from the mental health court.

Once a client has been found eligible and screened, the next step is for the clinical staff to devise a treatment plan. Depending on the needs identified during the assessment, the plan could require the client to be placed at a residential treatment facility or in the community—at a supportive shelter, with family or friends, or at home while enrolled in outpatient services. The treatment plan will outline the goals sought, specify the therapies and programming for the client, as well as the providers of that treatment. Additionally, this plan will recommend continuation of medications that are prescribed, as well as their dosage. Treatment plans can include a client being assigned a team of professionals who will assist them and supervise them daily, as well as individual and group therapies. You should inform your client as to the intensity and level of intrusion of treatment. Some localities allow the input from the nonclinical staff, but many rightly leave the science to those who practice it.

As the defense attorney, you must review the treatment plan and share any concerns about it with clinicians based on your specific knowledge of your client, as you do not want to set your client up for failure. For example, if your client struggles in groups of people, you can advocate for more individual verses large group therapy. You can also ensure they know of your client's community support and the level of supervision and assistance they would receive if permitted to live at home. If your jurisdiction does not follow evidence-based best practices, you could also advocate for the use of trauma-informed care, clinicians being empowered to devise treatment plans, and harm reduction practices. Clients new to medication should be advised that they are not always easy to take; often there are side effects such as weight gain, and for some, lowered self-esteem and depression. If your client prefers to not take medication, it is worth suggesting alternative therapies, but be mindful that if prescribed, courts almost always require medication compliance.

Once the treatment plan is in place, your client may sometimes immediately be placed and begin treatment. In virtually every jurisdiction a plea or plea agreement must be executed first. These closely resemble traditional "repleader" agreements, specifying the plea to which a client will admit guilt, the sentence that is to be deferred, and the charge and sentence the client will receive upon completion of all phases of treatment delineated by the court. In many instances clients will end up with a misdemeanor and time served; in some cases, the charges are dismissed entirely. In more rare instances, they might end up with a felony conviction and time served or probation. As defense counsel, you must negotiate the terms of the plea, zealously advocating for a lesser charge and sentence as you would in any plea bargain negotiation. Critically, if a prosecutor requests plea to the top charge in mental health court, but there had been a pre–mental health court offer of a lesser charge, argue that your client should not face a worse outcome simply because they have mental health, cognitive, or intellectual disabilities.

There has been a recent movement to allow participation in diversion without a guilty plea, and some states have codified this. Detractors may claim that this removes both the court's leverage and your client's accountability. However, not requiring a guilty plea in order to be allowed to participate in treatment is proven to avoid the coercive aspects inherent in that, as well as sparing a client from terrible collateral consequences, such as triggering dire immigration actions (including a client's deportation), creating issues of employment or licensing eligibility, or the stigma and difficulties of navigating housing, employment, and the world in general with a felony conviction. All of those serve as barriers to your client's stability in the community and lead to a greater likelihood of recidivism.

Once the client is in treatment, they will come back to court periodically to update the court on their progress. Attorneys should ensure the client is prepared for the high level of supervision by the court and treatment staff throughout their participation in mental health court as well as the system of graduated sanctions and rewards. When clients do well—meaning, they remain active and engaged in treatment, are compliant with medication, and test negative for any mandated toxicology screenings (always required if a client has a dual diagnosis of a mental health condition and chemical addiction)—they often receive "rewards" such as advancement to the next phase of diversion, further privileges within their programs, certificates of completion, and public commendation. If a client is noncompliant with mandates, courts impose "sanctions." These range from essay-writing assignments, to suspension or removal of privileges, to incarceration for fixed periods of time, and in cases of rearrest and new indictments, ejection from mental health court and sentencing upon the original plea. Where not codified, advocates should demand due process for any sanctions and request to be allowed to present evidence that counters or extenuates the claims on which the client is being sanctioned. When that is not possible, attorneys should endeavor to negotiate a lesser sanction using any available mitigation arguments. It is important to remind the court and prosecutor that "relapse is part of the recovery process," and to educate them as to the forms relapse might take in someone with mental illness or cognitive or intellectual disabilities.

If your client successfully navigates their way through the phases of mental health court, they will graduate. In some places this is a very informal process with the top charge or case being dismissed on the record; in others, all stakeholders are given an opportunity to make statements of commendation, including the client, before the matter is disposed of officially per the plea agreement.

Mental health courts may be codified by statute or exist by creation of the prosecutor's office or the court administration. When a mental health court statute is in place, it makes it possible to safeguard against stigmatization, arbitrary rejection, punishment, and expulsion. Such laws can address issues of inequity depending on locality, and make it more likely that diversion is evenly applied across the state. Codification of this specialized court, if done right, could also assure protections against racial and economic disparities, or discrimination against members of the LGBTQIA community. If the statute was written empowering judges to rely on clinical and scientific bases in accepting participants, those most in need would have a greater likelihood of receiving treatment. If codification includes a mandate that no up-front plea is required, coercive elements of the plea process would be obviated and collateral consequences stemming from such conviction could be avoided, which both reduces a client's exclusion from employment, housing, and education opportunities and increases their overall stability so that they don't reoffend, which ultimately benefits the public.

If the mental health court statute includes evidence-based best practices, mental health courts may employ such innovations as a "harm-reduction" approach towards substance use relapse rather than the zero-tolerance principle more generally used. The latter method is proven to be ineffective and even counterproductive. Using the modern scheme reduces deaths and illnesses caused by the negative aspects of drug use, and allows for individualized treatment for the specific individual in the instant case.

Legislating mental health courts also solve issues of funding and a lack of capacity that exist when there is no statutory authority, as state funds would be available, easing the burdens on small localities trying to find ways to financially support ad hoc courts.

In some jurisdictions, no mental health courts exist. However, that does not mean your client has no ability to obtain treatment instead of incarceration. Attorneys can craft a repleader, employ clinicians or forensic experts to do psychosocial assessments and reports, devise treatment plans, make program placements, and set the terms of the plea agreement similar to what mental health courts require, with an outright dismissal or conviction of a lesser charge and time served as the final outcome upon completion or the alternative carceral sentence imposed if not.

What If Mental Health Court Is Not a Good Fit for My Client?

If your client is ineligible for mental health court, you may still be able to avoid the horrendous, traumatizing, and destabilizing effects of incarceration and harm to the greater community via resulting recidivism through other problem-solving courts. Drug court is the most common and an in-depth discussion of it follows here; other specialized courts will be reviewed more briefly.

Drug Courts

The United States currently operates more than 3,500 drug courts, about half of which are adult treatment courts. The typical mission of adult drug courts is to end the participant's abuse of alcohol and illicit drugs and their criminal legal involvement, by combining treatment with phase advancements, enforcement-based sanctions, an abstinence approach, and incentives to have the charges dismissed or reduced to avoid incarceration. Ongoing drug court participation is believed to improve quality-of-life issues such as family support, aftercare, and stability. Like mental health courts, a dedicated multidisciplinary team of professionals manages the daily operations of the drug court, including conducting clinical evaluations, making treatment referrals, and providing supervision services. The drug court "team" typically includes the presiding judge, contracted treatment court representatives, defense attorney, and assistant district attorney.

Unlike mental health courts, drug courts throughout the United States are often codified into law, giving judges discretion to accept or reject an applicant even over the prosecutor's objection. Acceptance into drug courts requires a diagnosed substance use disorder. While drug court statutes may specifically authorize a co-occurring mental health diagnosis and although there is no empirical justification for excluding applicants with co-occurring mental health conditions, in reality, serious mental illnesses (SMI) such as schizophrenia, schizoaffective disorder, and bipolar disorder frequently disqualify an applicant from consideration. Rejection based on SMI then shifts the decision on whether to divert to prosecutors who serve as "gatekeepers" for consideration of entry into a mental health court, assuming one exists in the jurisdiction. As we know, given that some jurisdictions in the United States do not have mental health courts, many otherwise eligible duly diagnosed drug court candidates are ultimately jailed or imprisoned for criminal "behavior" due to untreated substance dependence and mental health conditions.

Eligible charges for drug court consideration are determined by local jurisdictions. Most frequently, only low-level, nonviolent felonies or misdemeanors, particularly drug- or property-related charges, are allowed admission. Candidates with violent charges or prior violent felony convictions are unlikely to be considered for or accepted into drug courts despite studies which show that drug courts should target high-risk candidates and this class of applicants are as likely to succeed in drug courts as those charged with nonviolent crimes. This fearmongering around "public safety" perpetuates a falsehood that people with mental health conditions are more likely to commit a violent act then those without mental illness; whereas it bears repeating that individuals with mental health conditions are ten times more likely to be the victims rather than the perpetrators of violence. Existing research, similarly, shows that participants in drug courts, no matter the charge, have significantly lower rates of recidivism than if they were sentenced to the destabilizing and traumatizing carceral alternative, which is a recipe for instability, increased drug use, and future criminal legal involvement. Unfortunately, drug courts fail to serve those most in need due to rigid eligibility criteria.

Once a referral has been accepted by the drug court judge, an assessment or evaluation is ordered in which the candidate is screened by a Credentialed Alcoholism and Substance Abuse Counselor (CASAC), social worker, forensic psychologist, or another clinician, who will then prepare a nonconfidential report for all the parties. The report contains the applicant's psychosocial history and an opinion as to whether the candidate has a mild, moderate, or severe substance use disorder as defined in the *Diagnostic and Statistical Manual of Mental Disorders*, 5th edition (DSM-5).

Additionally, most jurisdictions require the showing of a "nexus" between the criminal allegations and the applicant's substance use. As such, the assessment team may directly ask the applicant about the criminal charges, which is problematic because there is no guarantee of acceptance into drug court. The applicant's response to this inquiry is memorialized in a written report, which can potentially be used against them should the applicant be rejected and the case proceed to trial.

After the parties have received the completed assessment, the defense advocates for their client's admission into drug court, while the prosecution may support or oppose the application. If the judge agrees to accept the applicant into drug court, the case is adjourned for completion of the court assessment team's "treatment plan," which may recommend a set period of long-term residential treatment, outpatient programming, or a combination of both.

Drug courts in the United States widely differ in their residential mandates, with many judges relying on the individualized clinical recommendations of treatment providers. However, some employ what appears to be a "one size fits all" approach to programming. For example, in some jurisdictions, the drug court requires every participant receiving residential programming to be in the program for a set period of one year, despite studies that show that treatment planning must be unique to the individual clinical needs of the participant. Drug court applicants must then decide whether to accept the court's "offer," which will require a plea to the charge(s) with a predetermined jail or prison sentence for failure to succeed, an enhanced jail sentence if the participant is rearrested, or a dismissal or reduction of the charge(s) if they are successful. Importantly, the research indicates that a person coerced to enter treatment by the criminal legal system is not as likely to succeed as one who volunteers. That said, drug courts entertain a widespread belief that the plea of guilty and the prospect of jail will incentivize the participant and bring about a successful result.

Drug court plea contracts and accompanying drug court handbooks in the United States contain a multitude of expectations of the participant, many of which are punitive and enforcement-based should the participant, for example, test positive for drugs or alcohol. However, contemporary policy makers, research analysts, and prosecutors are increasingly adopting a "harm reduction" response to drug use to be less punitive and to put medication and treatment decisions in the hands of clinicians and medical professionals. Yet many drug courts continue to utilize an outdated relapse sanction-based model that is at odds with what is known about the nature of substance use disorders and the ways that harm reduction, rather than complete abstinence, are worthy goals that can reduce overdose deaths.

In many drug courts, participants are expected to fully abstain from illegal drugs, alcohol, and unprescribed medications. Even when medical professionals recommend controlled substance medication for the treatment of pain, for example, these are frequently disallowed notwithstanding the risk that the participant may instead turn to their preferred illicit substance to manage their pain, risking the potential for overdose. Drug courts nationwide consider abstinence one of the most important treatment goals. In the beginning months of treatment, drug courts utilize "therapeutic adjustments" in response to "relapse." These can include additional counseling sessions, an essay on why the relapse occurred, or changes to the treatment plan. Unfortunately, drug courts often instead resort to more punitive sanctions including the loss of hard-earned compliance time and jail rebranded as "therapeutic remand." Such sanctions stigmatize the participant's addiction and fail to address that substance dependence is a brain disease. Indeed, by definition, substance use disorder is a mental disorder that affects a person's brain and behavior, leading to their inability to control the use of substances.

Many drug courts in the United States prohibit participants from using methadone, suboxone, or other forms of medication-assisted treatment (MAT) during the mandate. Yet MAT is proven as an effective treatment for opioid dependence that combines the use of prescription medications with counseling and education. MAT is shown to reduce drug overdose deaths as well as criminal activity among opioid addicted persons. Most critically, it saves lives. While in theory drug treatment courts offer treatment as a humane and pragmatic alternative to arrest and incarceration, this widespread refusal to permit MAT for participants is misguided, dangerous, and fails to recognize the disproportionate impact of drug policy and mass incarceration on Black and Brown individuals, families, and communities.

Most drug courts employ a multiphase treatment process, generally divided into levels of treatment during which participants earn compliance time so that they can be promoted to the next phase and then ultimately graduation. As part of the mandate, participants are referred to treatment services and required to submit to frequent and random drug and alcohol testing, often used for the purposes of whether to sanction as opposed to therapeutic reasons. Participants progress through phases, with an average of 12–18 months or longer for the mandate, and are expected to meet their case manager, attend court, and follow their treatment plan. To graduate, participants must typically obtain legal housing and full-time employment (unless they receive Social Security disability benefits), complete a period of community service, obtain a high school diploma, and submit a graduation application to the court.

The use of drug courts has grown dramatically over the past several years thanks to inspiring success stories and enthusiastic proponents within the criminal legal system. These success stories should be celebrated, but they provide only a partial picture. Drug addiction, also called substance use disorder, is a debilitating disease that affects a person's brain and behavior and leads to an inability to control the use of illegal drugs or alcohol. There are many psychosocial, societal, and even genetic reasons why people become addicted to drugs or alcohol, including but not limited to past trauma, socioeconomic status, untreated mental health conditions, a family history of substance use, being born addicted to drugs, and family rejection of sexual orientation or gender identity. More broadly, when major "systems" such as health care, child welfare, and education repeatedly fail a person during their life, resulting in substance dependence, the criminal legal system should consider the use that led to criminal legal involvement as a matter of public health equity. This, along with contemporary studies on how to most effectively treat substance dependence, should guide drug courts as they seek to fulfill their mission of curbing substance use disorders and recidivism.

Community Courts

Many community courts were borne from frustration that traditional courts did not stop the "revolving door" dynamic wherein people convicted of low-level violations and misdemeanors are sentenced to nominal incarceration, subsequently released and then rearrested and reconvicted of the similar charges shortly thereafter. This dynamic contributes to backlogs in criminal courts with such trivial charges, diverting resources away from more serious cases and offering no improvement for the communities where the crimes took place.

Acknowledging that incarceration for petty crimes has little or no deterrent effect, community courts function by having those convicted of mostly public order and low-level property crime charges connect instantly with resources to help them attain stability in housing, mental health and substance use treatment, employment assistance, and medical and child care, while beginning their sentence immediately. A sentence could be a specified number of treatment sessions or hours of community service. Most community courts are self-contained, with service providers and community service hubs located on-site. In many jurisdictions, the community is involved, be it through their input on the structure and programming of the diversion or by participating with the court itself. Community courts are usually geographically located within the community whose problems they aim to solve, as opposed to in the downtown commercial areas where most traditional courthouses are situated. The goal is to seek partnership between an individual "offender" and the community impacted by their crime, while importantly addressing the underlying systemic bases for the criminal behavior to avoid reoffending.

Youth Courts

As Chapter 12, "Youthful Offenders," explains in greater detail, advances in neuroscience can be credited for the now commonplace understanding that the brains of young people work differently than those of adults age 25 and older. Young people are physiologically primed to be more vulnerable to reward-driven, peer-pressured, and impulsive behavior. Significantly, as the juvenile brain is still developing, juveniles involved in the criminal legal system are acknowledged to be capable of maturing and evolving as they age, as opposed to being stigmatized with labels such as "super-predator" at the age of 17. Additionally, the research demonstrates that prosecuting youth as adults and seeking harsh sentences for juveniles leads to high rates of recidivism.

Over 1,000 youth courts currently exist in the United States. The structure of these diversion programs differs, but the central dynamics of all are to ensure that with early intervention and supports, using peer pressure and community resources, the young person remains arrest-free, safeguarding communities from repeat offenders.

Some youth courts are comprised of peer volunteers who serve as advocates, jurors, and judges, focusing on minor criminal charges diverted from family or criminal court. These tend to be extra-judicial constructs where sentencing takes the form of service to the community that has been harmed and necessary supportive resources are given to the youth in need. The volunteers playing court roles often get school or community service credit while benefiting from the process by both witnessing the consequences of unwise choices and also being trained in leadership and the legal process. In such courts the youth accused benefit from being diverted from the criminal legal system and experiencing personal growth via positive reinforcement for achievements and being sanctioned through extra mandates or expulsion from the program for noncompliance.

Other youth specialty courts have a conventional court structure of judge, defense, and prosecuting attorneys, but like other problem-solving courts have social service and clinical providers on-site. In these, participants receive educational, housing, vocational, psychological, and family counseling support. The peer pressure aspect of these courts exists indirectly wherein the interplay between the accused and the court, advocates, and programs occurs on the record and before an audience of other youths awaiting their court appearances, as well as observed by visiting students or youth interns intentionally present in the courtroom.

Sex Trafficking Courts

Sex trafficking courts are unique in that they offer immediate and direct recognition of the defendant as a victim—here, of being transported for the purpose of sexual exploitation—as opposed to the indirect acknowledgment of the accused as a victim of systemic failures by other specialty courts. The focus in this diversion part is on trauma-informed treatment and therapeutic jurisprudence aimed at reducing the likelihood of further exploitation, while diverting the accused from incarceration—and in most cases criminal conviction—to avoid additional harm to the individual.

Identifying the survivor is the first complication these problem-solving courts face. Often, the court, defense lawyer, and prosecutor or other reviewing organizations can easily determine whether someone has been trafficked if they are charged with prostitution, but importantly, charges such as shoplifting, panhandling, assault, truancy, and drug possession or sale can also raise the red flag that the accused is also a victim. A client's undocumented immigration status, paltry or no community ties, and language barriers are also indicators advocates should be aware of and thoroughly examine when assessing eligibility to refer them to such diversion.

Once someone has been identified as a victim of trafficking, they are connected with stabilizing support for housing and mental health and substance use counseling, as well as legal assistance for those with immigration matters. Sex trafficking court participants are also frequently referred for medical treatment. The duration of involvement with such courts may be shorter than with other problem-solving courts in deference to proportionality. For example, someone facing a 90-day maximum sentence for a charge would attend programming for the equivalent time, rather than for the year or more as in other diversion courts. As with other specialty courts, there is frequent communication on the record, monitoring and updates at court appearances, mandates to programming, requirements of compliance, and graduated sanctions and rewards.

Sex trafficking courts are criticized as not addressing whether decriminalizing sex work would be more beneficial for the individuals they serve. Critics charge that they inherently support the racial profiling, arrest, and "forced emancipation" of those who choose sex work. They also complain that such courts are less effective in helping those trafficked than nonjudicial organizations because it is difficult for participants to build trust when they know that punishment is an ongoing "threat" for noncompliance with judicial mandates while their cases are pending.

Domestic Violence Courts

Most domestic violence courts differ from traditional problem-solving courts in that they focus on the needs and wishes of the domestic violence complainant instead of those of the accused. The complainant and victim advocacy groups tend to be consulted at most stages of the process in such courts. Complainants are connected with housing, counseling, and other services, and are given legal protections such as restraining orders in these courts. Defendants are still served by such specialty courts in the form of a mandate to counseling and anger management, parenting classes, and substance use treatment instead of carceral sentences.

Domestic violence courts have been criticized for not being focused on the accused and for using progress reports and judicial monitoring as accountability measures for the complainant's sake instead of the client's therapeutic treatment. However, it is still true that the therapeutic jurisprudence approach generally taken by these courts is documented to result in benefit to the individual charged, as well as reduced rearrest for domestic violence.

Sex Offense Courts

Sex offense courts differ by jurisdiction but the main goals are the same: offering early intervention, strict supervision, and mandated programming for the individual accused, and protecting both the individual accused and victim's rights and the public from further victimization. In many jurisdictions these courts collaborate with the defendant, dedicated clinical staff, and advocates, as well as with victim service providers and the department of probation or parole. Generally, these courts only accept those charged and convicted with sex-registry registerable felony sex offenses, although currently there is an emerging trend towards accepting people convicted of misdemeanor sex crimes.

While social service supports are offered as in other specialized courts, the main provider here tends to be intensive sex offender mental health programs. In some jurisdictions the use of polygraphers and constant risk-evaluation are employed; in others the focus remains on the offender's accountability. This is operationalized through overt acknowledgment of their guilt and the harm caused by their actions, immediate and frequent court updates, and exacting mandates with prompt sanctioning for noncompliance. Participants are often restricted from using the internet, using alcohol or legal drugs, accessing sexually stimulating media, and having any contact with minors. If they have children, courts sometimes still allow only supervised meetings with these minors.

Unlike many other kinds of specialty courts, these are generally not considered "diversion" courts as most participants do not opt-in but are ordered by the court to participate. Clients rarely have their plea vacated, nor do they receive an alternative to incarceration if they are not already eligible for a noncarceral sentence or dismissal.

Parole Reentry Courts

The United States currently has almost two million people sentenced to incarceration, costing over $30,000 per detainee per year. Approximately 25 percent of those released from jails and prison are arrested again within the same year. The research overwhelmingly proves that recidivism is impacted significantly by a lack of post-release access to critical resources for managing poverty, homelessness, substance use, and mental illness—all of which are further exacerbated by carceral sentences. Reentry courts aim to lower these massive costs and reduce prison and jail populations by ensuring that formerly incarcerated people receive the support they need to transition back to living in the community. Crucially, such resources are provided at the time they are released. Doing so is proven to reduce recidivism and make communities safer.

Some reentry courts focus on people facing technical violations only, while others recruit participants from rosters of detainees set to be released. In the latter kinds of parole reentry courts, the court is an extra-judicial proceeding staffed by administrative law judges and parole office staff. In the former, a judge or judicial officer presides and the client is represented by counsel, but the role of prosecutor may be served by a parole officer. For all reentry courts, court appearances are frequent. Risk needs assessments are conducted, resulting in targeted treatment for the individual. Courts monitor progress intensely.

Greater success is seen with reentry courts that use graduated rewards and targeted sanctions within a harm reduction model. For example, rather than sending someone to jail for testing positive for illegal substances, they are instead sent to a detox or rehab. Reducing parole or probationary supervision time and instead being monitored by these courts has also been met with more positive outcomes than not employing this approach. Participants who are terminated from the nonadversarial extrajudicial courts are subsequently referred to face technical violations as they would have before. Those who "graduate" such courts are often allowed to finish parole supervision earlier or continue under such monitoring in the community rather than being incarcerated again on a technical violation they faced at the outset of their participation.

Ethical Issues for the Practitioner

Having a client participate in a problem-solving court presents unique ethical challenges for the criminal defense practitioner. Ingrained in most criminal attorneys is the idea that we should never allow our clients to say something that may work to self-incriminate. Yet all specialized courts require frequent colloquy between the court and the client. It is therefore important to advise your client to be careful of what they say or how they say it, while also not censoring their right to have their voice heard. Anticipating what may be asked and going over the myriad of ways different word choices might lead to different outcomes is necessary, especially with clients whose disability includes a lessened ability to read social cues.

Similarly, most defense attorneys used to the adversarial structure of conventional courtrooms might find themselves at a loss when faced with the collaborative dynamic of specialized courts. Attorneys should be cognizant at all times that even in such a team-oriented setting, the ethical rules protecting a client's confidential communications are still in effect. Moreover, the defense attorney should never lose sight of the penultimate goal of providing the client with the most effective representation possible. Attorneys should maintain their zealous advocacy and ensure the client's needs are being met.

Other ethical issues arise concerning coerced treatment—when a client chooses treatment instead of a long sentence of incarceration—and the too-often long delay before incarcerated clients can be placed into community-based programs. Practitioners should approach these the same as they would in any other plea-bargaining situation: Endeavor to find the least restrictive and most beneficial options for your client, explain these choices to them thoroughly so that they are fully informed, offer legal opinions as to preferred options, and ultimately respect their right of self-determination to make the choice they believe is best for them.

Criticism of Mental Health and Other Diversion Courts

Aside from knee-jerk opposition to "helping criminals who deserve to be locked up," much of the early critique of specialty courts is that there have not been enough repeated evaluations with rigorous scientifically sound methodology. While previously there was a complete dearth of data pertaining to such courts, more information is available to show that the aspirations of problem-solving courts are indeed being realized. However, further methodologically sound data collection and assessment must continue in order to enable more longitudinal studies on which to rely in shaping refinements and improvements to these courts.

Valid critique exists concerning the plight of those who do not succeed at diversion after they are terminated from participation. However, in many instances a different approach in the individuated treatment might have better filled the critical gaps that often cause such lack of success. Additionally, reforming the approach of some courts, increasing their capacity, staff, and training, and augmenting their resources to expand their reach beyond the specific problem they are tasked with solving—while incorporating evidence-based best practices into their structure to address the systemic issues that contribute to criminal legal system involvement in the first place—have been found to reap better results.

In general, the studies of mental health court outcomes consistently reflect positive effects for successful participants such as reduced recidivism, improvements in psychological functioning, reliance on beneficial resources versus poor coping mechanisms, and a reduction in substance use, homelessness, and other indicia of instability. Drug courts, which have existed longer than other diversion courts, have the most data to support their efficacy: In general, they significantly reduce recidivism and future drug use. Community court evaluations tend to show significant reductions in rearrest and greater engagement of the community in support of these. Youth courts are heralded with reducing the harm done to young people who biologically lack the ability to process decision-making while also significantly lessening repeat offenses, though peer-run youth courts are statistically less effective than more traditionally structured ones. Sex trafficking courts succeed in reframing perceptions of those arrested for these crimes, offering needed services to the survivors of trafficking, and sparking a conversation that may ultimately prove to usher in greater reform in the decriminalization of sex work. Domestic violence courts show that offenders are less likely to be rearrested for domestic violence and that batterers' programs improve engagement. The expansion of sex offender courts is seen to reduce recidivism and promote greater reporting by victims. Reentry court evaluations reflect a reduced new conviction and reincarceration rate within the first year of release.

Problem-solving courts are also critiqued for not going far enough. For statutorily created courts, a common criticism is that eligibility is too narrow and arbitrary. Moreover, some statutes are too static and do not allow for the evolution of these courts, even as social science progresses. For example, for drugs courts created before the latest evidence-based best practices, approaches widely employed within the field, such as harm reduction, cannot be utilized. For those courts that are creations of prosecutors' offices or court administration as opposed to statutory institution, issues of non-specialty-trained gatekeeping, a lack of due process, and uneven application from jurisdiction to jurisdiction within the same state—which in turn negatively impact participation rates—ensue. Ad hoc courts created by prosecutors or courts also tend not to have the same funding sources as those funded by the state, resulting in less effective results. Additionally, social science supports the notion that a person's involvement in the criminal legal system is not due to one issue alone. Thus, courts that focus on the specific "problem" that is before them to solve may be ignoring the vast systemic issues that create or exacerbate the mental illness or drug use in the first place. Critics offer that a systemic approach to diversion must be taken in all of these courts and work done to eradicate poverty, the lack of stable housing, and the lack of support to families with children resulting in adverse childhood experiences and other trauma.

Some of the greatest obstacles to the success of problem-solving courts in general are the lack of statutory creation and a dearth of funding to expand capacity or appropriately staff the dedicated courtrooms. This may be attributed in part to campaigns of disinformation waged against those involved in the criminal legal system. There is both financial and political profit in the support of the carceral system. As such, much time and money are spent working to undermine and highlight only the missteps or failures of specialty courts and minimize their success. These same actors perpetuate tactics rooted in racism, LGBTQIA discrimination, and economic injustice and foment fear of "The Other," portraying those accused of crimes as "bad," "dangerous," "lazy," and "animals." Moreover, there are vast swaths of the population simply uninformed of the dynamics of revolving door justice, trauma and harm caused by incarceration, systemic oppression, and how justice is not attained for either individuals or communities by continuing to support mass incarceration.

Attorneys who do the work of representing people with mental health or other challenges must expand how we see our role as advocates. We must take it upon ourselves to educate the ill-informed, whether this be members of the public, other lawyers, or members of the judiciary or legislative branches. Engaging in social media discussions on such topics, writing op-eds, or being interviewed for print, television, radio, or podcast media are ways to disseminate truths, correct misperceptions, and thwart misinformation. Joining movements that work to draft, get support for, and pass legislation protecting the rights of people with mental health, cognitive, and intellectual disabilities through codification or expansion of problem-solving courts is another way. Participating in local and state legislative hearings on behavioral health and mental, cognitive, and intellectual disabilities is an additional way to share information and dispel inaccuracies spouted by agenda-driven alarmists.

Conclusion

Social science proves that problem-solving courts are generally successful in achieving the desired goals for individuals and communities. As the social science evolves, so too should the approach of specialty courts. We should increase the capacity of those already in existence and advocate for the creation of new dedicated courtrooms where needed. Importantly, we must further educate our fellow members of the Bar as well as the public that innovations that serve to stabilize and support individuals also create stability in our society, reduce crime, are more cost-effective, allow courts the capacity to function optimally, and appeal to the best of our humanity. Continuing to base the administration of justice on social science rather than fearmongering will serve the best interests of not only the individual participants, but our collective communities, addressing public health while ensuring public order and safety.

• • •

Katherine LeGeros Bajuk, Esq., is the mental health attorney specialist for New York County Defender Services (NYCDS). Ms. Bajuk has been a public defender in New York City for almost 30 years, advocating for indigent clients at all stages of the criminal process. Her practice since 2015 has focused on representing NYCDS clients with mental health, cognitive, and/or intellectual disability issues in Manhattan Mental Health Court, the Alternatives to Incarceration Court, Manhattan Drug Court, and at forensic competency evaluations. Additionally, Ms. Bajuk serves as a resource for NYCDS attorneys by consulting on cases with clients with mental health and cognitive issues and conducts trainings and provides practice tips and updates on mental health law. She routinely teams with NYCDS administration, attorneys, corrections specialists, data research and IT, forensic social work, investigation, immigration, juvenile defense, paralegal, reentry, special litigation, and interns to achieve the best outcomes for clients. In 2018 she partnered with Vanessa Tejero and Wendy D'Amico Fisher to launch a wellness initiative to lessen the effects of vicarious trauma on office staff, implementing in-office programs such as meditation and the creation of wellness spaces. Ms. Bajuk participates with the National Association for Public Defender Well-Being Summit Workgroup and collaborated on *Principles for Creating Sustainability in Public Defense Offices* guidelines for public defender offices.

Ms. Bajuk is involved in mental health policy formulation through her work with the New York City Mayor's Office for Criminal Justice workgroups on 730s and behavioral health, appearances before the New York City Council, and collaboration with the NYCDS policy team and the greater coalition in drafting and supporting the Treatment Not Jail Act. Ms. Bajuk also provided input to the Center for Court Innovation for the development of Manhattan Drug Court's mental health track and Manhattan Misdemeanor Mental Health Court. She has written op-ed pieces in the *New York Law Journal*, *City Limits* (co-author), and *Honey* magazine. She is also quoted in numerous stories in national and local print and electronic media and podcasts.

Ms. Bajuk is co-chair of the New York State Bar Committee on Mandated Representation Mental Health Committee, a member of the NYSBA Task Force on Mental Health and Trauma Impacted Representation, and co-chair of the Women's Bar Association Criminal Law Committee. Born in New York City, Ms. Bajuk received a Bachelor of Arts from McGill University, a Juris Doctor from Rutgers University School of Law-Newark, and certification in Mental Health First Aid by MHFA New York. Ms. Bajuk lives in New York City with gratitude for her family, *Calzar* and found *Familia*, and Stormy the dog. Ms. Bajuk can be contacted at kbajuk@nycds.org.

Jeffrey Berman, Esq., is a mental health attorney specialist at the Legal Aid Society's (LAS) Manhattan Criminal Defense Practice. A public defender in New York City since 1998, Mr. Berman zealously represents indigent clients throughout the criminal legal process, from arrest through arraignments, to plea negotiations or hearings and trial. Mr. Berman is the primary resource to colleagues advocating for treatment-based dispositions for clients diagnosed with mental health, cognitive, and substance dependence health conditions. Mr. Berman advises attorneys on how to effectively prepare bail applications to procure clients' release from detention, as well as on issues related to client competency, psychiatric defenses, and the retention of expert witnesses. Mr. Berman routinely conducts internal and external trainings on best practices in representing clients with mental health conditions and develops and shares practice advisories in his area of expertise. He also presents to students, faith leaders, and others on advocating for treatment as opposed to incarceration for clients with mental health diagnoses.

Mr. Berman has been interviewed by local and national media on issues related to his expertise. He has authored or coauthored articles related to his advocacy for changes to New York's criminal legal system's treatment of people who live with mental health diagnoses, including an op-ed for *City Limits* titled "Opinion: For the Sake of Public Health and Safety, Pass the Treatment Not Jail Act" and an essay with Practicing Law Institute titled "Problem-Solving Courts and Bail Reform: A Defense Perspective."

Mr. Berman has testified before the New York State Senate and Assembly and the New York State Attorney General's office on issues related to criminal justice reform. He participates in LAS state policy strategies and recently co-drafted the Treatment Not Jail Act, which if passed will significantly expand New York State's Judicial Diversion drug court statute and legislate mental health courts in the state. Mr. Berman participated in developing the Manhattan ATI Court, Manhattan Misdemeanor Mental Health Court, and Manhattan Drug Court's mental health track.

Mr. Berman is a co-chair of the New York State Bar Committee on Mandated Representation Mental Health Committee and a member of the New York State Bar Association's Task Force on Mental Health. Born in Washington D.C., he was raised in the D.C. metropolitan area. Mr. Berman received his Bachelor of Arts from Clark University and a Juris Doctor from Chicago-Kent College of Law. He resides in Brooklyn, New York with his wife, two boys, a Bernedoodle, and two guinea pigs. Mr. Berman can be reached at jberman@legal-aid.org.

Chapter

14

Veterans Courts

Julie Marie Baldwin

The following chapter by Professor Julie Baldwin on veterans courts is an update of the version that appeared in the first edition. Of particular significance is the addition of the Military Information Questionnaire, Needs Questionnaire, and Eligibility Worksheet at the end of the chapter.

Veterans courts are an important type of problem-solving court—one that provides a valuable service to men and women who have served this country but who face a variety of mental health and substance use issues that have embroiled them in the criminal legal system. These courts have unique procedures and personnel, and this chapter provides valuable guidance for the criminal defense lawyer.

• • •

Veterans treatment courts (VTCs) strive to improve the lives of military veterans and service members who end up in the criminal justice system. Although this is their general purpose, VTC programs are unstandardized, varying even in fundamental aspects such as target population and structure. As such, the overall goal of this chapter is to provide you with pertinent information and tools to help you better serve these clients and navigate VTC programs.

The chapter begins by conceptualizing VTCs with a general explanation of their purpose and basic functioning. The targets of these programs (i.e., individuals and their needs) are then examined through an illustration of the constellation of issues and their interrelatedness. Contributing to this portrait, various group and subgroups of offenders and nonoffenders with and without a history of military service are comparatively examined in terms of demographics and legal and extra-legal challenges. With the VTC concept and its target generally established, several challenges facing defense counsel in their work with VTCs are addressed. These issues were identified by the author's research, which primarily consisted of self-report data from various types of defense counsel in contact with VTCs, as well as some nonparticipant observation. The remaining sections of this chapter address some of the particular issues that emerged and are organized by the following themes: (1) client identification, (2) case transfers and program identification, (3) eligibility, (4) admission, and (5) involvement (defense counsel participation and roles).

The Veterans Treatment Court Concept

Veterans treatment courts are a specialty court within the United States criminal court system, originally created through judicial initiative in the mid-2000s. To date, there are approximately 616 VTCs across the nation, including several federal VTCs. The VTC has been characterized as a hybrid of drug courts and mental health courts due to similarities in philosophies, objectives, goals, and procedures. Paralleling other specialized courts, VTC program participation is theoretically voluntary, with those eligible offered the choice to participate and having the ability to drop out at any time.

VTCs also utilize the specialty court model: divert their participants from the traditional criminal justice system to nontraditional channels of justice that address the potential underlying causes and correlates of their criminal behavior in an effort to reduce, if not eliminate, future contact with the criminal justice system (see Figure 14.1). This nontraditional route not only involves connecting participants with services that target the correlates of their criminal behavior, but also mandating and monitoring their participation in those services. These services include those traditionally associated with therapeutic specialty courts (e.g., mental health

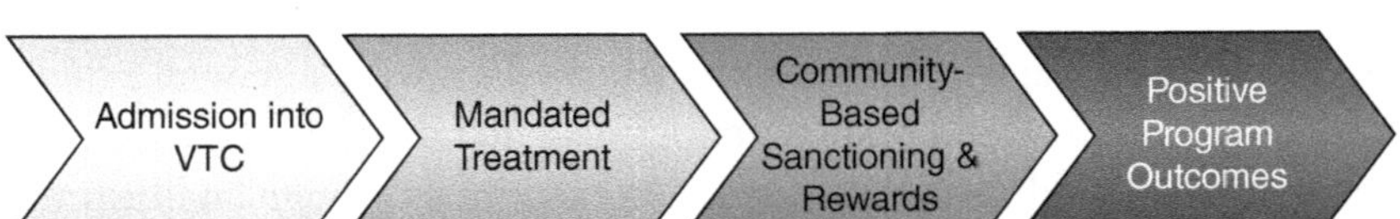

FIGURE 14.1 VTC process model.

counseling and substance abuse treatment). For participant accountability, rewards and sanctions are administered in correspondence with compliance and noncompliance. This process (linkage, requirements, supervision, and accountability) is facilitated through a "team" approach—in other words, individuals with often opposing roles and goals collaborate in a nonadversarial manner to implement the program.

Beyond these similarities, the VTC is a unique model with elements distinct unto itself. First, other specialized courts utilize specific criminal offenses or issues to define their general model's overall target population. For example, drug court begins to identify potential participations with drug offenses or issues in drug court, mental health court with mental health issues, DUI court with DUI or DWI offenses, and domestic violence court with domestic violence offenses.

However, the VTC target population is primarily defined by military status, not type of offense or issue. Generally speaking, VTC participants must have an official record of U.S. military service. Once this criterion is met, different VTC programs incorporate additional requirements to further define their specific target populations. Military record aside, *no* other eligibility criteria are currently standardized across all VTCs (see "Eligibility"). As such, its basic model allows for VTC programs to attempt to address as many of their participants' needs as their resources will allow, and as seen in the next section, the host of issues is complex and intertwined. Depending on the target issues and population and resources available, these programs vary from fairly basic to highly complicated in their impact goals, objectives, and service providers. The Impact Model (Figure 14.2) illustrates the intended impact of many VTCs overall, meaning that individual VTC programs may attempt varying degrees or components of this model.

The second distinguishing feature of the VTC is its inclusion of additional stakeholders and team members not previously seen among other specialized court programs. Although they vary from program to program, these can include the U.S. Department of Veterans Affairs (VA), state-level offices or departments of veterans affairs, state-level veterans councils, Veterans Justice Outreach Specialists (VJOs), Veterans Service or Benefits Officers (VSOs or VBOs), and veteran mentor coordinators. Third, some VTCs incorporate services specific to the status of military history, such as VA benefit enrollment, attempts to resolve VA benefit issues, expedited linkage and/or access to VA services, and treatments

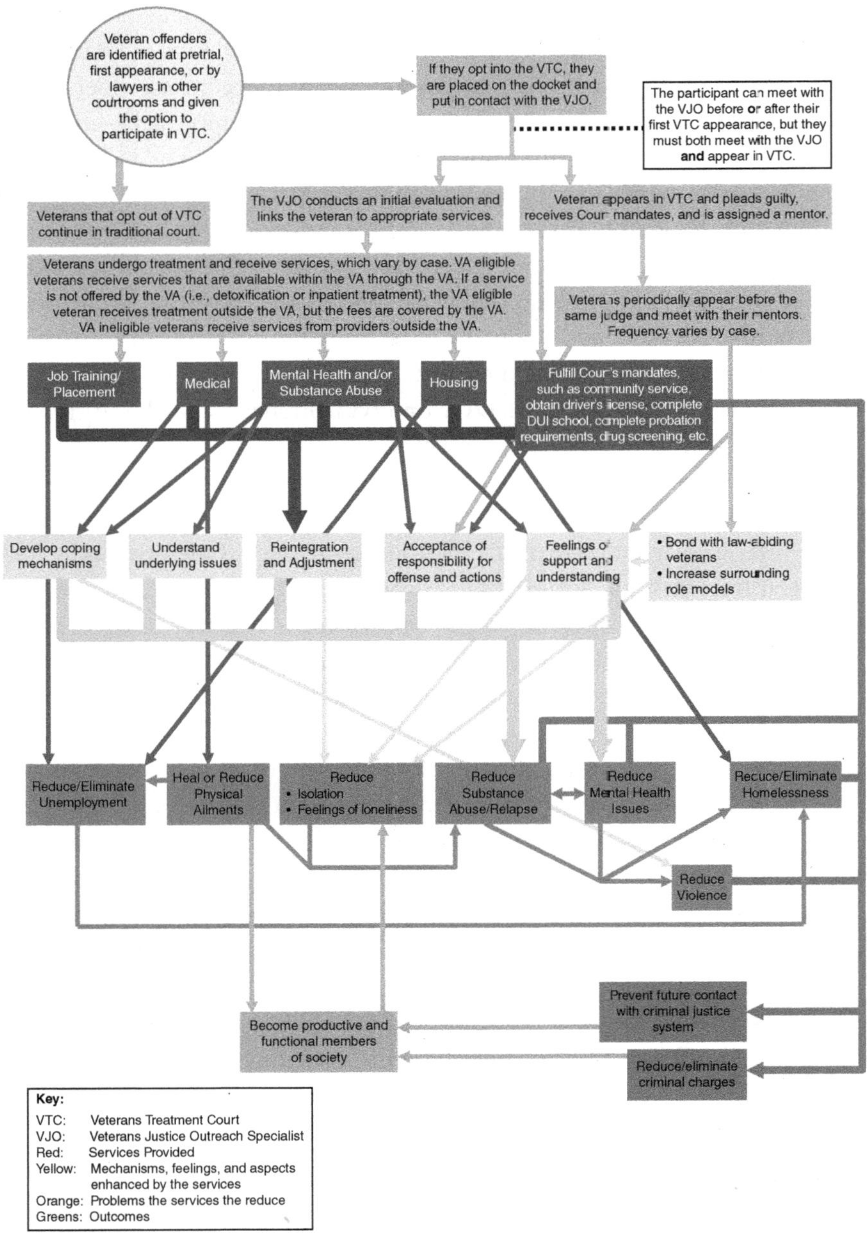

FIGURE 14.2 VTC Impact Model.

Source: Julie Marie Baldwin, "Veterans Treatment Courts: Studying Dissemination, Implementation, and Impact of Treatment-Oriented Criminal Courts" (PhD diss., University of Florida, 2013), 298.

focused on addressing the effects of conditions that may be related to military service, such as post-traumatic stress disorder (PTSD) and traumatic brain injury (TBI). Fourth, many VTCs utilize veteran peer mentors. In many programs, a mentor coordinator matches mentors to VTC participants, oversees the mentors, and serves as a liaison between the VTC team and the mentors. Finally, overtones of military culture and its camaraderie are both evident and employed as motivating factors for compliance, a support system, and a familiar environment. VTCs often encourage their participants to engage in veteran-specific events, as well as organize some of these events for their participants and the local community.

However, as noted at the outset, VTC programs are highly variable, meaning that all of these particulars—both similar to and distinct from other specialized courts—can differ from VTC to VTC. As such, the following description of VTC operation is general and programmatic variances significant to defense counsel are addressed throughout the sections of this chapter to help you navigate various types of VTC programs. Generally, when potentially eligible participants are identified (see "Client Identification"), their cases are transferred to the VTC for review (see "Case Transfers and Program Identification"), and the VTC team offers participation and program terms to those deemed eligible (see "Cost and Benefit of Admission"). Program terms frequently include participation in a variety of therapeutic services (e.g., mental health and substance abuse treatment), monitoring for program compliance (e.g., probation and drug screens), adjudication terms, potential sanctions for noncompliance, frequent court appearances, and additional mandates, such as paying restitution, obtaining a valid driver's license, and relinquishing firearms. Those deemed eligible can decline (opt-outs) or accept (participants) the participation offer (see "Cost and Benefit of Admission"). Opt-outs have their cases returned to the original court of jurisdiction without additional penalty (see "Case Transfers and Program Identification"). Those who want to participate in the VTC must then agree to the program terms, often by signing a behavioral contract (see "Cost and Benefit of Admission") and agreeing to appear at the next VTC session. Following the decision to participate, the VTC program begins for the participant.

Please note that only a general program operation for participants is subsequently described as programs vary in their methods, means, procedures, and time ordering. The VTC team links the participant to his or her mandated treatments and activities. The participant must then attempt to engage with the appropriate entities, often prior to his or her next appearance, to be deemed compliant. For the duration of the participant's time in the program, the VTC team implements the prescribed supervision methods to monitor the predetermined aspects of compliance. To perform this function, the VTC team reports on and subsequently assesses participant compliance, progress, and challenges (see "Defense Counsel Involvement") at each team meeting (called "Staffing"), which often takes place immediately prior to the VTC session.

Often in Staffing, the VTC team determines whether rewards or sanctions should be applied in response to their determinations of compliance. Tolerance for some noncompliance is built into the VTC model, meaning a single noncompliant act does not result in removal from the program (i.e., termination). Instead, many VTCs use graduated rewards and sanctions where consistent compliance receives rewards of increased significance up to final program graduation and repeated noncompliance garners sanctions of increased severity that can eventually lead to stints of incarceration and ultimate program termination. For VTC programs with tracks or phases, graduation (i.e., positive transition) to a less stringent level can be utilized as a reward, while demotion (i.e., negative transition) to a more intensive level can be applied as a sanction. Participants do not attend Staffing and are not directly privy to these discussions.

Participants are scheduled to frequently appear in VTC sessions, which are also open to the public. As everyone convenes prior to VTC session start, VTC team members and mentors can touch base with certain participants for a variety of purposes, such as to discuss elements of the team's discussion, obtain further updates, or offer support. VTC team members, mentor coordinators, mentors, and representatives from various organizations can make announcements.

In the VTC sessions, scheduled participants are called to appear before the bench where the VTC judge then summarizes recent progress aloud. The level of interaction and dynamics between the judges and participants varies both intra- and inter-program; judges may ask questions, make statements, and/or converse with participants, team members, or other members of the audience (if present). Regardless of the level and dynamics of interaction, the judge administers rewards or sanctions (if any) and imparts any feedback or advice he or she has during this face time. When a participant successfully completes the full program, he or she graduates during a VTC session or graduation.

Often, larger VTCs with many participants graduate participants as necessary throughout the regular VTC sessions; smaller programs often schedule graduates as a group in a dedicated graduation ceremony. Regardless of the type of gathering or number of graduates, the judge typically speaks about the graduate's change and accomplishments through the program and then asks the graduate to address the audience. The graduate speaks freely or reads a self-written statement, followed by receipt of some type of graduation token (e.g., a certificate or challenge coin), applause, and verbal praise. Paperwork is then signed to confer any graduation benefits that were predetermined for the participant's case at the time of VTC program entry (e.g., case dismissal). If a participant is terminated, the case is returned to its criminal court of origin, and the terms of the program agreement tied to termination are effectuated, meaning that all contractual penalties corresponding with termination go into effect (e.g., automatic sentencing upon return appearance in original court; see "Cost and Benefit of Admission").

Your Clients: Offenders and the Accused with a History of Military Service

Although the majority of veterans' reintegration journeys are devoid of formal contact with the criminal justice system, the group that does make contact has garnered attention from both inside and outside the criminal justice system. To most accurately reflect the group of interest in this chapter, as well as address this book's audience, this group is referred to as "clients (offenders and accused) with a history of military service." This term is intentionally employed for its inclusiveness because VTC programs are inconsistent in their specific target populations (see "Eligibility"), as well as their program requirements and adjudication policies (see "Cost and Benefit of Admission").

Although previously employed, the terms "justice-involved veterans" and "veteran defendants" have not always accurately reflected the groups to which they have referred. For example, "veteran" excludes currently enlisted military personnel (service members) that have been included in the group of focus. "Veteran defendant" has also been interpreted as those with previous experience in the defendant role regardless of military history. Further, "veteran" has numerous definitions that cause problems with self-identification, and some have criticized the phrase "justice-involved" as downplaying the seriousness of the criminal offenses of which members of this group have been accused or plead guilty (see "Cost and Benefit of Admission").

The U.S. Army has referred to the complex relationships between military experiences, extra-legal issues, and criminal behavior in several iterations of *Combat and Operational Stress Control Manual for Leaders and Soldiers*, a field manual for education on combat and operational stress control (COSC) and reactions (COSRs), including how to identify, manage, and prevent particular stress, reactions, and related issues.[1] The 2006 publication replaced the term "battle fatigue" with COSR and illustrated several relationships between stress behaviors and reactions that include criminal acts (see Figure 14.3). The 2009 version no longer contains the figure and explanation but instead states that the specific extra-legal issues of alcohol use or abuse (specifically addressed next), financial problems, and relationship issues can lead soldiers to commit criminal acts.[2] Both relationships described are understood within the context of environmental stressors (i.e., military combat and/or operations), but the latter places extra-legal (personal) issues as the direct cause of crime.

The correlation between higher rates of alcohol consumption and military service is supported by academic research and well-known to the public and the military.[3] Studies have discovered nearly half of veterans in some recent samples have participated in dangerous alcohol use and nearly half of some active-duty personnel samples satisfy the classification criteria of binge drinker. Identified trends show military personnel experience steady and significant increases in heavy drinking.[4] As previously noted, alcohol has been dubbed one of the "signature substances" of Operation Iraqi Freedom (OIF), Operation Enduring Freedom (OEF), and Operation New Dawn (OND; recent and current era) veterans.[5] The prevalence and behavioral trends are also meaningful in terms of crime as the Army has noted that the "majority of crimes that soldiers commit involve the use or abuse of alcohol."[6]

Other research has identified additional group differences and relationships. In contrast to unincarcerated veterans, incarcerated veterans

1. Dep't of Army, *Combat and Operational Stress Control Manual for Leaders and Soldiers*, FM 4-02,51 (July 6, 2006). Publicly available at https://fas,org/irp/dodcir/army/fm4-02-51.pdf.

2. *Id.* at 2–18.

3. *See, e.g.*, Bray, R. M., et al. 2009a. 2008 Department of Defense Survey of Health Related Behaviors Among Active Duty Military Personnel. Research Triangle Park, NC: RTI International; Bray, R. M., et al. 2009b. Department of Defense Survey of Health Related Behaviors Among Active Duty Military Personnel: A Component of the Defense Lifestyle Assessment Program (DLAP). Research Triangle Park, NC: RTI International.

4. Bray et al., *supra* note 3.

5. Inst. of Medicine (2012), https://psycnet.apa.org/record/2003-03854-003.

6. Dep't of Army, *supra* note 1.

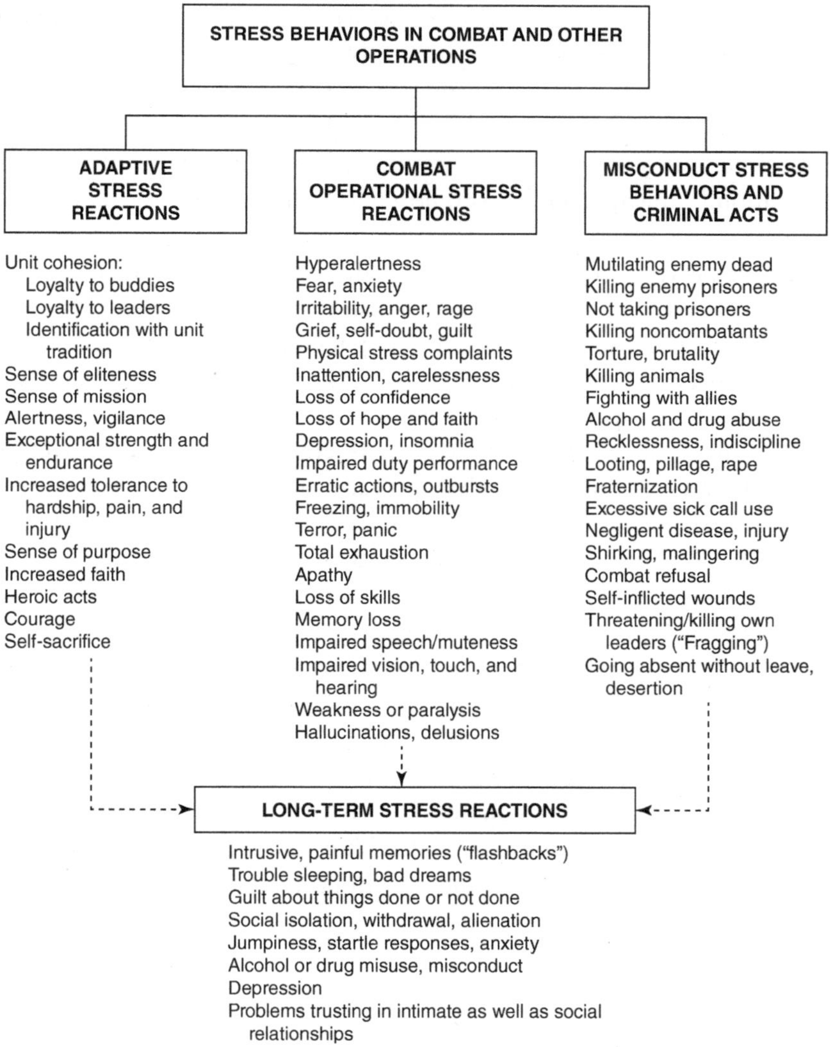

FIGURE 14.3 Stress behaviors in combat and other operations.
Source: U.S. Dep't of Army, *Combat and Operational Stress Control Manual for Leaders and Soldiers*, FM 4-02.51 (July 6, 2006). https://fas.org/irp/doddir/army/FM4-02-51.pdf.

have been found to have more issues with their families,[7] employment,[8] and substance abuse,[9] and were less likely to be married or satisfied with

7. Benda et al. (2003); Gondolf & Foster (1991), https://psycnet.apa.org/record/1992-21241-001.

8. Shaw, D. M., Churchill, C. M., Noyes, R. Jr., & Loeffelholz, P. L. (1987). Criminal behavior and post-traumatic stress disorder in Vietnam veterans. *Comprehensive Psychiatry*, *28*(5), 403–411. doi:10.1016/0010-440X(87)90057-5

9. Elbogen et al. (2012); Erickson et al. (2008); Shaw et al. (1987).

their marriages.[10] Incarcerated veterans who have PTSD were found to also experience more severe legal troubles, worse physical health, and higher lifetime substance abuse rates compared to incarcerated veterans without PTSD.[11] Incarcerated veterans may have a higher risk for suicide than either the general veteran population or the general incarcerated population.[12] Suicide continues to be a major threat to veteran and service member populations.

In the previous edition of this book, this chapter provided an overview of multiple subgroups of clients with a history of military service, as well as compared them to the general veteran population and incarcerated nonveterans (see previous edition Tables 12.1–12.3). Specifically, four groups were examined and compared: the national veteran population and three client samples (those in contact with VTCs, veteran inmates, and nonveteran inmates). Areas examined included age, race, ethnicity, legal issues (offense type), and extra-legal issues (mental health). For that information, please see pages 205–209, including Tables 12.1–12.3, in the original edition.

Although complicated relationships between military service, crime, and extra-legal issues have been found to challenge clients with a history of military service, it is important to note several limitations. These and other statistics related to the larger group of offenders and accused with a history of military service and its subgroups have been considered underestimations due to challenges in data collection, primarily identification issues.[13] The recent conclusion of individual military engagements and ongoing status of the overall OIF/OEF/OND[14] era must also be considered when interpreting findings. In particular, recent incarceration

10. Greenberg & Rosenheck (2009); Shaw et al. (1987).

11. Saxon et al. (2001).

12. Frisman & Griffin Fennel (2009); Wortzel, Binswanger, Anderson, et al. (2009). Suicide Among Incarcerated Veterans, *The Journal of the American Academy of Psychiatry and the Law* (Vol. 37).

13. Baldwin (2015).

14. Government sources vary in their conflict definitions. For example, one VA source lists OEF as October 2001–December 2014, OIF as March 2003–November 2011, and OND as September 2010–December 2011 (https://www.va.gov/vetsinworkplace/docs/em_datesNames.asp), while another VA sources defines OEF as 2001–present, OIF as 2003–present, and OND as September 2010–present (https://www.mentalhealth.va.gov/communityproviders/docs/conflicts.pdf). However, the Congressional Research Services recently defined OEF from October 7, 2001–December 28, 2014, OIF from 2003–2010, Operation Freedom's Sentinel from January 1, 2015–?, Operation New Dawn from September 1, 2010–December 15, 2011?, and Operation Inherent Resolve from October 2014–?; *see* Barbara Salazar Torreon, U.S. Periods of War and Dates of Recent Conflicts (September 29, 2016).

statistics reveal only a small percentage of OIF/OEF veterans.[15] However, many of these studies were conducted while these most recent conflicts were still ongoing, while some took place even before others began. Accordingly, it is expected that our statistics will be subject to change as time continues to progress.

Client Identification: The Responsibility Is Yours

The majority of VTCs, let alone the larger criminal justice system, do not have a systematic procedure for identifying a history of military service, and barriers to self-identification also exist. Instead, military history has been primarily identified by criminal justice agents, including judges, defense counsel, probation officers, and law enforcement, at various time points ranging from arrest to postconviction. Of all potential identifiers (regardless of affiliation with the criminal justice system), "defense counsel" has consistently been named the most frequent identifier of military status among those in contact with VTCs. This means that, in most cases, it is unlikely that you will be informed about a client's military history, not even by your client. Therefore, it is up to *you* to proactively identify these individuals.

There are three elements that are key to initial identification: who, when, and how. Whom should you ask? *Ask all of your clients*. You cannot anticipate who may have a military record. Although the comparative demographic data give us some insight into subgroups, we also know that the full portrait is incomplete, as well as expected to change over time (i.e., increasing in numbers, needs of current era service members peaking, and proportion of females). When should you ask? *Ask at your initial meeting with the client*. It is important to identify early to better serve your client, since the documentation necessary to begin the VTC process can take some time to retrieve. We will return to this issue in a moment. How should you ask? Use of the appropriate terminology is critical! *Do not use the term "veteran."* It is not inclusive, and many do not identify with the

15. *See, e.g.*, Noonan, M. E., Mumola C. J. (2004). *Veterans in State and Federal Prison, 2004*. Washington, DC: Bureau of Justice Statistics; White M. D., Mulvey P., Fox A. M., Choate D. (2012). *A Hero's Welcome? Exploring the Prevalence and Problems of Military Veterans in the Arrestee Population*, Justice Quarterly, 29, 258–86.

term. *Employ more inclusive language*, such as "Have you ever served in the uniformed services, armed forces, or U.S. military?"

Now that your identification procedure is in place, you may have clients that indicate a history of military service. What do you do if your client indicates that he or she *does* have a history of military service? You begin the process of determining your client's potential eligibility (see "Eligibility"). The first step of this process requires you obtain additional information about your client from your client; this information can also be used to identify other programs and services for which your client may qualify.

For your clients that have declared military experience, you should first administer the Military Information Questionnaire. This can be completed either as an interview (you ask your client the questions and transcribe his or her responses on the form) or as a survey (you give the form to your client to read and write his or her responses). However, I recommend employing the interview format for several reasons. You can immediately ask for clarification, which may be especially helpful if you are unfamiliar with military jargon, abbreviations, or acronyms. Relatedly, it allows you to ask follow-up questions and engage in an immediate conversation about a nonlegal topic, which can help establish or increase rapport. Additionally, you may find it easier to read your own handwriting than someone else's.

The Military Information Questionnaire is self-explanatory in that it contains items about your client's military history. On completion of the questionnaire, you should be able to answer most, if not all, of the initial questions the VTC might have concerning your client. The VTC will also ask for criminal offense information, but this is not included in the questionnaire since it is likely that you already possess this information as defense counsel. The first numbered item asks whether your client has a copy of his or her DD-214; the majority (if not all) of your military clients will know this term. The DD-214, or "DD Form 214, Certificate of Release or Discharge from Active Duty," is the Report of Separation from the military (discharge papers or separation documents) that serves as a verified record of active and reserve service history.[16] It is used by numerous government

16. Similar forms were used prior to January 1, 1950, including the WD AGO 53, WD AGO 55, WD AGO 53-55, NAVPERS 553, NAVMC 78PD, and NAVCG 553; *see, e.g.*, U.S. Dep't of Veterans Affairs, National Cemetery Administration, Veterans Military Discharge Documents Individuals, *available at* https://www.cem.va.gov/hmm/discharge_documents.asp. Those who have served solely in the Army National Guard or Air Force National Guard (Air Guard) will

and nongovernment agencies, including the VA. Your client possessing his or her separation paperwork can greatly reduce time to enrollment in programs and services, including VTCs. VTCs require a verified record of U.S. military service for enrollment. If a client does not have his or her separation documents, you should reach out to the VTC's VJO. Although your client can request the records, fulfillment time varies, and can exceed six months depending on service era and archiving. However, the VJO is a valuable contact because he or she can obtain a potential participant's DD-214 or otherwise verify military history in much less time.

The remaining items on the Military Information Questionnaire focus on information pertinent to different types of VTC programs. These items target various eligibility policies across VTCs related to discharge status (#2 and #3; both are also on DD-214) and potential combat experience (#4, #5, and #6; all are also on DD-214). VTC teams will also be immediately interested in information related to VA enrollment and services (#7, #8, and #9), as it provides insight into VA eligibility (in conjunction with #2 and #3), extra-legal challenges and needs, ability to access services, and documentation that may be available.

The Needs Questionnaire, as its name indicates, contains items regarding experiences with extra-legal and legal challenges and needs. This information equips you to answer additional questions from the VTC team, as well as link your clients to services. Similar to the Military Information Questionnaire, the Needs Questionnaire can be administered in either an interview or survey format. However, the survey format may be preferable for the Needs Questionnaire depending on your rapport with the client. Although the VJO may review these issues later with eligible clients, you should administer the questionnaire because you can use the information to help identify potentially applicable VTC programs for your clients (see the next section, "Transfer/Program Identification") and assess their eligibility (see "Eligibility" section). Further, not all VJOs assess each potential (or actual) participant. Therefore, to easily obtain the most valuable and useful client information early on, the Needs Questionnaire should be utilized in conjunction with the Military Information Questionnaire.

---

received an NGB-22 ("NGB Form 22, Report of Separation and Record of Service" from the National Guard Bureau) at separation.

Case Transfers and Program Identification

Legal cases cannot originate in a VTC. As stated at the outset of the chapter, the VTC is an alternative program into which eligible participants voluntarily choose to enroll. Therefore, a case must be transferred from the court of original jurisdiction (what I call the "Home Court") to a VTC program. There are several routes of transfer. The most common transfer occurs within a single jurisdiction: from the Home Court to a VTC program in the same jurisdiction (what I refer to as the "Home VTC"). Additionally, eligible cases can be transferred between (1) a Home Court in one jurisdiction to a VTC program in another jurisdiction (what I call an "Away VTC") and (2) VTC programs in different jurisdictions.

Why would participants be transferred to an Away VTC? Reasons vary, but some examples are as follows:

- Your client may not meet the eligibility criteria the Home VTC but may satisfy the requirements an Away VTC.
- The Home VTC may not be accepting new participants, but an Away VTC is taking new cases.
- The Home VTC may not offer the particular services your client needs but an Away VTC does.
- Your client may not live in or near the jurisdiction in which he or she was arrested, but there is an Away VTC operating near his or her residence.
- Your client is moving far from where the Home VTC is located, but there is an Away VTC located near his or her new residence.

In lieu of transferring, cases have been "shared" between VTC programs. In practice, this means that one VTC legally possesses a participant's case, while a different VTC monitors or supervises that participant's progress. Although sharing is rare, this can occur for the same reasons as interjurisdiction transfers.

I categorize transfers into two categories based on their impetus: positive transfers and negative transfers. Positive transfers are initiated because of client needs or circumstance. The transfers discussed up to this point are positive transfers. Conversely, negative transfers are initiated by the VTC as a programmatic sanction in response to participant noncompliance. Negative transfers occur less often but primarily result from program termination due either to the VTC's application of its ultimate VTC sanction or to the participant's desire to drop out of the program. For a variety of reasons, the VTC team may decide to remove the client from the program. To terminate, the VTC (Home or Away) returns the case to the Home Court. Initiation of a negative transfer brings all program terms tied to termination into effect. Similarly, if a participant drops out, the VTC (Home or Away) returns the case to the Home Court, and termination terms activate (see "Cost and Benefit of Admission").

The ability to transfer and share cases means that to best advise your client you should be knowledgeable about any Home and Away VTCs that could serve your client. To start, you need to initially identify these VTC programs. At this stage, relevant program information includes the VTC name, location, jurisdiction, and contact information. However, you should structure and maintain your VTC program list in a format that is most accessible and efficient for you.

There are several resources you can utilize to obtain this basic program information. Some of these resources include the following:

- Internet search engines: Search using the following combinations of terms:
  - Veterans court + city name + state
  - Veterans court + county name + state
- Office of Court Administration: Your OCA should have a list of VTCs operating within its jurisdiction.
- National Drug Court Institute (NDCI): As a division under the National Association of Drug Court Professionals (NADCP), NDCI maintains a map of VTCs.
- National Drug Court Resource Center: The Justice Programs Office serves as the clearinghouse for specialized courts and maintains a website that contains a map of specialized court programs, including VTCs (ndcr.org/database/).
- Your network: Ask your colleagues whether they know of any VTCs in the area.

Please note, VTCs continue to be implemented, as well as cease to operate, and the accuracy of the maps referenced depends on how frequently they are updated, which is unknown.[17] Therefore, you should *use multiple sources* to draft your initial program list and *consistently update* your

17. Baldwin, J.M. (2013). "Veterans Treatment Courts: Studying Dissemination, Implementation, and Impact of Treatment-Oriented Criminal Courts" (doctoral dissertation, University of Florida, Gainesville, Florida).

list. While this and the previous sections have addressed initial identification of both clients with military history (see "Your Clients") and VTC programs, the next step is to determine program eligibility.

Eligibility: Can My Client Enlist?

Directly related to the definition of offenders or the accused with a history of military service, the following are the only standard requirements for eligibility across all VTCs:

- The existence of a criminal offense or infraction
- A history of military service evidenced by military separation report (see "Client Identification")

Beyond these two standard requirements, VTC programs can restrict eligibility through a myriad of additional criteria. These restrictions may be related to military discharge status, type, or length of military service, VA service and benefit eligibility, criminal history, current criminal charges, substance-abusing behavior, and mental health issues. Further, some programs require a nexus between certain issues. Figure 14.4 illustrates how programs can vary in their eligibility criteria and the target populations subsequently created.

The reasons behind particular exclusions or requirements are similarly diverse and can include the availability of resources, VTC team or judicial preference, and directives per law or policy. For example, many VTCs include VA eligibility as a criterion for VTC admission. VTC programs may adopt this requirement because they do not have partnerships with community treatment providers to service VA-ineligible participants (resources), prefer to use the VA as the sole treatment provider (preference), consider VA-ineligible participants to be too high of a risk (preference), and/or are required to by statute or chief/administrative judge order (directive). VTC program exclusions may be contributing to differences in factors such as offense type and extra-legal issues between certain groups and subgroups.

As defense counsel, you are responsible for being familiar with VTC admission criteria even though they can highly vary and you may not currently have them in your possession. What types of information are relevant to eligibility across VTCs, and how do you obtain that information? An "Eligibility Worksheet: Things Defense Counsel Should Know about VTC Eligibility Requirements" is included as an Appendix.

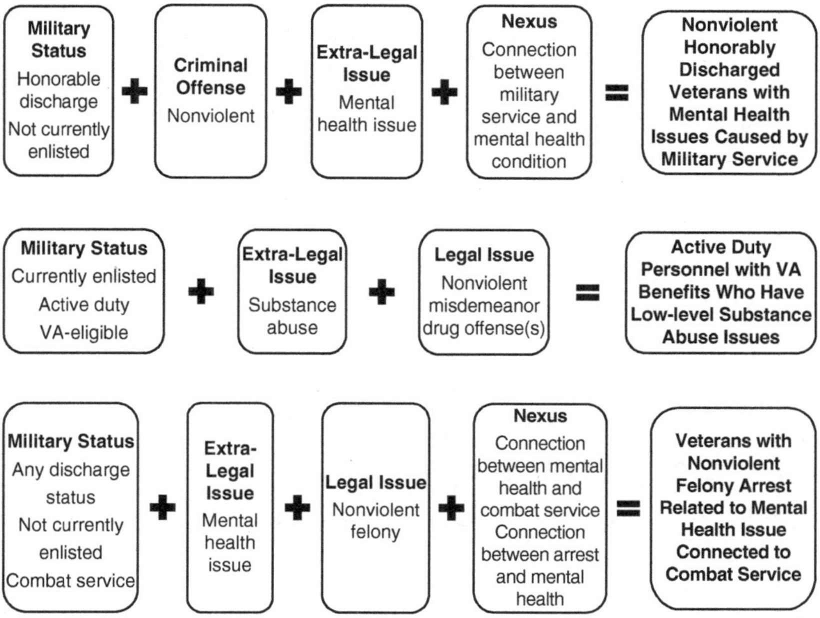

FIGURE 14.4 Examples of eligibility criteria and resultant target populations.
Source: Eligibility and target population data come from the author's national survey of VTCs conducted in 2012. See Baldwin (2015, 2015-Online First).

The items on the Eligibility Worksheet address most topics requisite to eligibility requirements across different VTC programs, spanning legal, extra-legal, and military domains, as well as relationships between domains. Additionally, VTCs may require documentation for certain requirements to be met. Simply reviewing the items provides further education on the type of information that may be relevant to eligibility. Moreover, the Eligibility Worksheet was designed to function as your information collection tool. To obtain the necessary eligibility information, contact each program using your list of VTCs and complete an Eligibility Worksheet for each program. Once completed for specific programs, they can be saved for continued use, as well as updated accordingly.

Armed with your client-specific information (Military Information Questionnaire and Needs Questionnaire) and program eligibility information (Eligibility Worksheets), educated deductions about a client's eligibility for VTC programs can be made. To confirm your hypotheses and satisfy any of your eligibility questions, work with your VTC contacts (i.e., your list of VTCs). Note, the Eligibility Worksheets indicate—and once completed should reveal—components that may be negotiated in certain circumstances (e.g., downgrading charges to satisfy requirements).

Determining eligibility *is* important, but it is not *all* about eligibility! As defense counsel, you have a commitment to assessing whether things are in the best interest of your client, including participation in a particular VTC program. Your consequential role brings us to the costs and benefits of admission.

Cost and Benefit of Admission: Should My Client Enlist?

Regardless of the type of transfer completed or sharing agreement created (see "Transfer" section), terms must be agreed on by the participant and all courts involved (i.e., Home Court and all affected VTC teams—Home Teams and Away Teams) for admission to transpire. For your VTC-eligible clients, your role is to evaluate whether enrollment (or transfer) into a VTC program is the best option for your client. While the VTC concept may appear to be a wonderful opportunity for those eligible, VTC program participation is often a time-consuming commitment that entails both costs and benefits. Therefore, the specific program requirements should be carefully considered in conjunction with your client's personal situation.

Eligibility and program requirements are distinct. Eligibility criteria focus on participant characteristics (e.g., legal, extra-legal, and military) that determine whether program admission can be offered, while program requirements define what is expected of your client and to what he or she will be subjected in the program. Similar to eligibility, a few trends exist among the multitude of program requirements that vary between programs. Typically, the terms are determined by the combination of program policies and VTC team recommendations.

Frequent court appearances and participation in mandated treatments and services are two common requirements across programs. Additionally, potential participants must agree to receive sanctions for future noncompliant behavior without due process if they enroll. However, the frequency of court appearances, types of sanctions, and treatment frequency, type, and level often differ between both participants and programs. Program length varies across VTCs (generally 12 to 24 months), but is normally dictated by policy for everyone in the program, or on a specific track (if they exist). Participants must agree to participate for the entire duration of the program through graduation or face penalties at termination (i.e., if they drop out or are kicked out). Termination penalties are important because of their severity, such as automatic sentencing triggered by "negative transfer" (see "Case Transfers and Program Identification") to the Home Court or incarceration.

Supervision, adjudication, and additional court mandates are highly variant at both the program and individual level. The former can consist of different forms of probation, mentorship, drug/alcohol testing, drug/alcohol monitoring, location monitoring, medication level testing, and home visits (other than those done by probation). Adjudication and case disposition can differ between particular cases and may be related to the particulars of the charges. Programs may require participants to plead guilty to the original charges, accept plea agreements or diversionary plea agreements, withhold adjudication, or pend/defer charges until program completion. Paying restitution or program fees, attending victim impact panels, surrendering weapons, completing community service or an aftercare program, residing within the jurisdiction, abiding by curfews, obtaining a valid driver's license, maintaining employment, or attending school have also been required in various cases.

VTC programs are intentionally designed to be rigorous, and some potential and actual participants are aware of their intensity. Reasons for potential participant opt out and participant drop out tend to be the same. Program difficulty, in particular, is the leading reason potentially eligible participants opt out and actual participants drop out (e.g., some believe it is easier to just do their time and move on). For both opt outs and drop outs, difficulty is followed closely by not wanting treatment or the belief that treatment is not necessary. Additional rationales of interest include not wanting to plead guilty and the ability to get a better deal in the traditional court system. Although a smaller proportion of cases end in termination as compared to graduation, it does occur, and termination penalties can be severe, which necessitates the careful weighing of client need and circumstance with the particular requirements.

What can my client get for program participation and graduation? As VTC programs ultimately intend to rehabilitate their participants and improve their life circumstances, your clients can receive the treatments and services they may need but may not otherwise receive. Depending on the case, further benefits can include:

- Diversion from incarceration
- Preferable adjudications, dispositions, or sentences
- Option for records to be sealed or expunged
- Early probation termination
- Reduction in court or supervision fees
- Sentence modification
- Benefit and claim assistance
- Opportunity for favorable military discharge/retention (active duty only)

You want to consider all the costs and benefits of participation, termination, and graduation for client advisement but you should also know that requirements can be inconsistent across programs and between participants in the same program. What types of information are relevant to program requirements across courts, and how do you acquire such information? Often, VTCs have a program contract or behavioral agreement that must be signed by the participant to enroll in the program, and this is a good place to start.

However, not all programs may have one, and these will most likely be general terms not covering additional requirements that may be added by the team. Therefore, you should contact the VTC programs (i.e., your list of VTCs) to request their general contract, as well as ask additional questions on pertinent program requirement areas. This list can also be used as a checklist of topics to address when making contact:

- Potential for litigation
- Adjudication and disposition options
- Penalties for termination (by program, by client)
- Frequency of court appearances
- Residency restrictions
- Length of program
- Treatments and services offered by which providers
- Required fees
- Supervision methods

- Rewards and sanctions
- Graduation requirements
- Grounds for termination
- Mentoring

Additionally, the "Program Worksheet: Things a Criminal Defense Lawyer Should Know about VTC Program Requirements," contained as an Appendix, is an information-gathering tool for program requirements. This Program Worksheet contains specific items that cover the aforementioned domains. The worksheet can be completed for each program and saved for continued reference, as well as updated as necessary.

Defense Counsel Involvement: Will You Participate?

The previous sections have addressed challenges defense counsel experienced in the preliminary stages of the VTC process, including discerning potential VTC-eligible clients, identifying and obtaining significant information, and becoming familiar with the components of VTC programs. The remaining section of this chapter is dedicated to defense counsel's communication and involvement with VTC teams and participants.

Can you be a part of the VTC team? Most VTC teams include dedicated nonprofit defense counsel; however, the majority of VTCs also report a need for more resources. If you are interested in becoming involved in your Home VTC(s), do not hesitate to contact the VTC. Your interest will likely be welcomed. Additionally, participants can, and frequently do, choose to maintain their own hired or pro bono counsel throughout their VTC participation. However, some "outside" counsel have indicated difficulties in knowing who everyone is on the VTC team, let alone getting to know its members.

In many VTCs, nonteam defense counsel representing VTC clients are not required to attend the VTC Staffing or Session and often do not. How are you supposed to get to know the VTC team if you never see them? It is your responsibility to bridge the gap! Reach out to team members using your growing VTC contact list (i.e., your list of VTCs) or review their policy manual for a list of team members (see "Case Transfers and Program Identification"). Although members vary across VTCs teams, the following are some roles to search for: VTC coordinator, court coordinator, and case manager. You can also set up a meeting with the judge (through the clerk or assistant, of course). When you make contact with team members, including the judge, make it known that you are interested in attending Staffing to provide updates on your client and discuss his or her progress if you have a VTC client. Team members often build strong relationships amongst themselves in programs that utilize frequent communication in their attempts to achieve program goals. You, too, can become a valued member and better advocate for your client if you are involved. If you do not yet have a VTC client but are interested observing a Staffing, all you have to do is ask. Most VTCs allow observers to attend some meetings. These avenues give you face time with the team and more opportunities to communicate with its members than just appearing in VTC Sessions. Additionally, with Staffing attendance, you become privy to behind-the-scenes action and dynamics of the VTC process.

Observing VTC Sessions also provides insight into the culture of the program and how to participate. In visiting nearly 40 VTCs across the country, I have found each VTC's culture to be unique due to the personalities of the VTC team, especially the judge in some cases. Distinct to each VTC is its opening ceremony, fashion, décor, or lack thereof, as well as the language and interactions between the VTC judge, team members, participants, and other attendees. Some VTCs do not have an opening ceremony aside from all present rising for the VTC judge, whereas others have an opening ceremony that can include a flag ceremony, Pledge of Allegiance, and service calls either individually or some combination thereof. The courtroom décor and attire of the VTC team and participants also contributes to the culture. Some VTCs have added flags (including ones specifically created for their courts) or balloons in red, white, and blue, and others have looked exactly like standard court without any additions to the setting. I have seen teams and participants dressed professionally and casually dressed in their own clothing and garments depicting their VTC name, as well as participants and mentors wearing hats, shirts, and jackets emblazoned with military service eras, service years, service organization logos, and military patches. Extremely unique have been enlisted personnel appearing with commanding officers in combat uniform and a judge in a camouflage robe.

Relatedly, can defense counsel advocate for their clients in absentia? This refers to both physical presence and action. Nonteam defense counsel have cited the frequency of VTC Staffing and Sessions (often twice a month) as a reason for nonattendance. In a minority of cases, team defense counsel may not even attend Staffing or may have been physically present but not have participated in any fashion. Some have indicated that their role is not necessary in a court that employs a team approach. However, because you are defense counsel, you retain the power and responsibility to advocate for your clients' best interests even in a nonadversarial environment. If you are not present and participatory in VTC, you cannot fully advocate for your client.

A troubling number of VTC participants have indicated that they do not know who their attorneys are.[18] How are clients supposed to know their defense counsel if they do not interact? Regardless of whether you are on the VTC team, make yourself known to your client and attempt to maintain consistent contact. You should touch base with your VTC clients prior to each VTC session. Stay current on your clients' progress and challenges, so you can update the VTC team and help connect your client to services. Further, many VTC participants and potential participants possess low levels of knowledge about the VTC programs they are participating in or with which they have had contact. What can be done to increase participants' knowledge of their program? The answer lies with you. One of your many responsibilities includes reviewing and discussing the VTC requirements and the behavioral contracts with your clients.

While VTC programs are a drastic departure from the traditional criminal court system, defense counsel is a vital component of VTCs. Nonadversarial does not equate to nonpresent or nonparticipatory. Rather, it refers to working as a team to effectuate the most positive change in participants. Full collaboration cannot occur if team members are missing.

You have a great responsibility to your clients, as well as your team members, and your involvement is key.

---

18. Baldwin J.M., Hartley R.D. (2022). National Institute of Justice's Multisite Evaluation of Veterans Treatment Courts: Systematic Assessment of Implementation and Intermediate Outcomes. Available at https://nij.ojp.gov/library/publications/national-institute-justices-multisite-evaluation-veterans-treatment-courts.

Eligibility Worksheet: Things Defense Counsel Should Know about VIC Eligibility Requirements

VIC: ______________________

LEGAL ISSUES	
1. Are there requirements *or* exclusions for current arrests or charges? YES *(go to 1b)* NO *(go to 2)*	1b. Specify Requirements, Exclusions, and Necessary Documentation:
2. Are there requirements *or* exclusions for criminal history? YES *(go to 2b)* NO *(go to 3)*	2b. Specify Requirements, Exclusions, and Necessary Documentation:
3. Will the VTC team collaborate to downgrade charges? YES *(go to 3b)* NO *(go to 4)*	3b. Types and Additional Information:
4. Is victim consent required? YES *(go to 4b)* NO *(go to 5)*	4b. In what circumstances is it required?
5. Any other legal requirements *or* exclusions? YES *(go to 5b)* NO *(next section)*	5b. Specify Requirements, Exclusions, and Necessary Documentation:

EXTRA-LEGAL ISSUES	
Are there any requirements *or* exclusions regarding:	
6. Mental health? YES *(go to 6b)* NO *(go to 7)*	6b. Specify Requirements, Exclusions, and Necessary Documentation:
7. Substance abuse or addiction? YES *(go to 7b)* NO *(go to 8)*	7b. Specify Requirements, Exclusions, and Necessary Documentation:
8. Homelessness? YES *(go to 8b)* NO *(go to 9)*	8b. Specify Requirements, Exclusions, and Necessary Documentation:

9. Family issues? YES *(go to 9b)* NO *(go to 10)*	9b. Specify Requirements, Exclusions, and Necessary Documentation:
10. Employment, education, or school enrollment YES *(go to 10b)* NO *(go to 11)*	10b. Specify Requirements, Exclusions, and Necessary Documentation:
11. Other extra-legal issues? YES *(go to 12b)* NO *(next section)*	11b. Specify Requirements, Exclusions, and Necessary Documentation:

MILITARY HISTORY	
12–17. Are there requirements or exclusions regarding:	
12. VA eligibility status? YES *(go to 13b)* NO *(go to 14)*	12b. Specify Requirements, Exclusions, and Necessary Documentation:
13. Currently enlisted military personnel? YES *(go to 14b)* NO *(go to 15)*	13b. Specify Requirements, Exclusions, and Necessary Documentation:
14. Military discharge status? YES *(go to 15b)* NO *(go to 16)*	14b. Specify Requirements, Exclusions, and Necessary Documentation:
15. Combat experience? YES *(go to 16b)* NO *(go to 17)*	15b. Specify Requirements, Exclusions, and Necessary Documentation:
16. Trauma? YES *(go to 17b)* NO *(go to 18)*	16b. Specify Requirements, Exclusions, and Necessary Documentation:
17. Branch of service? YES *(go to 18b)* NO *(go to 19)*	17b. Specify Requirements, Exclusions, and Necessary Documentation:
18. Length of service? YES *(go to 19b)* NO *(go to 20)*	18b. Specify Requirements, Exclusions, and Necessary Documentation:
19. Other Military Factors? YES *(go to 20b)* NO *(next section)*	19b. Specify Requirements, Exclusions, and Necessary Documentation:

NEXUS QUESTIONS	
20. Do we have to show whether any relationships exist between arrest/charge, extra-legal issue, and/or military service? YES *(go to 21b)* NO *(next section)*	20b. Specifically what relationships and documentation necessary?
ADDITIONAL INFORMATION	

Program Worksheet: Things a Criminal Defense Lawyer Should Know about VTC Program Requirements

VTC: ____________________

DISPOSITION ISSUES
1. Can the case be litigated prior to *or* after VTC enrollment?
2. For Program Admission, what adjudication methods are required or available for which clients? *Mark all that apply* __ Must enter a guilty plea (current offense, plea agreement): *Which clients* ______________ __ Deferred or pending until program end: *Which clients* ______________ __ Adjudication withheld: *Which clients* ______________ __ Nolle Prosequi (nolle pros, no pro, dropped, dismissed): *Which clients* ______________ __ Other: *Specify* ______________
3. At Program Graduation, what adjudication methods are required or possible for which clients? *Mark all that apply* __ Had to plead guilty (current offense, plea agreement) to participate: *Which clients* ______________ __ Adjudication withheld: __ Nolle Prosequi (nolle pros, no pro, dropped, dismissed): *Which clients* ______________ __ Records sealed: *Which clients* ______________
4. If the participant is terminated from the program (kicked out or drops out), what adjudication methods and additional termination terms are required *or* possible for which clients?

<table>
<tr><th colspan="2">STRUCTURE & CONTRACTS</th></tr>
<tr><td colspan="2">5. What is the length of the entire program?</td></tr>
<tr><td>6. Are there different program tracks?
YES (go to 6b)
NO (go to 7)</td><td>6b. Track Information (Track Name, Length, What Types of Clients):</td></tr>
<tr><td colspan="2">7. Does the participant have to live within the VTC's jurisdiction? YES NO</td></tr>
<tr><td colspan="2">8. How often does the participant have to appear in the VTC?</td></tr>
<tr><td colspan="2">9. Aftercare:
__ None required
__ Required but included in program length
__ Required but not included in program length: Indicate addition time: _________</td></tr>
<tr><td colspan="2">10. Does the participant have to sign a contract ? YES (request a copy) NO</td></tr>
</table>

<table>
<tr><th colspan="3">MONITORING, SANCTIONING, GRADUATION, TERMINATION</th></tr>
<tr><td colspan="3">11. What are the requirements for graduation?</td></tr>
<tr><td colspan="3">12. What are grounds for termination (kicked out)?</td></tr>
<tr><td>13. Is probation mandatory for all participants?
YES (go to 13b-13c)
NO (go to 14)</td><td>13b. Who must be on probation and for how long?</td><td>13c. Who is exempt?</td></tr>
<tr><td colspan="3">14. Aside from probation, what other methods of supervision or monitoring can be imposed?</td></tr>
<tr><td>15. Are participants responsible for fees?
YES (go to 15b)
NO (go to 16)</td><td colspan="2">15b. Describe reason for fees and amounts:</td></tr>
<tr><td colspan="3">16. What sanctions can be applied?</td></tr>
<tr><td colspan="3">17. What therapeutic treatments or services can be mandated (e.g., mental health, substance abuse, mentoring) for whom?</td></tr>
<tr><th colspan="3">ADDITIONAL INFORMATION</th></tr>
</table>

Military Information Questionnaire

Name:

Date:

1. Do you have your DD-214 or Discharge/Separation Papers? Circle one: YES NO

2. What is your discharge status? __ Currently Enlisted __ General __ Other Than Honorable __ Honorable __ Dishonorable __ Bad Conduct __ Officer Discharge __ Entry Level Separation - ELS Other: Write in ___________	3. Branches of service: __ Army __ Air Force __ Coast Guard __ Marine Corps __ Navy __ Reserves: Which _________ __ National Guard: Which ______

4. Era served and/or entry & exit dates: ________________________________

5. Deployment locations: ___________________________________

6. Combat service or hazard pay: YES NO

7. Enrolled with the VA or VA Medical Center: YES (go to 8) NO (stop)

8. Have you participated in VA services or received any benefits: YES (go to 9) NO (stop)

9. VA Services, Programs, Benefits you participated in or received:	
Currently:	Previously:

Needs Questionnaire

Have you ever had an issue with: Check all that apply

__ Alcohol (binge drinking, driving while intoxicated, drinking to escape problems or issues)
__ Drugs (illegal or prescribed, self-medication)
__ Homelessness
__ Mental health (insomnia, anxiety, depression, PTSD, suicidal thoughts)
__ Employment (unemployment, unstable or inconsistent employment)
__ Family (lack of support, strained relationships, estrangement, abuse, aggressive altercations, child abuse, child custody)
__ Spouse/significant other (lack of support, strained relationships, estrangement, abuse, domestic violence, verbal altercations)
__ Education (inability to complete high school diploma or vocational training)
__ Other (please list): ______________________________

Ever experienced traumatic event in service? Circle one YES NO

What LEGAL ISSUES would you like to address in your life?

What NON-LEGAL ISSUES would you like to address in your life?

What SERVICES OR TREAMTMENTS would be helpful to YOU?

What SERVICES OR TREATMENTS would be helpful to YOUR FAMILY?

• • •

Julie Marie Baldwin, PhD, is a Research Professor for American University's Department of Justice, Law, and Criminology. She is the leading national expert in the area of VTCs, conducting multi-site evaluations and national surveys and working with courts, agencies, researchers, practitioners, and legislatures in this area since 2010. Her research interests primarily include courts, military service and crime/delinquency, and drug policy and use/misuse.

Dr. Baldwin has obtained more than $55 million in external funding for her collaborative projects with more than $20 million dedicated to her VTC work. Her research has been funded by the National Institute of Justice (NIJ), Bureau of Justice Assistance (BJA), National Institute of Corrections, Substance Abuse and Mental Health Services Administration, and National Science Foundation, as well as a variety of state and local entities. In addition to a variety of externally funded single-site and statewide collaborations, Dr. Baldwin is currently the principal investigator of the NIJ's Multisite Impact and Cost-Efficiency Evaluation of Veterans Treatment Courts and BJA's Veterans Treatment Court Risk and Need Enhancement Initiative (VTC Risk and Need Assessment Project), was the principal investigator of the NIJ's Multisite VTC Process Evaluation, and conducted the first comprehensive national survey of VTCs. Her articles have been published in the *Journal of Criminal Law and Criminology*, *Criminal Justice and Behavior*, *Criminal Justice Policy Review*, and *Drug and Alcohol Dependence*.

Dr. Baldwin earned her PhD from the University of Florida in criminology, law, and society (2013). Prior to her doctoral work, she was a court analyst (2008–2009) for the New York State Supreme Court Appellate Division and a paralegal and Freedom of Information Law administrator (2007–2008) for the Kings County District Attorney's Office in the Appeals Bureau. She obtained her MA from John Jay College of Criminal Justice (2007) and BA from the University of North Florida (2004). She can be reached at baldwin.juliemarie@gmail.com.

Chapter

15

Standby or Advisory Counsel

Dr. Elizabeth Owen and Dr. Erica Weissman

The following chapter by Dr. Eizabeth Owen and Dr. Erica Weissman is virtually the same as the version that appeared in the first edition of this book. Indeed, Dr. Weissman and Dr. Owen's work remains one of the most comprehensive treatments of this subject to date.

The American Bar Association, namely through the Defense Function Standards drafted by its Criminal Justice Section in 2017, has attempted to deal with questions by counsel about the nature of their role when appointed standby counsel. Defense Standard 4-3.9 states that standby counsel "should permit the accused to make the final decisions on all matters, including strategic and tactical matters." However, standby counsel "may bring to the attention of the accused matters beneficial to him or her." Still, standby counsel should "assist a pro se accused only when the accused requests assistance" and "should not actively participate in the conduct of the defense unless requested by the accused or insofar as directed to do so by the court."

For the typical criminal defense lawyer, all this is easier said than done. How many of us find ourselves calling out, if not jumping from our seats during legal shows and movies, stating in frustration: "That's not how it really happens!"? Dr. Owen and Dr. Weissman's chapter examines the case law that has evolved around the issue of standby counsel. It also provides insight into the psychological makeup and motivation of individuals who choose to represent themselves. Finally, the chapter provides examples from the authors' own experience evaluating pro se defendants.

• • •

Criminal defendants have a constitutional right to counsel—and a constitutional right to dispense with counsel and represent themselves. As the United States Supreme Court explained in *Faretta v. California* (1975):

> [U]nless the defendant agrees to representation by counsel, the defense presented is not the defense guaranteed by the Constitution, for, in a very real sense, it is not his defense. The defendant, not his lawyer or the State, will bear the personal consequences of a conviction. It is the defendant, therefore, who must be free personally to decide whether in his particular case counsel is to his advantage.

If a defendant is competent to stand trial under the standard established in *Dusky v. United States* (1960), he or she is also competent to choose self-representation, as long as he or she does it "knowingly and intelligently" after having been informed of its "dangers and disadvantages" (*Godinez v. Moran*, 1993). The defendant in *Godinez* wished to represent himself and enter a guilty plea, and the court reasoned that the decision to plead guilty is just one of the many decisions that any competent defendant may have to make, so a defendant who is competent to proceed is also competent to plead guilty.

But what about a pro se defendant who plans to go to trial? Pro se defendants must follow the same procedural and substantive rules as represented defendants, must make arguments that are legally cognizable, and must maintain the same standard of courtroom decorum. *Faretta* and *Godinez* only speak to the capacity to decide on self-representation, not to the ability to actually represent oneself as a lawyer would. In 2009, the ABA Coalition for Justice surveyed almost 1,000 state court trial judges about the perceived impact of the economic downturn on the way defendants were represented in court. Sixty percent of the judges reported that they were seeing more self-representation by civil litigants, and there was a "strong consensus" that self-representation had a negative impact on court proceedings, as pro se litigants often failed to present necessary evidence or object to improperly introduced evidence; made procedural errors; did not examine witnesses effectively; and did not make effective legal arguments. A substantial majority of judges also felt that going pro se has a negative impact on the court because of the amount of time court staff must devote to assisting such parties; they also cited the difficulty of ensuring a fair trial when the facts are not properly presented. Although it appears that this study did not ask specifically about the judges' experience with pro se criminal defendants, it is very likely that the same problems arise in those situations.

In *Indiana v. Edwards* (2008), the Supreme Court, addressing the question that *Godinez* sidestepped, held that even when a defendant has been found competent to stand trial (and would therefore also be competent to enter a guilty plea), a court may require him or her to accept representation by counsel if he or she lacks the "mental competency" to conduct a defense. Left unaddressed were questions such as what constitutes mental competency to conduct a defense; how that might differ from competency to stand trial; how such competency (or lack thereof) would be assessed; and whether the *Edwards* holding applies only to defendants with mental illness, or also to defendants with intellectual or developmental disabilities. These questions have yet to be answered with any clarity.

Since all parties, including the court, have an interest in fair, dignified, and timely proceedings, the court may decide to appoint standby counsel in criminal cases. This is an attorney who is present throughout the proceedings, can advise the pro se defendant if needed, and is prepared to step in if the defendant—or the court—decides that self-representation is no longer appropriate. Even if the defendant objects to having standby counsel, the appointment can be made without violating the defendant's right to self-representation, provided the defendant retains "actual control" of the case (i.e., makes all relevant decisions and speaks for himself or herself) and standby counsel does nothing that would cause the jury to think otherwise (*McKaskle v. Wiggins*, 1984).

It is relatively rare for a criminal defendant to go pro se. In reviewing the records of over one million federal felony cases conducted between 1996 and 2011, Goldschmidt and Stemen[1] found that only 2 percent of defendants were self-represented at the time the case terminated. As a result, there is little published data in this area. In fact, according to a recent study of patterns and trends in federal pro se defense,[2] no state

1. Goldschmidt J. and Stemen D. *Patterns and Trends in Federal Pro Se Defense, 1996-2011: An Exploratory Study*. 8 Federal Courts Law Review (2015).
2. *Id.*

publishes such data. An empirical study by Hashimoto[3] based on records of over 200 state felony cases and over 800 federal felony cases in which the defendants had gone pro se, concluded that between 3 and 5 percent of defendants represent themselves in state and federal court. Misdemeanor cases are a different matter. Some states (e.g., South Carolina, Tennessee, Florida) and some cities, due to fiscal constraints, are unable to provide counsel for indigent misdemeanor defendants. In Utah, nearly 75 percent of such defendants are unrepresented.

In her review of state and federal felony cases, Hashimoto found no evidence that most pro se defendants suffered from mental illness or chose to represent themselves for irrational or delusional reasons, even though competency evaluations were ordered for them at a slightly higher rate than for other defendants—usually, after they had announced their intentions of going pro se. However, when defendants do choose to go pro se because of eccentric, irrational, or even delusional beliefs, the role of standby counsel may become quite difficult. Standby counsel may have to watch helplessly as a defendant rejects assistance and pursues a losing course; may have to actively assist a defendant whose approach to the case seems bizarre or self-defeating; or may have to raise the issue of whether the defendant remains competent to stand trial or even whether the defendant's right to self-representation should be limited by the court.

In seeking to assist pro se defendants as standby counsel, it is crucial to understand why the defendant has opted for self-representation. It is also important to understand one's own reactions to the defendant's decisions and the defendant's behavior. Pro se defendants tend to fall into one of the following groups:

- Those who are unable to hire a private attorney and/or think ill of public defenders
- Those who are charged with relatively minor crimes and/or crimes where the likely sentence is not in question
- Those who struggle with personality disorders and/or think laws do not apply to them
- Those who are delusional or otherwise psychotic

3. Hashimoto E.J. *Defending the Right to Self Representation: An Empirical Look at the Pro Se Felony Defendant*, 85 North Carolina Law Review 423–87 (2007).

Indigent or Mistrustful Defendants

It is our opinion that it is better for an indigent defendant to be represented by a dedicated court-appointed attorney (and we have found that most are dedicated) than to scrape together the family funds to hire a perhaps less-than-desirable private attorney who is struggling to "make it." However, plenty of defendants have had what they perceive as bad experiences with assigned counsel or are significantly distrustful of the "system" as a whole. Some reasons for defendants' disillusionment or mistrust include:

- A belief that the criminal justice system is racially biased. For example, a 2011 report by the Bureau of Justice Assistance, U.S. Department of Justice, noted that most research shows "blacks are less likely than whites to receive reduced pleas."
- Wanting more face time with their attorneys. According to a Bureau of Justice Statistics Special Report on defense counsel in criminal cases (November 2000), prison inmates spoke to court-appointed lawyers later in the proceedings, and less often, than they spoke to private attorneys.
- Wanting longer interactions with their attorneys. Lawyers are used to making concise points and moving on, but most defendants need things explained more than once, in very plain (but not patronizing) language. They will also need time to process the information—especially if it does not comport with their understanding of or hopes for the case.
- Hearing from other detainees that someone else got a much better plea offer for what seems like the same or similar charge.
- Not understanding (or appreciating) aspects of the charges and/or evidence against them.
- Wanting to file motions that are inappropriate or ill-advised and being discouraged by their attorneys from doing so.
- Thinking that since all court personnel (except privately retained attorneys) are paid by the state, they all are "in cahoots." As evidence of this, they will often refer to having seen attorneys, prosecutors, and sometimes judges talking collegially with each other in court. In some respects, this perception is accurate. A 2011 report from Bureau of Justice Assistance, U.S. Department of Justice found that "[t]he

overwhelming majority (90 to 95 percent) of cases result in plea bargaining and to some defendants, plea bargaining seems like a collusion between defense and prosecution."

- Discomfort with attorneys who suggest that a plea bargain is the best legal option—before exploring each and every other possible approach in minute detail. A little legal knowledge can be a dangerous thing. Remember, many incarcerated defendants are able to spend a great deal of time reading legal materials in the law library, talking to "jail-house lawyers," and thinking about their cases, often without understanding the fundamental principles of the law.

Case Example: Clarence Earl Gideon

While technically not a pro se case by defendant choice, we cannot discuss self-representation without including Clarence Earl Gideon, of *Gideon v. Wainwright* (1963) fame. An indigent drifter, he was charged in Florida with committing a nonviolent felony. His request for a court-appointed attorney was denied because under Florida law at the time, this was only permitted for indigent defendants facing capital cases.

Gideon represented himself at trial and was convicted. While incarcerated, he filed a habeas corpus petition with the Florida Supreme Court, which denied it. Gideon appealed this decision to the United States Supreme Court, which accepted the case—this time, argued by a court-appointed attorney—and unanimously held that under the Sixth Amendment, states must provide all indigent criminal defendants with counsel, regardless of the type of charge. Gideon's conviction was overturned, he was represented by counsel at his second trial, and he was acquitted. This is both an example of when self-representation can work and when things are best left to a professional.

Case Example: N.M.

N.M., who had immigrated to the United States, had a wealthy and highly respected family still living in his country of origin. When he was charged with a serious felony, he eschewed a public defender, claimed that he could not afford a private attorney whom he trusted, and chose to represent himself. Mr. M., who had been in jail awaiting resolution of his charges for over two years, spoke frequently about how his family was "everything" to him and how all he wanted was to be released and reunited with his children. When he refused an offer of time served, everyone was confused. His stance seemed so irrational that the court ordered an evaluation of his competency to proceed with trial, and Dr. Owen was assigned to examine him.

After several frustrating sessions, she was finally able to ascertain that in his mind and culture, pleading guilty and admitting wrongdoing would bring shame on him and his family back home, irreparably tarnishing its good name and social standing. In this case, the defendant's recalcitrance was not due to a personality disorder or disillusionment about the system, but had a cultural basis. He maintained his innocence through what was a relatively short trial, thus preserving his family's reputation; and was sentenced, with head held high, to time served.

TIP: Always be polite, respectful, and aware of possible cultural issues. Some careful research, including interviews with the defendant's family or community, if available, can assist in differentiating between beliefs and behaviors that are genuinely culturally normative for the defendant, and those that are idiosyncratic and may indicate psychopathology.

Personality Disorders/Laws Don't Apply

As conceptualized in the *Diagnostic and Statistical Manual of Mental Disorders*, 5th edition (DSM-5), a personality disorder is "an enduring pattern of inner experience and behavior that deviates markedly from the individual's culture, is pervasive and inflexible, has an onset in adolescence or early adulthood, is stable over time, and leads to distress or impairment." Eleven different personality disorders are included in the DSM-5, but two of them seem to be overrepresented among those who decide to fend for themselves in court on criminal charges: narcissistic personality disorder and paranoid personality disorder.

In brief, someone with narcissistic personality disorder has a grandiose sense of self-importance, an exaggerated belief in his or her superiority, and often behaves in a haughty or arrogant manner. A person with paranoid personality disorder harbors pervasive, unfounded beliefs that others are attempting to exploit, harm, or deceive him or her, and therefore interprets benign events or remarks as demeaning or threatening. Other characteristics include being quick to take offense; counterattacking when feeling threatened; and being reluctant to confide in others out of fear that the information will be used against him or her. With narcissistic and paranoid personalities alike, the issue of psychological and legal autonomy—the "dignity of individual choice," as Justice Scalia wrote in his *Edwards* dissent—may be a primary motivating factor.

As their own counsel, they have the final say in every legal matter that affects them—for better or worse. The narcissistic defendant believes that no lawyer can represent him or her as well as he or she can represent himself or herself (or perhaps, that there is no lawyer worthy of representing him or her); the paranoid defendant believes that no lawyer is trustworthy, so he or she must do the job himself. (There is, as one can surmise, some overlap between this group and those who are disillusioned with the criminal justice system.) That being said, some pro se defendants who lose at trial will later claim ineffective assistance of counsel, or claim that they were denied the right to an attorney because the court should have known that they were ill equipped to represent themselves. To our knowledge, these arguments have never succeeded.

TIP: Listen to what the defendant has to say. This can act as an effective sedative for an irritable client.

Case Example: Ted Bundy

Ted Bundy, perhaps the most famous (or infamous) serial killer in the United States, decided to represent himself at one of his trials. Psychological profiles of him are in abundance. A study in 2006, using a brief vignette of Bundy's life, found that of the 73 psychologists participating, 95 percent thought he met DSM criteria for both narcissistic and antisocial personality disorders.[4] He likely wanted to demonstrate his perceived superior intelligence by representing himself. It is noteworthy that this also allowed him the opportunity to further terrorize his surviving victims by examining them on the stand. Needless to say, he lost both the trial and his life.

---

4. Samuel D.B., Widiger T.A. *Clinicians' Judgments of Clinical Utility: A Comparison of the DSM-IV and Five-Factor Models*. 115 Journal of Abnormal Psychology 298–308 (2006).

Case Example: C.B.

The growth of "sovereign citizen" ideology has proved vexing, to say the least, to court staff on many levels. This is not an organized "movement"; it is more akin to a leaderless resistance, in which the concept of "sovereign citizen" has many versions and offshoots. They all, however, have some things in common. One of the central ideas is that "sovereign citizens" owe no allegiance to laws or governments, with the possible exception of locally elected sheriffs. When in court, they will not acknowledge the authority of the judge, attorneys, clerks, or court officers. Some have tried to represent themselves, with unsurprisingly poor results, while others eventually relent and accept legal advice or even representation.

They use unusual language: "The court lacks territorial jurisdiction over me . . . the name on the charge is all in capitals—it is a corporation. I am a live man, flesh and blood." They may evoke Admiralty Law or the Uniform Commercial Code as the means by which to "settle accounts" in a criminal case. Legal terms thrown in with what sounds like gibberish can drive even the most patient judge or attorney to levels of frustration usually reserved for toddlers at the end of a hard day. "Sovereign citizens" may refuse to use the words "I understand" in a legal context, or answer any question that begins "Do you understand . . . ?" on the premise that answering will be tantamount to acknowledging that they "stand under" the law whose legitimacy they deny.

One example of this is C.B., a person who, after a competency to stand trial evaluation, was thought to be fit but also a "true believer" and not merely using the ideology as legal strategy. Charged with breaking and entering, he represented himself using "squatter's rights," by taking over several foreclosed houses and buildings, claiming ownership, repairing them, and then offering them for sale. There are certainly indications of a narcissistic personality disorder in this individual.

TIP: Be curious. Ask such defendants what specific words mean to them and how they came to have their beliefs. Dr. Owen was able to come to a compromise with one "sovereign citizen" during a competency evaluation by asking him not if he understood, but if he comprehended the role of the judge. He was delighted to show her just how much he "comprehended" about the criminal justice system (some accurate, some clouded by sovereign citizen misinterpretations of the law and Constitution), without feeling he was betraying his beliefs by saying he "stood under" the rule of law.

Case Example: Nidal Malik Hasan

Nidal Malik Hasan, an Army psychiatrist, having rejected several attorneys, both civilian and military, represented himself at trial on charges that he killed 13 people and wounded more than 30 others during a shooting at Fort Hood in 2009. He did not deny his guilt, but suggested that he was justified as his "oath of office . . . compels [him] to at least speak out against these illegal and unconstitutional wars [in Iraq and Afghanistan]."[5] As he did not call any witnesses, chose not to take the stand, and failed to make a closing statement, this can be viewed as a "suicide by trial." He was convicted and sentenced to death, possibly to obtain martyrdom status, which was somewhat controversial, as the military could have been seen as contributing to his martyrdom by sentencing him to death.

TIP: Try to find out why your client decided to go pro se. There could be something in his or her reasoning that the court would find instructive.

The Psychotic Defendant

Broadly speaking, "psychosis" denotes a mental condition in which a person has lost contact with reality. Symptoms may include delusional beliefs, hallucinations or other disturbances of perception, thinking that is very irrational or disorganized, bizarre speech, dramatically inappropriate displays of emotionality, bizarre or grossly inappropriate behavior, and poor self-care. There are a number of different psychotic disorders, some of which are not readily evident from the person's outward demeanor but become obvious when he or she begins to express his or her thoughts.

Case Example: Colin Ferguson

The case of Colin Ferguson cannot be ignored when discussing defendants who choose to go pro se against all advice and logic. Ferguson, who was arrested in 1993 at the age of 35, was a well-educated Black man from a well-to-do family in Jamaica, West Indies, and had immigrated to the United States some 20 years earlier, settling in New York City. He felt

---

5. Fernandez, M., *Fort Hood Gunman Told Panel That Death Would Make Him a Martyr*, N.Y. Times, Aug. 12, 2013.

frustrated by series of personal misfortunes, including his family's financial decline after his parents' deaths, his own divorce, and difficulty finding work apart from menial jobs, which he attributed to racism. On December 7, 1993, carrying a loaded gun, he boarded a Long Island Railroad commuter train with, as he later said, the intention of killing Caucasians. He succeeded in killing six people and wounding 19 others before being restrained by three uninjured passengers.

Despite some indications that he held paranoid and irrational beliefs, he was found fit to stand trial. He went through an appointed attorney and, sequentially, two well-known attorneys who offered to work pro bono on the case before deciding to represent himself. Standby counsel was appointed for him, but he refused to make use of the attorney. During trial, he demonstrated irrational thinking and paranoid delusions by making absurd arguments, such as claiming that he was charged with 93 counts because the incident occurred in 1993 and that had it occurred in 1925, he would have been charged with only 25 counts. There was an assertion from a parapsychologist that a chip had been planted in Mr. Ferguson's brain causing him to shoot, but Mr. Ferguson decided not to call him to testify (possibly because it would have contradicted his defense that he was not the shooter). Not surprisingly, he was convicted and sentenced to several life terms in prison.

Case Example: J.B.

J.B. was a defendant with a diagnosis of delusional disorder, which indicates that the person has fixed, false beliefs that are "encapsulated," meaning that they only pertain to a specific topic and do not necessarily affect all areas of the person's functioning. Because J.B. seemed able to set his delusions aside when discussing his case, he was found fit to proceed. He requested to represent himself and, partly because of the finding of fitness, was allowed to do so. The charge was attempted murder and there seemed to be plenty of evidence against him. Unfortunately, at times encapsulated delusions can be accompanied by a very inflexible type of thinking, and J.B. insisted on going to trial.

During jury selection, he made odd statements and asked unusual questions that alluded to his idiosyncratic version of the events leading up to his arrest. He frequently had to be advised that he was not phrasing his questions properly, and he sometimes became upset and belligerent, necessitating temporary removal of the potential jurors. Fortunately, due to a somewhat patient judge, he was able to "have his day in court" to the point that he was finally able to fully appreciate his chances at trial. By the end of what must have been an extremely frustrating week for all involved, J.B. decided to accept the offer made by the prosecutor.

TIP: Be patient. Sometimes all defendants want is their day in court—to be heard.

Conclusion

So how do you interact with a difficult pro se defendant when assigned as standby counsel? First, remember that this is *not* about you. If the defendant feels the need to rant about injustices, his or her own competence, or conspiracies, so be it. Provide a neutral sounding board. You do not have to take the bait.

TIP: Do not get into a power struggle. In most cases, no matter how logical you are, you won't be able to win. It is not about logic. Recognize that and free yourself from the expectation that you can change their mind.

TIP: Remain calm while your "client" possibly says and does outrageous things in court. It is up to the judge to manage the courtroom.

Should you try to provide legal advice if the defendant doesn't ask for it? Opinions differ. However, it is in both parties' interests to find a way for the pro se defendant to learn about courtroom procedures and effective legal arguments. This may best be approached by suggesting sources of information rather than attempting to directly educate the defendant. Remember, this is someone who, for whatever reason, wants to do this himself or herself. Respect that wish, do not let it anger you that your vast knowledge is being ignored, and provide as much positive feedback as possible. Once defendants realize the complexity of what they are facing, you have a better chance of gaining their trust and being able to act as a coach and step in, if necessary. Serving as standby or advisory counsel can be educational and rewarding when approached with a calm and open mind.

• • •

Elizabeth Owen, PhD, is the director of the Kings County Forensic Psychiatry Service and past president of the Forensic Division of the New York State Psychological Association. Her 16 years of forensic experience includes having provided assessment and treatment to detainees on Riker's Island, as well as at the Queens and Brooklyn Houses of Detention. She has published in peer-reviewed journals on different aspects of competency to stand trial, and has presented at both national and international conferences, as well as more local venues such as the Legal Aid Society, New York's Judicial Institute, and various law school classes.

A graduate of Columbia University's clinical psychology doctoral program, she teaches at Columbia University's Teachers College, the State University of New York's Downstate Medical School, and Brookdale Hospital Medical School, providing supervision and courses in the areas of psychopathology, forensic psychology and psychiatry, and clinical applications of social psychology. Her private practice includes evaluation of disputed confessions, sex offender risk assessments, mitigation, psychiatric defenses, and immigration issues. Dr. Owen has testified in New York State, Federal, and Immigration Courts, where she has been qualified as an expert in clinical and forensic psychology. She can be reached at eao8@tc.columbia.edu.

Erica Weissman, JD, PsyD, is director of student mental health services and associate professor at Touro College, New York, and maintains a private practice in forensic psychology. At Touro College, she has taught graduate courses in research methods and in the theory and practice of individual and group psychotherapy. As a longtime adjunct assistant professor in the forensic psychology master's program at the John Jay College of Criminal Justice, CUNY, she taught graduate courses in forensic psychology and family violence. She has served as the unit chief of the forensic psychiatry service at Kings County Hospital in Brooklyn, New York; clinical director of the forensic psychiatry service at Bellevue Hospital in New York, New York; and director of quality improvement for Bellevue Hospital's Department of Psychiatry. As a forensic examiner, she has conducted numerous evaluations for cases in state and federal courts, focusing on competency to stand trial, mental state defenses, and sentencing issues, including risk assessments. Before becoming a clinical psychologist, she was a practicing attorney. She may be reached at Erica.Weissman2@touro.edu.

Complete citations are available from the authors upon request.

Chapter

16

Jail and Prison Conditions

Henry Dlugacz, Esq.

It has become a cliché to say that this country's jails and prisons have become de facto mental institutions. Indeed, jail and prison may be the worst place for our clients: Persons with intellectual or developmental disabilities may be preyed on by other inmates, and persons with mental illness may be punished for acting out the symptoms of their disabilities. Access to appropriate medication may be problematic and treatment is sometimes minimal. The criminal defense lawyer is often the only person appropriate and available to advocate for an incarcerated client. In this updated chapter, attorney Henry Dlugacz explains how to navigate the insular environments of jail and prison from a client's admission to release. Attorney Dlugacz updates many statistics, as well as discusses in detail the ethical dilemma of requesting support for a client who may be likely to harm themselves.

• • •

This chapter focuses on practical issues that arise when a client with a mental disability is detained in a jail awaiting disposition of a new case or parole violation, or is serving a sentence, which generally takes place in a prison. Specifically, this chapter will discuss ways in which an attorney can advocate for his or her client short of pursuing litigation. Of course, the success of a given advocacy strategy will vary depending on the needs and receptiveness of the client, as well as the resources and the receptiveness of the correctional system in which he or she is confined. In all instances, however, success requires an individualized assessment of the client's needs and wishes matched against a detailed understanding of how the jail or prison operates. All advocacy approaches must be tailored to ethically and effectively address these factors, understood in the context of a client's legal situation.

TIP: A good rule of thumb to remember is that clients with mental disabilities require the same advocacy as any other client, but may require further advocacy specific to their mental disability.

A good rule of thumb is that clients with mental disabilities require the same advocacy as any other client, but may require further advocacy specific to their mental disability. The correctional environment can be harsh and destructive, particularly for those with mental disabilities. Additional advocacy may be aimed at securing needed treatment or support services such as medications, or it may be connected to efforts to secure accommodations that simply allow the person to have the same rights as people without a mental disability. An example of the latter would be additional support during a disciplinary proceeding. In other words, when advocating for an incarcerated client with a mental disability, we should not allow the disability to define the person for us.

In short, clients with mental disabilities, like all others, are individuals with their unique needs and right to self-determination, and ought to be treated as such. This principle should guide our advocacy for the client in the same way that it would guide our other criminal defense efforts. The ways in which these two areas can come into conflict will be discussed later in the chapter.

REMINDER: Clients with mental disabilities, like all others, are individuals with their own unique needs and right to self-determination, and ought to always be treated as such.

Background Scope of the Problem

Although we should not allow a client's mental disability to serve as the sole defining characteristic of that client, we must ensure that we understand, to the best of our abilities, the difficulties they often encounter. These difficulties run the gamut of the entire criminal justice system, from confinement to ultimate release into the community. Additionally, we must acknowledge that people with mental disabilities are disproportionately overrepresented within the criminal justice system. An understanding of these issues underscores the likelihood that the criminal defense attorney will need to address advocacy for his or her client. Moreover, it can help alert the attorney to situations in which advocacy may be required.

Overrepresentation in the Criminal Justice System

At the end of 2021, the United States had approximately 5,444,900 people under the control of adult correctional systems.[1] In the spring of 2021, 1,774,900 were confined in prisons and 647,200 in jails.[2] Although this represents a decline from historical high levels in 2008 when we confined 2.3 million people on any given day, the United States still confines 537 people per 100,000 residents.[3]

REMINDER: At any given time, close to seven million people within the United States—a number approximating nearly the entire population of Hong Kong—are under the control of the criminal justice system.

Estimates of the prevalence of serious mental illness among this mass of humanity vary according to the methodology and definitions employed. However, it is estimated that between 8 percent and 19 percent of all prisoners in the United States have a serious mental illness resulting in a significant functional impairment, with an additional 15 percent to 20 percent requiring some type of psychiatric intervention during the course of their incarceration.[4] In the jail population, a conservative estimate is that 14.5 percent of men and 31 percent of women come into jail with current symptoms of serious mental illness.[5]

1. E. Ann Carson and Rich Kluckow, *Correctional Populations in the United States, 2021—Statistical Tables*, U.S. Department of Justice, Office of Justice Programs, Bureau of Justice Statistics (2023).
2. Jacob Kang-Brown, Chase Montagnet, and Jasmine Heiss, *People in Jail and Prison in Spring 2021*, Vera Institute of Justice (2021).
3. *Id.*
4. Jeffrey L. Metzner, *Class Action Litigation in Correctional Psychiatry*, 30 Journal of the American Academy of Psychiatry and the Law, 19–29 (2002).
5. Henry Steadman, Fred Osher, Pamela Clark Robbins, Brian Case, and Steven Samuels, *Prevalence of Serious Mental Illness among Jail Inmates*, Psychiatric Services, 60 (2009).

This group also has elevated rates of substance abuse and homelessness. Their physical illnesses are found later, and at more advanced stages in life, as compared with others. One study found that released prisoners are 13 times more likely to die within the first two weeks after release than others of similar demographics.[6] Another study found that two-thirds of offenders with serious mental illnesses are rearrested and one-half hospitalized within 18 months of release.[7]

Policing practices and the characteristics of this group all too often lead to contacts with law enforcement related to quality-of-life crimes such as trespassing or public urination. As a group, criminal defendants with serious mental disabilities spend longer periods of time in jail awaiting a disposition of their charges and serve longer sentences as compared to others charged with comparable offenses. The location of the detention facility may make visitation by counsel or family difficult, further stressing already frayed social supports.

This group of offenders is disproportionately victimized while incarcerated. At the same time, they are involved in more rules violations than others, leading to high rates of segregation, which in turn can make access to visitation, programming, and needed treatment much more challenging. This group is cited more than others while on parole, often for technical violations such as failure to report for mandated treatment or failure to meet with parole officers. And so, the vicious cycle of incarceration continues.

The focus of this chapter is on practical issues, but effective approaches to advocacy are impossible without comprehending the nature of correctional institutions. Even well-run facilities are isolated, closed institutions designed to separate from society the individuals confined in them. The life of an inmate takes place in a small, tightly controlled, rigidly monitored setting, with a multitude of rules, regulations, and unspoken norms. An inmate is told when to wake up, when to go to sleep, when to look up, and when to look down. Such complete control and isolation of inmates tends to distort normal human interaction.

---

6. Ingrid A. Binswanger, Marc F. Stern, Richard A. Deyo, Patrick J. Heagerty, Allen Cheadle, Joann G. Elmore, and Thomas D. Koepsell, *Release from Prison—A High Risk of Death for Former Inmates*, 356 New England Journal of Medicine, 157–165 (2007). doi:10.1056/nejmsa064115.

7. Stephanie Hartwell, *Short-Term Outcomes for Offenders with Mental Illness Released from Incarceration*, 47 International Journal of Offender Therapy and Comparative Criminology, 145–158 (2003).

In such a setting, an appropriate request for accommodation made by an inmate or on behalf of an inmate by his or her representing attorney may be interpreted by custody staff as an affront to their authority, paradoxically leading to a further degradation of confinement conditions. This does not mean that advocacy should be eschewed, only that the way it is undertaken needs to be tailored to the specific situation. Sometimes, an informal discussion with correctional staff is most effective. At other times, the system will only respond to intervention when an official becomes convinced that the attorney will demand accountability. In such cases, a well-placed letter showing a strong command of the facts as well as the applicable policies is the only way of penetrating barriers.

TIP: In order to be fully effective, advocacy must always be tailored to the needs of a specific situation.

There is an often-unspoken current underlying many interactions between advocates and correctional officials: The attorney may see a client with a mental disability in pressing need of treatment, services, or accommodations, while security personnel see an inmate who is faking or exaggerating his or her condition in order to game the system. In the attorney, the officer may see a gullible do-gooder taken in by an antisocial client, while the attorney sees a callous jailer denying their client needed services. Inmates caught in the criminal justice system have sometimes learned that, in order to be heard, they have to make their complaints in dramatic fashion. Wholesale repetition of the client's claims stated as if they are proven facts can foster disdain for the attorney by custody staff. At the same time, it is critical not to buy into the notion that inmates are inherently trying to manipulate their way into preferential treatment. Remaining firm but facts-based is usually the most effective approach. For this and other reasons, time spent gathering objective information from collateral sources such as family or community treatment providers can not only promote better treatment but can also be the most useful means of establishing need and gaining a constructive response.

While clinical staff working in facilities can be great allies in securing needed care and treatment for the incarcerated client with a mental disability, such support cannot be taken for granted. Unfortunately, some clinical staff may overidentify with the custody function and adapt this same disparaging view of the patients they serve.

TIP: When dealing with clinical staff in an advocacy role, two key points are critical to keep in mind:

1. While some inmates may perceive benefit in overselling their degree of disability, many others will see wisdom in hiding it.
2. Behavior that is viewed pejoratively as "manipulative" may in fact be the only means the correctional system makes available to someone to get his or her legitimate needs met. Countless inmates in numerous correctional systems have told me that their mental health needs were ignored until they said they were "suicidal." Objective, firm, and responsible advocacy can help to create more socially acceptable ways of getting legitimate needs met.

As this brief overview makes clear, the problems associated with advocating for this group of clients lies not in finding areas where advocacy is needed, but instead in focusing on the places where the attorney's efforts will be most useful and effective in any given situation.

Know the Law

Advocates can work to obtain assistance and relief outside traditional legal methods. A good starting point, however, is a fundamental knowledge of what the constitution and local law require. It is always critical to understand state and local statutes, rules, and regulations as well as local policy and practice. An additional complex issue is the tendency of some judges and lawyers to use competency examinations (which is not an affirmative defense but rather an issue that should be raised by any party, including the court, sua sponte) as a way of accessing treatment resources for the client. The lack of adequate treatment facilities, coupled with court's concern about reversal on appeal should the competency issue not be sufficiently addressed, make this an area ripe for inappropriate use, however well-intentioned.

Preserving the Right to Bring Suit

Although this chapter focuses primarily on advocacy short of litigation, a critical part of advocacy and client education revolves around helping clients preserve their future right to file litigation. The Prison Litigation Reform Act (PLRA) restricts a prisoner's right to sue successfully with respect to prison conditions in a number of significant ways. Chief among them is the requirement that prior to bringing suit, the prisoner must exhaust all available administrative remedies:

> No action shall be brought with respect to prison conditions under 42 U.S.C. section 1983 or any other Federal law, by a prisoner confined in any jail, prison, or other correctional facility until such administrative remedies as are available are exhausted.[8]

This is the most common reason why prisoners find their cases dismissed under the PLRA. Prisoner may feel that a facility's grievance system is stacked against them and rarely leads to a meaningful remedy of the complained about condition. They may find the pursuit of appeals and the coordination and maintenance of required paperwork difficult. In some cases, prisoners with mental disabilities can find this task daunting and frustrating. Yet, should they wish to preserve their right to bring suit at some point in the future, the full exhaustion of available remedies, and the paper trail to prove that it was done, is essential.

TIP: The hard work of advocacy necessitates never keeping the prospect of litigation fully in abeyance; the advocate must be cognizant of any and all future remedial opportunities.

REMINDER: While often cumbersome, full exhaustion of all administrative remedies is a prerequisite for successfully bringing suit.

Many obstacles await the inmate trying to exhaust his or her facility's remedial systems. Timeframes for filing grievances and appeals of adverse findings are frequently tight. It is not always clear which grievance system is appropriate to a specific complaint. A complaint about the mental health care provided, for example, will likely require a different form and use of a different system than an appeal of a disciplinary proceeding decision. Staff at the facility may incorrectly inform an inmate that a certain area of concern is not "grievable." Sometimes, an inmate is appeased by a promise that something will be "taken care of," which may or may not turn out to be correct. Proper forms may not be made available to the inmate. Allegations of staff "intercepting" grievances or appeals before they reach the proper authority surface from time to time. Some inmates have even reported threatening behavior by staff who seek to intimidate them into not continuing with a grievance.

---

8. 42 U.S.C. § 1997 e(a).

Unfortunately, failure to comply with the mandatory requisite standards of exhaustion, even under circumstances such as those just described, will automatically bar the contemplated suit; indeed, the standards of exhaustion demand that even in the event of intentional obstruction, one must seek remedy elsewhere, either by breaking the corrections chain of command or shining a public light on a case through media outreach. Some systems require that specific people complained of be named, while others do not.[9]

REMINDER: Under the PLRA, futility does not excuse failure to exhaust administrative remedies.

The exception sometimes found in administrative law that exhaustion is not required where it would be futile does not apply to prison condition cases, even where the process cannot give the relief sought. Some courts have even held that when an inmate prevails administratively but has not been granted all relief possible, he or she has not filled the exhaustion requirement.[10]

Deadlines

At the same time that all available administrative remedies, including all appeals, must be pursued, the inmate contemplating a future lawsuit needs to become aware of and keep track of the statute of limitations for the particular claim. The lawyer can assist the client by making him or her aware of these strict requirements. Assistance completing and filing paperwork within timeframes can also be helpful, as can tips about organizing and maintaining files. The lawyer can assist the inmate in organizing and cogently presenting and in sufficient detail. While some of this is simply good lawyering skills, those skills must be brought to bear with knowledge of the system's requirements. The level of detail necessary in a grievance to comply with the grievance procedures will vary from system to system

9. John Boston and Daniel E. Manville, *The Prison Litigation Reform Act: Prisoners' Self-Help Litigation Manual* (4th ed., 2010), 600, note 421. Though conceived as a guide for prisoners, this thorough and well-documented book is an invaluable resource.

10. *Id.* at 568, note 253.

and claim to claim, but it is the prison's requirements, and not the PLRA, that define the boundaries of proper exhaustion.[11]

TIP: It is critically important that clients never lose track of deadlines.

Although perhaps not the first thing one associates with advocacy work, helping clients devise methods to keep track of deadlines and maintain strong organization benefits the client in a number of ways. First, the client may gain the relief sought through the proper use of the grievance system. Second, the facility's awareness of the lawyer's involvement may be constructive with respect to accountability. Third, in the event of an unsuccessful grievance, the inmate's future right to sue may be preserved and protected.

Dealing with the Risk of Suicide

An inmate, with or without a mental disability, may become suicidal at any point during his or her incarceration and require emergency assessment and intervention. For the lawyer, it is crucially important to remember that common high-risk periods for suicide often overlap with the lawyer's own involvement.

REMINDER: Many common periods of high risk for suicide frequently overlap with the lawyer's involvement.

Although the natural inclination is to ensure that a client receives the assistance he or she requires to avoid a suicide attempt, some defense counsel remain hesitant to bring such issues to the court or jail's attention. Information that the client may be at elevated risk may lead to the person being stripped of all possessions and placed in a bare cell under constant observation. These conditions may be viewed as punitive by some offenders, which could in turn cause the client to mistrust the attorney. Additionally, concern about an offender's mental health and/or suicide risk may cause some judges to favor a treatment alternative to incarceration. However, this may not be welcomed by some defendants who would prefer to be released without conditions, especially those that may lead to increased

11. *Id.* at 587, note 357 (citing Jones v. Bock, 549 U.S. 199, 219, 127 S. Ct. 910 (2007)).

surveillance with its attendant likelihood of rearrest. Further, even when a treatment alternative is a client's goal, some judges may view a suicide risk as arguing for continued incarceration where the person is at least in a controlled environment where he or she can be observed.

This is not to say that help should not be sought; rather, like many other situations in this area of advocacy, there are multiple considerations—often related to attorney-client relations, legal strategy, and ethical dilemmas—to sort out. These ethical dilemmas are highly complex.[12] Consultation with an expert in legal ethics or seeking an advisory opinion from the relevant bar association may be warranted. In addition, consultation with an expert in correctional conditions, correctional mental health care, and/or a custodial suicide expert can be highly useful in guiding counsel.

Arrest and incarceration may precipitate a crisis. The person is wrenched from his or her environment and support system. Sometimes arrest is accompanied by violent interactions with police. Family of the incarcerated may not know where their loved ones are or why they did not return home. Children, or even beloved pets, may be left unattended, and prescription medication dosages may be missed. Some arrestees may suffer from withdrawal, some from guilt surrounding an embarrassing arrest. For some people in positions of prestige, the arrest may precipitate a fall from a respected position, which engenders feelings of hopelessness and suicide. The uncertainty of the situation and outcome leads some to despair. When confronted with a client who expresses thoughts of self-harm or otherwise appears at increased risk, the lawyer should act. Bringing concerns to the attention of a judge during arraignment can be effective in having the court issue a request or order for a "suicide watch" and assessment by correctional mental health staff. Where this is not an option, a well-placed telephone call followed by a faxed, emailed, or hand-delivered letter may prompt action on the part of staff.

TIP: When confronted with a client who expresses thoughts of self-harm or otherwise appears at increased risk, the lawyer should act, or decide not to act with full knowledge of the consequences.

---

12. Lisa Griffin, *Suicide in the Criminal Justice System: Ethical Considerations*, *Suicide and Its Impact on the Criminal Justice System* (Elizabeth Kelley and Francesca Flood eds., 2021).

The goal is to ensure that the person receives a timely assessment by qualified staff, and that he or she is placed in an appropriate setting commensurate with the degree of risk (i.e., the more likely it is that the inmate will harm themselves, the greater the risk). Also important is that the person is observed in a suicide-resistant setting pending assessment. Unfortunately, this can be a blunt instrument. An inmate may be stripped of his or her clothing and placed in an uncomfortable observation cell pending evaluation.

As in all other forms of advocacy seeking to obtain evaluation or services for the client, specifics are important. If a client is exhibiting suicidal tendencies, here are some important questions to keep in mind before determining the best course of action for your client:

- What is known about previous behavior and risk?
- What did the client say (assuming that this does not breach confidentiality requirements)?
- What do family or outside providers say about this?
- What history is known?

Although there may be times when confidentiality rules bar the disclosure of some of these specifics, jail staff will find details more useful and more convincing than bald assertions—a concept that should be familiar to the attorney making an argument.

There are, of course, other high-risk times for suicide. These include, but are not limited to:

- Receipt of bad news regarding an inmate's personal affairs
- Receipt of bad news regarding the case
- Immediate entry into administrative segregation or other restrictive housing

When there are negative developments in a client's case to which he or she reacts in a way that elevates concern, it can be useful for the attorney to promptly bring this issue to the attention of both the court and/or jail staff. The evening the person returns from court following a negative development can be a crucial time when prompt intervention is needed.

Many of these considerations come into play with respect to the possibility of transferring a case to a mental health or other problem-solving court. While these dispositions may very well facilitate access to treatment, which would appear to be in the client's best interest, they also come with treatment requirements and ongoing court supervision. Especially when the charge carries a relatively minor criminal penalty, some clients will prefer to simply "do the time" and be done with it.

Intake

On admission, most medications are taken away from new inmates, who are seen as exhibiting so-called drug seeking behavior, faking their illness in order to gain access to illicit drugs.[13] Reports frequently arise of an arrested individual bereft of needed medication for an extended period of time over the course of the arrest, arraignment, and jail processing procedure. This can include medication for somatic conditions, medication for psychiatric conditions, or medications such as methadone for maintenance. Again, specifics—both orally and in writing—are most effective.

The advocate can forestall this confiscation of property by providing the intake person with as much specific information as possible. The first goal is to have the inmate promptly assessed by a qualified professional. If the inmate has a physician or other healthcare provider in the community, providing this information to the person assessing the inmate is useful. Family, too, can help with specific information. Following are some useful questions to keep in mind when gathering specific information to present to the intake person:

- What medication does the person take?
- What is your client's specific diagnosis?
- Why does your client require this medication?
- Who prescribes the medication for your client?
- What are the side effects associated with taking the medication?
- What are the side effects associated with medication withdrawal?
- When was the last dose?
- What is the contact information of the community prescriber?

13. These circumstances will typically arise when representing people incarcerated in jails while awaiting trials or serving shorter sentences, but the principles apply to those in prison as well.

The answers to these questions, and more, can reduce the amount of time preceding the inmate's assessment and help limit the amount of time he or she does not receive needed medications.

Some barriers that may be encountered include:

- Skepticism by jail-based staff that the inmate really requires medication, rather than simply being engaged in drug-seeking behavior
- Concerns that certain medications have resale value within the correctional environment and are therefore inappropriate to prescribe
- Limitations on "formularies" available to jail-based prescribers (i.e., limitations on the range of medications they are permitted to prescribe)

When met with restrictions of this nature, it may be necessary to inquire as to the local procedures for approving "formulary exceptions" (i.e., the process for a higher up to approve prescription of a medication not usually available).

REMINDER: Some smaller jurisdictions may permit family or friends to bring the inmate's own medication to the jail or detention facility. These should always be brought in original containers. Even when not permitted, they offer useful information about medication, dosage, and the physician who prescribed them, all of which can serve to get the person needed medication more quickly.

As is applicable to most of these areas of concern, the intervention of caring family and a firm advocate can help focus the jail staff on the individual and his or her needs. Anything that humanizes the inmate and gives staff the message that they may be held to account for their decisions and actions is generally constructive in differentiating this particular inmate (your client) from the masses of other "new admissions."

TIP: Anything that (1) humanizes the inmate and (2) gives staff the message that they may be held to account for their decisions and actions is generally constructive in differentiating this particular inmate (your client) from the masses of other "new admissions."

Once again, these issues can be tricky and multifaceted. Medication, while often helpful to a person's mental state, may control the person's behavior sufficiently to undermine a successful insanity defense because the person is not acting in a manner laymen associate with someone who is "mentally ill." Similarly, they may blunt the person's emotions so that they appear to the jury to be apathetic to the suffering of the alleged victim, thus creating prejudice. Additionally, treatment with psychotropic medication is a primary driver of controlling symptoms of mental disability sufficiently so that the defendant becomes competent to stand trial. While of a questionable ethical nature, it is not unheard of for defense counsel to use competency evaluations as a way of securing needed treatment for clients and/or creating delay in criminal court proceedings. What should a lawyer do when advocacy for the clear psychiatric needs of his or her client may conflict with successful legal strategy?

Time of Release

Some of the same concerns present on intake to corrections are mirrored upon release. Attorneys can facilitate successful reentry to the community in several ways. Correctional staff attempting to make reentry plans for inmates with mental disabilities face many obstacles. Unlike discharge planning in a hospital setting, which is governed by clinical progress, discharge from corrections is not. The standards of all major organizations addressing correctional health care require that staff attend to discharge planning. Although the contours of the requirements are still being developed by law and practice, it is certainly a best practice and probably at this point the standard of care to provide some discharge planning services.

Especially for detainees, discharge may occur quite precipitously for a number of reasons, such as:

- Dropped charges
- Paid bail
- A court-ordered alternative to incarceration

TIP: For an attorney who finds himself or herself in this situation, one highly effective form of advocacy is also one of the most simple: communication.

The attorney can assist efforts to plan for reentry and continuity of care by communicating with jail staff about developments that might affect the timing and/or conditions of release. The treatment, social services, and legal systems are complex and fragmented. While we should always strive to educate and inform the client about the status of his or her case and plans for release, putting all these moving pieces together can be very challenging for any client, particularly one with a mental disability. Providing status updates about upcoming court dates, efforts at arranging alternatives to incarceration (ATI), and other relevant developments can assist staff in creating individually tailored plans.

Jail staff who are aware of case developments apropos of possible release can better plan for having a supply of needed medications and prescriptions available for the detainee upon release. This is one of the more universally implemented aspects of discharge planning from corrections and, at least as interpreted by the Ninth Circuit Court of Appeals, is required by the United States Constitution.[14] The staff can then attempt to release the inmate during hours that permit him or her to attend programs or find shelter. Discharge at a reasonable time of day can assist program or case management staff in meeting the inmate upon release to assist in getting them to a program or appointment that has been arranged.

REMINDER: The time of release is a high-risk juncture, when a client can easily get lost to services, be victimized, or succumb to urges to engage in destructive behaviors such as substance abuse.

Staff can prepare written discharge plans that clearly delineate referrals and appointments for ongoing care that has been arranged. The attorney can communicate with the jail about case developments and advocate that these things occur.

Benefits Advocacy

No discharge plan means much if the person lacks the means to pay for needed services. The attorney can advocate that staff assist the person with benefits applications, at least starting the process before release. These can include Medicaid, Social Security benefits, veterans benefits, or public assistance. All require documentation to support applications and the attorney can assist in both prompting staff to explore these benefits and possibly in facilitating the collection of needed supporting documentation.

TIP: If a client lacks the means to pay for needed services, the attorney can advocate on his or her client's behalf for staff assistance with benefits applications.

---

14. Wakefield v. Thompson, 177 F.3d 1160 (1999).

Housing

Housing is a critical component of successful reentry planning that can be advocated for by the attorney. One of the most destructive collateral consequences of incarceration can be loss of apartments, rented rooms, or supportive housing placements. Some programs prematurely attempt to use incarceration as an excuse to dismiss the person from services. A well-placed telephone call or letter may assist in preventing or at least forestalling homelessness.

The Americans with Disabilities Act

While litigation under the Americans with Disabilities Act (ADA) is well beyond the scope of this chapter, the requirements of the ADA and Section 504 of the Rehabilitation Act[15] can assist the lawyer in advocating for his or her incarcerated client. Both apply to inmates and prisons. Title II of the ADA requires that "no qualified individual with a disability shall, by reason of such disability, be excluded from participation in or be denied the benefits of the services, programs, or activities of a public entity, or be subjected to discrimination by any such entity."[16] The Rehabilitation Act says that "[n]o otherwise qualified individual with a disability shall, solely by reason of her or his disability, be excluded from the participation in, be denied the benefits of, or be subjected to discrimination under any program or activity receiving Federal financial assistance or under any program or activity conducted by an Executive agency."[17] So, if you get federal funding, which is usually the case even for small sheriffs, you are subject to the Rehabilitation Act.

TIP: Become well versed with the ADA and the Rehabilitation Act.

Furthermore, the same standards are used for both the ADA and the Rehabilitation Act in determining a violation:

> The standards used to determine whether this section has been violated in a complaint alleging employment discrimination under this section shall

15. Section 504 of the Rehabilitation Act (29 U.S.C. § 701 et seq.).
16. 42 U.S.C. § 12132.
17. 29 U.S.C. § 794 (a).

be the standards applied under title I of the Americans with Disabilities Act of 1990 (42 U.S.C. 12111 et seq.) and the provisions of sections 501 through 504, and 510, of the Americans with Disabilities Act of 1990 (42 U.S.C. 12201-12204 and 12210).[18]

Thus, while primarily associated with litigation, familiarizing oneself with the requirements of the ADA and the Rehabilitation Act, and using that knowledge proactively on behalf of one's client, can be an extremely efficacious technique for the advocate to employ. Of course, the person must be qualified and there are many restrictions, but the broad requirements of these statutes provide the basis for advocacy short of litigation in a number of areas. Disparate treatment or disparate impact can form the basis for litigation, but as a matter of advocacy, failure to reasonably accommodate the inmate's disability can sometimes be an effective issue to raise when advocating for the incarcerated client.

What the ADA Does

The ADA provides protections for people with disabilities "who, with or without reasonable modification to rules, policies, or practices, the removal of architectural, communication, or transportation barriers, or the provision of auxiliary aids and services, meet the essential eligibility requirement for the receipt of services or participation in programs or activities provided by the public entity."[19] Thus, the protections afforded under the ADA are potentially broad.

For example, say your client requires assistance in order to communicate effectively and take part in services and programs offered to nondisabled inmates. If this is the case, then your client is likely entitled to accommodations to help facilitate participation, or non-exclusion. Depending on the needs and eligibility of your client, such accommodations can be far reaching, including everything from hearing aids and wheelchairs to a staff or inmate assistant. These can affect almost any area of prison life.

---

18. 29 U.S.C. § 791.
19. 42 U.S.C. § 12131.

Access to Programs under the ADA

The ADA requires what is referred to as meaningful access to programs. In a well-developed prison system, an array of programs may be available, such as educational or vocational programs. Even jails with quick turnover will often have jobs available for inmates. Programming may include recreational or therapeutic groups that address specific client needs.

Programming and meaningful access are critical in a number of ways and represent a worthy focus for advocates. Participation can make incarceration tolerable. Skills that promote successful reentry and recidivism reduction may be taught, meaning that exclusion can have long-term deleterious effects on the person's ability to lead a lawful life after release. Also (and this fact is usually not lost on clients), being able to successfully demonstrate participation in programming may be useful with respect to calculation of "good time" and the calculation of remaining sentence time, or may help sway a judge; the person is a good candidate for an ATI.

Rules Violations and Use of Force

Unfortunately, inmates with mental disabilities are disproportionately involved in use-of-force incidents and rules violations, resulting in their being disproportionately held in restrictive, punitive housing and further reducing their access to services. The hearings associated with such violations therefore arise often. This is a highly complex and fraught issue in corrections, much of which is beyond the scope of the individual attorney advocating using nonlitigation techniques.

This, however, is not to say that the advocate has no role to play in this process. Indeed, merely by familiarizing oneself with the ADA and the Rehabilitation Act, as recommended, and using that knowledge to ask incisive questions, the advocate can prove particularly helpful. Following are some questions an advocate may want to consider when tasked with aiding a client who has been involved in a violation of rules or a use-of-force incident:

- Was your client receiving needed mental health services that might have helped to avoid the underlying incident?
- Were efforts made to de-escalate the incident that led to the use-of-force and/or rules violations?
- Did the hearing officer hear and consider evidence about the potential role the client's disability may have played in the incident?

- Was a staff assistant involved to assist the person to effectively advocate for himself or herself?
- If found "guilty" of a rules violation, what are the local policies concerning placement of inmates with mental disabilities in segregation and were they followed?
- What is the client's current access to needed treatment, programs, and time out of cell, and do they comport with policy?

Related to the issue of exhaustion, the attorney can assist with respect to the preservation and gathering of needed evidence. With respect to use-of-force and rules violation incidents, this may include writing to counsel for the corrections department about preserving any video recordings of the incident and attempting to ensure that the client has access to incident reports and other documents that may be needed to mount a defense.

Media Outreach

On occasion, an incident involving the treatment of a client may strike the attorney as so egregiously disconcerting that consideration of contacting the media or oversight bodies outside of the local corrections chain of command may be warranted. While an impassioned advocate's first instinct may be to immediately contact the press or go outside the chain of command, it is important to remember that such outreach must not be done hastily or reflexively, as it can lead to unintended consequences for the client, including unwanted backlash or scrutiny.

However, there are circumstances that may warrant media outreach. The details will naturally depend on the attorney's local media contacts and the local system for correctional oversight; a good rule of thumb to keep in mind is that outreach of this nature should be taken with extreme precaution and, generally, only after all other options have been exhausted.

TIP: Before deciding to contact the press or go outside the chain of command, make sure to exhaust all other options.

The inspector general of the department may investigate certain allegations of wrongdoing. Some jurisdictions, such as New York City, have created independent oversight bodies. If a system or facility is accredited by organizations such as the American Correctional Association, the

National Commission for Correctional Healthcare, or the Joint Commission, they might be contacted concerning possible remedy. A state or local legislature will usually have a committee with oversight of corrections and may be contacted if a violation is particularly flagrant.

Privacy and Confidentiality

The issues of privacy and confidentiality are complex, requiring research not only of legal but also of ethical requirements. In this section, we will address the issues of privacy and confidentiality from two perspectives: the client's perspective and the medical staff's perspective.

Apropos of the client's perspective, courts have generally found that there is a constitutional right to privacy under which prisoners are not excluded with respect to medical information.[20] A number of implications should follow from this: for one, the practice of using inmates to file papers in the client's medical records should be prohibited, as should the use of correctional officers in accessing confidential medical files. The issue also arises, meeting with mixed reactions from courts, about the propriety of using other inmates or correctional staff as interpreters where the inmate's primary language is other than English.

Clinical staff working in corrections, by contrast, are often reluctant to discuss medical information. This can stem from legitimate concerns about patient privacy. The Health Insurance Portability and Accountability Act (HIPAA) requires covered entities to keep patient's health information private.[21] When state laws are more stringent than HIPAA, they preempt. Also, the ethical codes of conduct for many clinician professions likewise have requirements to keep health information private.

However, sometimes misinterpretations of these laws and rules cause staff to act in ways that go beyond the legitimate and, in fact, required protection of information, which can impede better treatment outcomes for your client. For example, there is nothing in confidentiality requirements stating that staff cannot listen to—as opposed to disclose—information being provided by others. Should an attorney or concerned family member find that it is useful and proper to impart information to staff, therefore, the staff members are not prohibited from taking notes.

20. Boston and Manville, *supra* note 8, at 101, note 754.
21. 42 U.S.C. §§ 1320d et seq.

Additionally, even HIPAA has exceptions that might permit staff to disclose the patient's information. So long as the patient does not object, HIPAA permits health care providers to communicate with a patient's family members, friends, and others involved in his or her health care; in some instances, disclosure is permitted even without the patient's consent.[22] Providers in the community could possibly lawfully respond to a request for protected health information made by a correctional institution having custody of the inmate if they represent that such information is needed to provide health care to that person.[23]

Conclusion

As we have seen, advocating for a client with mental disabilities can present attorneys with a vast array of ethical, procedural, and practical challenges. There is, of course, no one-size-fits-all method when it comes to advocacy work; a successful advocate must consider a variety of factors when developing a strategy, many of which will be heavily dependent on the institutional context and the individual client. Some rules, particularly the protection of the client's individual autonomy, are, irrespective of context, inviolable. However, much else rests in the hands of the attorney and his or her ability to both craft an individualized assessment of the needs of the client and understand the correctional context in which his or her client is ensnared.

This emphasis on individualization is particularly important for clients with mental disabilities who may require additional advocacy specific to their disability, often just to be on a level playing field with other inmates. However, while never losing sight of the fact that a client has a mental disability, it is likewise a mistake for an advocate to allow that disability to define the client entirely.

This chapter has sought to bring the reader closer to a general understanding of the requirements necessary when advocating for incarcerated clients with mental disabilities. It has attempted to do so by providing the reader with an overview of the context in which decisions must be made, which can be used as a jumping-off point in developing a strategy for advocacy.

The successful advocate will develop a strong understanding of two things: (1) the correctional context and (2) the individual needs of the

22. 45 CFR 164.510 (b).
23. CFR 164.512 (k) (5).

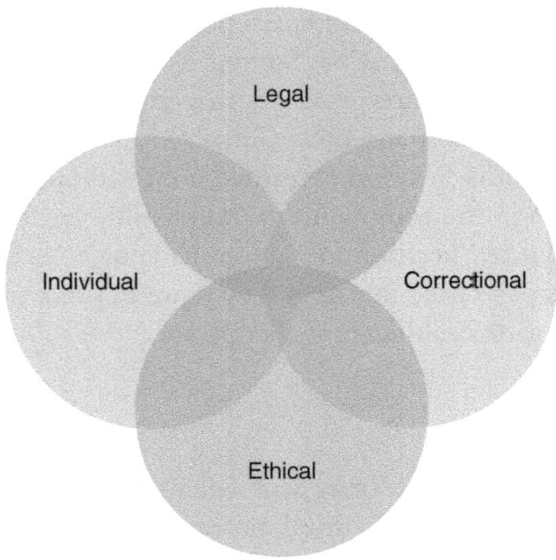

FIGURE 16.1 Foundations of advocacy.

client. Additionally, there are two issues underlying every institutional or personal decision: (1) the legal issue and (2) the ethical issue. These four form an interconnected base from which the work of advocacy rests (see Figure 16.1).

A summary of the main recommendations presented in this chapter follows. Certain issues are more specifically legal, while others demand a greater emphasis on ethical considerations. All require close consultation with the client.

Correctional Context

- Know the Law
  - First and foremost, any attorney-advocate must be familiar with the letter and the spirit of all relevant law, including the U.S. Constitution, state and local statutes, rules, regulations, and local policy and practice.

- Preserve the Right to Bring Suit
  - While litigation is outside the bounds of the advocacy described in this chapter, ensuring that the client maintains his or her right to bring suit is not. Starting with the first principle, we see that if the

client does not comply with the strictures of the PLRA regarding exhaustion of all administrative remedies, they will be unable to bring suit in the future if they decide to.

- Be Mindful of Deadlines
  - Building on one's knowledge of the law and legal procedure, an advocate seeking to preserve the right of the client to bring suit must help the client to always be mindful of the particular claim's statute of limitations. Not only is this important in a number of respects (including, inter alia, preserving the right to bring suit, and alerting the facility to the fact that a lawyer is now involved), but failure to comply with the statute of limitations could potentially result in malpractice claims against the attorney.

Individualized Assessment

- Suicide Prevention
  - While preserving the right of the client to bring suit is an important and necessary step, one can argue that preserving the client's life is a paramount concern. Thus, an advocate must develop a personalized understanding of the client's situation and advocate for needed services and assessment in order to reduce the possibility of client self-harm, including suicide.
  - It is crucial to understand not only when the common high-risk periods are (many of which often overlap with the lawyer's own involvement, including intake and release), but also what are the appropriate and necessary precautionary steps.
- Respecting Client Autonomy
  - At least four major issues invariably arise during the representation of any client; however, there is one overriding ethical principle to which all others are generally subordinated: the central value of client autonomy.
  - The centrality of client autonomy does not dissipate merely because the client has a mental disability. As we have seen, the attorney must maintain, as the ABA Model Rules indicate, the integrity of client autonomy "as far as reasonably possible."

• • •

Henry Dlugacz, MSW, JD, is an attorney and social worker who has devoted most of his career of over 35 years to improving correctional mental health and reentry services in the United States. He is a partner at the New York law firm of Beldock Levine & Hoffman LLP, and a clinical assistant professor of psychiatry and behavioral sciences at New York Medical College.

Mr. Dlugacz is a former adjunct professor of law at New York Law School and St. John's University School of Law, the cofounder and former cochair of the New York State Bar Association's Health Law Section's Committee on Mental Health Issues, and the former director of mental health and acting assistant program director for the St. Vincent's Hospital Prison Health Services. Prior to these experiences, Mr. Dlugacz provided direct clinical treatment and assessment services on both an inpatient and ambulatory care level to people with mental disabilities confined in the New York City correctional system.

Mr. Dlugacz teaches, writes, and lectures on related topics nationally and internationally. He is active as a court-appointed monitor of the remedial phase of institutional reform class action lawsuits involving correctional mental health care, forensic hospital care, and reentry planning for inmates with mental disorders. Mr. Dlugacz can be reached at hdlugacz@blhny.com.

The author acknowledges the contribution of Scott Griffin Held and Sophie Nettesheim, paralegals at the law firm of Beldock, Levine & Hoffman LLP, for their invaluable assistance.

Chapter

17

Working with Families

Elizabeth Kelley

Some people with mental disabilities don't have families. Or they had families, but for a variety of reasons, the family is no longer involved in their lives. However, for those clients who do have families, establishing and maintaining a productive working relationship with the family is vital and, indeed, can be instrumental in achieving a good resolution. Conversely, dealing with angry, demanding, or unrealistic families can be draining and time-consuming. Moreover, even the best-intentioned family member can impede progress on the case.

Over the years, I have identified some common challenges when working with families who have a loved one with a disability. Some of the challenges, as well as the strategies I have developed, are presented in this chapter. These strategies may not work for you. But if nothing else, perhaps recognizing the issue will be of assistance.

Bitterness, Guilt, and Denial

When the family comes to you, they may be suffering from tremendous bitterness, guilt, and denial. Often, by the time a family meets you, that family has endured years or even decades of misunderstanding. The family has had to deal with neighbors, schools, and employers who do not understand the nature of their loved one's disability. Their loved one may have been bullied. The fact that their loved one has now been charged with a crime may have caused them to isolate themselves from others, or at least keep the charges as private as possible. You as the attorney must maintain your professionalism, but you must also show that you care. It is a delicate balance.

Many families have spent their entire lives protecting their loved one. Criminal charges are their worst nightmare. They may very well blame themselves, for instance, for not knowing what their young son on the autism spectrum was doing while on the internet or not realizing the depth of their father's bipolar disorder before he snapped during a period of mania. Some parents may say that they will gladly go to prison instead of their son or daughter.

There may come a point when you can no longer ignore a family member's extreme statements or anxiety. You may fear for your client's safety. You may worry that the family member's anxiety will be transmitted to the client, who is already struggling with the trauma of the charges. You cannot simply tell a parent that he or she should seek counseling. You may want to enlist the assistance of other family members. You may want to acknowledge that you know they are going through a hugely traumatic experience, but that they should not go through it alone.

Other families may simply not accept what their loved one has done. (Obviously, here I am not talking about cases where the client is likely innocent or the case is likely overcharged.) With time, some will accept the situation. Others never will. In these situations, it would be easy to say things you will later regret. Insofar as possible, remain professional.

Documentation and Information

Often, the family has tons of documents and loads of information. This is where the family can be most valuable. Ask them if they have any of the following:

- Medical records
- Names and contact information of medical providers
- Any mental health evaluations or records
- Information about the receipt of any community services
- List of schools attended
- Places of employment
- Housing situations
- Past interaction with the criminal justice system, including prior victimization

Some of this will be useful for your expert. Some of this will be useful for both of you. Both you and your expert will be able to decide what is relevant. It is better to have too much information than not enough. Beyond that, family members will have loads of stories. Invest in the time to listen. It may take time for them to build trust and rapport with you. This may require multiple visits. It is often the story that is prefaced with "This may not be important, but . . ." Many times, I say "Be sure and tell doctor so-and-so that . . ." And as often as practical, the meetings should be in-person.

Respecting Client Privilege and Confidentiality

This is difficult water to navigate, but remember that the family is not the client. Consult your ethical rules. However, unless you are specifically representing a family member, the client is indeed the client with all that this implies. Even if the family is paying the lawyer's fee, the family should abide by this. Everything the lawyer does concerns the best interest of the client. Ethically, a lawyer cannot allow the person who is paying the fee to interfere with the lawyer's independent professional judgment on behalf of the client.

At times, there may be a conflict between what the family wants and what the client wants. The lawyer has an ethical duty to work on behalf of the client, regardless of what the family thinks is the best course of action. Although the family can be a part of the conversation, it is still the client who makes the final decision. Beyond that, the family may have other goals such as "letting the court know what they think" or "promoting social change." But families must be told that your primary duty is to promote the client's best interest as regards the current criminal case. Moreover, families must be warned that some actions can backfire, perhaps to the client's detriment.

The lawyer also has an ethical duty to uphold attorney-client privilege and confidentiality. The attorney-client privilege is a rule that preserves the confidentiality of communications between a lawyer and their client. The purpose of the privilege is to encourage clients to communicate with their attorneys in an open and honest manner so that an attorney can provide the best representation possible. The lawyer cannot share any written or oral communications they have with their client without their client's consent.

Lawyers also have a duty of confidentiality. This duty means that they cannot, even informally, discuss information about their client's case regardless of whether the information came from the client. The client must keep private all information regarding representation in the case absent the client's consent.

When you are representing someone with a disability, the parents often handle most of the communication with the attorney. Nonetheless, the attorney needs to build a relationship with the client and must be given the opportunity to speak privately with the client if needed. This is often difficult for many parents to accept. The family's desire to shield a loved one varies depending on the age and nature of the disability. But assuming that the client is an adult and that they are competent to proceed, the attorney must be allowed to do their job.

Understanding the Legal Meaning of Competency and Sanity

Often, family members state that "he doesn't get it" or "he doesn't know what is going on." True enough, but this is not the legal definition of incompetent to proceed. In most jurisdictions, the standard for competency is low. Even if the accused has an intellectual disability, developmental disability, or mental illness and cannot understand the complexity of the criminal justice system, they may not meet the standard of incompetent to proceed. In short, competency typically requires (1) the ability to understand the nature of the charges and (2) the ability to assist counsel. Even if someone is found incompetent, that does not mean that the prosecutor will automatically dismiss the charges. The defendant will have to undergo a period of court-ordered restoration.

While the standard for competency is low, the standard for insanity at the time of the act is high. Every state plus the federal government has its own definition of insanity. However, generally speaking, insanity means the individual did not know what they were doing at the time of the act. Insanity is often a misnomer for someone with an intellectual or developmental disability. In short, a diagnosis of a mental disability does not automatically mean that one can be declared incompetent to stand trial or insane at the time of the act.

At this point, you will have to explain that the standard categories that the criminal justice system currently offers—incompetent to proceed and insane at the time of the act—may not apply to or serve your client well. Nonetheless, the materials and information provided to the mental health experts working on the case may provide strong arguments for lesser charges, diversionary options, or sentencing mitigation.

Involving the Media or Other Organizations

Sometimes the family wants to involve the media or pursue something other than resolving the criminal case. In some cases, the media may be valuable. And in some cases, the media will come to you, invited or not. Nonetheless, you should explain to your client and their family that your jurisdiction has certain ethical rules governing contact with the media. Beyond that, particularly if your client is charged with a sexually oriented offense, the media or the response to coverage may not be friendly.

The family may also have other targets of anger, such as a school that didn't provide accommodations or an institution that discharged their loved one. Their complaints may be legitimate. But your challenge is to focus the family's energies on resolving the criminal case.

Unrealistic Expectations

Generally speaking, the criminal legal system is the worst place in the world for someone with a mental disability. That being said, if an individual with a disability is charged with a minor offense, they might be able to be diverted out of the system. But if the individual is charged with a major crime such as a crime of violence or sexually oriented offense or in federal court, that is a different matter. The family may be willing to accept a plea, but they want the sex offender registry requirement taken away. Or, they want the charges dismissed. You need to be frank with them up-front and perhaps remind them as needed. The danger is that they will hear what they want to hear or that they will seek new counsel who may very well make unrealistic promises.

Demands on the Expert

You engaged the expert or expert to conduct independent forensic examinations. Certainly, your expert may be compelled by your client's mental status and the circumstances of their case. However, other than arranging logistical details such as ensuring the client makes the interview appointment and providing collateral information, the family's contact with the expert should be limited. This needs to be made clear.

Concluding with Gratitude

This chapter is not intended to be negative, and I want to conclude on a positive note. The majority of families will welcome your involvement. For many, it will be the first time someone listened and understood their loved one. They will appreciate that you are fighting for them. They will do anything they can to assist you in that fight, whether it be to bring you a cup of coffee while you are at the courthouse, return your call as soon as humanly possible, or do whatever they can to retain the experts you suggest. They want you to see them as more than the family of someone charged in a criminal offense. They want you to recognize that they may be a successful professional, or have interesting hobbies, or simply be a person who would otherwise be a friend if it were not for the pendency of their loved one's legal situation. Maintain your boundaries, but recognize their humanity.

• • •

Elizabeth Kelley is a criminal defense lawyer with a nationwide practice focused on representing people with mental disabilities. She is the editor of three previous books published by the American Bar Association: *Representing People with Mental Disabilities* (2018); *Representing People with Autism Spectrum Disorder* (2020); and *Representing People with Dementia* (2022), as well as co-editor with Francesca Flood of *Suicide and Its Impact on the Criminal Justice System* (2022). She serves as a vice chair of the ABA's Criminal Justice Section and edits the section's annual publication, *The State of Criminal Justice*. She is a frequent speaker on the intersection of mental disabilities and the criminal legal system.

Chapter

18

Post-Conviction Remedies

Richard W. Levitt and Zachary Segal

Criminal defense lawyers are known for having yet one more strategy for securing relief for our client—or at least reducing damage. However, generally, the farther along in the criminal proceeding, the greater the obstacles. This chapter by criminal defense lawyers Richard W. Levitt and Zachary Segal thoroughly explains the obstacles involved in filing federal post-conviction petitions, including motions for compassionate release.

The first part of the chapter is devoted to providing guidance to the deadlines and other procedural hurdles involved with filing post-conviction petitions. Although the chapter focuses on federal practice, many of the principles are applicable to state practice. Aside from the substantive details of this discussion, a larger takeaway is that missed deadlines and failure to follow particular procedures can be fatal. This challenge may be even greater for persons with mental disabilities whose executive functioning is further impaired by incarceration.

The second part of the chapter focuses on litigating issues of mental disability in the post-conviction context, namely competency and sanity. Also included is a discussion of raising issues of mental disability in the post-conviction context, in particular, the failure of the Federal Bureau of Prisons (BOP) to provide adequate mental health treatment.

• • •

If you are seeking a post-conviction remedy for your client, you've already met with multiple failures. Your client pleaded guilty or was convicted at trial, the intermediate court affirmed the conviction (or perhaps your client waived appeal), discretionary direct review, if any, has been denied, and the final mandate has been issued. So, you are now hoping for a miracle—that the damage can somehow be undone or at least mitigated. You still have some tools in your litigation belt in the form of post-conviction remedies, a term we use here to describe any remedy that may be available after direct appeals from conviction and sentence have been denied.

The most common form of post-conviction review—and one upon which we principally focus in this chapter—is a writ of habeas corpus, codified at 28 U.S.C. §§ 2254 (state prisoners) and 2255 (federal prisoners). Bringing a successful habeas petition, however, is, to put it mildly, difficult. Broadly, you must show that your client's constitutional rights were violated in procuring the conviction and/or sentence. But, before a federal district court can consider whether your client's constitutional rights were violated, you must navigate around several land mines imposed by Congress in the Antiterrorism and Effective Death Penalty Act of 1996—the dreaded AEDPA—including the statute of limitations, issue exhaustion, and various procedural requirements and possible defaults.

We'll discuss these habeas-related hurdles and ways a client's mental health problems may help surmount them in the succeeding sections, but it's important to keep in mind that numerous additional forms of post-conviction remedies exist that, while not "undoing" the conviction or sentence, nonetheless can provide meaningful relief to clients from a variety of the collateral consequences of conviction. Although most of these additional remedies are beyond the scope of this chapter, it is well to keep them in mind. For example, while all states provide some means to pursue post-conviction remedies, which, if successful, would result in vacatur of conviction or sentence, many states and municipalities also now provide for the sealing of criminal records after a period of good behavior. *See, e.g.*, New York Criminal Procedure Law § 160.59. Additionally, many states and cities have passed "ban the box" laws, which prohibit employers from asking job applicants whether they have a prior conviction, at least before the employer makes a preliminary determination to hire the applicant.

In the second part of this chapter, we'll discuss applications for compassionate release under 18 U.S.C. § 3582(c)(1)(A), pursuant to which courts may grant federal inmates sentencing reductions or outright release upon a showing of extraordinary and compelling circumstances.

Federal Habeas Corpus Proceedings

Clients serving state or federal court sentences may bring federal habeas corpus proceedings under 28 U.S.C. § 2254 and 28 U.S.C. § 2255, respectively. There are both similarities and differences between these two statutes. Principally, because the AEDPA puts a premium on comity, showing considerable deference to state court judgments, state defendants are required to jump through additional hoops to obtain habeas relief, any one of which can preclude relief. As we will see, however, your client's mental disabilities may, in unusual cases, help surmount the various procedural obstacles and may themselves provide a basis for a substantive habeas claim.

Section 2254 Prerequisites

One-Year Statute of Limitations

The procedural hurdles to bringing a successful § 2254 petition, imposed by the AEDPA, include a one-year window for filing the petition. *See* 28 U.S.C. § 2244(d)(1). Certain events stop this one-year clock, the most significant of which is the time during which a post-conviction motion, such as a motion under Art. 440 of the New York Criminal Procedure Law, is pending in the state court. *See* § 2244(d)(2). The limitations clock can begin anew if the ground for the habeas is newly discovered evidence that could not have been discovered previously through the exercise of due diligence or is a new Supreme Court case declared retroactive.

Additionally, the one-year clock may be equitably tolled upon a showing of extraordinary and exceptional circumstances. Because the AEDPA's one-year limitation is not jurisdictional, the Supreme Court has held a petitioner is "entitled to equitable tolling if he shows (1) that he has been pursuing his rights diligently, and (2) that some extraordinary circumstance stood in his way and prevented timely filing." *Holland v. Florida*, 560 U.S. 631, 649 (2010). Equitable tolling is also available for federal prisoner proceeding under § 2255. *See Estremera v. United States*, 724 F.3d 773, 775 (7th Cir. 2013). Every circuit to consider the question of whether mental illness may be considered an "extraordinary circumstance" to justify equitable tolling has responded in the affirmative. *See Ata v. Scutt*, 662 F.3d 736, 742 (6th Cir. 2011) (collecting cases from First, Second, Third, Fourth, Fifth, Ninth, and Eleventh Circuits).

To obtain equitable tolling of the AEDPA's statute of limitations based on "mental incompetence," "a petitioner must demonstrate that (1) he is mentally incompetent and (2) his mental incompetence caused his failure to comply with AEDPA's statute of limitations." *Scutt*, 662 F.3d at 742. The Third Circuit, in *Wallace v. Mahanoy*, 2 F.4th 133 (3d Cir. 2021), adopted a non-exhaustive list of relevant factors: (1) whether the petitioner was adjudicated incompetent and, if so, when did the adjudication occur in relation to the habeas statutory period; (2) whether the petitioner was institutionalized for his mental disability; (3) whether the petitioner handled or assisted in other legal matters that required action during the federal limitations period; and (4) whether the petitioner supported his allegations of mental disability with extrinsic evidence such as evaluations and/or medications. *Id.* at 144. Equitable tolling, however, is rarely granted. *See Taylor v. Lightner*, No. CIV.A. 14-00156-WS-N, 2015 WL 3407622, at *4 (S.D. Ala. May 27, 2015) (collecting cases).

In one of the rare instances when equitable tolling based on mental disability was granted, the Ninth Circuit in *Forbess v. Frank*, 749 F.3d 837, 839 (9th Cir. 2014) agreed that the defendant, convicted of kidnapping his wife, suffered from delusions causing him to believe his wife was working for a drug cartel, he was working with FBI to help arrest her, his prosecution was staged to effectuate his wife's arrest, and he had to remain in prison until the FBI freed him once his wife was successfully prosecuted. Other examples of where the one-year limitations period can be surmounted can be found in 9 A.L.R. Fed. 2d 343 at § 8.

Exhaustion of State Remedies

Another of the hurdles imposed by the AEDPA is the requirement that state habeas petitioners first exhaust their state remedies before filing in federal district court. Exhaustion requires the petitioner to have first presented their issue(s) to the highest state court having authority to consider it, even if only on a discretionary basis. *See* 28 U.S.C.A. §§ 2254(b), (c). The Second Circuit has held that this requirement is satisfied "if the legal basis of the claim made in state court was the 'substantial equivalent' of that of the habeas claim." *Daye v. Att'y Gen. of State of N.Y.*, 696 F.2d 186, 192 (2d Cir. 1982) (citations omitted). Many courts have applied the exhaustion requirement strictly, leading some judges to observe "the requirement for exhaustion is not intended to exhaust the petitioner or his or her lawyers . . ."

Procedural Defaults

Habeas corpus will also be unavailable if the last state court to consider the issue found it to have been procedurally defaulted, as, for example, by finding the issue waived because it was not raised in the trial court. In some instances, a state court's finding of procedural default may be disregarded if the rule invoked by the state court to find the default is not uniformly applied or was employed "exorbitantly" in a given case.

For our purposes, the doctrines of exhaustion and procedural default may, in certain circumstances, and in certain circuits, be excused due to the client's mental illness. The Second and Tenth Circuits, although never having weighed in on whether mental illness per se excuses procedural default, have a standing rule that a substantive competency claim can never be subject to a procedural default. *See Silverstein v. Henderson*, 706 F.2d 361, 368 (2d Cir. 1983); *Lay v. Royal*, 860 F.3d 1307, 1318 (10th Cir. 2017). Those courts were persuaded by the language in *Pate v. Robinson*, 383 U.S. 375 (1966) that "it is contradictory to argue that a defendant may be incompetent, and yet knowingly or intelligently 'waive' his right to have the court determine his capacity to stand trial." *Silverstein*, 706 F.2d at 366 quoting *Pate*, 383 U.S. at 384. The circuits in disagreement, *see United States v. Basham*, 789 F.3d 358, 379, n.10 (4th Cir. 2015) (canvassing split), maintain the language in *Pate* is limited to a waiver, which requires voluntary abandonment, whereas procedural default does not. *See Hodges v. Colson*, 727 F.3d 517, 540 (6th Cir. 2013).

Additionally, a procedural default may be excused—though rarely—upon a finding of "cause and prejudice," that is, that there was excusable cause for the default and that the petitioner suffered actual prejudice or that a miscarriage of justice will occur if the federal court does not consider the claim. *See Coleman v. Thompson*, 501 U.S. 722, 750 (1991). Cause is ordinarily shown by demonstrating that "some objective factor external to the defense impeded" defense counsel or the pro se defendant from compliance. *Murray v. Carrier*, 477 U.S. 478, 488 (1986). A habeas petitioner demonstrates prejudice by establishing that the constitutional errors "worked to his actual and substantial disadvantage, infecting his entire trial with error of constitutional dimensions." *United States v. Frady*, 456 U.S. 152, 170 (1982).

Unlike equitable estoppel, the circuit courts of appeal are split on whether mental illness can excuse a procedural default. The debate focuses on whether mental illness satisfies the "cause" prong of the aforesaid analysis. Those courts that have rejected the notion that mental illness can serve as cause for procedural default rely on the "external to defense" requirement. *See, e.g.*, *Gonzales v. Davis*, 924 F.3d 236, 244, n.4 (5th Cir. 2019) ("Neither [Petitioner's] illiteracy, nor his deafness, nor his lack of training in the law amounts to cause either, because none of these factors was *external* to [Petitioner's] defense."); *see also Hull v. Freeman*, 991 F.2d 86 (3d Cir. 1993). Rather, as these courts see it, mental illness is *internal* to the petitioner. *See Harris v. McAdory*, 334 F.3d 665, 669 (7th Cir. 2003) ("[s]omething that comes from a source within the petitioner is unlikely to qualify as an external impediment.").

Other courts, following the lead of the Eighth Circuit, apply the following test when deciding whether mental illness excuses procedural default:

> Our cases establish that, in order for mental illness to constitute cause and prejudice to excuse procedural default, there must be a conclusive showing that mental illness interfered with a petitioner's ability to appreciate his or her position and make rational decisions regarding his or her case at the time during which he or she should have pursued post-conviction relief. . . . Mental illness prejudices a petitioner if it interferes with or impedes his or her ability to comply with state procedural requirements, such as pursuing post-conviction relief within a specific time period.

Holt v. Bowersox, 191 F.3d 970, 974 (8th Cir. 1999) (internal citations omitted) (remanding with instructions to consider procedural default due to mental illness). Few cases recognizing mental illness as "cause" have directly addressed *Murray v. Carrier*'s "external to the defense" language, but the Supreme Court of Connecticut recently did so in finding the language not preclusive. *See Saunders v. Comm'r of Correction*, 343 Conn. 1, 22 (2022).

Although the test applied to excuse procedural default due to mental illness is similar to that for equitable estoppel, courts are less willing to excuse procedural default out of respect for federal-state comity. In *Schneider v. McDaniel*, 674 F.3d 1144 (9th Cir. 2012) this dichotomy was front and center where the federal district court equitably tolled the one-year limitations period for filing the habeas petition based on the petitioner's mental illness but rejected the argument, citing comity, that the same mental illness excused petitioner's failure to exhaust his issue in state court. *Id.* at 1154 ("One might ask, how is it that Schneider's mental conditions so impeded his ability to file post-conviction petitions as to justify the application of equitable tolling, but did not so impede his ability to file a state post-conviction petition as to demonstrate cause for a procedural default? . . . Principles of comity require federal courts to respect state procedural bars to post-conviction relief"); *but see id.* at 1156 (Noonan, J., *dissenting*) ("Comity cannot convert lack of focus, pace, consistency of direction and organizational skills into capabilities now enjoyed by the state petitioner. Comity cannot turn incompetence into competence.")

Reaching the Merits: Demonstrating a Violation of Federal Constitutional Rights

Assuming you surmount all the procedural hurdles and show your client's constitutional rights were violated, do you necessarily win? Not necessarily. The federal habeas corpus statute presumes the finality and correctness of state court proceedings and will disturb them only where the state court acted "unreasonably," either by applying the law or unreasonably determining the facts. *See* § 2254(d).

Courts have said that the "unreasonable application" standard "falls somewhere between 'merely erroneous and unreasonable to all reasonable jurists.'" *Brown v. Alexander*, 543 F.3d 94, 100 (2d Cir. 2008). In other words, it's not sufficient to show the state court was merely wrong, but, then again, you need not show the state court was incompetent, either.

With those basic rules in mind, let's look at some cases in which an inmate's mental illness played a part in an effort to obtain habeas corpus relief.

Ineffective Assistance of Counsel

The Sixth Amendment to the United States Constitution guarantees the effective assistance of counsel and this right applies to the states through the Fourteenth Amendment. Under the Supreme Court's decision in *Strickland v. Washington*, 466 U.S. 668 (1984), courts are instructed to analyze ineffectiveness claims using a two-part analysis, asking whether: (1) counsel's representation was unreasonable under prevailing professional norms; and (2) there is a reasonable probability that but for counsel's unprofessional errors, the result of the proceeding would have been different. *Id.* at 690. A "reasonable probability" does not require a showing of "more likely than not" but rather requires the court to ask whether counsel's ineffectiveness undermines the court's confidence in the verdict. However, as noted, assuming the state court reached the merits of an ineffective claim, to prevail in a § 2254 proceeding a petitioner must not only satisfy the *Strickland* standard but must demonstrate that the state court's rejection of the ineffectiveness claim was based on an unreasonable application of *Strickland* or was based on an unreasonable application of the facts. *See* § 2254(d). Additionally—and often problematically—the presumption of state court reasonableness also applies to harmless error analysis; therefore, if the state court found that the asserted error was, in any event harmless, that finding of harmlessness will itself be entitled to the presumption of correctness. *See Davis v. Ayala*, 576 U.S. 257, 269 (2015).

Bear in mind that ineffectiveness claims are not limited to claims relating to guilt or non-guilt; many concern counsel's ineffectiveness at sentencing for having failed, for example, to bring the client's mental disability to the court's attention. After all, "[e]vidence of organic mental deficits ranks among the most powerful types of mitigation evidence available." *Littlejohn v. Trammell*, 704 F.3d 817, 864 (10th Cir. 2013). *Row v. Miller*, No. 1:98-CV-00240-BLW, 2021 WL 4553117, at *71 (D. Idaho Sept. 30, 2021). When analyzing such potential claims, it is well to remember that effective sentencing advocacy begins long before a sentence is imposed; effective counsel often is positioning the client for the best sentencing outcome when negotiating a plea; when communicating with a probation officer assigned to interview the client and write the presentence report; when submitting a defense presentence memorandum; and when appearing in court for sentencing. An attorney's prejudicial blunders at any of these stages may provide grounds for an ineffectiveness claim. However, left unsettled is whether the Supreme Court's jurisprudence regarding the availability of habeas relief where a lawyer fails to investigate facts relevant to sentencing applies in non-capital cases. *See, e.g.*, *Millington v. Lee*, No. 11 CIV. 499 LGS DCF, 2015 WL 1402133, at *12 (S.D.N.Y. Mar. 26, 2015) (discussing cases).

With those preliminary thoughts in mind, let's examine some of the more oft-cited claims of ineffectiveness based on a client's disability.

Failure to Investigate Mental Illness

In non-capital prosecutions, courts have found counsel ineffective in failing to raise and investigate mental illness at sentencing and move for an appropriate departure from the United States Sentencing Guidelines. Such was the case in *Rogers v. United States*, 949 F. Supp. 2d 879 (D. Iowa 2013) where the court was unaware of defendant's "intermittent explosive disorder" diagnosis before upwardly departing due to the defendant's violent outbursts. Although the pre-sentence report mentioned the diagnosis, it was not corroborated and so the court explained counsel "performed deficiently" in failing to undertake his own investigation of his client's medical records. *Id.* at 893. The court found *Strickland's* prejudice prong met because "the sole basis for my upward departure was Rogers's history of violence" and "there is a reasonable probability that, if trial counsel had investigated Rogers's mental health issues more fully, I would have had more information regarding the possibly mitigating explanation for Rogers's previous violent outbursts and would have had reason to believe that there were potential successful treatments for this mental disorder, which would have led to a substantial likelihood that my upward variance in Rogers's case may not have been quite as significant, because I would have known that Rogers's mental health history was relevant to his violent history." *Id.* at 894.

Failure to Request a Competency Hearing

Counsel's failure to request a competency hearing may be found to deny a defendant the effective assistance of counsel only when "there are sufficient indicia of incompetence to give objectively reasonable counsel reason to doubt the defendant's competency, and there is a reasonable probability that the defendant would have been found incompetent to stand trial had the issue been raised and fully considered." *United States v. Brooks*, 2012 WL 2000792, at *13 (E.D.N.Y. June 4, 2012), quoting *Jermyn v. Horn*, 266 F.3d 257, 283 (3d Cir. 2001). At least one court has taken the position that prejudice naturally follows from a finding of incompetence. *See Bouchillon v. Collins*, 907 F.2d 589, 595 (5th Cir. 1990) (Because a claim of incompetence does not lend itself well to the outcome test in *Strickland*, "[w]ith respect to the prejudice prong of a claim of ineffective assistance of counsel, [petitioner] need only demonstrate a reasonable probability that he was incompetent, sufficient to undermine confidence in the outcome.")

The defendant in *Newman v. Harrington*, 726 F.3d 921 (7th Cir. 2013), met these requirements. There, the defendant's mother gave counsel "a two-inch stack of psychological and educational records concerning Newman's history of cognitive deficiencies" early in the criminal proceeding.

Putting the records aside, the court explained, the defendant's cognitive limitations were so obvious that counsel was deficient in not recognizing them. Addressing the prejudice prong, the court reasoned that, based on the report by the psychiatrist who evaluated the defendant, there was a reasonable possibility the defendant would be deemed incompetent. Applying the *Dusky* standard for competency, the court rejected the prosecution's argument that defendant's ability to identify his girlfriend's brother as a potential witness demonstrated he was able to assist in his defense. *Id.* at 935; *see also Becton v. Barnett*, 920 F.2d 1190, 1194 (4th Cir. 1990).

Courts have remanded for further inquiry when defendants have plausibly asserted counsel was ineffective in failing to seek a competency hearing prior to defendant's entry of a guilty plea, but the lower court denied relief without a hearing. *See, e.g., United States v. West-Bey*, 2 F. App'x 339, 340 (4th Cir. 2001) (granting certificate of appealability and remanding); *see also Cherys v. United States*, 405 F. App'x 589, 590 (3d Cir. 2011) (remanding for a hearing where petitioner raised colorable claim of ineffective assistance of counsel arising from his trial attorney's failure to seek a pretrial competency hearing).

Petitioners have also argued that counsel provided ineffective assistance at a competency hearing. In *Hull v. Kyler*, 190 F.3d 88, 92 (3d Cir. 1999), the court explained, "Whether Hull was prejudiced by his counsel's failure to cross-examine the government's single witness or to present any evidence of his possible incompetence is largely a function of whether Hull was in fact incompetent at the time." After agreeing the evidence established that he was, the court also concluded, "prejudice to a defendant is presumed when his counsel's performance is so deficient as to effectively constitute a denial of the right to counsel . . . [because] . . ., despite the strong evidence of Hull's incompetence . . . Hull's trial counsel 'agreed' at the conclusion of the competency hearing that Hull was competent to stand trial. This is essentially tantamount to constructive denial of the assistance of counsel altogether, [which] is legally presumed to result in prejudice." *Id.* at 112.

Failure to Pursue Insanity Defense

An attorney provides ineffective assistance by not pursuing an insanity defense even though aware that the client may have been legally "insane" at the time of the offense and no other defense was available. *See Hooper v. Garraghty*, 845 F.2d 471, 474 (4th Cir. 1988). Counsel's awareness must be clear from the record. *See Brown v. Sternes*, 304 F.3d 677, 692 (7th Cir.

2002) ("Where the record establishes that counsel had reason to know, from an objective standpoint, that a possible defense, such as insanity, was available, failure to investigate fully can constitute ineffective assistance of counsel."). Such was the case in *United States v. Kaufman*, 109 F.3d 186 (3d Cir. 1997), where counsel received a letter from the defendant's psychiatrist detailing his struggles with a mental illness but did "not pursue any investigation into an insanity defense." *Id.* at 190. Failing to raise an insanity defense or at least investigate such a defense based on "hints" that it might be available can amount to ineffective assistance, or in some circumstances at least require a remand to further explore the issue. *See Genius v. Pepe*, 50 F.3d 60, 60–61 (1st Cir.1995) (remanding for fact-finding).

Failure to Pursue Intoxication Defense

Where a state permits an intoxication defense, counsel could be found ineffective in failing to raise it. In *Miller v. Terhune*, 510 F. Supp. 2d 486 (E.D. Cal. 2007), habeas relief was granted to the defendant charged with second-degree murder in connection with shooting his friend upon his claim that his counsel was ineffective in failing to investigate and develop evidence of petitioner's extreme intoxication, to persuade the jury that he did not have the requisite intent to support the second-degree murder charge. Before trial, the defendant's attorney knew his blood alcohol level was .30, but never explored whether this level of intoxication could have disabled him from forming the necessary intent to support a second-degree murder conviction. Doing so, explained the court, was required because the intoxication constituted the sort of "mental impairment relevant to the case[.]" *Id.* at 499. The prejudice prong of *Strickland* was satisfied because an expert called at an evidentiary hearing testified that the defendant's intoxication disabled him from developing a specific intent to kill. *Id.* at 504.

By contrast, the Second Circuit, in *Waiters v. Lee*, 857 F.3d 466 (2d Cir. 2017), reversed a district court's grant of habeas, finding counsel was not ineffective in failing to raise the intoxication defense. There, distinguishing the facts from those of *Miller*, the Second Circuit explained the attorney's failure to seek out expert advice was not constitutionally deficient because the attorney requested and received an intoxication instruction and the expert testimony from the evidentiary hearing did not conclusively establish the defendant's toxicity level disabled the defendant from developing a specific intent to kill. *Id.* at 483–84.

Competency

In the previous section we discussed habeas claims of ineffective assistance of counsel, including claims based on counsel's failure to raise issues regarding competency. Here we discuss habeas claims based not on counsel's ineffectiveness, but rather on the defendant's assertion either that the court failed to conduct a required competency hearing or that the record evidence requires the conclusion that defendant in fact was legally incompetent.

Due process requires that a defendant be mentally competent to be tried, convicted, and/or sentenced. *See Drope v. Missouri*, 420 U.S. 172-73 (1975). The standard for competency—the *Dusky* standard—is whether the defendant has "sufficient present ability to consult with his lawyer with a reasonable degree of rational understanding" and a "rational as well as factual understanding of the proceedings against him[.]" *Dusky v. United States*, 362 U.S. 402, 402 (1960).

There are two types of competency claims cognizable in post-conviction proceedings that do not involve ineffective assistance of counsel: procedural competency claims and substantive competency claims. A procedural competency claim alleges the trial court failed to sua sponte conduct a competency hearing, or an adequate competency hearing, whereas a substantive competency claim alleges that the record establishes that defendant was tried and convicted while incompetent. *See McGregor v. Gibson*, 248 F.3d 946, 952 (10th Cir. 2001) (en banc).

Procedural Competency

Courts presented with procedural competency claims consider three factors when deciding whether the court should have ordered a competency hearing: (1) whether the defendant has a history of irrational behavior; (2) the defendant's demeanor at trial; and (3) prior opinions from medical professionals about the defendant's competency. *See Gonzales v. Davis*, 924 F.3d 236 (5th Cir. 2019) citing *Drope v. Missouri*, 420 U.S. 162, 180 (1975). To make this showing, "the accused must point to evidence before the trial court that raised a bona fide doubt about competency." *United States v. Flores-Martinez*, 677 F.3d 699, 706 (5th Cir. 2012).

One case in which this very high burden was met is *Maxwell v. Roe*, 606 F.3d 561 (9th Cir. 2010), where the court did not conduct a hearing even though the defendant "had a history of mental illness, frequently refused to take his prescribed antipsychotic medications, was unable to verbally or physically control himself in the courtroom and exhibited increasingly paranoid and psychotic behavior that impaired his communication with defense counsel and reasoning regarding his defense. Furthermore, during the trial, Maxwell attempted suicide and spent a substantial portion of the trial involuntarily committed to a hospital psychiatric ward." *Id.* at 565; *see also Johnson v. Norton*, 249 F.3d 20, 27 (1st Cir. 2001) (decision not to hold competency hearing violated due process because the defendant was assaulted and suffered concussion on morning of jury selection, passed out, and was vomiting during break from trial); *but see Competency to Stand Trial*, 48 Geo. L.J. Ann. Rev. Crim. Proc. 540, 553, n.1438 (2019) (collecting cases where no violation found).

When the court sustains procedural competency claims, it must then fashion an appropriate remedy, which generally takes one of two forms: vacatur with instructions to hold a retrospective competency hearing or vacatur and remand for a new trial. Choosing between the two remedies largely depends on the availability of medical records created when the court should have held a hearing. The Tenth Circuit in *McGregor*, 248 F.3d at 962 (10th Cir. 2001) (en banc), enumerated a set of factors for courts to consider:

> (1) the passage of time, (2) the availability of contemporaneous medical evidence, including medical records and prior competency determinations, (3) any statements by the defendant in the trial record, and (4) the availability of individuals and trial witnesses, both experts and non-experts, who were in a position to interact with defendant before and during trial, including the trial judge, counsel for both the government and defendant, and jail officials.

Applying this test, the Tenth Circuit in *McGregor* vacated the defendant's conviction and remanded for a retrial, explaining, "We are influenced greatly by the lack of contemporaneous medical evidence in the record regarding McGregor's competency at the time of trial." *Id.* at 963. In at least one case, where the defendant passed out twice and vomited in the courtroom after being struck in the head earlier that day, the court made no mention of a retrospective hearing and just vacated the conviction. *See Johnson v. Norton*, 249 F.3d 20, 27 (1st Cir. 2001). Conversely, in *Reynolds v. Norris*, 86 F.3d 796, 803 (8th Cir. 1996), a capital murder case, although the court found the petitioner's procedural due process rights were violated by the court's failure to conduct an additional competency hearing after "Reynolds' meandering and irrational testimony at trial evidenced that his condition had deteriorated," it concluded that a retrospective hearing was deemed adequate (rather than an automatic grant of the petition without a hearing) because the defendant's hospital records created shortly before trial were available, as were the two doctors who created the records.

Substantive Competency

A substantive competency claim—where the defendant alleges they were convicted while legally incompetent—is even more difficult to establish than a procedural competency claim. To obtain a hearing, the defendant must present "clear and convincing evidence creating a real, substantial and legitimate doubt as to his competence to stand trial." *Medina v. Singletary*, 59 F.3d 1095, 1106 (11th Cir. 1995). The "standard of proof is high, and the facts must positively, unequivocally, and clearly generate the legitimate doubt about whether the petitioner was mentally competent when he was tried." *Wright v. Sec'y for Dep't of Corr.*, 278 F.3d 1245, 1259 (11th Cir. 2002). Further, "neither low intelligence, mental deficiency, nor bizarre, volatile, and irrational behavior can be equated with mental incompetence to stand trial." *Burket v. Angelone*, 208 F.3d 172, 192 (4th Cir. 2000). And the fact that the petitioner has been treated with antipsychotic drugs does not per se render him incompetent to stand trial.

This very high bar nonetheless was met in *McManus v. Neal*, 779 F.3d 634, 659 (7th Cir. 2015), another capital murder case, where the state court had failed to hold a competency hearing, and its competency findings were contrary to the *Dusky* standard. It was undisputed that the defendant's panic attacks and the medications used to treat them raised bona fide doubts about competency. The panic attacks were severe enough to require two trips to the hospital, and every medical doctor who testified agreed that the drugs used to treat the defendant had significant cognitive effects, most notably on perception, judgment, and memory. Responding to these circumstances, defense counsel moved repeatedly for a mistrial, arguing the defendant was "incompetent to proceed." *Id.* at 657. The court denied the motions in conclusory fashion; indeed, the trial court candidly acknowledged that the (unqualified) doctor it sent to informally assess the defendant was tasked with getting the defendant "'fixed up' enough to complete the trial." *Id.* at 659.

Ultimately, the error that required vacatur was the court's failure to employ the *Dusky* standard in finding the defendant competent. *Id.* ("The due-process inquiry asks whether the defendant had a present factual and rational understanding of the trial proceedings and the capacity to assist his lawyers with a reasonable degree of rational understanding. *See Dusky*, 362 U.S. at 402, 80 S. Ct. 788. Because the court never actually applied this standard, it too committed unreasonable error.")

Faretta Claims

In *Faretta v. California*, 422 U.S. 806 (1975), the Supreme Court held that the Sixth Amendment as made applicable to the states by the Fourteenth guarantees that a defendant in a state criminal trial has an independent constitutional right of self-representation and that he may proceed to defend himself without counsel when he voluntarily and intelligently elects to do so.

A defendant arguing a court violated *Faretta*, either by allowing or disallowing self-representation based on competency, is subject to a two-part analysis. The first involves applying the competency test laid out in *Dusky* and its progeny, followed by inquiring into whether the defendant knowingly and voluntarily waived his right to the assistance of counsel. *See Godinez v. Moran*, 509 U.S. 389, 400–401 (1993); *see also United States v. Garrett*, 42 F.4th 114, 118 (2d Cir. 2022). A trial judge, consistent with *Faretta*, can find the defendant competent to stand trial, but incompetent to proceed pro se and appoint counsel. *See Indiana v. Edwards*, 554 U.S. 164 (2008). However, the Supreme Court has not explained when a court may find a defendant competent to stand trial yet incompetent to proceed pro se, leaving the decision to the trial court's discretion. *See Dixon v. Ryan*, 932 F.3d 789, 804 (9th Cir. 2019). Precisely what differentiates a defendant who is competent to stand trial from one who can represent themselves remains a "gray area." *Edwards*, 554 U.S. at 172.

Lacking clear Supreme Court guidance, courts generally hold that "[a] state may . . . deny defendants the right to represent themselves where they suffer from severe mental illness to the point where they are not competent to conduct trial proceedings by themselves" even if they are competent to stand trial. *See Imani v. Pollard*, 826 F.3d 939, 946 (7th Cir. 2016) (cleaned up). *Imani* is part of the saga of Seventh Circuit decisions granting habeas to criminal defendants from Wisconsin based on the state court's improper conclusion that the criminal defendants were unable to represent themselves. *See Washington v. Boughton*, 884 F.3d 692, 703-04 (7th Cir. 2018) (granting habeas and recounting cases). In each of the Seventh Circuit cases, a *Faretta* violation was found because the record did not establish the defendant had severely deficient mental functioning. Criminal defendants have also successfully argued their mental illness disabled them from knowingly and voluntarily waiving their right to self-representation. In *Shafer v. Bowersox*, 329 F.3d 637 (8th Cir. 2003), the court affirmed the habeas grant because the state court's knowledge that the defendant suffered from mental illness required a more searching colloquy before finding the waiver was knowing and voluntary. *Id.* at 652 ("the Supreme Court failed to consider the impact of Shafer's mental health on his understanding and the need for the court to comply fully with colloquy standards."). See also Chapter 15, "Standby or Advisory Counsel."

Compassionate Release

Federal inmates have an additional avenue for seeking post-conviction relief: a motion for a reduction of sentence or "compassionate" release under 18 U.S.C. § 3582(c)(1)(A). Although as originally conceived a compassionate release motion could be brought on an inmate's behalf only by the warden and was limited to the grounds authorized in United States Sentencing Guidelines (USSG) § 1B1.13 (e.g., debilitating medical conditions or extraordinary family circumstances), the First Step Act, signed into law in December 2018, substantially expanded the availability of compassionate release, permitting defendants to bring their own compassionate release motions in the district court after first applying to the warden for relief and receiving the warden's rejection, or after the passage of 30 days without a response from the warden (although some courts have ruled that if the warden rejects the request within the 30-day time period the defendant must then exhaust administrative remedies before proceeding to district court). Additionally, since U.S.S.G. § 1B1.13 has not been (officially) rewritten to account for the First Step Act, most (but not all) circuit courts have held that district courts can grant compassionate relief for any "extraordinary and compelling" reason other than rehabilitation alone.

The United States Sentencing Commission proposed an amended § 1B.13, which was not objected to by Congress and took effect in November 2023. The proposed amendments, however, are unlikely to obstruct compassionate release motions based on mental illness because the new guidance retained the circumstances that if "the defendant is . . . (ii) suffering from a serious functional or cognitive impairment; or (iii) experiencing deteriorating physical or mental health because of the aging process, that substantially diminishes the ability of the defendant to provide self-care within the environment of a correctional facility and from which he or she is not expected to recover." U.S.S.G. § 1B1.13 (cmt) (Application Note 1(A)). Additionally, the proposed amendments added a circumstance for a defendant that "is suffering from a medical condition that requires long-term or specialized medical care that is not being provided and without which the defendant is at risk of serious deterioration in health or death." *See* https://www.ussc.gov/sites/default/files/pdf/amendment-process/official-text-amendments/202305_Amendments.pdf at page 3. Both of these definitions plainly encompass the mental illness circumstances commonly raised.

Before addressing those circumstances involving mental illness deemed extraordinary and compelling, it is worth noting that a compassionate release motion can be denied if the district court finds the statutorily prescribed factors to consider at sentencing—enumerated in 18 U.S.C. § 3553(a)—do not support a reduction. *See e.g.*, *United States v. Keitt*, 21 F.4th 67, 73 (2d Cir. 2021). Courts have found mental illness tilts the 3553(a) balance in favor of a reduction. In *Jones v. United States*, No. 217CR20608TGBDRG1, 2021 WL 4264763, at *3 (E.D. Mich. Sept. 20, 2021), the court granted the defendant's motion for compassionate release, observing, "First, the Court considers the history and characteristics of the defendant. Mr. Jones has a history of mental health problems, most notably depression, and mental disability including 'low average intellectual functioning and borderline to average memory functioning.'" Similarly, in *United States v. Moore*, No. 4:12CR00030, 2021 WL 3682312, at *2 (W.D. Va. Aug. 19, 2021), the court explained, upon reducing the defendant's sentence, "This sentence would be sufficient to punish and deter someone like Moore who, because of his mental disability, is more likely to suffer 'extra burdens' while incarcerated like violence, victimization, and manipulation."

Turning to the extraordinary and compelling circumstances, following are cases where mental illness has been successfully cited to show such circumstances. Although many of the cases spawn from complications related to the COVID-19 lockdowns, these cases retain their relevance.

For one, the lockdowns persist despite the conclusion of the federal emergency. And second, the effects of the disruptions in treatment when the lockdowns were more prevalent might very well persist.

COVID-19: Interruption of or Failure to Provide Treatment

In *United States v. Reyes*, No. 19 Cr. 66-LTS, 2021 WL 22717 (S.D.N.Y. Jan. 4, 2021), the court released the defendant after he served 90 percent of his sentence, adding a special additional term of four months' supervised release to be served in the residential reentry center (i.e., halfway house), in light of the BOP's failure to provide the defendant "substance abuse and mental health treatment," which resulted in his confinement at Brooklyn MDC "in circumstances that can exacerbate, rather than support the treatment of, his mental health issues." The court in *United States v. Hatcher*, No. 18 CR. 454-10-KPF, 2021 WL 1535310 (S.D.N.Y. Apr. 19, 2021), reached the same conclusion for the defendant, also confined at Brooklyn MDC. *Id.* at *4 ("While harsh conditions of confinement alone are insufficient, given Ms. Hatcher's serious mental and physical health issues, deprivation of these services for such a prolonged period of time rises to the level of 'extraordinary and compelling reasons' for compassionate release in this instance."). The availability of medication, said at least one court, does not mitigate the absence of appropriate programming. *See United States v. Richardson*, No. 20-CR-00276-SI-1, 2022 WL 2541275 at *3 (N.D. Cal. July 7, 2022) ("FCI is under 'Condition 3' restrictions preventing Mr. Richardson from receiving group therapy, counseling sessions, or anything beyond medication.").

COVID-19: Increased Risk of Bad Outcomes

Courts have also granted compassionate release where a defendant's mood disorders increase the likelihood of a bad outcome should defendant contract COVID-19. In *United States v. Richardson*, No. 20-CR-00276-SI-1, 2022 WL 2541275 (N.D. Cal. July 7, 2022), the court granted release because, per guidance from the Centers for Disease Control and Prevention (CDC), the court found that post-traumatic stress disorder (PTSD) and depression placed the defendant at increased risk of complications from a COVID-19 infection.

Even lacking clear CDC guidance, courts have accepted general scientific consensus that "a substantial subset of individuals with major depressive disorder and bipolar disorder exhibit atypical immune response" when agreeing to reduce a defendant's sentence. *United States v. Lavy*, No. 17-20033-JAR, 2020 WL 3218110, at *5 (D. Kan. June 15, 2020). Relief has also been granted where the defendant's PTSD has been exacerbated by lockdowns that prevent defendants from exercising the necessary caution to protect themselves from contracting COVID-19. *See United States v. Johnson*, 464 F. Supp. 3d 22, 39 (D.D.C. 2020) ("the mental and physical stress of being detained under the conditions of confinement . . . while dealing with established and serious physical and mental health issues, almost certainly thwarts Johnson's ability to provide the type of self-care within the prison environment that is needed now more than ever.").

Neglectful Medical Treatment

Courts have also found BOP's (or a state facility housing federal inmates) failure to provide adequate mental health treatment to be an extraordinary and compelling circumstance supporting compassionate release. In *United States v. Brocoli*, 543 F. Supp. 3d 563 (S.D. Ohio 2021), the defendant, sentenced to 30 months' imprisonment for cyber stalking, likely suffered from paranoid personality disorder resulting from childhood sexual abuse. Although charged and convicted in federal court, the defendant was circulated through a variety of state facilities, including one at which he was a victim of an attempted rape. A psychiatrist evaluated him following this encounter and the ensuing report highlighted the "importance of his receiving mental health services." *Id.* at 568. Despite this report, the defendant received only two counseling sessions over a period of six months. The court granted release because "the BOP has not offered Mr. Brocoli a consistent environment nor the mental health services he needs." *Id.* at 568-69; *see also United States v. Verasawmi*, No. CR 17-254 (FLW), 2022 WL 2763518, at *9 (D.N.J. July 15, 2022) (granting compassionate release to an inmate with major depressive disorder who was not being adequately treated, concluding, "Given the apparent severity of Verasawmi's mental health condition, the discrepancy in treatment compared to what she received outside prison adds to the Court's concerns regarding the level of care Verasawmi is receiving at FMC Carswell."); *United States v. Herrera*, No. 17 CR. 415 (PAC), 2023 WL 3614343, at *2–3 (S.D.N.Y.

May 24, 2023) (BOP failed to address psychological effects of sexual abuse by a BOP guard on an inmate, which included anxious arousal, depression, PTSD, defense avoidance, sexual disturbance, and insecure attachment).

Finally, in *United States v. Clay*, No. 6:17-CR-00286-MC, 2022 WL 3347037 (D. Or. Aug. 12, 2022), the government joined the defendant's motion for compassionate release based on BOP's neglectful medical treatment. The defendant suffered from schizoaffective disorder and anxiety, conditions that had been successfully treated, in part, by a regimen of antipsychotic medication. Upon arrival in federal custody at FDC Sheridan, he had not been receiving the dosages necessary to stabilize his condition, the joint efforts of his counsel and federal prosecutors notwithstanding. The BOP's refusal to administer the required dosages caused him to suffer auditory and visual hallucinations, insomnia, and general panic. Citing these failures, the government waived the requirement that defendant first submit his request for compassionate release to the warden and consented to immediate release, which the court granted the day of the filing. *See also United States v. Booker*, No. 18-CR-2611-GPC, 2023 WL 3186296 (S.D. Cal. May 1, 2023) (without government opposition, at least until the 30-day exhaustion period runs, the court grants release because the defendant was denied access to medication he relied on for seven years, the denial of which resulted in withdrawal symptoms including relapse in depression and suicidal ideation).

Conclusion

As can be seen from this brief discussion, defendants—and their counsel—have a long row to hoe as they seek post-conviction relief, but the cited cases reflect the willingness of at least some courts to remedy the most egregious failures of trial courts and defense counsel to protect the rights of defendants with mental disabilities. Additionally, many federal courts have demonstrated a willingness to grant compassionate release where a disabled inmate is put at risk through the BOP's failure to adequately discharge its obligations to them.

• • •

Richard W. Levitt is a criminal defense lawyer whose practice has spanned more than four decades. Focusing on trial and appellate advocacy and post-conviction relief, he is also the author of numerous articles on criminal law–related topics and lectures frequently for several organizations. Mr. Levitt's wide-ranging practice includes the defense of individuals charged with political corruption, money laundering, capital crimes, drug distribution, fraud, tax evasion, and other offenses. He is a past board member of the New York Criminal Bar Association and a past honoree of that organization, as well as a life member of the National Association of Criminal Defense Lawyers.

Mr. Levitt is the creator of the nationally renowned judge-rating website, The Robing Room (http://www.therobingroom.com). He is the author of the 1,500-page Second Circuit Criminal Law Sourcebook (North Law Publishers, 2021). Mr. Levitt received his JD from the University of Miami and his LLM from New York University. His website is http://www.levittandkaizer.com and he can be reached at rlevitt@landklaw.com.

Zachary Segal, an associate at Levitt & Kaizer, is a graduate of Touro Law Center, where he was a member of the *Touro Law Review*. While in law school, Zach interned with the Federal Defenders of New York in the Eastern District of New York, Brooklyn Defender Services, the Hon. Joseph F. Bianco (then–EDNY USDJ, now Circuit Judge, Second Circuit), and the Hon. Associate Justice Robert J. Miller (N.Y.S. App. Div., Second Department). Born in Montreal, Zach attended the University of Ottawa, where he double-majored in political science and history. After graduating, he worked at the Aleph Institute, a nationally recognized prisoners' rights organization. Zach is a fluent French speaker and is conversational in Spanish and Hebrew. With Levitt & Kaizer partner Richard Levitt, Zach publishes the Compassionate Release, COVID-19, and BOP Blog, accessible from the Levitt & Kaizer website, www.levittandkaizer.com. Since 2022, Zach has been a member of the Young Lawyers Committee at the Historical Society of the New York Courts.

Chapter

19

Ethics

Peggy Cross-Goldberg

In 2016, the ABA promulgated its Criminal Justice and Mental Health Standards. *These standards provide best practices for judges, prosecutors, defense lawyers, law enforcement, and mental health professionals. Admittedly, the standards are aspirational, but they can provide guidance and can be cited. Yet even the most experienced attorney after following these standards can be faced with an ethical dilemma.*

This chapter on ethics by federal public defender Peggy Cross Goldenberg is a close reading of ABA Model Rule 1.14, Client with Diminished Capacity. Other chapters in the book have discussed particular ethical issues, such as whether it actually helps a client to raise the issue of competency (see Chapter 1, "Competency to Stand Trial"), whether it harms a client who might be suicidal to reveal this information to the jail or court (see Chapter 16 "Jail and Prison Conditions"), or whether a criminal defense lawyer's participation in a problem-solving court compromises their duty of zealous advocacy and preservation of client confidences (see Chapter 13, "Mental Health Courts and Other Diversion Options").

Using Model Rule 1.14 as a lodestar, attorney Goldenberg acknowledges the infinite variety of ethical challenges and notes that "[o]ne-size-fits-all answers are nowhere to be found." But it is this editor's hope that by continuing to educate ourselves, seeking guidance from trusted colleagues, and holding fast to our duty to our clients, that we will achieve some modicum of justice for people with mental disabilities ensnared in the criminal legal system.

• • •

Representing individuals in the criminal legal system is challenging. Representing individuals with diminished capacity is challenging. The intersection of the criminal legal system and clients with diminished capacity creates some of the most challenging situations for defense attorneys. An approach that may lead to better mental health outcomes may mean a worse outcome in the criminal case, one that may result in the client spending additional time in custody and may lead to collateral and criminal consequences that will follow the client for the rest of their lives. And what may otherwise be the best disposition of the criminal case, such as a plea to a reduced charge, may not be possible in light of a client's diminished capacity. As the commentary to Model Rule 1.14 acknowledges, a "lawyer's position in such cases is an unavoidably difficult one." One-size-fits-all answers are nowhere to be found. But by centering and remaining loyal to the client's interests and building a robust, respectful client-lawyer relationship, attorneys can best meet their ethical obligations.

Model Rule 1.14 addresses special considerations that arise in representing clients with diminished capacity. Although Rule 1.14 addresses these special considerations, it is not the only rule that governs an attorney's duties in these representations. This chapter will cover the special considerations of Rule 1.14 as well as highlight challenges under other rules that may arise when representing clients with diminished capacity. Model Rule 1.14, Client with Diminished Capacity, states:

> Client-Lawyer Relationship
>
> (a) When a client's capacity to make adequately considered decisions in connection with representation is diminished, whether because of minority, mental impairment or for some other reason, the lawyer shall, as far as reasonably possible, maintain a normal client-lawyer relationship with the client.
>
> (b) When the lawyer reasonably believes that the client has diminished capacity, is at risk of substantial physical, financial or other harm unless action is taken and cannot adequately act in the client's own interest, the lawyer may take reasonably necessary protective action, including consulting with individuals or entities that have the ability to take action to protect the client and, in appropriate cases, seeking the appointment of a guardian ad litem, conservator, or guardian.
>
> (c) Information relating to the representation of a client with diminished capacity is protected by Rule 1.6. When taking protective action pursuant

to paragraph (b), the lawyer is impliedly authorized under Rule 1.6(a) to reveal information about the client, but only to the extent reasonably necessary to protect the client's interests.

An attorney representing a client with diminished capacity has a duty, "as far as reasonably possible," to "maintain a normal client-lawyer relationship with the client" (Rule 1.14). Maintaining a normal client-lawyer relationship includes maintaining effective communication (Rule 1.4), maintaining confidential client information (Rule 1.6), and remaining a loyal, zealous representative. A client with diminished capacity "often has the ability to understand, deliberate upon, and reach conclusions about matters affecting the client's own well-being" (Rule 1.14, cmt. 1). It is the attorney's responsibility to treat the client with attention and respect and to maintain effective communication (Rule 1.14, cmt. 2).

The commentary to Model Rule 1.14 acknowledges that "a severely incapacitated person may have no power to make legally binding decisions." Yet individuals facing criminal charges cannot simply avoid making decisions. Either decisions that lead to the disposition of the case, such as whether to plead guilty or proceed to trial, must be made, or the court must find that the client is not competent to make such decisions.

When faced with a client who may have diminished capacity, and determining what actions the attorney should take in response, the commentary directs the attorney to consider and balance several factors: the client's ability to articulate reasoning leading to a decision, variability of the client's state of mind and their ability to appreciate the consequences of a decision, the substantive fairness of a decision, and the consistency of a decision with the client's long-term commitments and values. When necessary, an attorney should seek the guidance of an appropriate diagnostician to assist in this consideration and balancing.

A client's capacity to engage in decision-making and assist in their defense may fluctuate over the course of the representation. Lawyers should continue to work to maintain the client-lawyer relationship throughout the representation, recognizing that different approaches to communication with the client may be more fruitful at different times. Where one approach is unsuccessful, attorneys should be willing to try other strategies to strengthen the client-attorney relationship. And where repeated attempts are necessary, attorneys should request adequate time to make the necessary attempts. This may involve requesting adjournments or additional time from the court and will require the attorney to balance the need for the request with preserving confidential client communication.

Effective communication is the backbone of any successful client-attorney relationship. It may facilitate communication and enhance the client-attorney relationship to involve family members or other members of a client's support system in discussions with the attorney. Where the involvement of others is "necessary to assist in the representation," their involvement will ordinarily not affect the attorney-client privilege that covers the communications. Although the attorney may involve others in conversations about the case and the decisions to be made, the attorney should look to the client, and not those others, to make decisions on their behalf (Rule 1.14, cmt. 3).

In some cases, attempts to involve others in attorney-client communications may undermine the client's trust in their attorney and lead to the deterioration of the client-lawyer relationship. And where a client has made clear their desire to not have family members involved in their case, such involvement against the client's will could be perceived as an ambush or breach of trust. Still, an attempt to involve members of a client's support system may be preferable to seeking withdrawal or raising competency concerns with the court.

Model Rule 1.14(b) allows a lawyer who reasonably believes that (1) the client's capacity is diminished; (2) the client is at risk of substantial physical, financial, or other harm unless action is taken; and (3) the client cannot adequately act in their own self-interest, to take reasonably necessary protective action. Model Rule 1.14(c) provides that attorneys are impliedly authorized under Rule 1.6(a) to reveal information about a client when taking protective action pursuant to Rule 1.14(b), but only to the extent reasonably necessary to protect the client's interests. And not all states have adopted this exception to preserving confidential information. California, for example, does not have an exception for impliedly authorized disclosures.

The Model Rules recognize that the disclosure of information related to a client's diminished capacity may adversely affect the client's interests. If the only interest of the client's that needs protecting relates to the client's mental health, it may be clear that the attorney is authorized to raise concerns about the client's diminished capacity in order to facilitate treatment. The question is more complicated, however, when the client is facing criminal charges. Simply raising concerns about diminished capacity may alter the court's view on whether the client poses a danger and may result in incarceration. Requesting a competency examination may actually require that a client be remanded for evaluation and may result in a longer period of incarceration than a simple disposition of the case might have. And a finding that a client is not competent to proceed may result in forced medication or an additional period of incapacitation in an effort to restore competency as well as involuntary commitment even after the criminal case is dismissed or otherwise resolved.

Given these challenges, attorneys representing individuals with diminished capacity in criminal cases may require additional training and specialized knowledge. Rule 1.1 requires an attorney to provide "competent representation." Competent representation "requires the legal knowledge, skill, thoroughness and preparation reasonably necessary for the representation" (Rule 1.1). The requisite knowledge and skill will vary depending on the matter, and when it comes to representing individuals with diminished capacity, attorneys may need special training to provide competent representation. Just as complex and specialized legal matters may require heightened levels of expertise, attorneys representing individuals in criminal matters have an obligation to understand how their client's mental health and mental capacity are impacting the representation and the client's decision-making.

One area of training relates to understanding a client's mental capacity and distinguishing when diminished capacity, as distinct from a difference of opinion or divergent goals, is affecting the representation. A client's disagreement with counsel over the goals of the representation or over the means of achieving those goals does not necessarily mean the client's diminished capacity is interfering with their decision-making. Involving others, including the client's family members, other defense team members, or mental health professionals, in the client-lawyer discussions can help the attorney distinguish between situations in which the client's diminished capacity is interfering with their decision-making and situations in which the client, for reasons the attorney may disagree with, wants to pursue a different course of action than that recommended by the attorney.

When the attorney reaches the difficult decision that the representation cannot continue, none of the available options is problem-free. The attorney can ask to be relieved of the representation. Model Rule 1.16 governs the termination of the client-lawyer relationship and what steps the attorney will need to take. In a criminal case, this would involve notifying the court of a breakdown in the attorney-client relationship and requesting the appointment of new counsel. In some situations, this will be the best course of action. It is possible that a different attorney, with different skills or training, may be able to forge an effective client-lawyer relationship and effectively represent the client. And even if this ultimately does not turn out to be the case, it may be in the client's best interest to have another attorney attempt the representation prior to taking the drastic step of raising capacity concerns with the court. In some situations, though, substitution of counsel serves to relieve the attorney of their responsibilities without enhancing the representation the client receives. When the attorney decides it is necessary to raise concerns about the client's capacity or competency with the court and seek an evaluation, they should.

Ultimately, the lawyer should be guided by their loyalty to the client and should act zealously on their behalf. Any disclosures made by the lawyer should be narrowly limited to those deemed necessary to carry out the representation after the attorney has determined that the potential benefit to the client outweighs the potential adverse consequences.

• • •

Peggy Cross-Goldenberg is a supervising trial attorney and director of training, providing advice, support, and CLE programming for assistant federal defenders and Criminal Justice Act attorneys in the Southern and Eastern Districts of New York. Ms. Cross-Goldenberg holds a BA in history and political science from Duke University and a JD from Columbia Law School, where she was a Kent Scholar and served as an articles editor on the *Columbia Law Review*. She clerked for the Honorable Lewis A. Kaplan of the U.S. District Court for the Southern District of New York and for the Honorable William A. Fletcher of the U.S. Court of Appeals for the Ninth Circuit.

Before joining the Federal Defenders in 2007, Ms. Cross-Goldenberg was an associate at Stillman, Friedman & Shechtman and a staff attorney in the Manhattan office of the criminal defense division of the Legal Aid Society. She teaches professional responsibility in criminal law at Columbia Law School.

Suggested Works

Following is a list of suggested works arranged according to chapter. These categories are not airtight, and some resources may be used in or applicable to other areas. In addition to exploring the works cited in individual chapters, readers are encouraged to explore the articles and books written by the various chapter authors.

Chapter 1: Competency to Stand Trial

Artha Gillis, Brian Holoyda, William J. Newman, Machelle D. Wilson & Glen Xiong, *Characteristics of Misdemeanants Treated for Competency Restoration*, 44 J. Am. Acad. Psychiatry & L. 442 (2016).

Lubna Grewal & Stephen Noffsinger, *Retrospective Postconviction Competency to Stand Trial Assessments*, 44 J. Am. Acad. Psychiatry & L. 491 (2016).

Shelley J. Hill, Sarah Homsy, Chad Woofter & Barbara E. McDermott, *Persistent, Poor Quality Competency to Stand Trial Reports: Does Training Matter?* 19 Psychol. Serv. 206 (2022).

Lauren Kois, James M. Wellbeloved-Stone, Preeti Chauhan & Janet I. Warren, *Combined Evaluations of Competency to Stand Trial and Mental State at the Time of the Offense: An Overlooked Methodological Consideration?* 41 Law & Hum. Behav. 217 (2017).

Devrey A. Martin, Cassandra A. Bailey, & W. Neil Gowensmith, *Ethical Considerations of Competency Restoration: The Risk of Decompensation in Correctional Settings*, 29 Psychol., Pub Pol'y & L. 62 (2023).

Nathaniel P. Morris, Dale E. McNeil, & Renée L. Binder, *Estimating Annual Numbers of Competency to Stand Trial Evaluations across the United States*, 49 J. Am. Acad. Psychiatry & L. 530 (2021).

Sarah Smith, *What Are We Going to Do About Tyler?* ProPublica (Dec. 28, 2017).

Sarah Treleaven & Beth Karas, "Unrestorable" (Podcast), 2023.

Chapter 2: Criminal Responsibility

Adjorlolo, S., Chan, H. C. O., & DeLisi, M. (2019). *Mentally disordered offenders and the law: Research update on the insanity defense, 2004–2019*. International Journal of Law and Psychiatry, 67, 101507.

Kahler v. Kansas, March 23, 2020 (SCOTUS blog), www.scotusblog.com/case-files/cases/kahler-v-kansas.

Mac McClelland, "When 'Not Guilty' Is a Life Sentence," *New York Times Magazine*, Sept. 27, 2017. https://www.nytimes.com/2017/09/27/magazine/when-not-guilty-is-a-life-sentence.html.

G. B. Melton, et al. (2018). Mental state at the time of the offense (pp. 266–341). *Psychological Evaluations for the Courts: A Handbook for Mental Health Professionals and Lawyers* (4th ed.). The Guilford Press (p. 413).

I. K. Packer (2009). *Evaluation of Criminal Responsibility*. Oxford University Press. https://academic.oup.com/book/1268.

Chapter 3: Mitigation

Advocating for People with Mental Illness in the New Jersey Criminal Justice System, located at https://www.naminj.org/wp-content/uploads/2013/02/Finding_Our_Way.pdf.

Criminal Justice Standards on Mental Health, located at https://www.americanbar.org/content/dam/aba/publications/criminal_justice_standards/mental_health_standards_2016.authcheckdam.pdf.

Janet Hinton, F.P.D. E.D. Mo., *Developing Mitigating Evidence*, located at https://moe.fd.org/Dev_Mitigation.php (containing a significant list of resources).

Edmond Howe, *What Lawyers Should Know About Clients with Mental Disabilities*, located at https://www.americanbar.org/publications/gp_solo/2014/march_april/what_lawyers_should_know_about_clients_mental_disabilities.html.

Mental Illness, Your Client and the Criminal Law. A Handbook for Attorneys Representing Criminal Defendants, located at https://ttu-ir.tdl.org/ttu-ir/bitstream/handle/10601/876/Shannon_Mental%20Illness%2C%20Your%20Client.pdf?sequence=1.

Post Traumatic Stress Disorder in Criminal Justice: From Vietnam to Iraq and Afghanistan. The Federal Lawyer, September 2010. This article discusses mitigating cases and information related to veteran issues.

The Changing Landscape in Possession of Child Pornography Cases, NACDL Champion Magazine, May 2011. This article also addresses a number of cases for mitigation.

Your Law Practice: Understanding Client's with Mental Illness, an online seminar located at https://osbar.inreachce.com/Details/Information/f35d1895-b2e2-497f-96d0-df16889b4640.

Chapter 4: Working with the Expert: From the Perspective of Experts

D. Canter, *Forensic Psychology: A Very Short Introduction*. Oxford University Press (2010).

D. Canter, *Investigative Psychology: Offender Profiling and the Analysis of Criminal Action*. Wiley (2009).

Y. Okamura., Y. Murahashi, Y. Umeda, T. Misumi, T. Asami, M. Itokawa, H. Harima, M. Mizuno, H. Matsunaga, & A. Hishimoto (2022). *Obsessive-Compulsive Disorder with Psychotic Features: Is It a Clinical Entity?* HEALTHCARE (Basel, Switzerland), 10(10), 1910, https://doi.org/10.3390/healthcare10101910.

Chapter 5: Working with the Expert: Guidance for Lawyers

Daubert v. Merrell Dow Pharmaceuticals, 113 S. Ct. 2786 (1993).

Frye v. U.S., 295 F. 1013 (D.C. Cir. 1923).

Kumho Tire Co. Ltd. et al. v. Carmichael et al., 526 U.S. 137 (1999).

Chapter 6: Assessment of Malingering for Criminal Defendants with Mental Disabilities

Emily Brown & Brie Pileggi-Valleen, *Malingering and Sentence Enhancement*, 49 J. AM. ACAD. PSYCHIATRY L. 277 (2021).

Christoph Leonhard, *Review of Statistical and Methodological Issues in the Forensic Prediction of Malingering from Validity Tests: Part 1—Statistical Issues*, 33 NEUROPSYCHOL. REV. 581 (2023).

Christoph Leonhard, *Review of Statistical and Methodological Issues in the Forensic Prediction of Malingering from Validity Tests: Part 2—Methodological Issues*, 33 NEUROPSYCHOL. REV. 604 (2023).

Richard Rogers, "Detection Strategies for Malingering and Defensiveness," in CLINICAL ASSESSMENT OF MALINGERING AND DECEPTION 18 (Richard Rogers and Scott D. Bender eds., 4th ed., 2018).

Richard Rogers & Kamar Y. Tazi, *Intensification of Impairment as an Elusive Malingering Presentation: Validation of the Trauma and Disability Scale for Impairment (TDSI)*, 16 PSYCHOL. INJURY & L. 320 (2023).

Chapter 7: Testing

American Academy of Clinical Neuropsychology (2021), "Position Statement on Race Norms," https://theaacn.org/wp-content/uploads/2021/11/AACN-Position-Statement-on-Race-Norms.pdf.

American Academy of Clinical Neuropsychology (2021), "Consensus Statement on Validity Assessment: Update of the 2009 AACN Consensus Conference Statement on Neuropsychological Assessment of Effort, Response Bias, and Malingering," https://www.tandfonline.com/doi/full/10.1080/13854046.2021.1896036.

American Educational Research Association, American Psychological Association, and National Council on Measurement in Education (2014), "Standards for Educational and Psychological Testing," https://www.apa.org/science/programs/testing/standards.

American Psychological Association (2023), "PTSD Assessment Instruments." Retrieved from https://www.apa.org/ptsd-guideline/assessment.

American Psychological Association Task Force on Guidelines for Assessment and Intervention with Persons with Disabilities (2022), "Guidelines for Assessment and Intervention with Persons with Disabilities." Retrieved from https://www.apa.org/about/policy/guidelines-assessment-intervention-disabilities.pdf.

American Psychological Association Task Force on Psychological Assessment and Evaluation Guidelines (2020), "APA Guidelines for Psychological Assessment and Evaluation." Retrieved from https://www.apa.org/about/policy/guidelines-psychological-assessment-evaluation.pdf.

American Psychological Association Task Force on Re-envisioning the Multicultural Guidelines for the 21st Century (2017), "Multicultural Guidelines: An Ecological Approach to Context, Identity, and Intersectionality." Retrieved from: http://www.apa.org/about/policy/multicultural-guidelines.pdf.

Boone, K.B., Sweet, J.J., Byrd, D.A., et al. (2022), "Official Position of the American Academy of Clinical Neuropsychology on Test Security," https://www.tandfonline.com/doi/full/10.1080/13854046.2021.2022214.

Glen, T., Barisa, M., Ready, R., et al. (2022), "Update on Third Party Observers in Neuropsychological Evaluation: An Interorganizational Position Paper," https://www.tandfonline.com/doi/full/10.1080/13854046.2021.1901992.

Pearson, "Pearson's Position on Responding to Demands for Copyright Protected Material," https://www.pearsonassessments.com/footer/legal-policies.html.

Psychological Assessment Resources, "PAR's Position on Responding to Demands for Copy-Right Protect Material," https://www.parinc.com/IP-Postion.

Chapter 8: Neuroimaging

Kevin Davis, *The Brain Defense: Murder in the Courtroom and the Dawn of Neuroscience in America's Courtrooms* (Penguin Press 2017).

Bessel Van der Kolk, *The Body Keeps the Score: Brain, Mind, and Body in the Healing of Trauma* (Viking 2014).

Stephanie Yarnell, Alexander Westphal & David A. Ross, *Scanning for Justice with Functional Magnetic Resonance Imaging*, Biological Psychiatry (Aug. 15, 2017).

Chapter 9: Structured Violence and Sexual Risk Assessment

Christian Baudin, et al. "A Static-99R validation study on individuals with mental disorders: 5 to 20 years of fixed follow-up after sexual offenses." *Frontiers in Psychology*, vol. 12 625996, 2 Feb. 2021.

Alex Buchanan, et al. "Psychiatric violence risk assessment." *American Journal of Psychiatry*, vol. 169, 3 (2012):340.

K. S. Douglas, S. D. Hart, C.D. Webster, & H. Belfrage, (2013). *HCR-20V3: Assessing risk of violence—User guide*. Burnaby, Canada: Mental Health, Law, and Policy Institute, Simon Fraser University.

Seena Fazel, et al. "Use of risk assessment instruments to predict violence and antisocial behaviour in 73 samples involving 24 827 people: systematic review and meta-analysis." *BMJ (Clinical research ed.)*, vol. 345 e4692. 24 Jul. 2012

Ryan C. W. Hall & G. Iannuzzi, "Prediction of violence: Part contagious disease, part unpredictable individual: Is a public health assessment approach an additional option and at what cost?." *Behavioral Sciences & The Law*, 10.1002/bsl.2611 (2023).

S. D. Hart, K. S. Douglas, & L. S. Guy (2017). The structured professional judgement approach to violence risk assessment: Origins, nature, and advances. In D. P. Boer, A. R. Beech, T. Ward, L. A. Craig, M. Rettenberger, L. E. Marshall, & W. L. Marshall (eds.), *The Wiley Handbook on the Theories, Assessment, and Treatment of Sexual Offending* (pp. 643–666). Wiley Blackwell.

Matthew M. Large and C. J. Ryan, "Violence risk assessment has not been shown to reduce violence." *The Australian and New Zealand Journal of Psychiatry*, vol. 49,1 (2015): 91.

John Monahan, et al. "Risk assessment in sentencing and plea bargaining: The roles of prosecutors and defense attorneys." *Behavioral Sciences & The Law*, vol. 38,1 (2020): 1–11. Doi:10.1002/bsl.2435

Charles Scott and J. Phillip Resnick, "Clinical assessment of aggression and violence." In *Principles and Practices of Forensic Psychiatry*, 3rd ed. (CRC Press, Boca Raton, Florida 2017).

Statistical Information about Recidivism Scale: Some Reflections on its Applications | Office of Justice Programs (ojp.gov)

Chapter 10: False Confessions and *Miranda* Waivers

Gisli Gudjonsson (2018). *The Psychology of False Confessions: Forty Years of Science and Practice* (New York: John E. Wiley & Sons).

Saul Kassin (2022). *Duped: Why Innocent People Confess – and Why We Believe Their Confessions* (New York: Prometheus Books).

Richard Rogers & Eric Drogin, *Mirandized Statements: Successfully Navigating the Legal and Psychological Issues* (American Bar Association 2014).

William Douglas Woody and Krista Forrest (2020). *Understanding Police Interrogation: Confessions and Consequences* (New York: New York University Press).

Chapter 11: Substance Use Disorder

G. Baranyi, S. Fazel, S. D. Langerfeldt, & A. P. Mundt (2022). The prevalence of comorbid serious mental illnesses and substance use disorders in prison populations: a systematic review and meta-analysis. The Lancet, 7(6), e557–8. https://doi.org/10.1016/S2468-2667(22)00093-7.

A. Bechara (2005). Decision making, impulse control and loss of willpower to resist drugs: a neurocognitive perspective. Nature Neuroscience, 8(11), 1458–1463. https://doi.org/10.1038/nn1584.

W. K. Bickel, M. L. Miller, R. Yi, B. P. Kowal, D. M. Lindquist, & J. A. Pitcock (2006). Behavioral and neuroeconomics of drug addiction: Competing neural systems and temporal discounting processes. Drug and Alcohol Dependence, 90(Supplement 1), S85–S91. https://doi.org/10.1016/j.drugalcdep.2006.09.016.

S. Fazel, I. A. Yoon, & A. J. Hayes (2017). Substance use disorders in prisoners: an updated systematic review and meta-regression analysis in recently incarcerated men and women: Substance use disorder in prisoners. Addiction, 112(10), 1725–39. https://doi.org/10.1111/add.13877.

G. F. Koob, & N. D. Volkow (2010). Neurocircuitry of addiction: A window into the network underlying neuropsychiatric disease. Neuropsychopharmacology (New York, N.Y.), 35(1), 217–38.

G. F. Koob, & N. D. Volkow (2016). Neurobiology of addiction: a neurocircuitry analysis. LANCET PSYCHIATRY, 3(8), 760–73. https://doi.org/10.1016/S2215-0366(16)00104-8.

A.T. McLellan, D. C. Lewis, C. P. O'Brien, & H. D. Kleber (2000). Drug dependence, a chronic medical illness: Implications for treatment, insurance, and outcomes evaluation. JOURNAL OF THE AMERICAN MEDICAL ASSOCIATION, 284(13), 1689–95. https://doi.org/10.1001/jama.284.13.1689.

R. Sinha (2001). How does stress increase risk of drug abuse and relapse? PSYCHOPHARMACOLOGY, 158(4), 343–59.

R. Sinha (2011). New findings on biological factors predicting addiction relapse vulnerability. CURRENT PSYCHIATRY REPORTS, 13(5), 398–405. https://doi.org/10.1007/s11920-011-0224-0.

N. D. Volkow (2020). Stigma and the toll of addiction. The NEW ENGLAND JOURNAL OF MEDICINE, 382(14), 1289–90. https://doi.org/10.1056/NEJMp1917360.

N. D. Volkow, G. F. Koob, & A. T. McLellan (2016). Neurobiologic advances from the brain disease model of addiction. NEW ENGLAND JOURNAL OF MEDICINE, 374(4), 363–71. https://doi.org/10.1056/NEJMra1511480.

Chapter 12: Youthful Offenders

Richard Bonnie et al., *Reforming Juvenile Justice: A Developmental Approach*, National Research Council Committee on Assessing Juvenile Justice, Division of Behavioral Sciences and Education (Washington D.C. 2013).

Burns Institute, *Youth Justice Reimagined, Recommendations of The Los Angeles County Youth Justice Work Group* (October 2020).

Center for Law Brain & Behavior (CLBB) at Massachusetts General Hospital, *White Paper on the Science of Late Adolescence: A Guide for Judges, Attorneys, and Policy Makers* (January 27, 2022), https://clbb.mgh.harvard.edu/white-paper-on-the-science-of-late-adolescence.

Robin Dahlberg & Lael Chester, *Arrested Futures: The Criminalization of School Discipline in Massachusetts Three Largest School Districts*, ACLU-Citizens for Juvenile Justice (Spring 2018).

Thomas Grisso et al., *Juveniles Competence to Stand Trial: A Comparison of Adolescents' and Adults' Capacities as Trial Defendants*, LAW & HUMAN BEHAVIOR (Sept. 2003).

Robert Kinscherff et al, *Promoting Positive Outcomes for Justice Involved Youth: Implications for Policy, Systems, and Practice*, Judge Baker Guidance Center, Boston (February 2019).

Meribah Knight, "The Kids of Rutherford County" (podcast), ProPublica, Serial, and Nashville Public Radio (2023).

Jill Lepore, *A History of Political Tragedy*, The New Yorker (Feb. 2016).

Dorothy Roberts, *Torn Apart: How the Child Welfare System Destroys Black Families—and How Abolition Can Build a Better World* (Basic Books April 2022).

Julie Rosenthal, *Understanding Psychological Trauma*, Pathways, PSYO, Portland, Oregon (Aug. 20, 2022).

Chapter 13: Mental Health Courts and Other Diversion Programs

Annual Report, Re-Entry Court, Eastern District of Pennsylvania, 2021.

Center for Court Innovation, available at http://www.courtinnovation.org.

NYSBA, "Report and Recommendations of the New York State Bar Association, Task Force on Mental Health and Trauma Informed Representation" (June 2023), available at https://nysba.org/app/uploads/2023/06/final-report-Task-Force-on-Mental-Health-and-Trauma-Informed-Representation-June-2023.pdf.

Urban Justice Center, *Reimagining Paths to Healing & Justice*, Perspectives on Community Diversion (Dec. 2023).

Chapter 14: Representing Veterans

Brocton D. Hunter & Ryan C. Else, eds., *The Attorney's Guide to Defending Veterans in Criminal Court* (Veterans Defense Project 2014).

Justice for Vets (a division of the National Association of Drug Court Professionals) provides training and technical assistance for veterans treatment courts, available at http://www.justiceforvets.org.

Karl Marlantes, *Matterhorn: A Novel of the Vietnam War* (Atlantic Monthly Press 2011).

Karl Marlantes, *What It Is Like to Go to War* (Atlantic Monthly Press 2010).

Chapter 15: Standby or Advisory Counsel

William Finnegan, *Defending the Unabomber*, available at https://www.newyorker.com/magazine/1998/03/16/unabomber-trial-ted-kaczynski.

Christopher Slobigin, *Mental Illness and Self-Representation: Faretta, Godinez, and Edwards*, 7 Ohio State Journal of Criminal Law 391 (2009).

Chapter 16: Jail and Prison Conditions

Alan Ellis, Todd Bussert & J. Michael Henderson, *Federal Prison Guidebook: Sentencing and Post-Conviction Remedies* (James Publishing 2015).

Alan Ellis & Maureen Baird, et al. *Federal Prison Guidebook* (2022–2023 ed.).

John Boston & Daniel Manville, *Prisoners' Self-Help Litigation Manual* (4th ed., Oxford University Press 2010).

Michael Perlin & Henry Dlugacz, *Mental Health Issues in Jails and Prisons* (Carolina Academic Press 2008).

Alisa Roth, *Insane Consequences: America's Criminal Treatment of Mental Illness* (Basic Books 2018).

Chapter 17: Working with Families

American Residential Treatment Association, available at http://www.artausa.org.

Lawrence A. Dubin, "ASD and Sex Offenses: A Father's Perspective," *Representing People with Autism Spectrum Disorders: A Practical Guide for Criminal Defense Lawyers*, Elizabeth Kelley, ed., American Bar Association (2020).

Pete Earley, *Crazy: A Father's Search Through America's Mental Health Madness* (Berkley 2007).

Sue Klebold, *A Mother's Reckoning: Living in the After-Math of Tragedy* (Crown Publishers 2017).

David Sheff, *Clean: Overcoming Addiction and Ending America's Greatest Tragedy* (Eamon/Dolan Mariner Books 2014).

Bedlam (film), Kenneth Paul Rosenberg, 2019.

Chapter 18: Post-Conviction Remedies

Brian R. Means, *Introduction to Habeas Corpus* (Barnes and Noble 2022).

United States Sentencing Commission's Compassionate Release data bank, available at https://www.ussc.gov/topic/compassionate-release.

Updated Compilation of Compassionate Release Grants, available at https://thefederaldocket.com/updated-compilation-of-compassionate-release-grants/.

The Sentencing Law and Policy Blog, available at https://sentencing.typepad.com/sentencing_law_and_policy/prisons-and-prisoners/.

Chapter 19: Ethics

American Bar Association, *Criminal Justice Standards on Mental Health*, available at https://www.americanbar.org/content/dam/aba/publications/criminal_justice_standards/mental_health_standards_2016.authcheckdam.pdf.

John Wesley Hall, *Professional Responsibility in Criminal Defense Practice*, Thompson Reuters (2023).

John D. King, *Candor, Zeal, and the Substitution of Judgment: Ethics and the Mentally Ill Criminal Defendant*, 58 Am. U. L. Rev. 207 (2008).

Christopher Slobigin, *The American Bar Association's Criminal Justice Mental Health Standards: Revisions for the Twenty-First Century*, 44 Hastings Constitutional Law Quarterly 1 (2016).